ARCHAEOLOGICAL SURVEY OF WESTERN INDIA, VOL. IV.

REPORT

ON THE

BUDDHIST CAVE TEMPLES

AND

THEIR INSCRIPTIONS

ARCHAEOLOGICAL SURVEY OF WESTERN INDIA, VOL. IV.

REPORT
ON THE
BUDDHIST CAVE TEMPLES
AND
THEIR INSCRIPTIONS

BEING PART OF
THE RESULTS OF THE FOURTH, FIFTH, AND SIXTH SEASONS' OPERATIONS
OF THE ARCHAEOLOGICAL SURVEY OF WESTERN INDIA

1876-77, 1877-78, 1878-79

SUPPLEMENTARY TO THE VOLUME ON "THE CAVE TEMPLES OF INDIA."

BY

JAS. BURGESS, LL.D., F.R.G.S.,
MEMBER OF THE ROYAL ASIATIC SOCIETY, OF THE SOCIETE ASIATIQUE, &C.
ARCHAEOLOGICAL SURVEYOR AND REPORTER TO GOVERNMENT FOR
WESTERN AND SOUTHERN INDIA

GYAN

Published by

Gyan Publishing House
5, Ansari Road
Daryaganj, New Delhi-110002
Phone: 011-47034999, 9811692060
E-mail: books@gyanbooks.com

Distribution Network
gyanbooks.com
India, USA, Canada, UK, Australia, France

ISBN : 978-81-212-2119-1 (HB)
First Published, 1975

2nd Impression 2021

Printed at: Gyan Press, Delhi.

Report on the Buddhist Cave Temples
and
Their Inscriptions
Author: Jas. Burgess

PREFACE.

As explained in the introductory chapter of this volume, it is not intended to be considered as a complete report in itself, but to afford much additional material for the study of Buddhist Cave Architecture which could not be comprised within the limits of the second part of the work on *The Cave Temples*, published last year, and to supply a tolerably complete account of the inscriptions found on the walls of these Caves. Much of the materials here supplied consists of drawings of architectural details—principally from the Caves at Ajaṇṭâ—which hardly require description. These drawings, with the woodcuts and autotype illustrations, speak for themselves, and show what a field for artistic study is presented by such remains of ancient Indian art.

It may be mentioned that the Buddhist Caves at Elurâ and some minor groups have not been alluded to in this volume. For the latter, there is scarcely any additional information or illustration to present beyond what is supplied by the volume on *The Cave Temples*, or in previous *Reports;* and for the former, it seems preferable to treat of the Elurâ Caves as a whole, and to describe the Caves—Buddhist, Brahmanical, and Jaina—found there, as a series complete in itself. Moreover, the number of inscriptions to be given in the next volume is so very much smaller that this arrangement will help to keep the volumes more nearly of the same size.

It remains to express my thanks to friends who have spared no pains to render me every assistance. James Fergusson, Esq., D.C.L., has taken the greatest interest in the work, and has helped very largely by revising the proofs of several whole chapters, and supplying many important additions; Professor G. Bühler, C.I.E., has not only translated anew the

Nâsik and Ajaṇṭâ inscriptions, but has revised and corrected the whole of the chapter on the inscriptions, while to him and E. Thomas, Esq., F.R.S., I am indebted for several suggestions in the chapter on Palæography; and to Paṇḍit Bhagwânlâl Indraji is due the credit of having prepared the facsimiles of nearly all the inscriptions now published.

The next volume will contain additional illustrations of the Elurâ Caves, and of the other groups of Brahmanical and Jaina Rock Temples.

JAS. BURGESS.

EDINBURGH, 25*th Oct.* 1881.

CONTENTS

LIST OF WOODCUTS.

NÂSIK CHAITYA CAVE AND ADJOINING VIHÂRAS (FROM A PHOTOGRAPH).

THE CHAITYA CAVE AT KONDÂNÉ (FROM A PHOTOGRAPH).

[Frontispiece.

REPORT

OF THE

ARCHÆOLOGICAL SURVEY OF WESTERN INDIA.

THE BUDDHIST CAVE TEMPLES.

INTRODUCTORY.

ONE of the principal objects sought to be attained by the publication last year of *The Cave Temples of India*[1] was to present to those interested in the study of Indian Archæology a general survey of all the known examples of rock-cut architecture in that country. As mentioned in that work, the number of these exceeds a thousand, and though by far the greater number of them are found in the Bombay Presidency and immediately adjoining districts, others exist, either singly or in groups, both in Bengal and Madras, but under forms as various as the localities are distant from the typical examples of Western India.

Another source of complexity arises from the caves being divided among the three principal religions which prevailed in India during the ages in which they were excavated. The oldest and most extensive series are those belonging to the Buddhist religion, whose votaries were the first, and for long the only, cave excavators. These were succeeded by the Brahmanical Caves, when that faith, in its turn, replaced the once dominant religion of the "Mild Ascetic." A smaller but hardly less interesting series of caves belongs to the Jains, who, at a later age, sought to rival the Brahmans in the magnificence of their rock-cut architecture. Their ages, too, are as various as either the localities in which they are found or the purposes to which they were dedicated. The oldest of all are the simple cells excavated for Buddhist monks during the reign of Aśoka (B.C. 263–225), or immediately after that date, in the granite rocks of Bihâr; and the series extends down to the most modern Bauddha caves at Ajaṇṭâ or Aurangâbâd, probably as late as 700 A.D. The Brahmanical Caves overlap these by a hundred or a hundred and fifty years, and may extend down to the tenth century, while

[1] *The Cave Temples of India*, by James Fergusson, D.C.L., F.R.S., &c., and James Burgess, F.R.G.S., M.R.A.S., &c. (printed and published by order of Her Majesty's Secretary of State for India in Council), 8vo. London, 1880.

the Jaina excavations, commencing about the same time as the Brahmanical, were continued in the rock at Gwalior down to the middle of the fifteenth century.

It was of course impossible within the limits of a single octavo volume, to which that work was necessarily restricted, to do more than point out the geographical arrangement of the various groups, their chronological characteristics, and to describe, as succinctly as was compatible with clearness, their principal architectural features, and the most interesting peculiarities of each of the various groups of caves, wherever situated, leaving the more detailed examination of individual examples for other opportunities.

Except in Mr. Fergusson's work on the rock-cut temples of India, published in 1845,[1] no such general survey of the whole subject had been previously attempted. The researches, however, which gave rise to that publication were terminated in 1839, and since then new series of caves have been discovered; others that he was not able to visit personally, have been described; inscriptions have been deciphered; and, generally, such progress has been made, that a new edition of his work—which this one on the Cave Temples practically is—had become indispensable. Neither of these works, however, pretend to exhaust the subject, but the latter will probably be found to be a useful manual for those who desire to obtain a general idea of this interesting class of monuments, and will enable any one who in future wishes to attempt a monograph of any single cave, or group of excavations, to dispense with any description of the whole series, and at once to assign to it its proper position among the Cave Temples of India. It cannot, however, for a moment be understood to supersede the necessity for more detailed descriptions of individual caves or of monographs of groups, which would occupy at least a dozen quarto volumes if carried out with the fulness which the interest of the subject seems to demand.

The present volumes are intended as a commencement at least of such a series for the caves of Western India. In the first it is intended to amplify and extend the description of some of the more notable groups of Buddhist Caves, which do not seem to have been hitherto sufficiently described, to illustrate them with additional details and drawings selected from the materials accumulated by the Survey, and to apply to the dates such rectifications as have only become apparent since the work on *The Cave Temples* was sent to the press. In the next volume it is proposed to apply the same process to the Brahmanical Rock-cut Temples—especially to the Kailâsa at Elurâ, the Jogeśvari Cave, and generally—with the Bâdâmi and other caves described in previous reports—to supplement the enforced brevity of the volume on *The Cave Temples.*

Owing to the very limited space available in *The Cave Temples*, it was found impossible to do more than allude in the most cursory manner to the numerous inscriptions that are found everywhere, especially in the earlier Buddhist caves, or to translate any of them, except some of the very shortest. In the present volumes this deficiency will be supplied: for though it is only too true that the cave inscriptions yield few facts of much historical value, and such data as they contain can rarely be affiliated to any known era, still, in the total absence of contemporary written records, they are, except the architectural indications, almost the only guides we have to lead us to a knowledge of the dates of the caves and of the objects for which they were excavated. Many of these inscriptions, it is true, have been

---

[1] *Illustrations of the Rock-Cut Temples of India;* 18 plates in tinted lithography (folio), with an 8vo volume of text, plans, &c. London: John Weale, 1845.

copied before, and various attempts made to translate them. The materials available were, however, generally only faulty eye-copies. During the progress of the present survey all, or very nearly all, have been recopied by impressions from the rock, so as to ensure their perfect accuracy in every respect, and the progress made during the last thirty or forty years in our knowledge of the Pâli language, in which most of them are written, renders the decipherment of them much more certain and satisfactory than has hitherto been the case. These cave inscriptions[1] are consequently intended to form a new and important feature in the present volumes.

As these volumes may be regarded as supplementary to that on *The Cave Temples*, it will be unnecessary to repeat the accounts there given of the different groups of caves, their localities, dimensions, &c. : in fact, most of the materials in this are additions to the illustrations there given, selected from the mass of materials collected by the Survey, and it is assumed that the volume referred to is in the reader's hands. In the case, however, of some of the more numerous but less known groups, a more minute enumeration will be given than space permitted in the general account.

CHAPTER I.

BHÂJÂ.

THE oldest cave probably in Western India is the small vihâra excavated at Bhâjâ in December 1879, and described in the Appendix to *The Cave Temples*. It possesses all the characteristics of the very early vihâras. It is small, as most of those at Junnar and the oldest at Ajaṇṭâ, Kuḍâ, Karâḍh, and Nâsik are; it has no pillars in the hall, and those of the verandah have been of the early square pattern with the corners chamfered off to near the bottom; the principal ornaments are the Dâgoba, Chaitya-arch, and rail-pattern; the jambs of the doors sloped slightly outwards towards the floor; there are stone benches or beds in the cell, a stone bench along one side of the hall, and a stone seat in the verandah, and there is no shrine nor image of the Buddha.

The general arrangements will be understood from the ground plan in the accompanying woodcut (No. 1). The hall is 16 feet deep by 16 feet 7 inches wide on the floor, and about 10 feet 9 inches high, with a bench 21 inches broad along the left side, and has two cells in the right and two in the back wall, and a fifth in the right end of the verandah. Three of these five cells have stone beds. In the portions of the wall not occupied by the doors of the cells are deep recesses, apparently intended either as seats or shelves on which to place articles, and each recess, like each door, is surmounted by the Chaitya-arch. Outside the vihâra, to the left, is a group of three small cells, each with its stone bed. These have evidently been excavated after the vihâra, apparently for

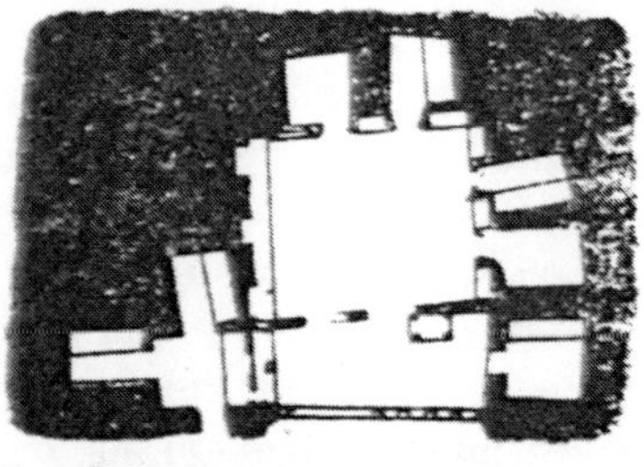

No. 1.—Ground Plan of the Small Vihâra at Bhâjâ. Scale, 25 ft. to 1 inch.

[1] A large number of these inscriptions have been recently printed by the Government of Bombay, under the title of "*Inscriptions from the Cave Temples of Western India*, by James Burgess, LL.D, and Bhagwânlâl Indrâji Pandit."

additional sleeping accommodation, and were entered, not directly from the hall, but by a separate door to the front.

All the sculpture about this cave is of that character which we find only in the earliest Bauddha works. The dâgoba is used ornamentally only, on the upper frieze of the back and end walls of the verandah, and is of the early simple type, without any abacus over the capital, but surmounted by an umbrella, and the dome surrounded by a festoon of flowers, while, in at least two cases, a garland of them hangs from the top over the front of it.[1] Between these dâgobas are Caryatid figures upholding the cornice above, which consists of four plain members, each about 2½ inches deep and projecting each about the same amount over the member below it. The lower of these has projections at short intervals representing the ends of a framework in a wooden house, from which this style of cornice has been literally copied. The Caryatids are male figures with a *dhoti* tied round the waist, heavy necklaces and bracelets, and large turbans. They stand in the recess, which is from 16 to 19 inches deep, incline slightly forwards, and in a few cases seem to have carried some ornament over their heads, which however is now damaged. It may have been the peculiar *triśûla* or trident head so common as a Buddhist symbol, though in one case at least it more resembles a grinning face.

On the front wall are three dwârapâlas very elaborately decked. The one between the two doors that enter the hall has, unfortunately, been much damaged. The upper portion of the wall was very thin and much cracked, and when the earth was excavated, it might easily have been pushed over, while large pieces on each side had dropped out, carrying away the arms of the figure.[2]

He wears an elaborately twisted bulky turban, and very heavy earrings consisting of four or five rings passed through a slit in the extended lobe of the ear, and to each earring are attached beads or pearls. He has a broad jewelled band about the throat, and another of a different pattern hangs on his breast, while a narrow ornamented belt or sash passes over the left shoulder and right side, probably to support the very broad sheath of a short sword, of which he holds the hilt in his hand. With the left hand he had held two spears, of which only the lower ends of the shafts are left. They probably had broad barbed points like those in the hands of the figure to the left of the second door. The feet are bare, but round the waist is tied an ample muslin *dhoti* which hangs in large loose folds around him.

On the right of the principal door is a stone seat, hewn out in full relief with moulded feet in front and against the wall, their projection up through the seat-board being also rendered in the stone. The edge of the seat is carved with a winding flower pattern and blossoms in the bays.

Over this is another dwârapâla very similarly dressed, his left hand on the hilt of the short broad knife or sword which he carries on that side, a bow in his right hand and a quiver on his back appearing over his left shoulder. He has heavy bracelets consisting of about five coils round the wrist, which on the right arm at least have been carved in some minute pattern. On the upper arm is a double coil to which are attached leaves or plates projecting upwards, and apparently of some precious metal graved or set with jewels. Owing to the seat in front, this figure is shorter than the other two.

---

[1] See *Cave Temples*, pl. xcvii.

[2] The wall was so rotted, that part of it fell soon after excavation, but it has been repaired, and a stone and lime one built behind to preserve it.

The third figure, to the left of the second door, or at the extreme left of the back wall of the verandah, is even more richly dressed than the other two; his head-dress is larger and more complicated, his bracelets and armlets are also larger, and have been finished with all the minuteness of carving that the stone would allow of; from the third of his ample necklaces hangs a pendant in the shape of an oblong jewel in a setting; he grasps the handle of his knife with his right hand, and with the left two spears, while two objects like bags hang from a knot on his girdle.[1]

The head-dresses of these and of all the other larger figures of this cave not only differ from all the sculptures in late caves, such as those of Ajaṇṭâ and Elurâ, of from the fifth to the seventh century, but even from the much older ones of Kârlê, Nâsik, the paintings in Cave X. at Ajaṇṭâ, and the sculptures of Amarâvati, and apparently belong to an earlier age.

The winged horse in the small sculpture in the left end of the verandah may be compared with those on the capitals in the Pitalkhorâ vihâra,[2]—also one of the very early caves. Such winged figures are exceedingly rare in Bauddha sculptures, and belong only to the earliest period.

The sphinx-like figures on the capitals of the pillar and pilaster in the recess at the left end of the verandah are also peculiar, and appear more archaic than those in Cave VIII. at Nâsik,[3] though related to them and to other similar figures found at Nâsik. These sphinx figures over the capitals, as shown in the annexed woodcuts (Nos. 2 and 3), have the bodies of bullocks with male and female busts. Their headdresses are very elaborate, with heavy earrings and armlets and jewelled necklaces; the females have also a beaded girdle. On the capital of the pillar a third head appears from behind the body of the front figure. The capitals themselves have a close resemblance to those of Pitalkhorâ;[4] and, as remarked by Mr. Fergusson, the whole pillar bears a marked family likeness to those represented on a portion of a gate-pillar at Buddha Gayâ.[5]

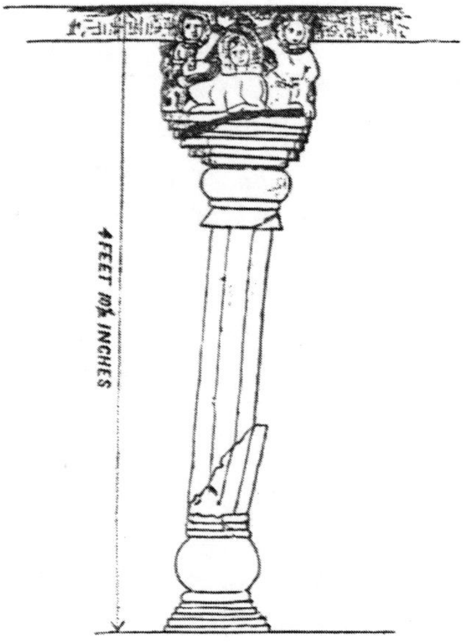

No. 2.—Pillar in the Verandah of Early Vihâra at Bhâjâ.

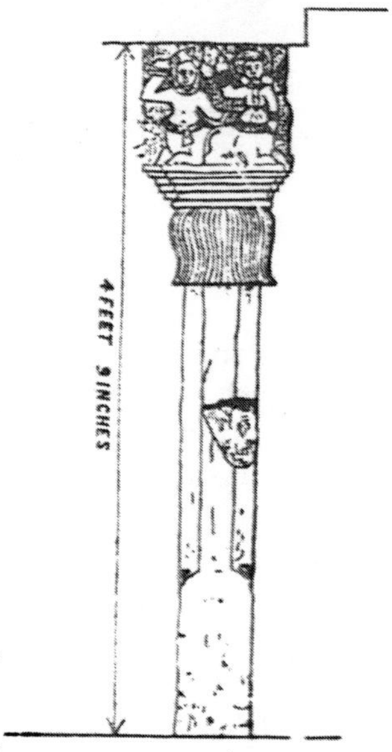

No. 3.—Pilaster in the Verandah of the Early Vihâra at Bhâjâ.

Curiously enough, too, on that fragment we also meet with the nearest approach to the style of the male head-dresses in the sculptures in this cave; and still further, as

[1] For these figures see *Cave Temples*, pl. xcvi. fig. 5, and pls. xcvii. and xcviii.

[2] *Cave Temples*, pl. xcvi. fig. 4, and pl. xvi. Also the horses and stags on the coping of the Buddha Gayâ railing. Cunningham's *Reports*, vol. iii. pl. xxviii.; *Bharhut*, pl. xxxvii. fig. 3.

[3] *Cave Temples*, pl. xxiii. fig. 3.

[4] *Cave Temples*, pl. xvi. figs. 1, 5, 6.

[5] Figured in Râjendralâla Mitra's *Buddha Gayâ*, pl. l., and Cunningham's *Reports*, vol. iii. pl. xxvii. fig. 1

Mr. Fergusson too has noticed the principal figure in the sculpture here (pl. vi. fig. 1), like Sûrya and his two wives on the Gayâ sculpture, is a male, seated between two women royally dressed, in a chariot drawn by four plumed horses, who are trampling down Râkshasas. Who these are, or the accompanying pair of horsemen, it is not easy to say. Mr. Fergusson also pointed out the resemblance of this sculpture to the carving on the brass lotâ represented in the accompanying woodcuts (Nos. 4 and 5), found in 1857, near Gundlâ in Kûlû, and now in the Kensington Museum.[1] It has no Râkshasas, but introduces three Bacchantes dancing and playing in front of the chariot, and two horsemen behind, carrying spears, and both with stirrups. Two horsemen also attend the chariot in the cave sculpture.

No. 4.—Ancient Brass Lotâ from Lahaul.

No. 5.—Engraving on the Ancient Brass Lotâ.

Behind the horsemen on the loṭâ is an elephant with some person of note and his attendant on it,—and on the right side of the cell-door in the same end of the verandah is another sculpture, the principal figure on which is seated on an elephant that carries aloft in its trunk a whole tree, wrenched up apparently by the roots. His attendant, seated behind, appears to carry two spears and a pennant, the head of the staff of which bears the Bauddha *triśûla*. The ropes of the housings have been carved in a way to indicate that they are of richer sort than usual, and the saddle-cloth is embroidered with figures of birds, &c. The turban, earrings, necklace, and garland of the chief figure here, like the dresses and ornaments of all the others in these sculptures, combine to indicate a period of great wealth and luxury when the display of riches was considered a mark of greatness.

The large number of small figures about the feet and in front of the elephant are not easily explained. Two Bo or Bodhi trees appear, one with a *chhatri* on the upper part of its foliage; the other with three people among the foliage, and others beside it or flying above; while in front is a man with turban and a long garland hanging from his neck, very like the rider on the elephant, seated on a *bhadrâsana* or cane seat, with a *chhatri* held over his head, and waited on by two females, one with a *châmara*, the other with a vessel in each hand—one of them shaped like a kettle; below, or in front of him, are three females dancing and playing, one on the same ḥarp-shaped instrument as the second figure on the Lahaul *lotâ* above noticed. To the right of these is the other Bodhi tree, and to the right of it, below the elephant, are two figures—a Kinnari or female with a horse's head[2] apparently striking at the shoulder or neck of a man who has a short sword in his right hand: below, behind, and beyond these are figures of monsters.

[1] *Jour. R. A. Soc.*, N.S., vol. v. (1871), pp. 367 f. These two woodcuts are from Dr. Birdwood's *Industrial Arts of India*, p. 154, and have been kindly lent by the author and Sir P. Cunliffe Owen.

[2] A similar figure appears on one of the pillars of the Buddhist rail at Buddha Gâya. See Cunningham's *Archæol. Surv. of India*, vol. i. pl. x.

The only other sculptures that have to be noticed here are the two figures in projecting panels over the bench on the left side of the hall. Each has a spear in his right hand, but the one has the rich armlets, earrings, necklaces, short and broad sword, and abundant headdress of the dwârapâlas outside (see pl. vi. fig. 2, 3), and the other has no ornaments whatever, and is more scantily clad. In later times, it is curious to note, when Bodhisattvas were represented as dwârapâlas, the one was also always richly clad, and the other without ornaments, or nearly so.[1]

No. 6.—Capital of a Dâgoba at Bhâjâ, from a Photograph.

Nearest to this small vihâra is the group of Dâgobas that form a peculiar feature of the Bhâjâ caves. They are fourteen in number, of which nine stand in an irregular line on a ledge of rock formed in cutting them out. The smallest of these nine are at the south-west end nearest to the small vihâra,[2] and are evidently the earliest. The capitals of several of them are broken off, but most of them have had nothing more than the representation of a box carved on the sides with the rail pattern, like the dâgoba in the Chaitya. Behind the seventh and eighth, other five are carved out under the rock, and of these—the two in front, have also only the square box-shaped capital. The ninth in the front row and the three behind the others under the rock have an abacus over the box supporting a small frieze; the latter have also *chhatris*, or umbrellas, cut in the rock over them, of which the staves have been of wood. The handsome capital of the ninth one outside is represented in the accompanying woodcut (No. 6). It is 3 feet 8 inches high and very elaborately carved.

On five, if not more, of them there have been short inscriptions[3] recording that they are stûpas of reverend Theras or Sthaviras—Buddhist abbots or high priests.

The oldest inscription found at this place, however, is over a cell-door on the right side of the vihâra numbered XVII. in the plan. The upper line is unfortunately damaged, but sufficient is left to enable us to read it with tolerable certainty. The letters of this inscription are of so early a form that we can hardly err in referring them to a period considerably anterior to the Christian era.

No. 7.—Front of the Cave at Bhâjâ, from a Photograph.[4]

The Chaitya cave here has been so fully described in *The*

[1] *Reports*, vol. ii. p. 46.

[2] See *Cave Temples*, pl. ix.

[3] See the transcripts and translations in the last chapter of this volume.

[4] From Fergusson's *Ind. and East. Archit.*, p. 111, also *Cave Temples*, p. 30.

Cave Temples (p. 223 f.), that nothing need be added here except to refer to the accompanying woodcut of the facade (No. 7) for the purpose of comparison with that of Kondâṇe, represented in the frontispiece. Plate vi. fig. 4 is a cross section of the Chaitya, showing the slant of the pillars in the aisles.

The upper-storeyed vihâra (No. IX.), to the left of the Chaitya, has been very much ruined, but a capital was found lying below, which must have belonged to one of the pillars of its verandah, and as it helps to indicate the style of the architecture—allied to that of several of the Nâsik caves—it is represented in woodcut No. 8.

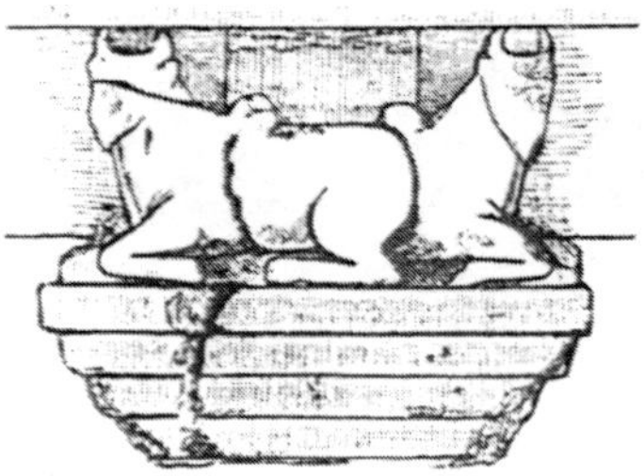

No. 8.—Capital of a Pillar at Bhâjâ.

Besides the archaic character of the architecture and sculpture in the Bhâjâ Caves, the stone benches or beds in almost all the cells of the vihâras is a very distinct indication of their early origin. The arches over the fronts of the cells, too, in Caves VI., X., and XIII., similar to those in Cave XIV. at Nâsik and Cave XII. at Ajaṇṭâ, are corroborative of this.

CHAPTER II.

KONDANE.

THE general characteristics of the Kondâṇê Caves have already been described in sufficient detail in *The Cave Temples of India*,[1] but as the Chaitya Cave there is one of the very earliest of its class, it seems to merit further description and illustration. Like Cave X. at Ajaṇṭâ, and the Pitalkhorâ and Bhâjâ Chaitya caves, it has no front screen left in the rock: in these four examples only were the screens wholly of wood. At Beḍsâ, Kârlê, Nâsik, and indeed all subsequent examples, this wooden front was replaced by one cut in the rock, and might consequently, even were there no other evidence, be safely assumed to belong to a subsequent period.

This Chaitya is further interesting, inasmuch as its façade—represented in the woodcut which forms the frontispiece to the present volume—is even a more literal reproduction of the wooden forms from which it was copied than that at Bhâjâ, which has of late been considered the most primitive of those known in the west, and in this respect equals the Lomaśa Ṛishi façade[2] among the Bihâr caves, which, there is reason to believe, was executed during the reign of the great Aśoka. Nothing could be more literal than the copying of the overhanging forms of the constructive parts of this façade, which show no trace of stone construction in any part, and which it would, indeed, be hardly possible to construct in masonry.

Every feature is essentially wooden in its form and derivation, and accords perfectly with the fragments of real wooden construction which still remain. Of this, however, unfortunately very little is now left. The wooden ribs that once adorned the interior of the roof have all disappeared, apparently in quite recent times, and of the open-work screen

---

[1] *Cave Temples*, pp. 220–223, pl. vii. fig. 2, and pl. viii.

[2] *Hist. of Ind. and East. Arch.*, woodcut, p. 109; *Cave Temples*, p. 39.

that ornamented the upper part of the great opening of the cave only a few pieces now remain *in situ*. These, however, are quite sufficient, when compared with the more complete examples at Kârlê and elsewhere, to render a restoration architecturally easy from them alone, even if we had not on the façade itself numerous repetitions of it, in the rock, on the heads of ornamental niches, and in various parts of the composition.

Besides these, the ornamentation of the façade consists of various string-courses and panels of the ordinary Buddhist rail pattern, and various constructive projections of very wooden form, with the brackets which simulate their supports. On the whole, in so far as the wood-work is concerned, it seems a more effective design than that of the Chaitya at Bhâjâ, and there is quite as little figure sculpture here as in that example. All the sculpture that is integral to the design is found in four panels on each side of the springing of the great arch, divided by compartments fitted with lattice-work. The two central compartments on each side contain each two figures, a male and female; the extreme ones on each side contain a single male; and the compartments next to the arch, three figures,—a man with a bow between two women.[1] In these the figures are but rudely cut; the head-dresses are of the same style as those on the façade of Kârlê and in the earliest caves. They do not appear to represent historical characters, and their only interest consists in their being apparently the prototypes of the groups of male and female figures we also find on the façades of the Hînayâna Chaityas at Kaṇheri and Kârlê and in Cave VI. at Kuḍâ. Below these,—on the spectator's left,—is the head of a single figure, represented in the accompanying woodcut. Doubtless it represented the excavator of the Chaitya, and is the earliest *śâlika*, or portrait statue, of which we have any remains; but unfortunately it has been entirely defaced. The elaborate and unique style of the head-dress—almost all that is now left of it—sufficiently indicates the care which the artist had bestowed upon it. The inscription to the right of the head, though short and of no historical value, is important as bearing out palæographically the early age which is assigned from its style to this cave. It is in the Maurya character, of about the second century B.C., and reads,—

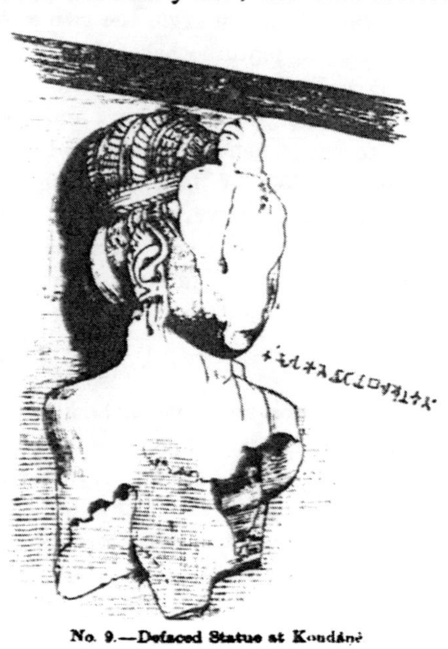

No. 9.—Defaced Statue at Koṇḍâṇê

Kaṇhasa aṁtevâsinâ Balakena kataṁ

and is translated, "Made by Balaka, the pupil of Kanha (*or* Kṛishṇa)"

Of Baluka and his master Kṛishṇa, of course, we know nothing. The name of Kṛishṇa could hardly have been unusual at that early date, for we have a Kṛishna among the very first of the Andhra dynasty, whom we have supposed to be contemporary with the earlier Śungas,[2] and, therefore, also to belong to the second century B.C.

---

[1] The compartment next the arch on the right-hand side is broken away.

[2] *Cave Temples*, pp. 26 and 275 n.

It is probable a similar figure (possibly a female) existed in a corresponding position on the right-hand side of the entrance, but the rock having rotted away from the action of the water there, all trace of it, if it ever existed, has disappeared.

Taken as a whole, this façade at Kondâṇê is one of the most complete and best-balanced designs, as well as the most interesting of those attached to these early Chaityas. Cave No. X at Ajaṇṭâ has no carving outside the great arch. Here, as at Bhâjâ, all the ornaments above the entrance screen are copied in stone, and in the subsequent Chaityas, such as No. IX. at Ajaṇṭâ and those of Beḍsâ, Kârlê, and Nâsik, the whole of the façades, including the entrance screen, are cut in the rock, though still retaining all the carpentry forms derived from the original wooden construction, and may consequently be regarded as mere wooden examples.

Internally this temple is a little longer and higher than that at Bhâjâ, but of the same width—this being 66½ feet long, 26 feet 8 inches wide, and 28 feet 5 inches high. The slope of the pillars and side walls of the aisles is decided, the pillars inclining inwards as much as 5 inches in a height of 11 feet, and the walls nearly as much in 8¼ feet, and from the close resemblance in style the two caves must belong to very nearly the same age.

The one feature that seems to indicate a slight difference of date is that the façade at Bhâjâ had apparently wooden ornaments attached to the horse-shoe fronton that surrounds the great window, and that at Kondâṇê had not, and no subsequent Chaitya seems to have been so ornamented in wood. This one fact may seem to indicate that Bhâjâ may be the older of the two, though the difference is so slight that they may be considered as contemporary or very nearly so. Be this as it may, these two are the finest among the four that are the very oldest specimens of Chaitya Cave Architecture in the west of India, and consequently worthy of any amount of attention that is likely to be bestowed upon them.

Cave at Ambivale.

The Ambivalê cave is about half a mile from the village of Ambivalê near Jâmbrug, north from Karjat, under the hill fort of Kotalgaḍh and to the east of it, and thus not far from Kondâṇe. Its age is uncertain, but it is considerably later than the last, and most probably belongs to about the first century of the Christian era. It may be noticed at this place, however, from its geographical position, and because it is not in any way very closely connected with any other caves. It is cut in a long low hill forming the concave side of a curve in the bank of the river. The cave overlooks the river, being about 20 feet above it,—the sloping rock leading up to it from the water. It consists of a large square hall, about 42 feet by 39 feet, and 10 feet high, having four cells off each of three sides—twelve cells in all. Around these same three sides runs a low bench similar to that in Cave XXXV. at Kaṇheri. Two doorways, a central and a side one to the right, lead into it from a verandah, 31 feet long by about 5 feet 10 inches deep, the eaves of which are supported by 3 feet 9 inches of the return of the wall at either end, and by four pillars. Between each pair of pillars (except the central pair, where the entrance is) and the end pillars and pilasters is a low seat, with a parapet wall running along the outer side and forming a back to the seat. The outside of the parapet wall was ornamented with festoons and rosettes, in the same style as Cave III. at Nâsik—which in all its arrangements the most resembles this one—but they are so damaged that but little now remains. (See plan, pl. vii, fig. 4.)

The pillars are of the same pattern as those of Nâsik—pot capitals with the flat tiles surmounting them, but roughly finished. The shafts, springing from the seats, have no bases. The central pair of pillars have octagonal shafts, the remaining two are sixteen-sided (fig. 5).

The doorways have had modern carved doors inserted at a late date, and within, in six of the back cells, are some built basements with carved figures on them. The cave has thus been converted into a Brahmanical temple. A Jogi, recently dead, long occupied it, the consequence being that the surface of the rock in the hall and verandah has been thoroughly coated with soot.

On the second pillar of the verandah, on the left of the entrance, is a short Pâli inscription in one vertical line, but much abraded and illegible.[1]

CHAPTER III.

PITALKHORA CAVES.

The quadrantal roof of the verandah in the small vihâra at Bhâjâ[2] shows that such roofs were not uncommon, and the arched cells at Pitalkhorâ[3] are also strictly in accordance with the style of the age; nay, if we look at the façade of one of these Pitalkhorâ cells (see pl. vii. fig. 1), we observe that the arches are not placed symmetrically over the doors, but extend from side to side between the capitals of the pilasters, and are intended to represent the extension, beyond or through the front wall, of the arched roof within. On comparing the section given in fig. 2 of one of these cells with the façades in fig. 1, it will be remarked that the arch in the latter is smaller than in the former, but this was necessitated here by the pilasters between the fronts being much thicker than the walls of the cells, and the intention is none the less evident that the outer arch was meant to correspond to that of the roof of the cell within. This is only another example, interesting because of its early date, of what we find continued into later works, namely, the distinct copying in these early monolithic works, never of stone buildings, but of constructions of wood. The "rail ornament" or *vêdikâ*, which covers so much of the façades at Kondâṇe, Bhâjâ, Beḍsâ, and Kârlê, too, is evidently the representation of a framing of wood, which probably was that in vogue in the construction of the walls of the better class of houses in the third and previous centuries B.C.

On two of the pillars of the Pitalkhora Chaitya are short inscriptions (Nos. 1 and 2) in the pure Maurya or Aśoka characters: they record the gifts of these pillars by two natives of Patiṭhâṇa,[4] the modern Paiṭhâṇ, which, as we learn from Ptolemy and the author of the *Periplus of the Ærythræan Sea*,[5] was a great commercial entrepôt in the beginning of our era.

---

[1] There are also some remains of letters on each of the central pair of pillars, but indistinct.

[2] See *Cave Temples*, pl. xcvii. figs. 2, 3.

[3] See *Cave Temples*, pp. 242–246, and plates xv., xvi. and xvii., figs. 1–3.

[4] See Inscriptions in the last chapter of this volume.

[5] Ptolem. *Geog.*, vii. i. 32; *Perip. Mar. Erthyr.*, § 51; and conf. *Report*, vol. iii. p. 54.

In the vihara, over the cell doors there are also five inscriptions (Nos. 3 to 7), two of them much mutilated, but all evidently recording gifts by Magila or Mṛigila, a râja's physician, whose mother was of the Vâchha or Vâtsa family, and of his daughter Dattâ and son Dattaka, who each contribute a cell in the vihâra.

In the remarks on the figure sculptures in the small ancient vihâra at Bhâjâ (*ante*, p. 5), reference has been made to the somewhat similar figures in this vihâra. At the left end of the back wall are a pair of winged sphinxes,[1] represented in the woodcut No. 10, along with half of the arch over the door and window of the cell. The one whose body is behind presents the teeth, as is usually done in the pictures of Yakshâs or Râkshasîs in Caves XVI. and XVII. at Ajaṇṭâ. The other has an ordinary human face, and the wing, like those on all the other figures in this cave, is not represented as a natural member of the body, but as an artificial addition. The figures filling the interspaces of the lattice-work in the arch should be noticed, and may be compared with the similar device in the arch over the Chaitya cave door at Nâsik.[2]

No. 10.—Winged Sphinxes, &c., at Pitalkhorâ.

CHAPTER IV.

CAVES OF KUDÂ AND THE SOUTH KONKAN.

A FEW additional details may be here given respecting the Kuḍâ caves,[3] 45 miles south of Bombay, though owing to their very plain character little will suffice. They are more interesting from their inscriptions than their architecture. These inscriptions, including all fragments, amount to about thirty, and the majority of them, being those of the excavators of the caves, are in Pâli—the language used in their inscriptions by the Hînayâna or earlier and purer Bauddha sect. They indicate that the caves are largely due to a family, apparently of local chiefs, named Mahâbhojas, and their official servants. But they yield no date or point of contact with any known dynasty. The alphabet of most of the inscriptions, however, is of so early a type as to justify our placing them early in the list of excavations.

Beginning with the lowest: Cave I. is a flat-roofed hall about 22 feet square, with a dâgoba in a cell at the back, separated from the hall by an antechamber the width of the hall, and about 7 feet 3 inches deep, divided from the hall by a low bench, on which stand two octagonal pillars (see pl. viii, fig. 1). The front of the verandah is destroyed, but it was

---

[1] Six other pairs of figures over the pilasters between the fronts of the cells are represented in *Cave Temples*, pl. xvi.

[2] *Cave Temples*, pl. xxv.

[3] *Cave Temples*, pp. 204–209. Pl. v. fig. 1; pl. vii. fig. 1

supported by two plain octagonal pillars and square pilasters with the sunk semicircles above and below a neck—a common ornament in the earlier Kaṇheri and other caves (pl. viii, fig. 6). In the left end of this verandah is a cell with a bench or bed, and over the door of it, close to the roof, an inscription in two lines (No. 1)[1] begins, and is continued along the back wall to the door.

Cave II. adjoins No. I.: the front room has a door and a large window, and there is a recessed stone bench or bed at the left end of it, and behind, to the right, is a sleeping cell with a stone bed in it. Cave III. is close to the last, and has a fragment of an inscription (No. 2) on the left-hand side wall, but all has peeled off except only the ends of two lines.

About four yards to the right, and at about 10 feet higher level, is Cave IV. It has a court in front with a bench on each side. The steps up to the verandah are broken. The verandah has two plain octagonal pillars with square bases, and square pilasters with similar ornament to that referred to in Cave I. A thin low parapet, with the rail pattern (fig. 8) outside, connects each pillar with its corresponding pilaster. In the back wall of the verandah a large central door leads into the hall, 34½ feet by 33¼, which is also lighted by a window on each side of the door. A stone bench runs round the three inner walls. In the back wall are three recesses roughly cut, as if it had been intended to complete this on the plan of some of the others, such as No. I. or VI. (see plan, plate viii, fig. 2).

Cave V. adjoins close by. In the left of the court of it is a recess over a tank of good water. Above the level, and to the right hand of this recess, is an inscription (No. 3). The *svastika* (卐) is formed at the end of the inscription. On the opposite or right-hand wall is another (No. 4), also much weatherworn, so that fragments only of a few letters in five lines are left. Still another inscription (No. 5) connected with this cave is in the left end of the verandah. It records the gift of a cistern by a nun, the niece of a Thera or senior priest, with her two disciples.

Cave VI. adjoins close to the last. A plan of it and detailed description is given in *The Cave Temples*. As stated there, the only sculptures that appear to be coeval with the cave, or nearly so, are those on the rail that separates the hall from the antechamber behind, the left half of which is represented on pl. viii, fig. 9,[2] and the figures (*śailarûpa*) in recesses on the back wall at the corner (fig. 7). The opinion expressed in *The Cave Temples* as to the early character of these sculptures has since been distinctly confirmed by the translation of the inscription (No. 6) in the left end of the verandah.

That inscription gives us a peep into the Bauddha social and religious life of perhaps a century before the Christian era: Skandapâlita is Mahâbhoja or local chief in the South Koṅkan, and in his service is a family, the sons of Sulasadatta—Śivabhûti, who is *lekhak* or writer, perhaps accountant, his next younger brother Śivaśarman, and four of his sons. They all bear names such as would only be found among the Saiva sect, indicating that though they (or their ancestors) may have been converts to Buddhism, they did not, as laics, feel bound to abjure all connection with the popular beliefs. One of them bears the name of Sarpila, from *sarpa*, "a snake," and probably pointing to serpent-worship,[3] which, however, was not inconsistent with his being a Śaiva. Śivabhûti constructs Cave I. for the use of the Bauddha monks, and perhaps also the *Bhikshugṛiha* Cave III. His brother Śivaśarman, emulating the religious munificence of his older brother, sets about the construction of Cave

[1] The translations of these inscriptions will be found in the last chapter of this volume, section 4.

[2] The other half was given in *Cave Temples*, pl. vii. fig. 1.

[3] One of the Rudras or terrific forms of Śiva is also called Sarpa.

VI.; and his wife and sons join him, and share the expense and the religious merit The prominence of the names of mothers and wives indicates that in ancient India women enjoyed a much more public and honoured place than they have done for centuries past; and this is in perfect accordance with the allusions to them in early Sanskrit and Pâli literature. Here the Mahâbhoja's mother's name, Vijayâ, probably of the Sâḍakara or Sâḍagaira family, is chronicled. Śivaśarman's wife is also called Vijayâ, and she, with their sons, undertake the sculptured work—the two pairs of figures on the back wall, and the front portions of two elephants at the ends of the façade—for these alone are coeval with the cave.[1] But this is not all: a share of the work is allotted to his four daughters, apparently daughters-in-law—for it seems more likely that they should be here called by the names of their respective husbands, than that he should have just four daughters called by feminine names corresponding to those of his four sons.[2] These women bear the expense of two plain octagonal pillars in the back of the hall, and other two in the verandah, with perhaps also the two pilasters. The family thus share among them the expense of a Bauddha chapel, plain indeed, but commodious, and one of the largest at this place; and though destined to last for at least two thousand years, there is no prayer attached to their inscription, or indeed to any of the earlier ones here, that the "merit of it may be for the attainment of supreme knowledge by parents and sentient beings." This idea, so frequently repeated in later donative inscriptions, seems to have been then unknown.

But other inscriptions in this cave, in a much later character and in the Sanskrit language, explain to us the origin of the other sculptures. These inscriptions being in Sanskṛit is sufficient proof that they were carved by members of the Mahâyâna sect, and are contemporary with the sculptures which belong to their mythology. On the front wall of the cave, at the left end and just behind the elephant, is a figure of Buddha, in low relief, 18 inches high, seated with his feet on a lotus over a wheel with three deer on each side, and upheld by Nâga figures, with other figures behind them. Beneath this and to the left is a fragment of a Sanskrit inscription, which has been but faintly cut, and is so decayed as to be illegible, except that it records a *deyadhammaṁ* or meritorious gift—probably of this sculpture.[3] On the left-end pilaster of the verandah has been carved a figure of Buddha, seated cross-legged, 13 inches high, with attendant *chauri*-bearers, that on the left being Avalôkitêśvara. Above is an arch, with Gandharvas on each side. The throne is a high seat with four legs, between which is a lotus, with a deer on each side of the stem. The legs of the throne stand on the semicircular ornament at the base of the pilaster, and inside this semicircle is a Sanskrit inscription (No. 7) stating that it was the donation of a female laic, and concluding with the prayer—so common in later inscriptions of this class—that the merit of it may be conducive to the attainment of the supreme knowledge by her parents, and, after them, by the whole sentient world.

On the face of the pilaster in the right end, near the top, are two Buddhas, each about 8 inches high, in compartments separated by a colonnette, and with a kneeling figure in the lower outer corner of each panel. Below these, seated on a *siṁhâsana* or lion-throne, with his feet on a lotus, is another Buddha, 13 inches high, attended by two *chauri*-bearers, one of them being Avalôkitêśwara, holding a lotus stalk as usual, and each standing on a lotus

[1] Is it possible that the very plain undecorated dâgoba was included in the *selarûpakamam*?

[2] Thus Sulasadatta's wife would be Sulasadattâ: Sivapalita's, Sivapalitâ; Sivadatta's, Sivadattâ; and Sarpila's, Sarpâ.

[3] See *Cave-Temple Inscriptions*, No. 6, p. 8.

flower. Overhead is a triple tiara, supported by two *Vidyâdharas*, with a *makara toraṇa* above; and over it, four more *Vidyâdharas* carrying garlands. Below, on each side of the lotus stalk, is a deer couched, with a man kneeling behind it and presenting some offering, and his wife at his back with joined hands. Below these are some other carvings, and in the semicircular ornament at the bottom is a Sanskrit inscription (No. 8) in three lines, faintly cut, and the right portion of it broken away. It appears to have borne the same donative formula as the last, only that the donor is a "Śâkya Bhikshu" or devotee, whose proper name is lost.

In the hall of the cave, as has been detailed, there is a good deal of late sculpture, all of the same type, consisting of seated Buddhas, teaching, with attendants. On the right wall near the back, under one of the sculptured panels, is another Sanskrit inscription (No. 9) in five lines, recording the donation of it by "the Śâkya-bhikshu Buddhasiṁha, for the benefit of his parents, the Bhaṭârka,[1] or high priest, and then of the world." Beside this is another piece of sculpture of similar character, with an inscription (No. 10), also in Sanskrit, partly on the left, and the rest on the right side of it. The character of the alphabet, the language, and the sculptures in the later carving in this cave, each independently point to about the fifth or sixth century A.D. as the period when they were added.

The next compartment represents a Buddha, 19 inches high, squatted on a lotus, the stalk of which is upheld by two Nâgas, behind whom are their wives, and below each two kneeling figures, and under them again a branched lotus (pl. viii, fig. 10).

Cave VII. is close to the last, but at a somewhat higher level, with a water cistern to the right of the entrance (pl. viii, fig. 3). On the left end wall of the verandah, which measures 17½ feet by 7¼ feet, is the inscription (No. 11) in four lines in Pâli of the same style as those first noticed. It records that the cave was excavated by a physician, Somadeva, his sons and daughters. The parapet wall connecting the pillars and right end pilaster is similar to that in the verandah of Cave VI., reprepresented in plate viii, fig. 8.

Just beyond the cistern outside Cave VII. is another, now dry, and the roof broken in. On the back of the recess over it is an inscription (No. 12) in three lines, of which, however, part of the first two are so worn as only to be read conjecturally,

Just beyond the last tank is Cave No. VIII., at a slightly lower level than the preceding. The door had a window on the left side of it: now the two are broken into one. This leads into an oblong chamber, with a door towards the right end of the back to a cell having a short recessed bench on the left side. In one end of this bench a box has been hollowed out, 21 inches square by 16 inches deep, with a counter-sunk lid 3 inches thick. This doubtless was for the concealment of valuables.

Close to this cave, but at a level 6 feet higher, is No. IX. (pl. viii, fig. 4). This is a small, flat-roofed Chaitya cave. In front the verandah, which measures 13 feet by 5 feet, had two octagonal pillars with the lotâ-shaped bases and capitals, and two plain half-octagon shafts in antis. A wide door leads into the irregular hall, 14 feet 4 inches deep, by 8½ feet wide in front and 11 feet at the back, with the dâgoba, 4 feet 4 inches in diameter, near the back, the abacus of its capital touching the roof. On the walls are traces of plaster. In the left end of the verandah is a cell, with door and window from the verandah as well as to the outer court; the front wall, however, is much broken. In the back of this cell is the usual stone bench or bed. On a smooth panel at the right end wall of the verandah is an inscription (No. 13) in one line.

---

[1] A corrupt form of Bhaṭṭâraka.

No. X. is close to the last, at about 5 feet lower level; the front wall is now destroyed but has had a door to the right, and a window to the left. Inside, the cave consists of an oblong room with a cell behind at the right end, having a stone bed in the back. Outside over the window, is an inscription (No. 14) deeply cut on a rough surface.

The next four or five caves are all in close proximity to one another, and in line; their fronts are ruined. The wall between the first two has been broken through, and the two together may be reckoned as No. XI.; the first has a verandah with an oblong room behind, having a stone bench along the back of it; the other is a larger room or deep verandah quite open in front. On the right end wall of the verandah to the first cave is a fragment of an inscription (No. 15) cut in two lines on a smooth panel, but much of it is broken away.

No. XII. is similar to the first portion of No. XI., but has a stone bench in the right end of the verandah. Partly on the back wall, and partly over the recess above this bench, is an inscription (No. 16).

No. XIII. is close to the previous one, and at a very slightly higher level; it has also an open verandah with a bench in the right end. The door is to the right, and the window to the left of it, and the nearly square chamber inside has a bench along the back wall. On the walls are traces of plaster. On the back wall of the verandah over the window is an inscription (No. 17) in one line terminating with a rude *dharma* symbol.

Cave XIV. is close to and on the same level with No. XIII., and is exactly similar in plan An inscription (No. 18) is lightly cut on a smooth panel on the left end wall, and extending along the back wall over the window. It records the gift of the cave by an ironmonger or blacksmith of Karâḍh, a town in the Sâtârâ district, which must have had a large and influential Buddhist population, as there are extensive Buddhist caves in the vicinity of it.

Just beyond this is a water cistern with an inscription (No. 19) deeply cut on a rough surface, but weatherworn and indistinct. It records the gift of this *Nânapoḍhi*[1] or bathing-tank for the bhikshus, by a merchant.

About seven yards from No. XIV. is a small recess (probably over a tank now filled up) with a much-effaced inscription on its rough, weatherworn surface. Eight yards farther is another similar recess nearly filled with earth and boulders.

Cave XV. is between fifty and sixty yards beyond No. XIV., at about 20 feet higher level, and is another dâgoba cave (fig. 5). The verandah, 23 feet 9 inches by 7 feet 4 inches, had four plain octagonal pillars, of which one is destroyed, and pilasters with the same ornament as before. At each end of the verandah is a cell with a stone bed or bench at the back. The shrine is about 13 feet 4 inches wide by 19 feet deep, and contains a plain dâgoba about 6 feet 4 inches in diameter, of which the abacus is attached to the roof. Deeply cut on a smooth surface in one long line on the left end wall and part of the back wall of the verandah, is an inscription (No. 20). It records the gift of the Chaityagṛiha by one Râmadatta, and of a cell by his wife, Velidatâ. There are traces of plaster on the roof and walls, and of painting on the columns.

The next four caves are in an upper tier, about 30 feet above the level of No. XV., and above the interval between that cave and No. XIV., but farther back. They are here numbered from left to right.

No. XVI. has an open court in front with a cistern at each side of it. Both tanks have

---

[1] Sans. *Snânapruhi.*

weatherworn inscriptions (Nos. 21 and 23) on the backs of the recesses over the openings into them,—one stating that the well was the gift of a gardener. A low stone bench runs across in front of the cave, which consists of an oblong chamber with a door from the court to the right and a window to the left, and has a bed or bench at the left end. Outside, between the window and door, is inscription No. 22, very clearly cut, and recording the benefaction of the cave by a nun, Sapilâ, with other females. A door near the right end of the chamber leads into a cell with a stone bed in the left side. On the walls of both the chamber and cell there are traces of plaster.

Cave XVII. is a little beyond the last, and is similar in plan, only it has a very large window. On the back wall of the chamber, close to the roof, and to the left of the cell door, is a partially effaced inscription (No. 24) stating that the cave was the gift of a trader and head of a family.

Cave XVIII. adjoins the preceding, and has a window on each side of the door, and also a window into the cell; otherwise it is like No. XVII. An inscription (No. 25) is cut on the left portion of the front wall, close under the roof, in two lines, with Bauddha symbols on each side of it. It states that the cave was the gift of a merchant (*seṭh*).

Cave XIX. is close to the right of No. XVIII., but about a foot and a half higher in level. The door is to the right of a large window, and enters a room 14 feet 9 inches by 6 feet 6 inches, with a passage 3 feet 9 inches wide leading back 8 feet 3 inches along the left end wall, and which has a recessed bed, 6 feet 2 inches long by 2 feet 3 inches broad, on the right side. To the right of the front chamber a door leads into a cell about 6 feet 9 inches square, with a recessed bench or bed at the back, 4 feet 8 inches long. Here, again, are traces of plaster on the walls.

Cave XX. is between fifty and sixty yards farther along, and at 10 feet higher level. It is difficult of access, and consists of a single small square room, the front wall of which is almost entirely destroyed.

Nearly thirty yards farther, and about 5 feet higher, is Cave XXI., an unfinished Chaityagṛiha. To the left of the front court is a cistern with a two-line inscription (No. 26) recording the gift by the same merchant as was the donor of Cave XVIII. The cave has two rough square pillars and pilasters in front of the verandah; and the hall, lighted only by the door, has a square mass left in the middle of the back wall, which, being partially worked out on both sides, was doubtless intended for a dâgoba.

Close to it, but at 3 feet lower level, is No. XXII., a single room with a bench along the back, and another outside on the left of the court.

Cave XXIII. is only separated from the last by sufficient room for a rock cistern in a recess. The cave has a door and two large windows into a small oblong room, at the back of which is a cell having also a window, and with a recessed bench at the back. Over the left window of the outer room is an inscription (No. 27), which states that the cave was the gift of a lady.

Cave XXIV. is only four yards further, and about 4 feet higher up, and is similar to the last, only the front is destroyed. The inscription (No. 28) is to the right of the door and partly on the right end wall: it is much weatherworn, but appears to record the gift of the cave, and perhaps a path to it, by a trader's son.

Close to it are the last two caves of the series: the verandahs of both are gone; each has a cell lighted by a window; and the first had a stone bench at the back; each verandah had also a bench at one end.

PALA OR MAHAD CAVES.

In the account of the Pâla caves near Mahâḍ or Mhâṛ (*Cave Temples*, p. 209) no illustrations whatever were given; and though they are not architecturally of much interest, it seems desirable, for the proper understanding of their character and arrangements, to give the drawings on plate ix., together with some notes of their numbers and sizes.

Fig. 1 is a plan of Cave No. I., which is supposed to be one of the latest excavations at this place. The rough square mass in the shrine was probably intended for a dâgoba, but a seated Buddha has been roughly sculptured on the front of it in low relief, with attendants at each side and the wheel and deer below, while other standing attendants are carved on the right and left sides of the block, and on the back another sitting figure of Buddha has been roughly indicated. The pilaster and the only finished pillar, at the left end of the verandah, are represented in figs. 8 and 9.

Fig. 2 gives the plans of Nos. II. and III., which are close together, to the north and above No. 1. No. II. has two pillars in front of a small verandah, 15 ft. 7 in. by 4 ft. 3 in., which gives access to a small unfinished cell. Cave III. has been very carefully finished, and consists of a raised verandah, beyond the front of which the rock projects a good way, giving ample shade. In the verandah are two pillars with square bases, and the remainder of the shaft octagon to the very top. This cave has been occupied in quite recent times, as the wall of the verandah is plastered and panelled in the Muhammadan style, shown in fig. 3. The inner room measures 17 ft. in length by 8½ deep and 7 high, and has a stone bed in the right end, the edge of which is beaded, and at the ends of it are moulded pilasters. From the right side of the court in front a stair has formerly led down to No. IV., and to the tanks in front of No. I., but the steps are now destroyed.

Fig. 4 gives the plans of Nos. IV. and V., which are at a considerably lower level. The pillars of the verandah of No. IV. are both broken; the room and cell behind are small. On the north or right wall was a large inscription about 3 ft. 10 in. by 2 ft., but only a few letters here and there can now be traced. In Cave V. the verandah—15 ft. 1 in. by 4 ft. 9 in.—has two octagonal columns with square bases, and the pilaster at the end has an ornament very frequent in early caves, and which is represented in plate ix, fig. 5. The verandah wall has been hewn very smooth, but the walls of the little hall—15½ ft. by 15 ft. 8 in. and 7¼ ft. high—are rough, and have been plastered. No. VI. is a recess in the rock, and No. VII. a very rudely finished verandah and cell.

The plan of Cave VIII. is given in fig. 6, and the section in fig. 7. It has been a Chaitya cave of the type so frequent at Kuḍâ. The two pillars of the verandah are destroyed, but part of the capital of one, still attached to the rock, and portions of the bases, show that they were of a type very similar to those in Cave VIII. at Nâsik and some of the Junnar caves. The pilasters have an ornament on the middle similar to that employed in Cave V. On the back wall is an inscription (No. 1) in pretty good preservation. It states that this *Chaityagṛiha*, a cave, and eight cells, with two cisterns, were the gift of a prince, Kânabhoä Vishṇupâlita. The dâgoba, however, has been hewn out of the shrine, and only the umbrella attached to the roof is left.

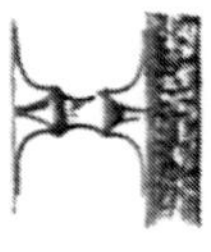

No. 11.—Pilaster ornament.

Cave IX. is south from, and above the level of, No. VIII. The verandah, 15 ft. 7 in. by 3 ft. 11 in., has two octagonal pillars in front, with corresponding pilasters. A door, with a small square window on each side of it, is pierced into the little hall, 15 ft. 3 in. by 6 ft.

9 in., which has a cell behind it. No. X. is very similar, but between the pillars and pilasters is a low parapet carved on the outside with the rail pattern, but much destroyed. Caves XI. and XII. have each two octagon pillars and two pilasters in front of the verandah, and inside an oblong hall with a stone bench.

Cave XIII. is under No. XII., and is similar in plan to No. IX. Cave XIV. consists of a verandah and a cell 10 ft. by 6 ft. 9 in. No. XIV. is a recess 4 ft. deep, containing a dâgoba 6 ft. 2 in. high and 4 ft. in diameter, in half relief. Cave XV. consists of a verandah 21 ft. 3 in. by 5 ft. 2 in., supported by two octagonal pillars, both broken, and a hall 18 ft. 8 in. by 15 ft. and 8 ft. high, with a bench round the three inner sides, and a cell off the east end of the south wall. The hall is lighted by a large square window on each side of the door. No. XVII. is an unfinished excavation; the verandah has two square pillars blocked out, but the hall is only commenced. Cave XVIII. is similar to Nos. IV., XIII., &c. No. XIX. is of the same pattern also, but the cell is unfinished; and No. XX. is only the oommencement of a cave.

In the lower scarp, about 30 feet beneath the preceding series, are the following:—Cave XXI., at the south end of this group, is a room 9 ft. 4 in. by 8 ft. 5 in. and 7 ft. high, with a dâgoba in the centre, 4 ft. 8 in. diameter, reaching to the roof. On the north wall is carved a figure of Buddha, of later date than the cave, seated with attendant *chauri*-bearers and *Vidyâdharas* holding a crown or mitre over his head; and over them is a *toraṇa* or wreath of flowers between the mouths of *makaras* on either side, as in Cave VI. at Kuḍâ. In the south wall is a cell with a stone bed.

No. XXII. is a plain verandah with a cell containing a stone bench. No. XXIII. is a copy of Cave X., with the rail pattern on the outer side of the parapet wall. The verandah is 15 ft. 2 in. by 4 ft. 9 in., and the hall, which has a square window on each side the door, is 14 ft. 10 in. by 6 ft. 7 in., with a stone bench in the north end. No. XXIV. was a room, of which the front has fallen, with two cells at the back. No. XXV. is a cell 9 ft. 3 in. by 7 ft. 10 in., with a square window. Cave XXVI. is a room with a window on each side the door, and a cell at the back, with stone benches in both. Cave XXVII. consists of a verandah 16 ft. 9 in. by 4 ft. 9 in., with two octagon pillars in front and pilasters, and a hall 17¼ ft. by 8¼ ft., with a cell at the north end of the back wall. Outside the verandah, on the north wall, is an inscription (No. 2), and on a raised bench, ornamented with the rail pattern, is a small dâgoba 4 ft. 2 in. high, in half relief. No. XXVIII. is a room 11 ft. 2 in. by 6 ft. 7 in., with a window on the south side of the door and a cell in the back wall.

From the above notes it will be seen that the Pâla or Mahâḍ caves are, like those of Kuḍâ, originally works of the Hînayâna sect, and that they have been occupied at a later date by the followers of the Mahâyâna school, but the alterations they have made are but of a trifling character.

Two small dâgobas, hewn out of single blocks, lie about the bottom of the hill, having been pushed from their bases. They are very plain, and similar to those found at Kaṇheri.

The Kol caves, south-east from Mahâḍ, are of similar type, but so very dilapidated as not to be worth enumerating. In the southern one of the two small groups are three inscriptions (Nos. 3, 4, 5 [1]).

---

[1] For transcripts and translations, see chap. xiv, sect. 5.

CHAPTER V.

KARÂDH CAVES.

Of the Karâdh caves, about 30 miles south of Satârâ, only two were illustrated in *The Cave Temples.*[1] To these may be added the drawings on plate x, where fig. 1 is a plan of Cave No. I., called by Sir Bartle Frere[2]—"Choka-Mela, the Mahâr's cave." It faces the south, and the pilasters at the ends of the front of the verandah have the same ornament as is mentioned in some of the Mahâḍ caves, and, with one exception, are the only ornamented pilasters or pillars among the Bauddha caves in this district. The pillars of the verandah have entirely disappeared. Nò. III. consists of a verandah 17 ft. by 6, with one cell behind, 6 ft. square.

Cave IV., named by Frere, "Lakshmîchi-Wâḍi," faces the south-east, and has a water cistern outside, on the right of the entrance. The verandah pillars are gone; the hall—17 ft. 5 in. wide by 18 ft. 7 in. deep and 6¾ ft. high—is lighted by two windows, and has two cells in each of the side walls, each with its stone couch, but the walls between the two on the right and the Chaitya Cave No. V. have been wrought so thin that they have broken down, and perhaps a door has been made from the front cell into the verandah of Cave V. Cave V. is the only Chaitya cave with an arched roof among these southern groups. It is about 13 ft. wide by 32 ft. long, and the window or opening over the doorway into the cave is about 4 ft. square.[3]

Cave VII., a few feet from No. VI., faces east, and has a cistern on the right of the entrance and a recess on the left. The fronts of the verandah and hall are much destroyed, but the former has had two pillars in front, each connected with its corresponding pilaster by a parapet wall; the pilasters have had the old ornament already described (p. 18). The hall is 20 ft. 7 in. wide by 9 ft. 7 in. deep and 7 ft. 10 in. high, lighted by a door with a window on each side of it. At each end of the room is a recess 7 ft. long, above the level of the floor, and with a projecting moulding up the sides in front. There are two cells in the back wall, each with its stone bed; and there is also a stone bench in each end of the verandah.

No. VIII. consists of a hall 19 ft. by 17½ and 6½ ft. high, with three cells, only commenced, on the left side. The front wall, which had originally two doors and no window, and the verandah are quite ruined.

No. IX. is across a watercourse from the last, and faces the south. It consists of a hall 16 ft. 9 in. deep by 20 ft. 4 in. wide, lighted only by the door, and having three cells in each side wall and two in the back, all with stone beds. In the centre of the roof of the hall of this and of Cave VII. are holes about 15 inches square and a few inches deep, the object of which is not understood. No. X., at a lower level than the last, is much filled up with earth, but is an irregular excavation. It seems to have been a large cell, or perhaps a tank with a covered approach to it.

---

[1] Pp. 213-217, and pl. v, fig. 2, and pl. vi.

[2] *Jour. Bom. B. R. As. Soc.*, vol. iii, pt. ii, p. 108, ff.

[3] For plan and façade of Cave V. see *Cave Temples*, plates v and vi; and for description of this and Cave VI. see pp. 214, 215.

Cave XI. is a flat-roofed Chaitya cave,[1] of which the plan and section are given in plate x, figs. 2, 3. Close to this is No. XII., approached by a passage from the front of No. XI., and by another from the south. The verandah had a bench at each end, and measured 26 ft. by 9, but the front has almost disappeared. The hall is 17¾ ft. by 5¾ and 6½ ft. high, with a stone bed at the left end, and has a small square window to the left of the door. At the back is a cell 5 ft. 9 in. by 3 ft. 9 in., with a stone bed, having a hole in the right end, 3 ft. by 2¼ ft. and 1 ft. deep, with a sunken edge for a cover. This was probably a place for concealing valuables.

No. XIII. is entered by a very narrow open passage 20 ft. long. It consists of three rooms opening into one another—the first, 14½ ft. by 4, and 6½ ft. high; the next, 12½ ft. by 6½; and the third, a cell, 7 ft. square, with a recess on the right. No. XIV. is a small outer room and a cell, 10 ft. 4 in. by 6 ft., with a bed in the right side; and No. XV., connected with it by an open passage outside, is very similar, the outer room being 15½ ft. by 7, with a recess in the left end and a window on the left of the door.

Cave XVI. is a flat-roofed Chaitya cave,[2] of which the plan and section are given (pl. x, figs. 4 and 5). It consists of the usual small verandah and hall, with a shrine quite open to the latter, as in some of the Kuḍâ caves. The square plinth, which serves as capital to the dâgoba, is connected with the umbrella carved on the roof by a short thick stone shaft. The next three excavations are mere cells, No. XVIII. being fully a hundred yards from No. XVII. and across a watercourse.

No. XX. is a vihâra, 28 ft. wide between walls and 35½ ft. deep, without pillars, but with a bench round the three inner sides. The plan and section are given in figs. 6 and 7. The front, if ever it had one of stone, is entirely gone, and there are sockets in the roof as if for wooden posts and frame-work, indicating, like some instances at Junnar and the Ebhal Maṇḍap at Talâjâ, that in the very early vihâras the fronts were probably in some cases of wood, or consisted of wooden screens between pillars. There appear to have been four cells in each side as well as in the back, with stone beds in them, but the front cells on each side have been altered. The remaining three caves of the first group are small and of no interest.

Cave XXIV., the first of the second group, has been finished with more care than almost any other of those here. It is in the bed of a watercourse, and faces the east-north-east. The details will be best understood by the drawings (plate x, figs. 8, 9, 10, 11). All the cells, except the central one in the back wall—of which the front has been cut out—have neatly carved stone lattice windows, about 15 in. square, the two cross-bars being rounded on the outside and the central portion of the two uprights fluted.[3] The next four caves are unimportant, and No. XXVIII. is about 150 yards beyond No. XXVII. Of the next eight, also of little interest, a sufficient account is given in the volume on *The Cave Temples*.

Fig. 12 shows the arrangements of Cave XXXVI., which is about a hundred yards west of No. XXXV., and which has an outer hall, 17 ft. by 13, with two cells, and an inner one, 9 ft. 4 in. by 12 ft. 7 in. and 6¾ ft. high, with five cells and two recesses. The next five caves are small.

In the third group, Caves XLII. to XLVI. are of little interest, and No. XLVII.[4] is

---

[1] See *Cave Temples*, p. 215.

[2] *Cave Temples*, p. 215.

[3] For further details see *Cave Temples*, pp. 215, 216.

[4] Sir B. Frere's No. XXXVI.; *Jour. Bom. B. R. A. Soc.*, vol. iii, pt. ii, p. 114.

chiefly important from containing some faint traces of inscriptions. On the left of the front is a cistern, and a wooden verandah has been at one time attached—the sockets for the four posts still remaining in the rock. The portico is about 12 ft. by 3, with a seat in a recess at each end, over which are faint traces of the rail-pattern ornament. On the back of the recess on the right are traces of an inscription, but only stray letters can be made out. Within is a room, 15 ft. wide by 11 ft. 2 in. deep and 7½ ft. high, with a bench in each end neatly cut, and with a slightly projecting edge. There is an unfinished cell in the back, and another in the left side, about 7 ft. by 6, and which has also a door to the front into the court. On the left or east side of the front of this is another inscription,[1] rather more distinct than the other. The letters are of a very similar type to those of the Kuḍâ inscriptions, but much worse cut, and record the gift of the cave by Saṅghamitra, the son of Gopâla. To the right side of the court of this cave was a stair leading up to Cave XLVIII.

Cave XLVIII. has been described in *The Cave Temples*, p. 216, and the sculpture by the side of the dâgoba there referred to, is represented in fig. 13, pl. x.

The rest of the excavations are small till we come to No. LVI. (figs. 14 and 15), which has a hall about 23½ ft. wide by 25 ft. deep and 9 ft. high, but has never been finished. Cave LXII. is still larger, measuring about 30 ft. by 38½, with about seventeen cells (see plan and section, pl. x, figs. 16 and 17). No. LXIII. is also a vihâra of some size, but choked up with earth.

CHAPTER VI.

BEDSA, KARLE, &c.

Respecting Beḍsâ caves, which belong to the series of groups around Bhâjâ, little need be here added[2] except to call attention to the longitudinal section of the Chaitya cave on plate xi, which exhibits the very plain and archaic character of the architecture of this cave. This Chaitya cave is interesting as one of the three or four examples of the class that retain the screen in front of the great window, which we may presume formed a marked feature in the wooden structures from which these Caves were copied. At Kârlê and Kaṇheri this screen consists of three openings below, and five above, rough hewn in the rock, and intended to be covered with wood-carvings, the mortices for which still remain. Here, and apparently here only, this screen is replaced by two pillars completely carved and ornamented with capitals bearing elephants, horses, &c.[3] It is not quite clear whether this indicates a more modern date than that at Kârlê, but it certainly marks a progress in style, and if the masses of rock in front were cleared away, it would show this to be—though small in scale —one of the most elegant and interesting Chaitya façades in Western India. The whole of the ornamentation in the end of the verandah, it will be observed, is a literal copy of wooden construction, and even the few figures that appear in the ends of the verandah and on the upper part of the façade at Kârlê, are awanting here. The pillars in the interior

---

[1] See below chap. xiv, sec. v, No. 6.

[2] *Cave Temples*, pp. 228–231 and pl. x.

[3] See woodcut No. 45 in *Cave Temples*, p. 229, or Fergusson's *Ind. and East. Arch.*, p. 113

are plain octagons and slope slightly inwards; and the dâgoba, though very similar in design, is slightly taller than that at Kârlê.

This cave possesses another peculiarity not observed elsewhere, in that the ridge of the roof slopes slightly inwards towards the dâgoba, which would certainly increase the perspective effect and tend to concentrate the light on the dâgoba.

At Beḍsâ there are only three inscriptions.[1] The characters are of an early type—the earliest being the line (No. 1) over the door of the cell in the right end of the verandah of the Chaitya, recording a gift—probably of the cell and its façade—by a person from Nâsik; the second (No. 2) is behind a small dâgoba outside, dedicated to the memory of a hermit; and the third (No. 3) is over a cistern close to the Chaitya cave, recording its being the gift of a Mahâbhoja's daughter. The first may date from before the Christian era, and the other two from about, or soon after, that date.

KARLE.

Since writing the account of Kârle Caves for *The Cave Temples* (pp. 232–242), the translation of the Inscriptions has helped to throw some light on the history of the great Chaitya. The inscription of the founder in the left end of the verandah, now satisfactorily read, informs us that this "most excellent rock-mansion in Jambudvipa," or India, was "established" by "Śeṭh Bhûtapâla from Vaijayantî." Vaijayantî is referred to both in Jaina and Brahmanical literature and in several copperplate grants, and seems to be the same as Banavâsi on the north-west border of Maisur,[2] in early times a very flourishing city. But whilst Bhûtapâla had a principal share in its construction, he was aided by numbers of devout Buddhists, who have left their inscriptions on the doors, and sculptures both inside the cave and outside, recording the donations of each. Thus under the feet of the elephants in the right end of the verandah is an inscription (No. 3)[3] stating that they and the rail-pattern ornament above and below were the gift of the reverend Indadêva; the right-hand door (Inscription No. 4) was the gift of a perfumer from Dheṇukâkaṭa; over the pair of figures in the extreme right of the verandah a short inscription (No. 13) tells us they were given by a mendicant named Bhadasama, who also gave the similar pair on the inside of the front screen facing them (Inscription No. 14). The base to the right of the central door, carved with rail pattern, called ***vêdikâ***, was the gift of a Bhikshunî or female mendicant (No. 15); and the similar piece on the left by another female (No. 16). Another belt of rail pattern on the inner face of the gallery or sill of the great window was also a female mendicant's gift (No. 12). On the remaining pillar of the open screen in front of the verandah it is stated (No. 5) to have been the gift of a housewife; and underneath is the record (No. 6) that a carpenter from Dheṇukâkaṭa made the doorway &c., but whether the doorway in the screen

---

[1] See *Cave-Temple Inscriptions*, pp. 26, 27, and chapter xiv of this volume, sect. vi.

[2] Dr. Bühler supposes Vaijayantî to be the same as the Buzantion of Ptolemy, which was on the coast. The Surab copperplates of Śaka 614, however, mention Vaijayantî (*Ind. Ant.*, vol. vi, p. 94; Rice's *Mysore Inscriptions*, pp. xxx, xxxix, 242) as an early Kadamba capital (*Ind. Ant.*, vol. vi, pp. 22, 25, vol. vii, pp. 36, 38; *Jour. Bom. B. R. A. Soc.*, vol. xii, pp. 319, 321), and it was evidently the same as Banavâsî, which is also often called Jayantipura in inscriptions of the middle ages. Here, in March 1880, I found a Pâli inscription dated in the reign of one of the Sâtakarṇi kings (*Cave-Temple Inscriptions*, p. 100). Vijayadurg, on the coast, may possibly have been the Buzantion of Ptolemy.

[3] See chapter xiv, sect. vii.

or that of the cave in the left of the verandah (which bears no inscription) is not clear. The lion pillar was the gift of Agnimitra, a Mahârathi (No. 2).

Inside, the third and fourth pillars on the left hand or north side were the gifts of Yavanas of Dhenukâkata (Nos. 7 and 10); the fifth (pl. xiii, fig. 1) was the gift of Sâtimitra, a Buddhist preacher of Sorpâraka, now Supârâ, a few miles north of Bassein (No. 8), and has a receptacle in it for relics (No. 9); and the seventh was also given by a native of Dhenukâkata (Inscription No. 11). All these are in an alphabet sufficiently early to be contemporaneous with the excavation of the cave, and they all relate to original features of it. The number of donors from Dhenukâkata suggests that it was some place not very far off, and as they are mostly Yavanas or "Westerners," we might look for it among the trading towns on the coast like Sorpâraka. It occurs too in inscriptions at Kanheri and Śailarwâdi, both in this part of the country. General Cunningham identifies it[1] with the old city in the lower valley of the Krishnâ, visited by Hiwen Thsang in the seventh century, and which he calls To-na-kie-tse-kia (Dhanakataka);[2] but the Pâli form of the name of that city, as found in inscriptions from Amarâvati, is Dhaṁñakata[3] or Dhaṁñakataka, quite a different name then from Dhenukâkata.

But after the temple had been finished, and, it may be, had been long in use, and the adjoining vihâras—all of them of the Hînayâna type—inhabited by a Saṁgha or congregation of monks, royal patrons bestowed lands in support of it. Doubtless Vihârgâńw, the village at the foot of the hill, belonged to it from the earliest times, and probably others, of which we have no record. But on the upper frieze, to the right of the central door and under the sill of the great window, is an inscription (No. 19)[4] of Usabhadâta, the son-in-law of Nahapâna, which bestows the village of Karajika on the Saṁgha for their support during the rainy season. Just below this, and among the prominences on the lower frieze, and afterwards partly cut away by a later piece of sculpture, is another inscription (No. 21),[5] which, from its position, must be of later date. Unfortunately, it is sadly mutilated, and the king's name is obliterated, but there is reason to believe the donor was Vâsishthîputra Pulumâyi, and it is dated in the nineteenth year of the reign. The object of this inscription is to confirm the rights of the monks of the Mahâsaṁghika school in the same village of Karajaka—probably Karañja, close to the Bedsâ caves in the Mâmâla or modern Mâvala district. Again, to the left of the central door, opposite to the first of these two, but on a worse surface (which would hardly have been chosen if the other side had not been previously occupied), is another inscription (No. 20) dated in the seventh year of the same Andhra king, recording the gift of some other village by a wealthy official. Plate xii gives an architectural elevation of the front of the great Chaitya itself inside the verandah, show-

---

[1] *Archæol. Survey Report*, vol. ii, p. 41; and *Anc. Geog.*, pp. 530 *seqq.* He reads the name as Dhanukakata, which is inadmissible. It is always spelt Dhenukâkata, but with the dental *n* or cerebral *ṇ* indifferently. In the fasciculus No. 10 on *Cave-Temple Inscriptions* (written in camp, January 1880), p. 32, this identification has been inadvertently adopted: it is of course erroneous. Dhenukâśrama is given in the dictionaries as the name of a place of pilgrimage.

[2] St. Julien, *Mém. des Cont. Occ.*, tome ii, p. 110.

[3] Equivalent to Dhaññakataka, Sans. Dhanyakataka (the city of wealth or of the wealthy—Daulatâbâd). The form Dhaṁñakata occurs on a marble now in the British Museum, photographed in Fergusson's *Tree and Serpent Worship*, pl. lxxxii, fig. 1; but the inscription, having been filled in with ink, is incorrectly represented; it is also copied pl. xcix, No. 20. The form Dhaṁñakataka occurs on a slab recently excavated.

[4] Chapter xiv, sect. ix, No. 6.

[5] See *Cave Temples*, pl. xiv, for the position of this as well as of the preceding inscription, and chapter xiv of this vol., sect. ix, No. 20, for the translation.

ing clearly the form of the wooden screen in the great arch, which is certainly the finest and most complete example still remaining in India. It is of teak wood, and no doubt original, and may therefore be 2000 years old. As at Beḍsâ, the ornamentation of the whole of the upper part of the façade consists of repetitions, on a smaller scale, of the design of the façade itself, or rather of the earlier example when the whole was in wood, and when the jambs and posts all sloped inwards.

The three doorways in the screen below, were all originally of the same height, and the central one about twice the width of the side ones. How the tympanum was ornamented is not quite clear—probably in painting. The only integral sculptures on this screen are the six panels, containing each a male and female figure like those in Cave VI. at Kuḍâ, on each side the spring of the great arch at Kondâṇe, and at Kaṇheri. They are placed one on each side of the three doorways, and, both from their style and the inscriptions attached to them, they appear certainly to be parts of the original design. All the others are subsequent insertions of the Mahâyâna school, and belong probably to the fifth and sixth centuries.

On plate xiii, fig. 2, is given a drawing of one of the pairs of figures above the elephants in the left end of the verandah. The style and quality of the sculpture in these panels is markedly superior to all the other more modern figures in the cave. They are in the same style of dress as the figures in the panels by the sides of the doors; and belonging to the original design, they prove that the latter are also part of it. There are two of these pairs in each end of the verandah, and a pair on each side of the great arch in the façade.

Some of the vihâras at Kârle are much ruined, the best preserved being the upper storeys. They have been described in *The Cave Temples* (pp. 240, 241), but the plans (pl. xiii) will illustrate their arrangements. The plan in fig. 3 is that of the first floor of a vihâra above the large ruined excavation to the north of the Chaitya cave. The stone benches in the cells are the only indication left of its age, for the front has all disappeared in the fall of the rock. Above this, and reached by a stair from it, is the cave of which the plan is given in fig. 4.[1] The pillars of the verandah are about 2 ft. 8 in. square at their bases, then a band 10 in. deep is octagonal, on which stands the neck of the capital, 2 ft. 7 in. high, with sixteen sides or flat flutes. This turns slightly out, and is surmounted by some narrow members and then by a torus 12 in. deep, but which does not project beyond the vertical lines of the pillar, and is crowned by two thin square plinths. In the east wall of the vihâra (fig. 5), which is still farther to the north and reached by a stair now broken, is an inscription (No. 22) of the time of the Andhra king, Puḷumâyi, who probably ruled about the middle of the second century A.D.

Fig. 6 is the plan of a hall to the south of the Chaitya, which has originally been 21½ feet deep, but, like No. XV. at Nâsik, has been afterwards enlarged to 33 feet, and by the Mahâyâna sect, for it has an image of Buddha on the back wall. This, and the later sculptures of the same character on the screen wall of the Chaitya, show that when the Hînayâna school either died out or lost the favour of a degenerating age, the more sensuous and less morally strict followers of the Mahâyâna school got possession of these Cave Temples and used them for their own services. This must have been at a later age, however, than Puḷumâyi's—possibly in the end of the fourth, or in the fifth century.

Of the Śailarwâdi caves,[2] 14 miles east from Kârle, nothing more need be said. The one inscription by a native of Dheṇukâkaṭa will be found in its place.[3]

---

[1] For a fuller account of these caves see *Cave Temples*, pp. 240, 241.

[2] *Cave Temples*, p. 246.

[3] Chapter xiv, sect. vii, No. 19.

CHAPTER VII.

JUNNAR CAVES.

The account of the Junnar Caves already given in *The Cave Temples*[1] need only be supplemented by a list of the various excavations in the different groups, with their dimensions and the inscriptions. As previously described, they are found in five different localities round the town of Junnar, and the number of separate caves is upwards of 130.[2] Of these there are between fifty and sixty in the Śivanêri Hill; about ten at Tuljâ Lenâ; thirty in the Gaṇêśa Lenâ; four in a spur of the hill a mile beyond it; and between thirty and forty in different parts of the Mânmoḍi Hill.

The small amount of sculpture, its character, the generally small size of the vihâras, the frequency of the early form of *Bhikshugṛihas* or mendicants' cells, and the stone beds in the cells, all combine to indicate that many at least of these excavations must be of very early date.

Caves in Sivaneri Hill.

Beginning with those near the base of the eastern scarp of the Śivanêri Hill, and commencing at its southern extremity, we have—

No. 1. A small cell some way up the scarp, and inaccessible.

2. At a short distance to the north, a cell about 7½ feet square by 6½ feet high, with an open verandah or court in front, and a dry cistern to the left of the front.

3. A cave 20½ feet wide by 19½ feet deep and 11 feet high, and with a door 6 feet wide, and containing the base of a dâgoba, 3½ feet high and 5 feet in diameter, with a hole sunk in the flat top.[3] The verandah is 16½ feet by 4½ feet, but one of each of its two free standing and two attached pillars are gone; they have had *lotâ*-shaped bases and capitals, with octagonal shafts.

4. A cell 8 feet 3 inches by 9 feet 6 inches and 7 feet 3 inches high.

5. Three cells with the front and dividing walls broken away. Outside to the left, but under the projecting eave, is a bench, and over it, on the end wall, is a short inscription (No. 1)[4] in two lines about 20 inches long, but the first three or four letters of each line have been broken away. It records the gift of a cistern (*pôdhi*), and perhaps of the cave.

6. At a higher level is a cell 8 feet square and 7 feet high, with a large recess in the back wall near one corner, and three slightly sunk panels on the remainder of the wall, which also bears faint traces of plaster.

7. Under the above is a large open cell 15 feet by 10 feet. 8. Next comes a small cell

---

[1] *Cave Temples*, pp. 248–262, pl. xviii, pl. xvii, figs. 4–5 and frontispiece.

[2] *Cave Temples*, p. 168. At p. 248 the number '57' is a misprint for 157; without counting wells and small recesses, there are about thirty more excavations than here estimated; and counting all unfinished cells, recesses, and cisterns, the total number must be nearly 200.

[3] *Cave Temples*, p. 249.

[4] For the facsimiles, transcripts, and translations of these inscriptions see chap. xiv, sect. viii, at the end of this volume.

with an open porch 4 feet square. 9. A cave 16½ feet wide by 15½ feet deep and 8 feet high, with a door 5½ feet wide. It has two small recesses in the back wall and faint traces of plaster.

10. A small recess broken through on the right into—11. An irregular-shaped excavation at a lower level, 7 feet wide by 11 feet deep and 5 feet high, with a stair within, on the right side, leading up to—12. Which consists of three cells, 7 feet to 8 feet square, and 6½ feet high, with a common open verandah in front, 16½ feet by 4 feet. There are faint traces of plaster in the third of these cells.

13. A cell above the last, but inaccessible, owing to the steps which led up from the outside of No. 11 being broken away.

14. A cell on the same level as No. 12, 7 feet square and 7 feet high.

15. A small recess, perhaps the entrance to an intended cistern; 16. Two small cisterns with water; 17. A recess similar to No. 15; 18. Three cisterns over 16 and 17, but filled with earth; 19. A recess begun at a high level; 20. A tank with water; 21. A recess begun; and 22. A chamber open in front, 9 feet by 8 feet and 6 feet high, with a bench on the left side.

From this point a path leads upwards and back over the lower caves to the upper scarp: there are also steps descending down from it. On reaching the base of the upper scarp over the preceding caves, and beginning again from the south end, we have first a small group of caves, viz.:—No. 23. Very high in the cliff, an open chamber, inaccessible. 24. Near the left of a narrow open gallery, ascended by steps at the north end, is a cell 6 feet wide by 8 feet deep and 6 feet high, with a bench along the back. The floor of the gallery in front is broken away and the footing precarious. 25. The commencement of three open cells at a lower level.

26. A two-storeyed vihâra cave, 24 feet wide by 22 feet deep and 7½ feet high, with ten cells, four in the back and three in each side, but half of them in an unfinished state. It is entered by a single door and lighted by two windows, and has in front an open verandah 23½ feet by 5 feet. In the right front corner a stair leads to the upper storey, which is a hall open in front, 21 feet wide by 11 feet deep and 7 feet high. On the pilaster on the left is one of those ornaments so frequent at Kaṇheri, Kuḍâ, and elsewhere; behind this is the commencement of a cell, and then along the upper part of the remainder of the wall (8 feet) is an inscription (No. 2), deeply cut, in one line, commencing with the Buddhist shield ornament. It tells us that this upper room was the *upasthâna śâlâ* or reception-room of the monastery.

27. Passing a cistern to the right of the last, we come to a cell; and then to—28. A second cell with a long open verandah.

At a rather higher level than these, and more to the north, is a third group, difficult of access, the footpaths to it being very steep and ending in steps cut along the scarp. It commences with No. 29. A small unfinished recess, next to which, and at a higher level is—30. Another, 12½ feet by 10 feet and 8½ feet high, over a dry cistern, with two openings into it and a low bench along the back wall between the openings. 31. Another cistern at the foot of the steps leading to No. 29, and beside it two others filled in.

32. Higher up is a small open chamber, about 8 feet square and 6½ feet high, with a bench along the left side. From this point steps in the rock formerly led up the scarp into

---

[1] *Cave Temples*, p. 250.

the fort, but they have been destroyed. On the face of the rock, between this and the next, are traces of two bas-reliefs of standing figures about 2½ feet high.

33. Another recess, 7 feet wide by 5½ feet deep and 7 feet high.

34. An open hall, 20 feet by 22½ and 8 feet 9 inches high, with a bench round all three sides, having an advanced seat at the back. The verandah is 18 feet long by 3 feet wide, with a pilaster at each end, into which a wooden front seems to have been fitted——probably this was another reception or assembly room: it has traces of plaster on the walls.

35. Is a room 15 feet wide by 11 feet 6 inches deep and 8 feet 3 inches high, with a bench along the left wall and half of the back. The walls are much ruined, being over a large water cistern, which extends out to the front of this and along to the next. There are traces of plaster on the walls.

36. A vihâra cave, 31 feet by 16 feet deep and 7½ feet high, with two cells in the left end and four in the back, the extreme right one being large, and with an ornamental door lintel let into the rock. The front wall is structural, with a carved doorway and lattice stone window. Outside is a stone bench in each end of the verandah, and on the right end wall has been an inscription beginning with the *dharma* symbol, but the letters are nearly all obliterated.

37. Is a recess or open room 10 feet by 6 feet and 5 feet high, at a rather lower level; and over it is a similar apartment 15 feet square by 7 feet high, with a well opening in the right-hand back corner into No. 38. It is probable that all these open chambers had wooden fronts.

38. Is a hall 20 feet by 13½ feet and 8 feet high, with a single plain door and a bench all round the inside. The verandah is broken in from above, and just beyond it to the right is an unfinished recess.

The next group on this scarp can only be reached from the preceding by descending the hill about half way and then going up right in front of them. It begins with No. 39 At some distance from the rest, high up, but accessible by steps from below, is a verandah 32½ feet by 7 feet, with a cell in the left end and a cell and unfinished chamber in the back.
40. A cistern, and a chamber 16 feet wide, 13 feet deep, and 9 feet high, with open front.
41. A smaller chamber, 9 feet by 7 feet and 7 feet high, also open in the front, and with a bench in the left side. There is also a bench in a recess between this and the next.

No. 42. A Bhikshugṛiha 9½ feet wide by 7 feet deep and 6½ feet high, with a bed or bench in the right side. The verandah is 14 feet by 5 feet, and has a large dâgoba in bas-relief in the left end. On the left of the cell door is an inscription (No. 3) in five lines about 6 feet 4 inches long, but unfortunately considerable portions of the last three are peeled off.[1] It has the *triśûla* or *dharma* symbol at the beginning.

43. An open verandah, 45½ feet long by 5 feet and 7½ feet high, with four cells at the back of it, the left one with an open window. Beyond this are three water cisterns.

44. Is directly over the preceding, and is a plain room, 15 feet 9 inches by 14 feet 9 inches and 7 feet high, having traces of plaster on the walls, with a verandah in front, which has had two columns in front, now broken, and two pilasters. It is reached by a stair from the verandah of the next.

45. Is locally known as the Bâra Kôtri[2] or twelve cells. It is a vihâra 36 feet 8 inches

[1] This is No. 15 of Lieutenant Brett's series, and divided into Nos. 8 and 9 of Dr. Stevenson's series, *J. B. B. R. A. S.*, vol. v, p. 163 f.; it is No. 6 of those copied by Colonel Sykes, *J. R. As. Soc.*, vol. iv, p. 287 f.

[2] *Cave Temples*, pp. 250, 251.

wide by 33 feet 5 inches deep and 9 feet 6 inches high. The cells are without benches, and one of them unfinished. On the ceiling are some remains of plaster, with faint and indistinct traces of painting in square reddish panels, with a light circular area in each. The divisions between the panels are also light.

46. A cell 7½ feet square, with an open verandah 15 feet 9 inches by 4 feet, having a stone-bench in the right end. There are a few patches of plaster on the ceiling showing traces of paint. Two dry cisterns are between this and the next.

47. A cell; 48. Another with a bench orbed on the left side; and 49. A large irregular recess.

50. A small vihâra, 19 feet by 18 feet and 7½ feet high, with three cells on the left side and two in the back, with a large dâgoba in bas-relief between them. On the left of the door was a large window; but the wall between is broken away. There are traces of plaster and paint on the ceiling and upper part of the walls.

51. Is a Chaitya Cave.[1] On the back wall of the open verandah, near the right end to the right of the window, is an inscription (No. 4), in 3 lines, about 5 feet long each, and complete, with a peculiar symbol at the commencement, also found in other inscriptions.

52. An unfinished recess above and an open cistern below. 53. After this is another cistern and three recesses in succession. 54. A cistern with a recess above it, and on the upper portion of the back wall of it is an inscription (No. 5) in one line, 4½ feet long and quite perfect, recording the donation of two such wells. 55 A cell 7½ feet square and 6½ feet high. 56. A dry open cistern with inscription (No. 6) on the rock above it. It is in two lines, and many of the letters are peeled off. It records the gift of two cisterns by a member of the Apaguriya sect and his wife.

Passing over the spur that strikes out to the north-east from Sivanêri, we reach the precipitous west side. The exact number of excavations here is doubtful; they are so hidden and choked up in front by prickly pear and thorny creepers as to be almost inaccessible. The first towards the north-east is No. 56. A hall, 30 feet 8 inches wide by 27 feet 6 inches deep, with two windows and a door. It has a verandah 4 feet wide, in which have been four wooden pillars. The abacus of four thin members is carved in the rock with a hole about 2½ inches square on the under surface to receive the tenon of the wooden shaft. On the ceiling of the hall is a fragment of painting, just sufficient to show that it has been the same in style as that in the Chaitya (No. 50) on the other side of the hill. There is perhaps another small excavation close to this.

At some distance to the west is No. 57. A group consisting of five wells and one vihâra with four cells, and with a mud wall built up in front of it; and 58. South from these are fragments of three or four others in a dilapidated state.

Passing round to the south side of the Śivanêri Hill, we come to the last group of excavations in its scarps.

No. 59. The first excavation now forms the shrine of a Hindu Temple in the second line of fortification, to which a tiled roofed mandap has been added.

60. A cell with the doorway half built up; and 61. An unfinished cell.

62. A Bhikshugṛiha, consisting of a cell with an inner one at the back, having a stone bed in the left side of it. The open verandah in front is 23½ feet long by 3 feet deep, and on its back wall on a slightly sunk panel is an inscription (No. 7) in two lines.

---

[1] This is described fully in *Cave Temples*, p. 251 and plate.

63. At a higher level than the last is another Bhikshugṛiha, with a stone bed in the back wall and a small window to the left of the door The verandah is 14 feet by 5 feet, and to the left of the cell is an open recess, 3 feet wide by 5 feet deep.

64. Close to the last, and partly broken into the verandah of it, is a recess 4½ feet by 5 feet, with a bench at the back. 65. A water cistern, of which the roof is broken in. 66. A small recess.

67. An open hall or refectory, 19 feet by 14½ feet and 8 feet high, with a bench round the three inner walls. A wall with a central door had been built in front some twenty or twenty-five years ago. On the left-side wall at the entrance is an inscription (No. 8) in four lines, each about 25 inches long.

68. Passing a water cistern, there is a small cell not quite finished, but with traces of plaster on the walls and ceiling.

69. Again passing three cisterns, there is a small Chaitya cave with a verandah, having had two octagonal pillars, with capitals in front, and two in antis, but only one of the latter on the left side is left. Over the door is an inscription (No. 9), in one line, easily read. A door leads from this into the next, No. 70, which is a hall, 24 feet by 22 feet and 8 feet high, with a bench along the back wall, lighted only by the doorway, which has sloping jambs—a very unusual feature—but found in very early caves at Bhâjâ, and near Kalyâṇ in the Dekhan. This has apparently been painted, but in later times it has been used as a Hindu shrine, and whitewashed.

No. 71. After passing an open cistern, we reach a Bhikshugṛiha, open in front, which was perhaps originally closed with boarding, with a stone bed in the left side and a cell at the back to the left; also a sort of passage going back on the right side of the cell. Here the fortification ends.

Below, and in front of these in the bottom of the scarp, are two or three more small excavations.

The total number of excavations in the scarps of the Śivanêri Hill, counting all the cisterns, &c., is at least ninety.

Tulja Lena Group.

The Tûljâ Lêṇa group has been described in sufficient detail in *The Cave Temples*. It is so dilapidated, and so much of the front rock has fallen away, that it is not easy to say how many separate excavations there may originally have been. The second is a vihâra, 17½ feet square and 7 feet high, with two cells at the back, two in the left side and one in the right. The front wall, however, has been all broken away. The third is the circular Chaitya.[1] Twelve or thirteen cells follow, and then a hall 23 feet wide and about 28 feet deep, with a bench round the three sides; the front is open, and there is one cell on the right near the front. Probably this was also a 'refection hall.' The absence of benches or beds in this series may possibly indicate that it is not so old as some in the other groups.

Caves in the Sulaiman Hills.

The Sulaimân Pahâr, or Gaṇêśa Lêṇa series, about three miles north-east from Junnar, has the characteristics of the earliest class of caves in their stone benches, absence of sculpture, and of pillars in the largest of the halls.

[1] *Cave Temples*, pp. 252, 253.

The first three are Bhikshugṛihas, or residences for single monks, the fourth is a room 16 feet by 11 feet and 8 feet high, with a window to the left of the door, and a bench along the right end.[1] No. 5 is a large hall, 26 feet wide, 29 feet deep and 8 feet high, with seven cells with stone beds. It has a bench all round the three inner sides, and over the left window outside is an inscription (No. 10), in one line; and outside the verandah, to the right, is a water cistern.

No. 6.[2] Is the principal Chaitya cave in this group, and forms a connecting link in the development of this type of caves. The necessity of defending the open fronts of the Chaitya caves from the rains had been learnt from earlier examples, such as those of Kondâṇe and Bhâjâ, but the solution of this problem attempted at Beḍsâ and Kârle, of setting the chapel well back behind a screen, seems not to have been arrived at, and some of the Chaityas are only flat-roofed rooms.

Here a verandah similar to that in the vihâras, with flat roof, supported by two free and two attached pillars in antis, forms the porch to the cave, from which a wide and lofty door—to give as much light as possible—leads into the arched nave of a Chaitya, 41 feet 3 inches long by 22 feet 6 inches wide, with a dâgoba of the same style as that at Beḍsâ, and animals over the capitals of the pillars in *rilievo*—an ornament which at Kârle and Kaṇheri is carried a step further by their being cut in almost entire relief. The same feature appears in the Nâsik vihâras, but in still later caves disappears with the introduction of the bracket capital. The next step to be made was to pierce the rock over the verandah with an arched window, and in this example it seems to have been thought of, but perhaps after the cave was finished—for a semicircular area has been sunk on the face of the rock above the verandah, but smoothed and never carried further; and whether or not it was intended to carve it similarly to the façade of the Mâṇmoḍi Chaitya, as seems not improbable, must remain doubtful. Above it are two smaller square recesses. As already stated in *The Cave Temples*, we may assign it to not later than the first century of the Christian era, or even earlier.

The close resemblance of the pillars in this cave to those of Cave VIII. at Nâsik would lead us to attribute both of them to nearly the same age, and this one is probably the earlier of the two. The Nâsik vihâra indeed is almost a copy of the larger vihâra close to this, and now used as a Hindu shrine of Gaṇêśa.

The single line of inscription (No. 11) in the verandah of this cave is in characters of an early type, before the letters began to have heads or *serifs* to the stems, but when the engravers were beginning to widen the strokes a little at the upper extremities, and slightly to turn round the down-strokes of *ka*, *ra*, &c.; but it has still the early or Maurya form of *e*.

No. 8 is only a recess; No. 9 is a verandah 19 feet long, with a recess in the right 4 feet wide and 12 feet deep, having a bench at the back and a cell to the left, with a bench recess on its left side.

10. A hall at a lower level, 31 feet 3 inches by 23 feet 2 inches and 9 feet high—the verandah of four columns totally gone except their bases. It has a door in the centre, and another at the extreme left, also a window on each side the central door.

11. Difficult of access, is a Bhikshugriha with an open verandah in front. It has a door

[1] Nos. 5, 6, and 7 are fully described in *Cave Temples*, pp. 253–256.

[2] *Cave Temples*, pl. xviii, fig. 10.

in the middle, with a window on each side, into a chamber 20 feet wide by 5 feet deep, with a bench in the left end. Behind this are two cells, that to the left having a bench at the back, and that to the right a bench on the left side. There are traces of plaster on the roof of the chamber.

12. Passing along a ledge of rock and over a small cistern, we come to a room 21 feet by 16 feet, quite open in front, and with a cell in the left end and a stone bed in it.

13. At a higher level, and very difficult of access, is another Bhikshugṛiha similar to 11, with stone benches in the left cell, and in the right ends both of the verandah and the front chamber.

14. Lower in the rock, the next has had two octagonal pillars in front of the verandah and a low screen wall. The pillars are gone, but on one of the pilasters left is the ornament. In the left end of the verandah is a short bench. The door leads into a room 10 feet by 7½ feet, with a stone bed in each end. Behind, on the right, is a plain cell, and, on the left, a passage 3 feet wide and 10 feet deep, with a recessed bench on the right side, and a seat at the extreme end of it.

15. The rectangular flat-roofed Chaitya cave, which is probably the oldest in this group,[1] and on the back wall of the verandah, to the left of the door and high up, bears a two-line inscription (No. 12), stating that this Chaityagṛiha was dedicated by a layman named Ânanda.

16. Somewhat higher up is a cell with a verandah in front, about 15 feet long by 6 feet wide.

17. Still higher is another cell, 10 feet by 8 feet and 7 feet high, with a stone bed in the right side; also traces of plaster on the roof and walls.

18. Consisted of a chamber 13 feet by 5 feet and 7 high, but the front wall is much destroyed. In the back, to the right, is a cell with window and door, and, to the left, a recess 4 feet wide and 7 feet deep, with a bench at the back. There are traces of plaster on the roof.

19. A nearly similar Bhikshugṛiha, the front chamber being 15 feet by 7 feet, with a bench in the right end; and the cell on the right opens from the recess, and has a stone bed in its right side. The recess is 4½ feet wide by 13½ feet deep, and has a seat at the back. A horizontal flaw in the rock has opened the upper part of the cell walls and of the dividing wall into the next cave.

20. A vihâra, 25 feet by 16 feet and 7 feet high, with a seat along each end, and two cells at the back, each with stone beds in the back. In the back wall at each end are also shallow recesses as if for cupboards. The front wall is all broken down, but was in line with the preceding two, and along the outside ran a stone seat the whole length of the three caves. Under the left front corner is a cistern, and outside is another.

21. Further along are three cisterns, and in the recesses over them are two inscriptions (Nos. 13 and 14),—the first stating that one was the benefaction of a goldsmith, a native of Kalyâṇa, near Bombay; and the second, that another was due to two married ladies.

22. A hall or refectory, 24 feet 3 inches wide by 29 feet 5 inches deep and 7 feet high, with a seat round the three inner sides and back. There are traces of plaster on the ceiling. Besides the door, two windows probably lighted it, but the front wall is much

---

[1] See *Cave Temples*, pp. 256, 257.

ruined; a bench ran along the front of it in the verandah. Under the left corner is a cistern with abundance of water.

23. A cell 6 feet by 8 feet and 6½ feet high, with a stone bed recessed in the right side. There is a cistern to the left of the entrance.

24. A room 31 feet by 10 feet and 6 feet high, open in front, and with a bench along the back part of the left wall.

25. Behind a cistern is a recess 4 feet wide and 8 feet deep, which opens on the right side into a cell 10 feet wide by 8 feet deep and 7 feet high, having a bed in the left end.

26. An open verandah 16½ feet by 4 feet, with a seat in the right end, gives entrance to a cell 10 feet by 7 feet and 7 feet high, with a bed in the left end. There are traces of plaster and paint on the roof and walls.

27. Is a cell 8 feet by 7 feet and 7 feet high, with a stone bed recessed in the back wall, and a small window in the left side, opening into a recess 4 feet wide by 10 feet deep and 9 feet high, going from the verandah of the cell, which is 33½ feet long by 4 feet wide. Near each end of this verandah in the back wall is a recessed bench, and on the wall to the right of the left bench is an inscription in three lines (No. 15), measuring about 2 feet by 8 inches, stating that the cave was the benefaction of Śivabhûti, a layman, who dedicated it to the Saṅgha or congregation at Kapichita—probably the name of the monastic establishment in this hill.

28. From an open verandah, 19½ feet by 4 feet, two cells enter; that on the right has a passage leading back in line with the right wall, with a recessed bed on the left side of it. On the back wall of the verandah, to the left of the door, is a smoothed panel, and inside the cell is a shallow recess exactly opposite the panel. The cell to the left has a recessed bed in the back wall.

29. Next comes a small recess; then a dry cistern; and a recessed bench. 30. Two cells at the back of an open verandah; difficult of access.

31. Lastly, and almost inaccessible, a recess similar to No. 25, with a cell opening to the left from it.

The fourth series in the eastern spur of the Leṇâdri hill consists of only four separate excavations, and is fully described in *The Cave Temples* (p. 257–8).

Caves in Manmodi Hill.

The series in the Mânmôḍî hill, to the south-west and south of Junnar, consists of three several groups.[1] Beginning at the north-west end of the first group and proceeding towards the south-east, we have—

No. 1. A cistern, and at a considerably higher level, two small cells.

No. 2. The Chaitya Cave[2] is 12 feet 6 inches wide between the pillars, of which three plain octagons are blocked out on the right side, and two just begun on the left. The whole depth is about 30 feet, and the width of the entrance about 10 feet. The dâgoba is plain, but, with the whole of the interior of the cave, has been left quite unfinished. Over

---

[1] Brett divided them into three groups, D, E, and F.

[2] Described, *Cave Temples*, p. 258–9.

the pillars an offset runs round the upper part of the nave, as if intended to support wooden ribs, as at Kârlê, Bhâja, &c. It faces north-east by north. The interesting details of the bas-relief sculpture on the façade are described in *The Cave Temples*, from which the accompanying woodcut (No. 12) is taken. In the central semicircle over

No. 12.—Manmodi Chaitya Cave at Junnar. From a photograph.

the open arch is a short inscription (No. 16) in characters of about a century B.C., recording that the façade was the work of a Yavana or foreigner named Chanda.

3. To the east of the Chaitya are two tiers of caves, of which, at the higher level, the

first excavation consists of five cells,[1] without stone benches, opening into a common open verandah 42 feet long and about 5 wide; three of the door heads, with part of another, and the connecting frieze, being carved with dâgobas, Chaitya windows, and rail pattern.[2]

4. Under this is a small vihâra nearly full of earth, with two cells in the right wall and one in the left, as also a cell in each end of the verandah. No. 5. The cell wall in the left side of the last is broken through into another small vihâra, 19 feet by 18 feet and 8 feet high, of which the front no longer exists. It has two cells in the left side and two back walls, of which the one to the right only has a stone bench along the back and right side. 6. At the higher level is an open chamber, with an unfinished cell at the back. 7. Over the last, and to the east of it, is another group of four cells without benches, each about 7½ feet square, entered from a common verandah, 34 feet by 4 feet. The pilaster at the right end of the verandah has the common ornament, fig. 11 (p. 18). The right end cell is broken into No. 6. No. 8. Three recesses, farther along, are at about the same level. No. 9. A cell under them, about 7 feet by 8 feet; and No. 10 consists of three unfinished recesses nearly full of earth.

Half a mile to the eastward, near where the face of the hill trends to the south, is the second group in this hill.[3] It is not a numerous one, and owing to the character of the rock, many of the chambers are much ruined; but it is particularly rich in inscriptions.

No. 11. Is the commencement of a cave with three pillars in the front of a verandah 17 feet long, but the hall has not been begun.

No. 12. At a lower level is a similar verandah, 18 feet by 6½ feet, with two free-standing pillars and two in antis. Outside, to the left, and close to the *lotâ*-shaped capital of the pilaster, is an inscription (No. 17), originally in ten lines, nearly 2½ feet in length, the first commencing with the *dharma* symbol, and the last ending with a *swastika*, having the points bent out; but many of the letters have peeled off, and render translation hardly possible. It records a gift by the Reverend Thera and Âchârya of the Gaṇa, the Tevidya Sulasa, and others.

13. Above this is a room about 12 feet square, with three doorways. 14. Close to it is a smaller one with two doors; and under this again is—15. A couple of cells opening into a verandah 15½ feet by 8 feet, on the back wall of which, between the cell doors, is an inscription (No. 18), in 1½ lines, extending about 3½ feet in length. 16. Close to the left side of this is a similar pair of cells, with a verandah 15½ feet by 5 feet, of which the front is broken away. An inscription (No. 19) occupies a similar position, in two lines, 3 feet 4 inches in length, with eight much smaller letters between them. 17. At a higher level than Nos. 13 and 14 are two cisterns.

No. 18. To the left or east of No. 16 is a large unfinished Chaitya cave,[4] measuring 26 feet up to the commencement of the dâgoba, and 13 feet across, without side aisles; but the interior cuts into a natural fissure in the rock, from which water drops during, and for long after, the rains, and this probably led to the abandonment of the work in its present incomplete state. The verandah is 20 feet by 9 feet long, with two octagonal pillars, and two attached ones in front of it. In this verandah are numerous inscriptions (Nos. 20 to 30)

---

[1] *Cave Temples*, p. 260 and p. xvii, fig. 5.

[2] See *Cave Temples*, pl. xvii, fig. 5. Between two of the doors is carved the date "988" over the name, "Muhammad Ali." The same also occurs in the next series of caves—probably the name of some visitor in A.D. 1580.

[3] Brett's series E.

[4] *Cave Temples*, p. 260.

recording gifts to the Bauddha community by individuals and guilds, which will be found in their proper place, with the translations. The façade of this unfinished Chaitya appears, in fact, to have been used as the special place for recording all land gifts and endowments to the Bauddha fraternity at Junnar.

No. 19. Close to the Chaitya is a room 10 feet by 12 feet, with a dâgoba in it.

20. Next to this are four open rooms, the fronts all more or less broken away; to the left of them some broken steps lead up to what may be considered as an upper storey, consisting of an open verandah, now much fallen away, 49 feet long by 7 feet wide, from which five small rooms are entered, of which two at the west end are now converted into one, which contains some rude Jaina sculptures of much later date than the cells.

21. Farther along is a small vihâra about 18 feet square, open in front, with two cells on each side and one in the back, also some other cells close to the left, but all broken through. Outside the vihâra hall, on the right, are fragments of an inscription (No. 31) in two lines. 22. A small inaccessible cell above the right side of the above.

On the eastern scarp of the hill, at a short distance from the preceding, we come to the last group.

No. 23. After passing an excavation just commenced between the last group and this one, we come to a room with two doors. 24. At a higher level, and nearly inaccessible, are seven cells close together, opening into a common verandah; between the doors of the cells (except the first and second) are small recesses for oil lamps. 25. Apart from the last is a solitary cell. 26. A recess with a bench round the three sides, and on the left wall is an inscription (No. 32)[1] in three lines, which is the most important at Junnar, for it is by Ayama, the prime minister of King Nahapâna, the great Satrap, and is dated "in the year 46." Now if Nahapâna dated from the same epoch as the later Kshatrapas, who are supposed to have used the Śaka era, this belongs to the year 124 A.D.[2] And, judging both from the character of the alphabets and the style of the caves, a large number of the Junnar excavations may be referred to about the same age.

No. 27. Two small recesses, and then a cistern, of which the roof is broken in. 28. A large cistern, of which the side is laid open by the rock having slipped away. Over it is a small recess, on the back wall of which is inscription (No. 33), in one line, stating that it was the benefaction of one Śivabhûti.

No. 29. At a lower level, but difficult of access, is a room with two plain square columns and pilasters in the verandah. 30. A hall 18½ feet by 16 feet and 7 feet high, with a bench along the right side. In the verandah there have been two plain octagon pillars, both broken, and one of the pilasters.

No. 31. Is an unfinished flat-roofed Chaitya cave.[3] There are traces of plaster on the roof, and on that of the verandah are fragments of painting in square panels. On the right wall outside the verandah are the remains of an inscription (No. 34) in three lines, 3 feet or more in length.

No. 32. Next is a small vihâra consisting of a verandah 20 feet by 4½ feet, with two octagonal pillars, and two in antis, having the usual lotâ-shaped bases and capitals; behind are three cells, of which one has a bench on the right side.

---

[1] See No. 11 in chap. xiv, sect. ix, below.

[2] *Cave Temples*, pp. 232, 265, 266, and note 4, next page.

[3] Described in *Cave Temples*, pp. 261, 262.

CHAPTER VIII.

THE NÂSIK CAVES.

THE Nâsik Caves, though one of the smallest groups, are of special interest from the number and character of their inscriptions. These had been translated in 1874 by Professor Râmakrishṇa G. Bhâṇḍârkar from the copies of the Messrs. West,[1] but it was desirable that they should be re-copied, and this has been done by Pandit Bhagwânlâl Indrâji, who joined my camp at the caves, and with the most patient and persevering care succeeded in preparing facsimiles which are probably unrivalled, and permit us to read them more satisfactorily than was hitherto possible.[2] The corrections, however, as might be expected, are of minor importance and give us no new facts or dates. One of the most material changes is that Sâtakarṇi Gautamîputra dates his grant from Beṇâkaṭaka, and not from Dhanakaṭaka,[3] as the name had been read. The history of the Andhra dynasty and its relation to the Kshatrapas, and of the latter to that of Usabhadata and Nahapâṇa,[4] thus still awaits further elucidation. It seems certain, however, that at the early date of the Chaitya cave and the small vihâra No. XIV.—perhaps 150 B.C.—the Andhras held the Nâsik district, but at a later date—in the time of Nahapâṇa and Usabhadata—both this

---

1 Bhâṇḍârkar in *Trans. Or. Congress*, 1874, pp. 306–354; West, *Jour. Bom. B. R. A. Soc.*, vol. vii, pp. 37–52 and plates.

2 The Pandit has been engaged for more than a year in preparing translations of these inscriptions, which were to have appeared in this volume, but not having received them up to the time of going to press, I was obliged to apply to my friend Professor Dr. Bühler, C.I.E., of Vienna, for the translations which appear in the sequel.

3 *Tr. Or. Cong.*, 1874, p. 324. Dhanakaṭaka, as the name of the Andhra capital, however, does occur once in Inscription No. 15.

4 The relation of Chashṭana to Nahapâṇa is as yet undetermined. Both use Baktrian-Pâli legends on their coins, and from this and the character of the coins we may infer that they probably belong to about the same age. We read often of Nahapâṇa's son-in-law Ushabhadâta, and once of his "minister Ayama, belonging to the Vachha-gôtra" (*Vachhasagotrasa Ayama;* conf. M. Müller, *Hist. Sans. Liter.*, pp. 380, 385); but no allusion is made to any son. Chashṭana, again, is the founder of the Mahâkshatrapa dynasty, up to whom the earlier kings always trace their origin. On his coins he is *Mahâkshatrapasa Ysamotikaputrasa Chashṭaṇasa*—but who his father Syamotika, or rather Ysamotika(?), was, we do not learn. Was he some minister of Nahapâṇa's, who got his son elevated to the throne after some invasion? Gautamîputra boasts of having "destroyed the Khakharâta race," and this may possibly refer to the extermination of the family of "the Khaharâta Khatapa Nahapâṇa." Again, Rudradâman, the grandson of Chashṭana, speaks of his "near relationship to Sâtakarṇi, lord of the Dekhan," which may point in the same direction; that is, Chashṭana may have been raised to the throne by Gautamîputra. If this be the true solution, it would make Chashṭana and Gautamîputra contemporaries, and Rudradâman contemporary perhaps with Mâdharîputra. This would place the first Sâtakarṇis considerably before the Christian era, and with this agrees the style of the alphabet used in the Nânâghâṭ inscription of Sâtakarṇi Vedisiri—the oldest Brahmanical record of the kind we have—and those in Caves XIII. and XIV. at Nâsik, one of which is of the time of Kṛishṇa, a Sâtavâhana, and perhaps the second king of the Andhra dynasty. Ayama dates "in the year 46," and Rudradâman in 72, &c.; now if Nahapâṇa's reign ended in 47, and Chashṭana ruled till 60 or 62, Jayadâman, his son, might rule till 71; Rudradâman, his grandson, till 100 or 102; and Rudrasiṁha till 118, as indicated by his coins, or even till 123, giving four reigns in from 71 to 76 years. Newton inserts a Jivadâman before Rudradâman, but the inscriptions do not contain his name (*Jo. Bom. B. R. A. Soc.*, vol. ix, p. 17), and it is evident that both the names and dates in Mr. Newton's list require the most careful testing and revision.

and the country to the south, about Junnar and Kârlê, were in possession of these Kshaharâtas, while soon after this again Śâtakarṇi Gautamîputra recovered the whole, and thus had ground for his boast of having "restored the fame of the Sâtavâhana race." This was probably in the first half of the second century A.D.; and it cannot have been very long after this that Caves III. and XV were excavated, while Cave VIII. was apparently the work of Nahapâṇa's family, and consequently of an earlier date. By what interval Caves VIII. and III., however, were separated is still undetermined, but from the fact of Usabhadata granting a village to the Kârlê monastery, and Puḷumâyi, in another inscription, referring to and confirming this grant, the interval was perhaps not very great.

The architectural details of the Nâsik caves are not very varied, and have been fairly illustrated in *The Cave Temples.*[1] The accompanying woodcut (No. 12), however, will convey a better idea than any architectural drawing of the style of the façades of Caves XII., XIII., and XV.,—No. XIII. being the Chaitya cave, and XII. the unfinished vihâra to the right of it.

The four pillars in the verandah of Cave XII.—two attached and two standing free—are so nearly identical with those of Cave VIII. that we can hardly suppose them to be far distant from it in date. They are, however, so similar to those in the interior of the great Chaitya cave at Kârlê, looking at the proportion of the base to the capital, and the perfection of the elephant sculptures and the figures they support, that they may possibly be even earlier, and are certainly among the most elegant of their class. The plan of this cave appears to have been changed during the excavation, and the hall extended considerably further to the right than was at first contemplated, leaving the door considerably to the left of the centre. Above the door and adjacent window is an inscription[2] (No. 19) in three long lines and a half, stating that it was the gift of Indrâgnidatta, a Yavana from the north, a native of Daṁtâmitrî—possibly the same as Demetrias, a town in Arachosia, mentioned by Isidore of Kharax.[3] The interior of the cave, we are told, was "a shrine for a Chaitya," but, beyond the hall, the shrine has only been commenced, and if intended for a Chaitya, the cave must have been planned on the pattern of those of Kuḍâ or of Bâgh—a dâgoba shrine at the back, with cells in the sides of the hall.

The façade of the Chaitya cave, which forms the centre of the picture, shows a considerable advance in design when compared with those of Bhâjâ, Beḍsâ, and even with that of

---

[1] Pp. 263–279, and plates xix–xxvi.

[2] The inscriptions from Nâsik caves are arranged with others in sections 9 and 10 of chapter xiv, where, for chronological reasons, two systems of numeration have been adopted,—one seriatim for each section, and another in which the Nâsik inscriptions are numbered continuously throughout both sections from 1 to 24; this latter is the only one referred to in this chapter.

[3] If Kandahar be the same as Alexandrianopolis, Demetrias was perhaps at Huramzai Sydani on the Helmand, 30 miles S.W.;—Conf. Isidori Characeni, *Mans. Parth.*, § 19, in Müller's *Geog. Gr. Min.*, vol. i, p. 254; Ritter, *Erd.*, vol. viii, p. 121, 61; Bayer, *Hist. Reg. Gr. Bac.*, p. 64; *Jour. A. S. Ben.*, vol. v, p. 389. In Wilson's map it is placed 100 miles S.S.E. from Kandahar, in about the same position as in the older maps; *Ariana Ant.*, p. 230. Prof. R. G. Bhâṇḍârkar points out that Dâttâmitrî is mentioned in the *Siddh. Kaum.* (under Paṇini, *Var.*, iv, 2, 76) as a Sauvira town; *Tr. Or. Con.*, p. 345. Sauvîra has not been satisfactorily defined; Wilson's map places it in the north of the Sindh-Sâgar Doâb, between the Indus and Jhelam, and Lassen's map names the same district, probably correctly, Sindhu Sauvîra; if Demetrias was in Sauvîra, the district probably included the modern Sewistân in Southern Afghanistan. This, however, is on the supposition that Bhâṇḍârkar's identification is correct. If the anusvâra is not superfluous, the Pâli Daṁtamiti may be the Sanskrit Dântâmitrî, as explained by Professor Bühler in the notes to the inscription.

Kârlê. Instead of simple rows of simulated Chaitya window openings resting on string courses, as in the upper row here, the central ones in this façade are supported by attached pilasters, copied apparently from stone construction, forming niches of very elegant appearance, each containing a dâgoba with a background of trellis-work. No feature so like stone construction is found in any of the earlier cave façades, though the paucity of examples prevents us from assigning it its exact position in the series.

It may be a question, which it is now not easy to answer satisfactorily, whether the great window of the façade was originally exposed to the open air as it is now. Judging from the examples at Beḍsâ, Kârlê, and Kaṇheri, it seems as if the great windows in the original wooden structures from which these Chaitya caves were copied were always covered by a screen in front, which partially hid them, while it protected them from the weather. This may have existed at Bhâjâ, Kondâṇê, Pitalkhorâ, and in No. X. Ajaṇṭâ, but in these cases would have been wholly in wood, and would consequently have long since perished. In the two later Chaitya caves at Ajaṇṭâ it was reduced to a portico over the entrance, leaving the upper part exposed, except in so far as a projecting frieze above might shelter it; and in the Viśvakarma at Elura it certainly was omitted. In attempting, however, to restore the original form of the wooden Chaitya halls of the earlier Buddhists, it is indispensable to take into account the advanced screens at Kârlê and Kaṇheri. They certainly were not singular or exceptional, but more probably, in some form or other, were applied to all Chaitya caves. If applied here, it may probably have been in the form of two advanced pillars, as at Beḍsâ. The returns of the rock at each side of this façade favour the idea that something in front was intended. These, however, have been broken away, apparently at the time when the vihâras on either side were subsequently inserted.

The façade of the vihâra No. XV. hardly requires any remark. It is the third of the larger vihâras, but which has been considerably extended inwards, and the shrine and antechamber added at a later date. The order of its pillars is an attenuated example of that employed in Cave XII.,—partly due at least to their having been re-hewn at the time when the back part of the cave was excavated,—and without any figure-sculptures about its capitals—indicative of the subsequent age at which it was executed, though even its date was in the time of the Andhra dynasty. The original inscription (No. 16) is over the left-hand side door and window on the back wall of the verandah, in three and a half lines, and is dated in the 7th year of Śrîyajña Śâtakaîṇi Gautamîputra.[1] It states that the cave was many years in a neglected state, but was finished by Vâsu, the wife of Bhavagopa, the commander-in-chief (*Senâpati*). Of very much later date, however, is a short Sanskṛit inscription (No. 25) on the left wall of the hall over the right-hand corner of the first cell door, stating only that the cave was "the meritorious gift of Marmmâ, a worshipper." This statement can only be true in the sense that she may have borne the cost of extending the old cave, and perhaps of adding the shrine for the Mahâyâna worshippers, probably as late as the seventh century A.D.

On the whole, though far from being of exceptional magnificence, the three caves represented in the woodcut form as interesting a group as any to be found among the minor caves in Western India.

---

[1] Śrîyajña Śâtakarṇi is also mentioned in the Kaṇheri Cave Inscriptions, and in the *Purâṇas* he is placed as the fourth in succession after Śâtakarṇi Gautamîputra, ascending the throne sixty-two or sixty-three years after the death of the latter.

The inscriptions in the Nâsik caves are of very various ages, the oldest being those in the Chaitya cave, and in the small vihâra, No. XIV. In the latter there is an inscription (No. 1), in two lines, over the stone lattice window to the right of the entrance; it is in two lines, with a rude form of the *triśula* symbol at the end of the second line, and records that a Mahâmâtra,[1] or officer, residing at Nâsik, made the cave in the time of Kṛishṇa, a king of the Sâtavâhana race. The style of the alphabet belongs to the early part of the second century B.C., and so supports the conclusion otherwise arrived at[2] as to the early age of this vihâra.

On the Chaitya cave, which seems to be almost contemporary with the small vihâra, there are three inscriptions. One (No. 3), on a projecting moulding to the left of the door-head, is much weatherworn and scarcely legible, but states that the rail-pattern moulding and the figure of a Yaksha below, by the side of the door, was the gift of a lady; a second (No. 2), over the entrance door, under the head of the arch, states that the door was the gift of a native of Nâsik; and the third (No. 4), in 3½ lines, is graven vertically on two of the octagonal columns to the right of the dâgoba, with one line on each face. It records the construction of the Chaitya temple by Mahâ-Hakusiriyâ, the daughter of one royal minister—possibly to Kṛishṇa or some other early Andhra king—and the wife of another officer of like rank.

The other inscriptions may be enumerated in the order in which the caves were described :—

In Cave II., close under the roof, and on a fragment of what was the back wall of the verandah of the cave in its original form, is a fragment of an inscription (No. 13), containing the date in the 6th year of Puḷumâyi;—the rest has been carried away with the wall, when the followers of the Mahâyâna school converted this old Bhikshugṛiha into a small chapel.

In Cave III., sometimes called Gautamîputra's, there are two inscriptions (Nos. 11, 14), containing four grants. One (No. 11) is on the left end wall of the verandah near the roof, and is in twelve lines, faintly cut and difficult to read in many places. It contains two grants,—the first by Śâtakarṇi Gautamîputra, "in the year 14," granting a field previously "enjoyed by Usabhadata" to the monks; and the second, a supplementary grant by the same king and his mother Balaśrî, in "the year 24," making over a second field in place of the first, which had gone out of cultivation. The other inscription is on the back wall of the verandah, over the left-hand side door and window, and contains two grants,—the first (No. 14) in 10¾ long lines, dated in the 19th year of Puḷumâyi, contains a long panegyric of his father Gautamîputra Śâtakarṇi, and the dedication of the cave to the monks of the Bhadrâyanîya school by his grandmother Balaśrî, and the grant by Puḷumâyi himself of a neighbouring village for their support. It is in this inscription that Śâtakarṇi is declared to have been king of Asika, Asaka, Surâshṭra, Aparânta, Anupa, Vidarbha, Avanti, &c., including all the countries along the Narmadâ and the Western coast. Among the mountains of which he was lord, are the Vindhyas, Sahyâdri or Western Ghâṭs, and Kaṇhagiri—that is, Kaṇheri in Salsette, where there was at that time a large Buddhist establishment. He is described as having "humbled the pride of the Kshatriyas, destroyed the Śakas, Yavanas, and Pahlavas"—tribes from beyond the north-west frontier of India—and as having "entirely destroyed the Kshaharâta race." The second

[1] Conf. Aśoka Edicts, V. and VI., *Report*, vol. ii, pp. 107, 110, and Senart, *Les Inscr. de Piyadasi*, tom. i, pp. 125, 156.

[2] *Cave Temples*, p. 275, and note.

grant beginning in the 11th line, where the first ends, extends to nearly three lines in much smaller characters, and records the refusal of the village by the Bhadrâyaniyas and its bestowal on Buddha. The second of these documents seems to leave no doubt that the cave was made by order of the great Śâtakarṇi himself.

Cave VI. is one of several caves here (I., IV., V., VI., part of VII., and XVII.) of which the floors have been cut down 6 or 8 feet or more—for what purpose it is difficult to conjecture—but it has ruined the caves. This cave has had a verandah supported in front by two octagonal pillars, with a frieze over them, similar to those in Caves IV. and V. Behind the verandah were three cells, and a fourth at the right end of it. On the back wall of the verandah, near the roof, and between the doors of the first and second cells, is an inscription (No. 24) in four lines, beginning and ending with the *svastika* symbol, stating that the cave was presented by a merchant, one cell by his wife, and another by his daughter.

To the left of the last remains the upper part of a plain chamber with a stone bench in it. On the left side of the door is a fragment of an inscription [1] in four short lines, faintly cut and almost illegible.

Cave VII. consists of a small verandah with one small cell at the left end and two behind, one of them leading into an inner one,—and with this we may include a cell to the right also, though it does not open into the verandah, but doubtless belonged to the same body. On each side the door of this latter is an inscription (Nos. 22, 23), that on the left being in two lines, and that on the right in one. Both state that the cave was the gift of Mugudâsa and his family, but the first calls him a layman of the Chetika school, and the second a fisherman; the first also records the grant of a field, from the proceeds of which a garment was to be provided for an ascetic.

Cave VIII., or Nahapâṇa's Cave, is the second large vihâra here, and one of the most interesting; it is purer in style and superior in execution to Caves III. and XV. On the side walls outside this cave are two inscriptions, and in the verandah are five more, two of them, however, identical. The largest (No. 5) is on the back wall of the verandah, extending the whole length of the cave, in unusually large and regularly formed letters; it has also two postscripts added in a line and half of much smaller letters over the right-hand window and door. This inscription records the construction of the cave and neighbouring cisterns by Usabhadâta, the son-in-law of the Kshaharâta king, the satrap Nahapâṇa, whose good deeds are enumerated, such as giving 3000 cows, presenting gold, constructing a flight of steps at the Bârṇâsâ river, giving sixteen villages to gods and Brahmans, feeding 100,000 Brahmans annually, providing marriage dowries for eight wives for Brahmans at Somanâth, building rest-houses at various places between Bharûch and Supâra, &c., establishing free ferries on six of the rivers between Surat and Dhanu, &c. The language then changes to the first person, and Usabhadâta says he went to Mâlaya to release the chief of the Uttambhadra Kshatriyas, who was besieged by the Mâlayas. Then in the rainy season he went to Pokshara. In the second addition, he records the gift of a field, north-west from the town, purchased for 4000 *kârshâpaṇas*, which is to provide food for the occupants of the cave.

A second inscription (No. 8) in three lines is on the right end wall of the verandah over the cell door; and a third (No. 9) in the same words is graven in two lines on the left end, above part of the next inscription to be referred to. Both these state that the cells

[1] No. 23 in West's copies, and left out as incomplete in Professor Bhândârkar's versions.

are the gifts of **Dakhamitrâ**, the daughter of **Nâhapâṇa** and wife of **Usabhadâta**. The fourth (No. 7) is partly on the left end wall of the verandah under the preceding, but it extends along the back wall as far as the left window, and has hitherto been copied as two distinct inscriptions. It is dated "in the year 42," and records certain investments at 5 and 7½ per cent. with the guilds of weavers at Govardhana, to provide a garment for each of the twenty mendicants residing in the cave during the rainy season. There are only 18 cells in the cave and verandah, but probably the small cave (IX.), with two cells close to the left, was regarded as part of the accommodation. Other large bequests are enumerated as having been made in the preceding year and in the year 45. Outside the verandah, on the left-hand wall, is a large fragment of still another inscription (No. 6) of the same Usabhadâta, recording his charitable deeds, but much weatherworn; and lastly, on the opposite wall, over a plain recess is another (No. 10) in Sanskrit, dated in the 9th year of king **Îśvarasena**, an **Abhîra**, the son of Śivadatta, when a lady made certain investments for medicines for the priests.

On the front wall of the small cave No. IX., to the right of the door and close under the roof, is an inscription (No. 21) in two lines, beginning and ending with the *svastika* symbol, and recording the gift of this cave by Râmanaka, a writer.

Beyond this are some five cells (No. X.) which perhaps belonged to two small contiguous vihâras, of which only these cells are now left. The first probably consisted of two cells at the back of a verandah, in the left end of which is an inscription (No. 20) in five and a half lines, stating that the cave was the benefaction of a merchant, who also deposited a sum of money in the hands of the townspeople to provide a garment for the ascetic living here during the rains.

Having already noticed the inscriptions in Caves XII., XIII., XIV., and XV., we pass the large and ruined excavations (No. XVI.) full of Mahâyâna sculptures and also a small rude chamber. About 45 yards beyond the latter is a recess containing an inscription (No. 12), perhaps originally in five lines, but the lower portion is much peeled off, and little more than the date, in the 2nd year of **Puḷumâi**, is left, except the statement that a husbandman executed some work in front of this, which has now disappeared.

Cave XVII. is another of those caves, of which the floor has been quarried out, converting it into a deep tank. Close under the roof, on what has been the back wall of the verandah, and between the doors of the two cells, is an inscription (No. 17) recording the gift of the cave and two cisterns by a native of **Daśapura**—one of the tanks for the spiritual benefit of his parents. On the back of a recess, some way to the right of this cave, is another inscription (No. 18) recording the gift of another cistern by the same individual; the rock below, however, where there probably was a covered cistern, is now quarried away.

AJANTA CAVE TEMPLES FROM THE NORTH.

CHAPTER IX.

AJANTA CAVES.

The account of the Bauddha Rock Temples at Ajaṇṭâ given in the volume on *The Cave Temples* occupies three chapters,[1] and is illustrated by 25 plates and 10 woodcuts; these, however, do only scant justice to the numerous features of artistic and mythological interest in this important group of monasteries and temples, with their varied architecture, sculptures, and paintings, exhibiting so much of the history of Indian art for a period of so many centuries. The following additions by no means exhaust the subjects of architecture and sculpture alone, but they add details that could not be described without the accompanying plates, and, with those in *The Cave Temples*, convey some idea of the wealth of decoration on doors, columns, windows, and façades. But as every door and pillar differs from every other in some details, to exhibit fully this profusion of beautiful ornamental design it would be necessary to delineate each of them individually.

The relative positions of the different caves, their proportionate dimensions, and the general disposition of the whole, will be much better understood by the general plan given on pl. xiv. To the proper understanding of this plan it must be borne in mind that the caves vary much in level, No. VIII. being the lowest, and the level generally rising towards each extremity of the group. But Cave III. is considerably higher up than either Nos. II. or IV. and difficult of access; Cave V., again, is quite below the level of No. IV., and there is a stair down from the front of No. VI. to No. VII.; Cave XI. is considerably above the level of XII., and its floor much above that of the large Chaitya cave No. X.; No. XIV., an unfinished vihâra, is just over No. XIII., and so could not be represented. From No. XV. to XIX. the level does not vary greatly, but Cave XX. is at a higher level than XIX.; Cave XXII., again, is higher than XXI. or XXIII.; and Cave XXV. is over the chapel and cell in the right end of the verandah of Cave XXVI., while Cave XXVII. is at a like high level on the other side. No. XXVIII. is only the beginning of a cave, very high in the scarp and now almost inaccessible.

The accompanying autotype plate (pl. i) will give some idea of the face of the rock in the glen, and of the appearance presented by those very remarkable rock-cut temples. It is taken from the platform in front of Cave XX., and represents the lower or northern end of the series, the first excavation on the left being Cave XV., and the last at the right of the view being the splendid vihâra known as No. I. of the series.

The Earlier Caves.

The earliest group of caves at Ajaṇṭâ consists of only four excavations,—two Chaitya caves, Nos. IX. and X., and two vihâras, XII. and XIII.,—which, as explained in the work on *The Cave Temples*, were all excavated certainly before the Christian era, though it is

---

[1] Pp. 280–347.

not quite certain which is the earliest of the four, inasmuch as it seems most probable that in the various groups of Buddhist caves, the *Bhikshugṛihas* or Vihâras—the lodging for the monks—would be commenced as early as the Chaitya cave or chapel, if not even before it, and thus we may presume that, generally at least, it would be the first finished. At Ajaṇṭâ, Caves XII. and XIII. are acknowledged to be of the earliest type of monastic abodes, and No. XIII. is so very plain and primitive-like, that it may safely be regarded as the oldest here. Its walls differ from those of all the more modern caves in not only having been chiselled perfectly smooth, but in being polished,—a clear index that it was not contemplated to plaster them or even to cover them with paintings, and perhaps we have here an attempt to imitate the polish given to the caves in the granite rocks of Bihâr.[1] In none of the later caves has this been done, but their walls are left roughly tooled, so as the better to retain the thin coating of plaster with which they were covered in order to prepare them for the paintings with which they were decorated. The stone beds arranged in the cells of these two caves and the absence of pillars in the halls, are also indicative of their early position in the history of Cave Architecture.

The ground plan of Cave XIII. is given on pl. xxviii, fig. 3. The hall or *upâśraya* only measures 13½ ft. by 16½, and is 7 ft. high, with seven cells round it. The façade and verandah—if it ever had one, which is probable—have entirely disappeared with the fall of the rock.

In No. XII.,[2] which is much larger, and bears a close likeness to the small vihâra at Bhâjâ, there is an inscription on the side of the door of the cell at the right end of the back wall. It is evidently of very early date, but so corrupt in spelling and perhaps defective, that there is some doubt about the sense of it. Apparently it records the gift of the cave—cells and hall—by a Baniya or trader. This cave has been sufficiently described in *The Cave Temples* (p. 291, and plate xxvii). These two caves are the only ones at Ajaṇṭâ in which the stone beds of the earliest monastic abodes are found.

Chaitya Cave IX.

Of the small Chaitya cave No. IX., the drawing of the façade (pl. xvii) illustrates its extreme simplicity as compared with that of Caves XIX. and XXVI. (plates xxx and iii) for example. It is even plainer than that of the Nâsik Chaitya (woodcut No. 12, p. 38). The few figures of Buddha inserted in this façade, and even the dâgobas at the ends of the side walls, are evidently of very much later date than the cave. Dâgobas and figures of Buddha have also been sculptured in the faces of the side walls, facing the court; and again to the left of the façade a small low shrine or chapel has been excavated with figures of the latest Mahâyâna type; and just above this is another recess, in which the sculpture is left unfinished.

The walls and pillars of this cave and also of No. X., like the walls of XII. and XIII., have been hewn quite smooth. A very thin coating of plaster, or perhaps of paint, has been put on them, which easily peeled off from the even surface, so that it had early to be renewed, and we can detect portions of painting of at least three different ages. As mentioned in *The Cave Temples* (p. 291), a piece of the oldest painting is on the inside of the front wall, extending

---

[1] *Cave Temples*, p. 42.

[2] A plan and section of Cave XII. is given in *Cave Temples*, pl. xxvii.

from the wall to over the left window; another piece in the same style extends from the front wall some way down the left side wall; then on the back wall is a large fragment of somewhat later date; while on the pillars and other parts of the walls the painting is mostly of a much later period, the characters in the inscriptions painted on them apparently belonging to the fifth and sixth centuries A.D. These painted inscriptions, of which there are above twenty in this cave, are mostly very fragmentary; all are donative and mostly in Sanskrit—the language being an evidence that they were the work of Mahâyânists. An exception, however, is found in what remains of the fragment of an inscription on the earlier painting on the back wall, which is in Pâli of faulty spelling.[1]

The transverse section (pl. xvii, fig. 2) illustrates the very simple style of the interior and of the dâgoba, which differs markedly from those in Caves XIX. and XXVI. The pillars slope very little, only an inch or two inwards from bottom to top.

Chaitya Cave X.

The façade of Cave X. is by far the simplest of all the large Chaitya caves. It belongs to the same early class as those of Bhâjâ, Kondânê, and Pitalkhorâ, which had only wooden front screens. In this façade it was probably at first of wood, but at a later date the lower portion of it, at least, was built of very large bricks. The great arch must have been similarly filled with those at Kârlê and Kondâṇê, and the whole interior was ribbed in wood. Outside the great arch there is no carving whatever, not even a piece of rail pattern (pl. xv, fig. 1).

The inscription on the right foot of the bargeboard or facing of the arch is in Maurya characters of as early a date as the first half of the second century B.C., and simply records that the cave front was the gift of Kaṭahâdi, the son of the wife of the Vâsishṭha family. No title or father's name is given, but we can hardly resist the inference that so brief a record must be that of some prince, probably of the Andhra dynasty.

Though a fourth part shorter than the great Kârlê Chaitya cave, this is only 4½ ft. less in total width, and it has two pillars more round the nave. The pillars slope inwards about 5½ in. from bottom to top.

The paintings on the two side walls are of much earlier date than the numerous figures of Buddha that adorn the pillars. This, too, is borne out by the old form of the characters in the fragment of a painted inscription in Pâli on the left wall. The painting on the right side is undoubtedly a representation of the *Chhadanta Jâtaka*, or story of Buddha, when in a previous birth he was born as a six-tusked elephant, or, as other versions of the story say, as a white elephant of the Chhadanta breed. Hiwen Thsang mentions[2] a stûpa near Banâras in commemoration of this. He says: "When the Buddha led the life of a Bodhisattva, and was a king of elephants with six tusks, a huntsman—wishing to obtain these precious teeth—put on a *kashâya* dress (the reddish-brown garment of a devotee) for a decoy, strung his bow, and waited for his prey. The king of the elephants, from respect for the *kashâya*, immediately tore out his tusks and gave them to him."

The more expanded *Jâtaka*, however, says, that in times long past a herd of elephants frequented the Chhadanta lake, one of the seven great lakes near the Himâlayas, and which

---

[1] Some specimens of the painted inscriptions will be given in chapter xiv, sect. 13, at the end of this volume.

[2] Stan. Julien, *Mém. sur les Cont. Occid.*, tome i, p. 360.

was surrounded by seven ranges of rocks. Of this herd the king was a white elephant with red mouth and feet, and his tusks shed rays of six colours. Having offended his younger queen one day, she desired revenge in a future birth. In her next birth she was the wife of the king of Banâras, and prevailed on him to send a huntsman named Sonuttara to kill the king of the Chhadanta elephants and bring his tusks. He was told that when he reached the summit of the seventh ridge he would see a huge Banian tree to the north-east of the lake under which the elephant king lived. Disguising himself as a priest, the hunter dug a pit, and, concealing himself in it, he succeeded in shooting the elephant, who roared with pain, at which the herd of 8000 assembled and roared too, then dispersed to seek the enemy. The elephant king himself, however, discovered him in the pit, and asked why he had done so. The elephant then gave him the tusks, which were carried to the queen. She, however, began to reflect that she had committed a very cruel deed; and remembering all the virtues of the elephant king, such deep sorrow overwhelmed her that she died the same day of a broken heart.[1]

The painting in Cave X. agrees with this story in all its chief features, and the elephant is painted as a white one with six tusks, as seen at the head of the herd in the upper section on plate xvi, and the head is repeated on the left of the lower one, so as to show the connection between the two. The huntsman is represented in the presence of the queen, and among the rocky ridges, also returning with the tusks; and the scene in the extreme right seems intended to portray the distraction of the queen under the remorse she felt for her cruelty. Though very much destroyed, and that wantonly, the reduced outline on plate xvi, of what can still be made out, will prove worthy of careful examination, and give some idea of the freedom of drawing in these paintings. To convey any complete idea of their interest, however, they must be reproduced in colour, and it may be safely asserted that few more interesting publications could be undertaken than a thoroughly well illustrated volume of the frescoes of Ajaṇṭâ, both decorative and picture compositions, for which purpose the materials are now nearly complete, and may be expected to be quite so in a year or two.

Some fragments of the early painting from the left wall of this cave were given in plates viii to xi of the *Notes on the Ajaṇṭâ Temples and their Paintings*, where also will be found the only detailed account of the frescoes in the other caves yet published.

The paintings[2] on the pillars and on those in Cave IX. are of about the same age, and on them are many short donative inscriptions in Sanskrit, indicating that they were the work of followers of the Mahâyâna school, and may probably belong to the fifth and sixth centuries.

---

[1] This outline is taken from the summary of the story given by General Cunningham (*Bharhut Stûpa*, pp. 62, 63), compiled from a translation supplied to him by Subhûti, a priest of Vaskaduve in Ceylon. Reference is made to the same *Jâtaka* in Upham's list (*Sac. and Hist. Books*, vol. iii, p. 269); in Alabaster's *Wheel of the Law*, p. 305; Mutu Coomara Swamy's *Dathavansa*, cap. iii, ver. 31, p. 50; and a different version is given in Beal's *Romantic Leg. of Buddha*, p. 367. This *Jâtaka* is No. 506 in the Copenhagen MS. The elephant which Mayâ saw in her dream on the conception of Buddha was a Chhadanta one; see *Cave Temples*, p. 288, note and citations there.

[2] For some further notes on the paintings see *Cave Temples*, p. 284 ff. 293, 294, and pl. xxix; and *Notes on the Bauddha Rock Temples of Ajaṇṭâ, their Paintings and Sculptures* (4to, pp. 112 and thirty-one plates), Bombay 1879.

Vihara Cave XI.

This vihâra is close to the Chaitya Cave No. X., and has evidently been inserted in its place, high above the level of No. XII., at a much later date than that cave, and, whatever its age, it belongs to the school of the Greater Vehicle. Possibly it is one of the earliest of the sect; but the absence of stone beds in the cells, the pillars in the hall, and the figure of Buddha in the shrine, all indicate their influence (see plan, pl. xxviii, fig. 2). The whole style of this cave, however, differs so much from that of any of the rest, that it is difficult to assign its place chronologically with any confidence. The door has only three plain fascias round it, but with a lion at each end of the threshold. The pillars in the hall are very clumsy, plain octagons, but like those of the verandah they have bases and capitals which are not otherwise known in early caves. The windows, too, are divided by colonnettes with moulded capitals and bases. The sculptures in the verandah are almost certainly of still later date than the cave, and cannot help us in any way to fix its age. Alterations were evidently made at a late date; the shrine at least was enlarged by a passage or *pradakshiṇâ* made round the image, and a secret cell was excavated high up in the left side of the shrine, possibly for concealing valuables connected with the ritual for great occasions. The image, though it has not the usual supporters, is not of a very early type, but has an attendant worshipper or *śâlika* in front, now much injured, but represented pl. xxxvii, fig. 1. It is a male figure of somewhat less than natural size, kneeling before the throne on the right hand of the image, with his hands joined in an attitude of devotion, but holding a cup or small bowl. More than half the head and right arm and part of the right leg are broken off. It was probably intended to represent the excavator of the cave, or at least of the shrine.

CHAPTER X.

THE LATER CAVES AT AJANTA.

In the account of the other excavations at Ajaṇṭâ, given in *The Cave Temples*,[1] an attempt has been made to arrange them chronologically, and though in some cases there may be room for slight differences of opinion as to the precise position of individual caves, there appears no reason to interfere with or modify the arrangement there laid down, by which the remaining caves, after those just described, were divided into two great groups:—the first or so-called "later group," comprising Caves VI., VII., and VIII., with those numbered XV to XX., and ranging in date from the fifth century to the end of the sixth; and the second or "latest group," consisting of Caves I. to V. at the one end, and XXI. to XXVIII. at the other,—all of which were excavated, or at least finished, within the limits of the seventh century. In adding to the illustrations there given of these caves, however, which is the object of this chapter, it is hardly necessary to follow the chronological arrangement rather than the topographical. This second and by far the largest series belong to the Mahâyâna school, and are distinctly marked off from the older group, to which belong Caves VIII., XII., and XIII., and the two Chaitya Caves IX. and X.

[1] Pp. 297–346.

Cave I.

Cave I., as described in *The Cave Temples* (pp. 320–332), is the most handsomely ornamented vihâra at Ajaṇṭâ or in all India, and at the same time one of the most modern, having probably been commenced in the beginning of the seventh century and not completely finished before 650 A.D. The plan detailed there (pl. xl) shows that it is a twenty-pillared hall with fourteen cells inside, and others in the verandah and connected with the cells outside.

The accompanying autotype plate (pl. ii) will convey a good idea of the façade with its richly carved frieze, the left side of which was illustrated by a drawing to scale in *The Cave Temples*, pl. xli. The return of this frieze over the left chapel outside is given in pl. xx, and is of interest, inasmuch as we can make out that when entire it represented the four predictive sights or visions which determined Gautama to leave his home and become an ascetic.[1]

The sculptures on the capitals of the pillars in this vihâra are remarkable, even among those of Ajaṇṭâ, for their variety and spirit. In *The Cave Temples* (pl. xxxviii, fig. 3, and pl. xlii, fig. 2) two of the pillars in the hall are represented, the second representing one of the most richly carved in the back aisle, just in front of the shrine, and the other, one of the plainer ones on the right side, but with an ingenious device on the capital representing four deer in different positions, to each of which the one head they have among them seems suitable. In pl. xviii are represented two more of the hall columns, and one of the pilasters of the verandah. The first column (fig. 1) is one of those in the back row, and is carved in the most elaborate style. On four sides, just under the neck, are small recesses in which apparently medallions have been inserted, whether of ivory or other material we do not know, as they have all been forcibly extracted. On the other four sides of the octagon the shields are smaller and bear each a small standing figure. Strings of beads are a marked feature in the ornamentation, a row, with pendants, surrounding each shield, another in festoons surrounding the pillar just below them, and a triple row festooned round the bottom of the sixteen-sided portion of the shaft. The bracket capital has in the centre two Nâgas, supporting with their hands and tails what appears to be a relic casket, and behind each is a small figure under a plantain-tree apparently with an offering. On the brackets of the capital are figures flying in the clouds—a male and female in each case. The rich grotesque on the base is worth attention.

Fig. 2 on the same plate is one of the corner pillars, and not nearly so richly ornamented. On the capital is Buddha in the *Jñâna mûdra* or meditative attitude, with an attendant *chauri*-bearer on each side; and on the wings are *śârdulas* or mythic lions, one of them with a rider. Two sections of the shaft are carved with shallow flutes which twist round the shaft and in opposite directions. On the corners of the base were little figures of lions, but some of them have been broken off.

Fig. 3 is an elevation of the front of the pilaster at the right end of the verandah, and is a good specimen of the beautiful carving with which the upper halves of the shafts of these are very frequently covered. A comparison of this with others both in this volume and in *The Cave Temples*,[2] will help the reader to form some idea of the great variety and

---

[1] For details see *Cave Temples*, p. 322.

[2] Pl. xlix, figs. 2, 3.

AJANTA — FRONT OF CAVE I.

beauty of these designs. In this case a short section of the shaft is semicircular, and carved with shallow flutes.

The accompanying woodcut (No. 14) represents one of the pillars in the right end of the verandah, and is an excellent specimen of the mode in which decoration is applied to these pillars. There is first the square base changing into an octagon, but not abruptly,—the passage from the one to the other being broken by four little figures of dwarfs, who reappear on the capital for the same purpose. Instead of continuing the usual system of again cutting off the angles so as to produce a sixteen-sided and then a thirty-two sided polygon, the shaft is here adorned with spiral flutes of singularly pleasing design, bound together with bands of jewelled ornaments of great beauty. The capital is ornamented with a square bas-relief in the centre, containing a religious scene, as is the case with most of those in the cave, supported by flying figures on the brackets, as is shown also on the left-hand figure in plate xviii.

No. 14.—Pillar in Verandah of Cave I., Ajantâ. From a photograph.

The richly carved door of the shrine in this monastery has already been given.[1] To this we now add the door of the hall (pl. xix). Though somewhat damaged below, the richness of the sculpture and its suitability to the different members of the mouldings will at once strike the eye. Inside, next the opening, is a band of the jewel ornament so frequently carved on the columns. Beyond that is a projecting member carved with the usual sculptured groups; first a single figure—apparently a Nâga—and above that five pairs of males and females standing in various attitudes; and on the lintel five more sitting, some of them playing on various musical instruments. On the outer edge of the design are the usual pilasters supporting two female figures standing on the heads of *makaras* or conventional crocodiles, suggesting their connection with the Hindu River Goddesses. In this instance they are less important than is generally the case, but are of more than ordinary elegance. They always stand under trees, usually the Aśoka and Mango: in this case, the tree on the left is the Aśoka, and that on the right the *Ambâ* or Mango tree. The figure-carving may seem too much devoted to music and dalliance for Western notions of monkish asceticism, but it is only the testimony of veracity to the social morality of the Buddhism of the age; an affected sanctimony and respect for orthodox teaching, a ridiculous tenderness for brute life, carried everywhere, and made the most important of all religious obligations, were not incompatible with

[1] *Cave Temples*, pl. xlii, fig. 1.

a casuistry that got rid of the obligations of secret purity, and even allowed the orgies of the Śâktas.

The side doors to the hall are much injured, but are among the only ones of the kind at Ajantâ that have any carving round them. The head of the left end one is represented in fig. 1, plate xx, and the right-hand one on plate xv, fig. 2. The mouldings are few and simple, the principal member being carved with human figures, mostly single, and on the lintel having three dâgobas, each worshipped by several kneeling figures.

The longitudinal section of this cave in pl. xxi, fig. 1,[1] when compared with the plan on pl. xi of *The Cave Temples*, will help to the clear understanding of its arrangements, passing as it does through the centre of the porch and hall and through the image in the shrine, and giving all the detail possible on so small a scale. The doors of the cells are seen beyond the pillars of the hall.

Cave II.[2]

Cave II. is a considerably smaller hall than No. I., being one of only twelve pillars, as shown in the plan on pl. xliv of *The Cave Temples*. The transverse section given of it in pl. xxi, fig. 2, shows in front the pillars, and behind the entrances to the shrine and the two side chapels, the back walls of which are covered with two large sculptures. That on the right contains the sculpture of Suddhodana and Mahâprajâpatî with the infant Buddha on her knee. That in the left chamber is represented in fig. 2, pl. xxiii, where two portly figures with royal head-dresses are represented seated together, with attendant female *chauri*-bearers, and over their shoulders *Vidyâdharas* or Bauddha cherubs, while each has before him a heap of some substance, perhaps food.

The pillars of the hall and verandah of this cave are equally varied in details with those in Cave I., though generally similar in design.

Cave IV.[3]

This is one of the largest vihâras at Ajaṇṭâ, being a twenty-eight-pillared hall, about 85½ ft. wide by 87 ft. deep, but the front is about 93 ft. long. Much of the cave, however, is unfinished, and only a few of the pillars of the hall have any carving upon them. Most of the pillars of the hall, like those of the verandah, are plain octagonal shafts with bracket capitals. A projecting frieze that once ran along the front, with the Chaitya window ornament at intervals, each containing a human head, has all fallen. The main door is represented in pl. xxiv. It is larger and more elaborately sculptured than any other cave door at Ajaṇṭâ, but not perhaps in better taste—the sculpture rather overloading the design, and the inner lines of moulding being reduced to give room for it. The lintel is ornamented with little figures of Buddha and other sculptures, and the side jambs with the usual pairs of figures. The attendants below are female figures, while in some caves they are Nâgas, and of the two females above, standing under foliage behind the *śârdûlas* or mythic lions,

---

[1] The size of the page necessitated the breaking of the drawing and giving the section of the inner part or shrine in the second portion.

[2] *Cave Temples*, pp. 332–336, and pl. xliv, fig. 2, pl. xlv, figs. 1, 2.

[3] *Cave Temples*, pp. 337, 338, and pl. xlvi, xlvii, and xlviii.

one is attended by a dwarf with a crooked staff—a figure often repeated not only in late Bauddha sculptures but also in Brahmanical ones at Elurâ and Elephanta.

The two windows, nearly square, that help to give light to this great hall, are surrounded by a very neat architrave. Half of one of these windows is represented in pl. xxiii, fig. 4.

The Bauddha Litany, sculptured in a panel to the right of the principal door, is represented in fig 3, pl. xxiii. Above, in a horse-shoe arch with a tall spire over it, Buddha is represented seated; and in the large panel Avalôkitêśvara or Padmapâṇi occupies the centre, with a *Vidyâdhaara* on a cloud over each shoulder. The sides of the compartment are carved with representations of the "eight forms of evil" from which he delivers—elephants, lions, fire, hooded snakes, thieves, fetters, drowning, and demons.[1] Above these compartments are figures of Buddha seated on the lotus.

CAVE V.

The next cave is at a much lower level, and is a quite unfinished vihâra. The door, however, merits notice for the richness of the surrounding carving, the details of which may be studied in pl. xxv. It differs principally from most others here from the bold manner in which the two female figures standing on *makaras* or mythic crocodiles, one accompanied by a boy and the other by a girl, project beyond the line of the general ornamentation, giving it considerable breadth and dignity. The same arrangement, slightly modified and not on so extended a scale, occurs in Caves XXII. (pl. xxxii) and XXIV. (pl. xxxv). The same figures, but enclosed in the ornament, occur in Cave VII. (pl. xxvii), and may generally be considered as most characteristic of the style. They possibly, as in Hindu sculpture, represent river goddesses, but it is not easy from their emblems to discriminate whether both are intended for the same or represent different rivers.

CAVE VI.[2]

Cave VI. is the only two-storey cave in this group. The whole façade and verandah of the lower storey have disappeared; but it would seem that the verandah was wide and had a cell in the left end, from the door of which the steps now descend to Cave VII. The lower hall is large, but instead of its pillars being arranged round the sides of a square, they are placed in four parallel rows of four each, distributing the weight to be sustained over short bearings. The pillars are plain octagonal shafts for fully three-fourths of their height, the remainder being sixteen-sided with a cincture round the top. The section on pl. xxvi will illustrate most of the details. Round the image in the shrine is a passage for circumambulation.[3]

The upper storey has on its walls, over the cell doors, and in the sides of the antechamber and shrine, &c., a great deal of sculpture, all of the style of the later Mahâyâna sect. The front of the verandah, except one pilaster[4] in the right end, is entirely destroyed.

---

[1] Conf. *Arch. Rep.*, vol. iii, p. 75; *Ind. Ant.*, vol. x, p. 187; *Cave Temples*, pp. 311, 342, 358, 380, and pl. lv.

[2] *Cave Temples*, pp. 301, 302, plans of both storeys are given on pl. xxxii, the shrine door on pl. xxx, fig. 2, and pilaster, pl. xlix, fig. 3. To these the reader is referred.

[3] The door of the shrine is given in *Cave Temples*, pl. xxx, fig. 2.

[4] See drawing, *Cave Temples*, pl. xlix, fig. 3.

Outside of it, at both ends, were small chapels containing seated figures of Buddha, of which that at the right end is tolerably entire. Outside, on the left, is a projecting jamb, on the top of which there still remains part of a figure of a Nâga Râjâ. Somewhat lower, and outside the jamb, is a curly-headed figure holding up his left hand, which appears to have clasped the staff of a flag; above him again is another smaller figure. Doubtless provision was made over the façades of other caves also for flag-staves, on which, as over modern Jaina and Brahmanical temples, flags would wave during certain periods of the year, especially during *wasso* or the rains, when the Bhikshus resided in their monasteries.

Cave VII.[1]

The ground plan (pl. vii, fig. 1) of this vihâra will help the reader to understand its arrangements. As will be at once seen, there is no enclosed hall, but it consists of a verandah with two advanced porticoes, the cells and antechamber of the shrine all opening direct from the verandah.

The sides of the shrine and antechamber are covered with sculptures of Buddha in his various positions or *mûdrâs*, and the sides and lintel of the shrine door (as may be seen in pl. xxvii) are similarly covered with figures of him, almost to the entire exclusion of all other ornament. Possibly this feature itself is an indication that the cave is not of quite so late a date as those in which figures of the Bodhisattvas and other mythological beings are introduced. The sculpture on the left side of the antechamber has been illustrated in *The Cave Temples*, pl. xxxi; that on the other side is now given in pl. xxxvii, fig. 2. It contains in all sixty-five figures, viz., seven rows each containing seven Buddhas seated on lotuses, a row of five seated and one standing Buddha, and in the lowest line two seated Buddhas, two Nâgas, and six worshippers. The Buddhas are arranged symmetrically, or nearly so, there being five and four in alternate lines with their hands in the *Jñâna mudrâ* or attitude of meditation, and two and three alternately in the *Dharmachakra mudrâ* or teaching position—an exception occurring in the seventh row, where the third figure is in the *aśi mudrâ* or attitude of blessing. The lotus leaves and stalks are wrought in between the *bhâmaṇḍalas* or aureoles behind each head, in the same way as in the painted figures similarly arranged in the antechamber of Cave II., so as to fill equally and artistically all vacant spaces.

Cave XIV.[2]

This vihâra is just above Cave XIII., and is now only accessible by means of a ladder. It is probably a late excavation, and has been left unfinished. The peculiarity of the plan (pl. xxviii, fig. 4) is that, instead of a square area in the middle of the hall surrounded by pillars, this hall was intended to be oblong, 61 ft. wide by 25½ ft. deep, and the roof supported by six columns and two pilasters running along the middle of it and dividing it into two long cross aisles. The doors and windows are of a very plain type, and have not been finished.

---

[1] *Cave Temples*, pp. 299, 300.
[2] *Cave Temples*, p. 303.

CAVE XV.

This cave, again, is probably an earlier cave than the last or any that follow it. The verandah, however, is so ruined and the remaining architectural features so few that data are barely sufficient to form a very definite decision from. The sculpture on the door (pl. xxix, fig. 1) is allied in character more to that of Cave VII. than to any other, but it is much simpler. The dâgoba on the lintel protected by the Nâga hoods is unusual, and the birds above are more realistic than anything on the frieze of Cave I. It has no pillars in the hall, and the two in front of the antechamber are very plain, while the image of Buddha in the shrine is of the earliest type, without attendants, and with the soles of his feet turned up.

CAVES XVI. AND XVII.

The full account of Caves XVI. and XVII. given in *The Cave Temples*[1] renders much further detail unnecessary. The inscription on the left end wall outside the verandah has, however, been recopied with great care and translated anew by Pandit Bhagwânlâl Indrâji,[2] and again revised by Dr. G. Bühler, who has also translated the Chammak or Ilichpur copperplate grant of an earlier king of the same Vâkâṭaka dynasty. A combination of the genealogies in the copperplate grant and in this inscription gives us the following pedigree, which is more complete than that previously published :—

1. Vindhyaśakti, mentioned only in the Ajaṇṭâ inscription, probably cir. A.D. 285–310.
2. Pravarasena I. (son ?), mentioned also in the land grant, cir. 310–345.
   Gautamîputra, son, married the daughter of the great king, Bhavanâga the Bhâraśiva.
3. Rudrasena I., son of Gautamîputra, cir. A.D. 345–355.
4. Pṛithivîsheṇa, son, married Prabhâvatîguptâ, the daughter of the great king of kings, Dêvagupta, and conquered Kuntala,[3] cir. 355–400.
5. Rudrasena II., son (omitted in the Ajaṇṭâ inscription), cir. 400–410.
6. Pravarasena II., son ; the grantor of Seonî and Chammak land grants, cir. 410–440.
7. ——————, son (name lost), cir. 440–470.
8. Devasena, son, cir. A.D. 470–500.
9. Harisheṇa, son, conquered Kuntala, Avanti (Ujjain), Kaliṅga, Kosala,[4] Trikûṭa, Lâṭa, Andhra,[5] cir. 500–520.

Dr. Bühler and the Pandit agree in fixing, on palæographic grounds, the date of the inscription about the beginning of the sixth century, and that of the copperplates about eighty years earlier, and these conclusions perfectly coincide with the date assigned to the vihâra in the *Cave Temples* (p. 306). The country ruled by the Vâkâṭakas seems to have embraced the upper basin of the Tâptî, extending eastwards to about the Waingaṅgâ, or as far as Nâgpur and Jabalpur. The cave, however, was not excavated by the king, who was a Hindu, but by his minister, Varâhadeva, the son of Hastibhoja, who presents it, in the inscription, to the community of monks.[6]

---

[1] Pp. 303–315, with nine woodcuts, and pl. xxxiii–xxxv.

[2] *Cave-Temple Inscriptions*, p. 69, and chap. xiv below sect. 11, No. 3, p. 124.

[3] Placed by Lassen about Vijayanagara, and by Yule in the Bidar and Malkhed districts.

[4] The country about the sources of the Narmadâ and Chhatîsgaḍh.

[5] Trikûṭa has not been satisfactorily identified ; the Trikûṭakas are mentioned in the Kanheri copperplate. and Pandit Bhagwânlâl has suggested that Trikuṭa may be Junnar (*Cave-Temple Inscriptions*, p. 59). Lâṭa is well known as including the Surat and Bharûch districts ; and Andhra, at the date of the inscription, was probably the district about Warankal.

[6] See the translations in chapter xiv, sect. 11 p. 116. below.

The Nâgarâjâ in the shrine below the front of this cave is represented with a *mukuṭa* or head-dress, having a frilled circular ornament behind, which bears a close resemblance to the like objects in the images in the Bâdâmi caves, which belong to the second half of the sixth century. The pilaster in the right-hand end of the verandah is represented in pl. xxix, fig. 2.

The inscription in Cave XVII. has also been similarly examined,[1] and from it we learn that the vihâra was the work of a minister to one of a dynasty of kings apparently subordinate to the Vâkâṭakas, and was executed during the reign of Harisheṇa, and thus is of about the same date as Cave XVI. The inscription is so mutilated that the sense is not very clear, but it speaks of a "monolithic gem-like hall, in which a *Chaitya* has been placed," a "great reservoir of water," and, "on the other side, . . . towards the west, . . . a beautiful *Gandhakuṭî*" or temple.[2] Cave XVIII. has had a cistern below the level of its floor, and may be the reservoir referred to; but there is no *Gandhakuṭî* or hall for images immediately to the *west*, though there are sculptures of Buddha on the lower parts of the walls of the court.

Pl. xxix, fig. 3, represents one of the two pillars of the antechamber in this cave.

Chaitya Cave No. XIX.

This is the most richly sculptured cave at Ajaṇṭâ, and might not be unworthy of a separate monograph illustrative of its details. It belongs to the same group as Caves XVI. and XVII., and is probably of the same age. A plan and longitudinal section of it on a small scale will be found in *The Cave Temples*.[3] On pl. xxx an architectural elevation of the façade is now given, which conveys some idea of the amount and character of the sculpture upon it. The constituents of the ornament are not very numerous, and are mostly to be found on the façade of Cave I. also. On each side the great horse-shoe arch which lights the cave is a corpulent figure with a regal head-dress, very similar to the two male figures that appear in one of the small chapels of Cave II. That on the left in this case is doubtless Kubêra, the god of wealth; who the other is meant to represent I do not venture to say. The panels between the pilasters on each side the doorway are also covered with sculptures, all representative of Buddha. In that on the extreme left he is twice represented: in the upper part, as squatting with his hands in the teaching position, and attended by two Nâga figures; below, he stands in a meditative attitude, apparently in the front of a dâgoba. On the opposite side he is also represented similarly on the front of a dâgoba, the top of which is worshipped by little flying figures with Nâga hoods. On the panel next to the left of the door he is represented in the usual standing attitude, while two Vidyâdharas support a tiara or jewelled cap over his head. On the right side he is represented—as he also is in two or three instances in the frescoes—with his alms-bowl, in which a little boy is placing something, being put forward by his mother, who carries a small pennant with a *triśûla* or trident on the head of the staff.

---

[1] *Cave Temples*, p. 310; and *Cave-Temple Inscriptions*, p. 73.

[2] See the translation, p. 130; the inscription is so mutilated, however, that it is quite possible the cave or caves may have been executed under the tenth of these kings, whose name, however, is lost.

[3] Pl. xxxvi and xxxvii; also one of the pillars from the nave, pl. xxxviii, fig. 2; and the Nâgarâjâ from the left side of the court, opposite the chapel containing the capital shown in the woodcut No. 14, is given on pl. xxxix. See also pp. 315–318.

Plate xxxi, fig. 1, is a transverse section of this cave, showing the stone ribbing of the roof, which is without any trace of wood having been ever adopted in any part of the cave or of its ornamentation. The Dâgoba also has the umbrellas wholly in stone, reaching almost to the roof of the cave. No other dâgoba in any other cave has as many as three, and in the caves with arched roofs these are generally in wood. The side of the dâgoba is also represented in fig. 2. The pillars round the nave have mostly figures of Buddha in the centres, and flying figures in the brackets of the capitals, but two on the left of the dâgoba have representations of musical entertainments (see fig. 3), reminding us of some of the groups represented in the frescoes of the Bâgh caves,[1] only here none of the performers dance. The triforium is occupied by figures of Buddha in compartments separated by panels of arabesques, each differing in details from the rest. One of these panels is represented in pl. xxxi, fig. 4.

No. 15.—Capital in front of the side chapel of Cave XIX. From a photograph.

On the right hand as you enter this Chaitya cave, is a small chapel or room extending at right angles to the main façade, with two free-standing pillars, and two pilasters in front. The capitals of these pillars are of very graceful design, the corners of the lower half being ornamented each with a small bunch of mangoes lying over their own leaves. The upper portions have a grotesque face on each side and small dwarfs at the corners, as represented in the accompanying woodcut, No. 15.

Cave XX.

The arrangements of this small cave[2] will be best explained by the ground plan (pl. xxviii, fig. 6), from which it will be observed that two of the cells are quite unfinished, and that the antechamber is advanced into the hall. The doorway of the hall is represented on pl. xxxii, fig. 1, and differs very considerably from most others at Ajaṇṭâ, being simpler, consisting of only two fascias, but the foliage carved upon these is of a singularly elegant pattern. The two *makaras* or conventional crocodiles which usually support the river goddesses, are here spouting forth two forms which nearly meet in the centre, forming a cusped arch of striking elegance; between them is a small winged figure, though what it is intended to represent is by no means clear. A somewhat similar arrangement occurs on plate xxx of *The Cave Temples*, over the doorway of the shrine of Cave VI., but there it forms an arch of the usual jewelled ornament over a seated figure of Buddha with a snake hood.

There is not, in fact, much variety in the general design of the doorways of the later group of vihâras at Ajaṇṭâ, but they are all elegant and in good taste, and as pleasing specimens of doorway decoration as are to be found anywhere else in India, though they are far from so rich as many afterwards excavated in stone in the structural temples of the middle ages.

---

1 *Notes on the Ajaṇṭâ Paintings, &c.*, p. 95.

2 *Cave Temples*, p. 318.

Caves XXI.-XXIII.

Cave XXI. is a very much larger cave, being $51\frac{1}{2}$ feet wide by 51 feet deep,[1] but the whole of its verandah has been destroyed. The ground plan is given on pl. xxxiv, fig. 1. At each end of the verandah, in each side wall of the hall, and on each side of the shrine in the back, are small rooms with two pillars and pilasters in front, and a carved frieze above. These lead into cells behind. The introduction of these six cells, each with its antechamber adorned with two pillars *in antis*, gives a variety to the plan of this cave which is not found in any other of the vihâras at Ajaṇṭâ, and adds to its interior a richness of architectural decoration which is most pleasing. As a specimen of the façades of these rooms, that of the one in the left end of the verandah, with the adjoining pilaster of the verandah, is given in pl. xxxiii, fig. 1. The columns in this cave are of a heavier type than in most of the others here, but by no means too massive for their position. One of them is represented (pl. xxxiii, fig. 2).

Cave XXII. is a very small cave, and the sculpture is not of much merit. The doorway is represented on pl. xxxii, fig. 2, which is of the usual type, only that the figures of the females or river goddesses are smaller and more subdued than usual.

Cave XXIII. is a twelve-pillared vihâra of almost exactly the same size as No. XXI., and of very similar arrangement. (See plan on pl. xxxiv, fig. 2.)

Caves XXIV and XXV.

Cave XXIV., after No. IV., is the next largest hall in the series, being $73\frac{1}{4}$ ft. wide by 75 deep, and has twenty columns supporting the roof, but inside only the front aisle has been advanced towards completion, the pillars in the back and side rows being only roughly blocked out. The verandah, however, has been completed in a manner that shows it was intended to be one of the most beautiful and highly-finished monasteries of the group. As the interior is only finished in part, it is probably one of the latest excavated, and the style of its sculptures may be taken as a good index of the character of art at that period. Unfortunately the verandah was long choked up with earth, and all the pillars are destroyed except one, but the capitals, still attached to the roof, are carved with very considerable grace and beauty. The accompanying woodcut (No. 16)[2] will illustrate this. The

No. 16.—Capital from the Verandah of Cave XXIV., Ajaṇṭâ. From a photograph.

subjects of the sculpture are to be found repeated again and again on other capitals, but

---

[1] *Cave Temples*, p. 339.

[2] From *Cave Temples*, p. 157.

nowhere with equal life and finish, and in other caves the flying Gandharvas in the corners of the central compartment are awanting. This may be an indication of the lateness of the work, which may be assumed as belonging to the middle or second half of the seventh century.

The woodcut (No. 17) represents another and a more complete capital in this cave with the upper portion of the shaft. The bracket-capital itself is carved with much the same subjects as the other, though with scarcely equal finish. Its greatest interest lies in the bracket-capital with overhanging leaves, like Ionic volutes, which forms so marked a feature in all subsequent Indian architecture, but seems first to have been perfected about the time this cave was excavated. It is so like in details to those in Cave III. at Aurangabad,[1] that there can be little hesitation in assigning them to the same age, if not even to the same workmen.

No. 17.—Capital from Cave XXIV
From a Photograph.

No. 18.—Pilaster in the Verandah, Cave XXIV.

Another illustration of the wealth of sculpture lavished on the pillars of this verandah, is seen in the accompanying woodcut (No. 18), which is the pilaster at the left end of the verandah, and also bears a very close resemblance in pattern to one of those in the hall of Cave III. at Aurangabad.[2] They are about the most elaborate specimens of an art which was verging on decay from the very exuberance of detail with which it was overloaded, and which it seems to have been almost impossible to carry further in stone, but is still very admirable from the skill with which they are carved, and general good taste displayed in the ornaments.

Although no two are actually the same, there is a great similarity of design among all the pillars at both ends of the series at Ajaṇṭâ, those in Caves I. and II. being almost identical in design with those in Caves XXI. to XXVI., and a still more striking similarity to those in the latest caves at Aurangabad.[3] These two last woodcuts, with Nos. 13 to 15, may be taken as types of the last and most elaborate phase of Buddhist architectural decora-

---

[1] *Archæol. Rep. W. India*, vol. iii, pl. xliv, xlv, xlvii, and xlviii, p. 66.
[2] *Arch. Sur. W. Ind.*, vol. iii, pl. xlvi, fig. 10, and p. 69.
[3] *Arch. Sur. W. Ind.*, vol. iii, pl. xliv to xlvii.

tion just before the extinction of the style in Western India, in the middle or towards the end of the seventh century.

The doorway to this cave (pl. xxxv) is by no means so elaborate as the pillars of the verandah; it is conceived much in the same style as many of the others, but with too narrow a frieze, all the members of it being too much compressed. On the lintel are six Vidyâdharas bearing a tiara over the centre of the door. The side compartments are filled with the usual pairs of figures.

Cave XXV The plan of this small vihâra, which is high up in the rock. close to the right side of the Chaitya cave No. XXVI., is given in pl. xxxiv, fig. 4. It has never been quite finished and is of no architectural interest.

The Fourth Chaitya Cave, No. XXVI

The plan and some details of the Chaitya cave No. XXVI. were given in *The Cave Temples.*[1] The accompanying autotype plate (pl. iii) will convey a better idea of the façade than any detailed description. Its principal characteristic is the excessive multiplication of figures of Buddha, of every size and in every attitude, almost to the exclusion of every other ornament.[2] What carving there is, is nevertheless as rich as that of Cave XIX., but hardly so elegant nor so effective. Instead of a small advanced porch to the entrance, a verandah ran across the whole front supported on four columns and pilasters, with a gallery on a level with the sill of the great arched window, but this has been broken down. Like the great Kârlê Chaitya cave, it had side doors in a line with the aisles.

To the right of the central door in the upper part of the back wall of the verandah, is a Sanskrit inscription (No. 6), which, having been long protected from the weather by the roof of the verandah, is still mostly in fair preservation, and is ascribed on palæographic grounds to the end of the sixth or early part of the seventh century. It records that the cave was excavated by a monk Buddhabhadra, who was probably the head of a sect, and was on terms of friendship with Bhavvirâja and Dêvarâja, two ministers who successively held office under the Aśmaka[3] king. This would appear to connect it with the inscription in Cave XVII., which seems to supply the names of the Aśmaka dynasty.

In *The Cave Temples*, it was pointed out that there was a passage in Hiwen Thsang's itinerary, in which he evidently mentions the Ajaṇṭâ caves as being on the eastern frontiers of Mahârâshtra, and which refers to two elephants, probably those in front of Cave XVI.[4] This inscription mentions a Sthavira Achala as one of the early excavators of vihâras

---

[1] See pp. 341–345, and pl. xxxvii, xxxviii, l, and li.

[2] This frequent multiplication of figures of Buddha is the most striking peculiarity of the recently excavated vihâras at Jamalgiri and Takht-i Bâi near Peshawar. Does it indicate that they are of about the same age?

[3] The Aśmakas are mentioned by Varâha Mihira, *Brihat Samhita*, ix. 18, xi. 55, xvi. 11, xvii. 15, xxxii. 15; in xix. 22 he places them in the north-west; and, in a note on this verse, Dr. Kern identifies them with the Assekanoi of the Greeks.

[4] *Cave Temples*, pp. 282 and 306, note 3. Cunningham (*Geography*, pp. 555, 556) suggests that Ajaṇṭâ might be meant by Hiwen Thsang, but prefers to change "eastern" into "western" frontier, and identify the monastery referred to with Kanheri.

AJANTA—FRONT OF THE CHAITYA CAVE No. XXVI.

at Ajaṇṭâ, who is evidently the Arhat 'O-che-lo of Hiwen Thsang, who says he founded the monastery here.[1]

Longitudinal and transverse sections of this temple are given on pl. xxxvi. The former is of more than usual interest, as it shows the position of the sculpture, in the left-hand aisle, of the Buddha attaining *Nirvâṇa*, drawn to a larger scale on pl. l of the work on *The Cave Temples*. A little farther inwards, between one of the pillars and the dâgoba, may be seen the position of the temptation scene, also drawn to a larger scale on pl. li of the same work. This longitudinal section illustrates also, though on rather small a scale, the rich sculpture of the pillars and triforium. A better idea, however, of the style of the interior will be conveyed by the accompanying woodcut (No. 19), from a photograph, of three pillars on the left side, with their entablature. As will be seen, they are in the same style as the pillars in Cave I. (woodcut No. 14), but even richer and more minute in detail, closely resembling those in Cave XXV immediately preceding it in local position if not also in age.

No. 19.—Pillars on left side of the Nave, Cave XXVI.

The transverse section (fig. 2) shows the form of the dâgoba, of which the top or stone umbrella has been so completely broken that it is impossible now to restore its original form, or to ascertain whether the dâgoba was surmounted by one or by three umbrellas.

Cave XXVIII.

Two of the Ajaṇṭâ caves, numbered XXVIII. and XXIX., are almost inaccessible. Of these, No. XXIX. is along the scarp beyond No. XXVII., and No. XXVIII. is high up in the scarp between Nos. XXI. and XXII. It is only the commencement of the façade of a Chaitya cave, and is represented in the accompanying woodcut (No. 20), from a sketch made on the spot.

No. 20.—Cave XXVIII. at Ajaṇṭâ.

[1] See Dr. Bühler's remarks on the inscription, p. 132, *inf.*

GHATOTKACHH.

The large vihâra of Ghatoṭkachh near Gulwâḍâ, about eleven miles west from Ajaṇṭâ, is a twenty-pillared hall somewhat irregular in shape, but about 79 feet wide by 78 feet deep, as shown in the plan of this cave given on pl. lii of the volume on *The Cave Temples*. The pillars in front of the verandah have all disappeared. In each end is a small room with two pillars in front, and behind each is a cell. In the right side of the hall are four cells, and a room with two pillars in its front; and in the left are six cells, and a similar chapel or room with a cell behind. In the back is the antechamber to the shrine with two pillars in front, and two similar rooms to those in the verandah, each having a cell at the back, and that on the left side having also the commencement of a second cell in the left-hand wall. This hall is entered by a central and two side doors, and is lighted besides by a window on each side of the central door. The section (pl. xxxvii) will help to elucidate the architectural style and arrangements. They are generally inferior to those of the Ajaṇṭâ caves of about the same age.

To the left of the left door was a long inscription, of which only about ten lines are now legible. It gives the genealogy of Hastibhoja, the minister of the Vâkâṭaka king Dêvasena, who was the father of Harisheṇa, in whose reign Cave XVI. at Ajaṇṭâ was excavated. And it seems probable that Hastibhoja was the excavator of this cave, which would thus belong to a period only slightly anterior to the Ajaṇṭâ vihâra excavated by his son.[1]

CHAPTER XI.

KANHERI CAVES.

THE great number of the caves at Kaṇheri and their generally plain character would render any detailed description of each of them tedious and monotonous. Indeed, the account given in *The Cave Temples* (pp. 348–360) gives nearly all that the general reader will be likely to care for. To the Buddhist world in the days of Gautamîputra Śrîyajña Śâtakarṇi, however, the monasteries of Kaṇhagiri must have been among the most interesting places in Western India. Like the Nâsik group, most of the excavations, including all the earlier ones, and among these the great Chaitya cave, belong to the sect of the Hînayâna or "Lesser Vehicle." But there are many caves, probably excavated by the followers of the "Greater Vehicle" or Mahâyâna school, and others have been adopted and altered by them at a later date. Indeed, there are here two inscriptions dated in the latter half of the ninth century, which may be taken as evidence that Buddhism had not died out here even at that date; and the discovery by the Messrs. West of coins of a still later date in the stûpas of monks at the place must be regarded as going far to prove that it lingered on for perhaps another three centuries. This also is countenanced by the Dambaḷ inscription, a genuine Bauddha document dated in A.D. 1095.[2]

[1] See the inscription *infra*, p. 138.

[2] This inscription was noted by me when at Dambaḷ in April 1880, and afterwards an impression was taken by Mr. Cousens, my assistant. It appears, however, that a transcript of it had long since been made for Sir W Elliot. The text and translation have been published by Mr. Fleet in *The Indian Antiquary*, vol. x, pp. 185 ff. 273.

The great Chaitya cave is one of the most interesting here, and there can be little doubt that, originally, the only sculptures on the inner façade were those in the two panels between the doors. Each of these panels contains a group of four persons, two men and two women, whose clothing, and especially their head-dresses, correspond in design very closely with those of the early figures on the Kârlê façade, with the figures in Cave VI. at Kuḍâ, with the Yaksha figures beside the doors in Caves III. and XIII. at Nâsik, and with the early painted figures in Cave X. at Ajaṇṭâ, though the style of execution is very different, and shows nothing of that largeness of conception and breadth of execution which characterise the earlier examples. The peculiar capitals of the pilasters on each side the panels with animals over them, and the inscription on one of the pillars of the front screen mentioning Gautamîputra Śâtakarṇi, confirm the opinion that this cave belongs to a period not later than that of Cave III. at Nâsik. Why so much labour was bestowed on these two panels and on the capitals of seventeen of the columns inside, while not the slightest attempt was made to ornament any other part of the inner façade, is not quite apparent. Not even the fronton round the arch of the window has been traced out, while in other instances this was the first feature that was marked out and appropriately chiselled. In later times numerous figures of Buddha in different *mudrâs*, one of Padmapâṇi on the extreme left, and another Boddhisatwa above the right-hand sculptured panel, were inserted. Under one of the smaller sitting Buddhas, on the right side of the central door, is a Sanskrit inscription[1] in one line, in characters of about the fifth or sixth century, beginning with the symbol for "Oṁ," and recording the dedication of the figure by a Bauddha mendicant. There are also mortice-holes under the level of the window-sill, in which rafters have been inserted for a roof over the lower portion of the verandah.

On each side of the entrance to the verandah, on the two pillars of the outer screen, are inscriptions,[2] but both have been much injured by the cutting out of large portions of the stone, apparently to provide rests for the beams of some wooden erection in front. That on the right-hand side is the longer of the two, and commences with the same syllables as another in No. 81, where we read in full the name of Râja Gautamîputra Svâmi Śrîyajña Sâtakarṇi. The one on the right side mentions certain endowments in Sopâraka, Kalyâṇa, and Paiṭhâṇa. On the inside of the screen, in the left end of the verandah, is a standing figure of Buddha, and under it a Sanskrit inscription of three lines, in letters of about the sixth century,[3] stating that the image was dedicated by Buddhagosha, a mendicant and disciple of Dharmavatsa, a teacher of the *Tripiṭaka*.

On a small dâgoba in bas-relief, on the right hand side wall of the court, near the *stambha* or great pillar, is a short inscription in letters of about the fifth century, and consisting of the beginning of the Mahâyâna creed.[4] Again, in the small chamber in the left of the court, on a pilaster on the right-hand side of a standing image of Buddha, is another Sanskrit inscription in nine lines of about three characters each, recording a gift by a teacher (*âchârya*) named Buddharakshita.

The great sculptures of Buddha, over 21 feet high, in each end of the verandah, are evidently of much later date than the cave itself, and may belong to the fifth or sixth

---

[1] No. 7 of West's, and 18 of Brett's copies. It has been found impracticable to prepare all the Kaṇheri inscriptions for publication in this volume. They will be given in the next.

[2] Nos. 4 and 5 of West's copies; Nos. 4 and 19 of Brett's, and 12 and 13 of Stevenson's versions.

[3] West's No. 6, Brett's No. 2, and Stevenson's No. 1.

[4] West's No. 8, and Brett's No. 5.

century; so also with the sculptures on the inner side of the front screen, and those in the small shrine in the left side of the court.

Of the pillars of the nave, eleven on the left side have been finished with bases and capitals. One of the capitals is represented in the accompanying woodcut (No. 21).[1] It is considerably damaged, but when compared with some of the sculptures from Amarâvati, in Mr. Fergusson's work,[2] it will be seen that it represents the worship of the *pâduka* or sacred footprints on the *Vajrâsana* or throne of Buddha under the Bodi tree, where he attained to supreme knowledge, or rather the honouring of the *Bodhi* tree over the throne, by elephants pouring water upon it.

No. 21.—Capital of a Pillar from the Chaitya Cave, Kanheri.

Six other of these capitals are represented on pl. xli, among which it will be observed that fig. 2 represents the worship of the stûpa or dâgoba—also a favourite subject in the Amarâvati and Bharhut sculptures; and here also the worship is performed by elephants pouring water upon it,[3] which, as in the example given in the woodcut, is supplied by figures with Nâga hoods,—thus substituting the dagobâ and the tree in place of Lakshmî, in a group of frequent occurrence, especially at Sânchi.

On the end or jamb of the low screen wall in front of the court is a water-jar with flowers, which also finds its counterpart among the Amarâvati marbles.[4]

The care bestowed on the figures in the panels on each side the entrance door, which have a finish scarcely anywhere else displayed, suggests that they were meant to be portrait-statues of the excavators of the cave and their wives (see pl. xl, figs. 2–4).

It ought to be noted also that the pillars at least, and probably the verandah of this cave, have been covered with painting, as at Ajaṇṭâ. Little of it is now traceable, but there is a pretty distinct outline of a female in the right end of the verandah by the leg of the large standing figure of Buddha. The Buddhas themselves, and the ornamental sculptures over their heads, have been painted, and on the pillars of the nave, especially on the left side, numbers of faces can be traced.

The external appearance of this cave, as seen from outside, may be best gathered from the accompanying autotype plate (No. iv). There it will be seen that it possesses what no other cave in India does, a stone rail enclosing the outer courtyard. This is of a rather late and elaborate character, resembling in design that at Amarâvati. Inside this are two Siṁha Stambhas attached to the rock on either hand, and beyond these inwards, the outer screen, which, as at Kârlê, is rough-hewn only, but meant to be covered with woodwork. In this instance it is quite complete as far as the stonework goes; at Kârlê the right half

---

[1] From *Cave Temples*, p. 350.

[2] *Tree and Serpent Worship*, pl. lxiv, fig. 1; lxxviii, 2; xciii; xciv; xcviii, 2. In the Bharhut sculptures the worship of the tree and throne is represented, but the *pâduka* are not represented; Cunningham's *Bharhut Stûpa*, pl. xiii–xvii, xix, xxix, xxx, and xxxi, 3.

[3] This may have a reference to the Râmagrâma stûpa: see Beal's *Travels of Fah-hian*, p. 91; Julien's *Mém. sur Cont. Occid.*, tom. i., pp. 326–328.

[4] Fergusson's *Tree and Serpent Worship*, pl. xciii, and xcvi, fig. 4.

KANHERI — FRONT OF THE CHAITYA CAVE.

and lion pillar have fallen. Like the *stambhas* in front of it, and indeed all the architecture of this cave, it is poorer and less elegant in design than the corresponding features at Kârlê; but, as at Amarâvati, which it more nearly approaches in age, the sculpture shows more elegance and finish, though less vigour and freedom in design.

In addition to what is said in *The Cave Temples*, the following notes indicate nearly all that requires remark in these caves, taken in the order in which they have been numbered on the general plan in pl. xxxviii :—

No. 2, the long cave to the right of the Chaitya, has apparently been originally a group of perhaps five separate caves; three in the middle containing Chaityas or dâgobas, those at each end being monastic abodes with stone benches in the cells, and it is not improbable that the dâgoba shrines are the later, and were thrust in long subsequently. In the back wall of the monastic hall next to the Chaitya cave, above a long stone bench is an inscription [1] in two lines, recording a gift by a native of Nâsik; and a few feet to the north of it is another, in an alphabet apparently of later date, recording another benefaction by a goldsmith of Kalyâṇa.[2] Of the middle dâgoba only the base remains, and it is possible the upper part of it was structural. The left-hand one is almost a reduced copy of that in the great Chaitya cave, having no capital, while behind it is a good deal of Mahâyâna sculpture; and that to the right has an abacus over the box, with a short and very thick stone shaft connecting it with the umbrella or *chhatri* hollowed out in the roof.

No. 4 is a small room to the left of the Chaitya cave, containing the dâgoba of a Thera, with an early Pâli inscription on the abacus, recording that it is the stûpa of the Thera, the venerable Dharmapâla, dedicated by the wife of a goldsmith. This is in characters quite as early as any other here, and may belong to the second century B.C. Round the walls are inserted numerous later figures of Buddha sitting and standing, and there are traces of plaster and colour on the walls.

No. 5 consists of a tank with two openings with a recess over them, in which is an inscription in two very long lines, much effaced, but containing the name "Mahâkshatrapa," so that it may possibly be a record by one of the Kshatrapa kings. In the left end of No. 7, above two openings into a cistern, are two inscriptions, the first recording the gift of it by a merchant from Sopâraka, and the other stating that it was the gift of a goldsmith from Chemula. Probably the cistern was the work of both, but each records his name separately over one of the openings into it.

No. 10 is the Mahârâja's or Darbâr cave in the side of the ravine. The eight plain octagon shafts that support the verandah stand on a moulded basement about 3 ft. high. Besides the central steps there are flights also to the two end openings. In the left end of the verandah is a sort of chapel, with two slender pillars in front, and half ones attached to the side walls. They have moulded bases, and capitals of the Elephanta type—that is, with a very thick torus above a fluted neck, and over the torus a square member supporting a thin bracket. These pillars stand on a moulded basement and support a panelled frieze. In the left side of this chapel is a figure of Buddha on the lion throne, with four male and two female attendants and other figures. On the back and left side are similar sculptures. Inside the hall the pillars are square, with a thin bracket above, but have a thirty-two-sided neck (see plate xl, fig. 5). The shrine is filled with the usual figures which are repeated on the left wall of it. As pointed out in the volume on *The Cave Temples*,[3] this

---

[1] No. 2 in West's copies in *Jour. Bom. B. R. A. Soc.*, vol. vi, p. 3; No. 3 of Brett, and 2 of Stevenson. *J. B. B. R. A. S.*, vol. v, pp. 15, 16.

[2] West, *ut sup.*, No. 3; Stevenson (*ut sup.*, p. 15), No. 1.

[3] *Cave Temples*, p. 353 f., and plan pl. liv.

cave was not intended for an ordinary monastery, but for a Dharmaśâla or convocation hall for the community of monks. Both in the verandah and the hall there are traces of plaster and paintings. Over the recess of a cistern in the left of the front, is a long inscription in small letters of not very early form; under it is another in two lines, of about the ninth century; and on the architrave of the verandah is another, dated in Śaka 775 (A.D. 853), in the reigns of Amoghavarsha the Râshṭrakûṭa king, and his feudatory, Kapardi II. the Śilâhâra.

No. 11 has a small court in front, with two recesses in the right side, one over a water cistern. The verandah has two columns in front, is raised above the level of the court and entered by a flight of five steps. In the right end of it is a square cell, nearly its whole front being open; in the left side are some sculptured Buddhas. From this a small hall is entered, with a cell on the right side and a shrine at the back containing a dâgoba, the whole drum of which is moulded somewhat in the style of those at Bâgh. The doors of the hall, cell, and shrine have a double fascia chiselled round each.

No. 12[1] is apparently an early cave, and like many others here (*e.g.*, Nos. 35, 63, &c.) it has a parapet in front, the upper portion carved with the rail pattern and the lower panelled.

No. 14 still retains some fragments of painting on the roof, but from the style it is evidently not of very early date. The roof of the small hall appears to have been divided into nine panels, of which fragments can be traced; in the centre of one is painted a figure with six arms, resembling Śiva in the *Tândava* dance. The roof of the antechamber has been divided into five compartments, each painted with a Buddha seated on a throne with a high back-rail surmounted by *makaras*, over which are figures with high caps, somewhat of the style of those on the Elephanta dwârapâlas, saluting Buddha. The central one, which is the most entire, represents a fair-skinned Buddha, with *kashâya* or brick-coloured robe, seated in the *Bhûmisparśa mudrâ*, *i.e.*, with the right hand lying over the knee and pointing to the earth—the position in which he attained to Buddhahood. The pillars, both of the verandah and antechamber, in this cave, are of the same type as in the Darbâr cave, but more slender. The door of the shrine is a moulded one. To the left of this cave is a boulder with a short inscription[2] on it, recording the dedication of a path by a native of Kalyâṇa.

No. 16, like No. 4, is a small cell containing a dâgoba, with rail-pattern ornament round the top of the drum, and the capital connected with the roof by the short thick rod of the umbrella. On the walls and roof of this cell are considerable remains of painting, consisting chiefly of figures of Buddha, with red robes, standing on lotuses, and with glories round their heads.

No. 21, both from its architecture and arrangements, must be regarded as one of the later caves. Its front columns are quite of the Elephanta and Dheḍwâḍa (Elurâ) pattern, while those behind most resemble the pillars in the unfinished vihâra, No. XIV., at Ajaṇṭâ. In a recess to the right of the porch, with much sculpture in it, is the figure of Sahasrabâhulokeśvara, or Avalokiteśvara, with eleven heads,[3] and a Bauddha Litany. The doors both of the hall and shrine have two fascias round them, then a neat pilaster on each side, supporting a small frieze with the horse-shoe ornament. On the back wall, to the right of the shrine door, are fragments of a number of painted panels, each about 17 ins. square, containing seated Buddhas in a variety of *mudrâs*, or attitudes of the hands.

---

[1] *Cave Temples*, p. 356, where also remarks on Nos. 13 and 14 are given.
[2] West's No. 53, *Jour. Bom. B. R. A. Soc.*, vol. vi, p. 12.
[3] See *Cave-Temples*, p. 357, and pl. lv, fig. 2.

No. 27 is quite unfinished, and may, therefore, be considered as a very late excavation. Like No. 21 and the unfinished Chaitya cave, the two pillars of its verandah are also of the Elephanta pattern. On the wall is part of an inscription, painted in white,[1] of an alphabet as late as the ninth or tenth century, if not later.

No. 29 is just to the left of the great Chaitya, but at a higher level, and, with the next six, probably originally belongs to the earliest series of caves here. This is indicated by the stone benches and beds, the grated windows, the ornaments of the pilasters, the plain octagonal pillars, and the parapet walls in front of the verandah, carved only with the rail pattern. But into this and several others the followers of the Mahâyâna schools have introduced numerous figures of Buddha, with Nâga and other attendants, in some cases quite covering the walls with them. On the back wall of the verandah and between two grated windows is a long Pâli inscription, recording the dedication of the cave and cistern by a native of Kalyâṇa.[2]

No. 35 is one of the largest of this group, having a hall about 40 ft. wide by 45½ ft. deep, without pillars, with a bench or seat round three sides, and with four cells, each with a stone bench.[3] The verandah in front has four pillars-octagons with square bases, and a parapet wall carved with rail pattern in front over a panelled basement, which raises the verandah floor 3 ft. 2 in. above the level of the court. On each side of the court is a long stone bench, forming a pleasant seat in the evenings, with a magnificent view over Salsette to the westward, with the sea along the horizon. Two rows of holes across the court mark the position of wooden posts which supported a sloping roof raised against the front of the cave for further comfort during the rains. A cistern of excellent water close to the front of the verandah on the left side, would supply abundant water for the community. At a later date, however, the simpler early doctrines gave place to those of the Greater Vehicle, and the inner walls both of the verandah and the hall were covered with sculptures, mostly of Buddha, variously attended. One of the panels is given in the accompanying woodcut (No. 22). It represents one of the most common groups in this and several other caves,—Buddha seated on the lotus-throne (*padmâsana*), his hands in the *dharma-chakra mudrâ* or that of instruction, Padmapâṇi as chauri-bearer on his left hand, attended by Târâdêvî, and another Bodhisattva

No. 22.—Sculptured Panel from Cave XXXV

[1] No. 62 of West's copies.

[2] No. 18 of West's copies, and No. 7 of Brett's, but the latter is very inaccurate, and Stevenson's translation from it quite useless.

[3] *Cave Temples*, p. 358.

with his *śákti* on the right. On clouds above are two Vidyâdharas with garlands, while the stalk of the lotus is upheld below by two Nâgarâjâs, behind whom stand their Nâganîs or wives, and kneeling worshippers occupy the corners. This is the same group, in so far as design is concerned, as that inserted between the two original groups of figures on the left-hand side of the screen at Kârlê (pl. xii). It occurs also in several other caves here, in Cave II. at Nâsik, at Elurâ, and, in fact, in most of the latest Bauddha excavations. It belongs undoubtedly to the Mahâyâna school, and is probably in no instance older than the sixth or even the seventh century.

In the right end of the verandah is a small group, represented in woodcut No. 23, which is much less common in the sculptures in the Bauddha caves of Western India. It is the representation of a favourite Jâtaka or birth-story, found in the legends both of the northern and southern Buddhists,[1] and is represented on some of the sculptures from later monasteries on the frontiers of Kabul. According to the northern account, Megha,[2] a young ascetic, came to the city of Paduma at the time when Dîpaṅkara Buddha was expected, and wishing to make an offering of flowers to him, he found that none were procurable as the king had ordered all to be reserved for his own offerings. Seeing a dark-clad water-girl named Bhadrâ concealing a seven-stalked Utpala flower[3] in her pitcher, he attempted to purchase five of the stalks for 500 pieces of money, the price the girl had paid for the whole. The girl finally agreed to the bargain, with the further condition that he should offer the other two on her account, and that in every successive life he would take her as his wife, and, if he arrived at Buddhahood, permit her to follow him as a disciple. This being agreed to, he proceeded to meet Dîpaṅkara, who was entering the city, the flowers offered to him by the king and his followers forming a canopy over his head. He threw the seven stalks of Utpala towards the Buddha, and in accordance with his desire they remained in mid-air, the flowers standing upwards, crowning the canopy, and moving as he moved. Megha being repulsed by the crowd, who were spreading their garments in the way, Dîpaṅkara formed a muddy place in front of him, on which the ascetic immediately placed his deer-skin garment, and undoing his hair, spread it over the skin for the Buddha to pass over, who then granted his secret desire that he should become the Buddha Sâkya Muni. "Then Megha ascended into the air the height of seven Tâla trees, and did reverence to Dîpaṅkara." There is no difficulty in recognising this legend in the sculpture.

No. 23.—Dipaṅkara Jâtaka from Cave XXXV.

In No. 36, on the side walls outside the verandah, are two Pâli inscriptions of seven

[1] The southern or Singhalese version was translated by Childers, Rhys Davids' *Buddhist Birth-Stories*, p. 3 f.; and the Chinese one by Rev. S. Beal, *J. R. As. Soc.*, vol. vi, p. 377 f.

[2] He is called Sumedha in the *Buddhavaṁsa* version.

[3] The blue lotus, Nymphæa cærulea.

lines in early characters, and dated in the eighth year of Srîsena Mâḍharîputra,[1] one of the Andhra kings who is placed conjecturally after Puḷumâvi. The inscription on the left-hand wall is much injured, but both record gifts by natives of Kalyâṇa.

In Cave No. 37 the water oozes through a large crack in the rock at the back of the hall, and a drain has been cut out to carry off the water, which is led through the front wall under the left-hand grated window. It has evidently been covered over. The pilasters of the verandah have an ornament similar to that given in woodcut No. 11, from Mahâḍ.

No. 38 is the long terrace under the overhanging rock on the brow of the hill, where are the bases of numerous brick stûpas, being the monuments over the ashes of numerous Bauddha sthaviras or priests who died here. Two are in recesses in the rock, and one is in relief on the rock, but a vast number fill this gallery, which is about 200 yards in length; many of them, however, are covered over with the débris of decayed bricks and rock, and all seem to have been rifled long ago of any relics or caskets they contained. The general view of the widest portion of the gallery is represented in the accompanying woodcut (No. 24). One stûpa, larger than the rest, was built of stone, and was examined and described by Dr. E. W. West in 1861.[2]

No. 24—The Kaṇheri Bauddha Cemetery.

Cave 42 has two halls, each about 15 feet square, with stone benches along the back, and each has a benched cell. They open from a verandah about 37½ feet long, which had four pillars in front, now unfortunately destroyed, except the tops of the capitals, which have been sculptured in *bas-relief*, with elephants or tigers and human figures on each of the four sides, apparently in the style of the Kuḍâ rail (pl. viii, fig. 9), certainly in a much ruder style than any of the Nâsik capitals. Below this was the abacus and thick torus of capitals of the early type. The two pilasters were among the most richly carved at Kaṇheri; from the remaining fragments[3] we learn that each had a rosette in the centre and a large segment of another at the top and bottom, the intervals being

[1] West's Nos. 19 and 20; see *Cave-Temple Inscriptions*, p. 60, and *Jour. Bom. B. R. A. Soc.*, vol. xii, p. 407.

[2] *Jour. Bom. B. R. A. Soc.*, vol. vi, p. 116 f. See also *Cave Temples*, p. 359.

[3] See *Cave-Temple Inscriptions*, pl. xxviii, fig. 5, p. 56.

filled up with wavy leaves over three shallow flutes. A line of five small rosettes also finished off the upper end of the pilaster. In the ends of the verandah later sculptures of Buddha and attendants have been inserted, and in the back wall of the right-hand hall is a small arched recess as if for a metal image. In both rooms are remains of plaster all over the walls, and some traces of painting in that to the right.

In No. 43, close to the right of the preceding, there is also an arched recess at the back containing a sitting figure of Buddha on a lotus. Over a cistern on the right side of the court is an inscription in eight and a half lines.[1]

No. 45 has also four pillars in front of the verandah—square with a short neck, having eight sides—and the pilasters have the ornament so frequent in early caves, represented in woodcut No. 11 (p. 18). The cave consists of a Bhikshugṛiha to the left, entered from a neat hall with a bench along the back and most of the right side, terminating in a sort of sofa end.[2] In an arched recess in the back wall is a figure of Buddha in the *Bhûmisparśa mudrâ*. In the left end of the verandah is also some sculpture, but all of it is probably the work of a later age than the cave. A general plan of Caves 45 to 49 is given, pl. xl, fig. 8.

In No. 47 are remains of plaster on the walls, and some traces of painting; and on the left-hand side wall of the court of No. 48 is an inscription[3] in five lines, the ends of which are partially obliterated.

Cave 50 has a parapet wall, ornamented with rail pattern, in front of the verandah; the two pillars are octagonal with square bases, and the pilasters have an ornament somewhat more complicated than that in No. 45. The verandah is about 10 ft. deep by 20 ft. wide, and the hall is about 20 ft. square, with a bench nearly all round. The single cell on the left side has also a stone couch.

Cave 51 contains much plaster and some remains of painting, and also some sculpture. As a specimen of the ordinary style of façade among the smaller vihâras at Kaṇheri, this one is represented on pl. xl, fig. 6, and a drawing of part of the parapet wall on an enlarged scale in fig. 7.

Nos. 52 and 53 are very similar; each has two octagonal pillars in front of the verandah, connected with the ends by a parapet wall, and ascended to by a flight of steps; each has a seat in the right end of the verandah, and grated windows into the hall and cell. The halls are about 14 ft. square, with stone bench along two sides, and the single cells have each a stone bed. In the courts also are benches, and a round stone bowl for holding water to wash the feet of the visitor before entering. Outside, to the right of each, is also another seat cut in the rock.

No. 56 is a still larger cave, the hall being nearly 19 ft. square, and the verandah has four octagonal pillars in front, with square bases similar to those in Nos. 60 and 61, &c., rising from a parapet wall. In the back of the hall is a square niche with a moulded throne for an image in the style of the eleventh century. The pillars and pilasters are grooved all the way up for some sort of boarding or lattice screen between. This and the next have similar bowls and seats outside as the last.

No. 59 has a bench with an ornamental head as in No. 45 Over the cistern in the

---

[1] West's copies, No. 24.

[2] For the pillar and end of the bench see *Cave-Temple Inscriptions*, pl. xxviii, figs. 3 and 6, p. 56.

[3] West's No. 25.

court and on the back wall of the verandah are short Pâli inscriptions[1] dedicating the cave and well by a mendicant of Kalyâṇa. Nos 60 and 61 have each a low parapet wall in front, carved with rail ornament, and No. 61 has a similar frieze above.

No. 62 has had a bench along the back and right side, but a shrine has been cut in the back wall, with two roughly-formed square pillars in front.

No. 63 has a parapet wall in front, with rail ornament above and panelled below, and two octagonal pillars on square bases.

In Cave 64 the verandah is raised, like Nos. 60, 61, &c., above the court, and has a parapet wall in front. The pillars are plain octagons with square bases and the pilasters have a slightly modified form of the ornament so frequent on the pilasters here, and of which there are many varieties (see woodcut No. 25). The verandah walls are largely covered with the sculptures of the usual sort.

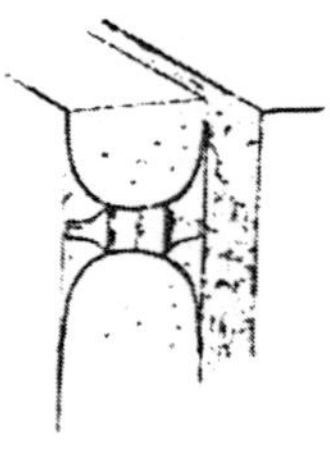

No. 25.—Pilaster Ornament in Cave 64 at Kanheri.

No. 66 is the cave having three Pahlavi inscriptions on its pilasters and well-recess. They have been deciphered and translated by Dr. E. W. West, and give a series of names of two parties of Pârsis who visited the caves in 378 and 390 of Yazdajerd (A.D. 1009 and 1021).[2] Fragments of inscriptions by the same party were also found at the large stûpa in No. 38. The interior of this cave is covered with Mahâyâna sculptures, among which is a fine copy of the Litany of Avalôkiteśvara, Buddha enthroned, and attendants,[3] dâgobas, &c.

Cave 67, close to the last, but at a lower level and similar in its arrangements, has two square pillars in front, with a very short neck of sixteen sides ornamented with circular grooves above and below. The walls of the verandah and hall are covered with figures of the usual sort and a few dâgobas. Beyond the hall is a small shrine, in the back wall of which is carved a seated Buddha, with smaller ones and dâgobas on the lower parts of the side walls, while the upper portions still retain portions of plaster and painted figures.

No. 68 has a façade similar to No. 60, with two grated windows into a hall about 13½ ft. square, with a bench along the back and right side, and a cell in the left also with stone bed and a window into the verandah. There is a cistern in the left wall of the court and an inscription in seven lines,[4] partially defaced, between it and the front of the cave There is no sculpture in this or No. 69, which is a similar cave with an ornament on the pilasters, and an indistinct inscription on the left-hand wall of the court. Outside Cave 70 there are also two long inscriptions, but large portions of them are worn away.

Cave 72 had two square pillars in front of the same pattern as in No. 67, of which one however is destroyed The door of the hall is surrounded by mouldings, and in the cell at the back is a seated figure of Buddha, covered with plaster which has been painted; there are also remains of plaster and painting on the walls of the hall.

Nos. 75, 76, and 77 are close together, each consisting of a small raised verandah with two octagonal pillars, and pilasters with an ornament more complicated than the usual type. but which also occurs in Nos. 51 and 69. To 76 and 77 additional cells have been added in the sides of the courts, but in neither of them is there any sculpture. and but a small

---

1 West's Nos. 32 and 33, and Brett's 15 and 14.

2 *Cave-Temple Inscriptions*, p. 62 f.; and *Ind. Ant.*, vol. ix. p. 265 f

3 See *Cave Temples*, p. 358, and pl. lv. fig. 1. and pl. lvi.

4 West's No. 35.

piece in No. 75. On the right side wall of the court of No. 76 is an inscription in nine lines by a native of Dheṇukakaṭa.[1] There are also inscriptions in Nos. 75 and 77.[2]

No. 78 is just opposite to the Darbâr cave No. 10, and has two long inscriptions on the architrave, one of them dated in the reign of Amoghavarsha the Râshṭrakûṭa king, S. 799 (A.D. 877). The two pillars and pilasters in front are of the Elephanta and Elurâ type, and the door in the back of the verandah has three chiselled fascias round it; the hall is about 14 ft. by 11; and in the shrine is a large sitting figure of Buddha on a bench, on which has been a very short inscription in much older letters than that on the façade of the cave, but only two or three are legible.

In No. 81, on the left-hand wall of the court, is an inscription of the reign of Gautamîputra Śriyajña Sâtakarṇi.[3]

No. 85 has a tank on the right of the court with two neatly hewn half-columns at each side of the recess; the pilasters or half-columns, too, of the verandah have their middle sections of seven sides.[4]

No. 86 has had two pillars and pilasters in front, of a pattern very similar to those in Caves 67 and 72. The hall is 21 ft. wide by 21¾ ft. deep, with a door recessed in the jambs. To the right of it, outside, are traces of a large circular painting, like the so-called zodiac in Cave XVII. at Ajaṇṭâ. It has had a figure of Buddha in the centre, and the area was divided into eight sectors, in each of which, if we may judge from what remains of one, were numerous figures variously employed. At the back of the hall are three small rooms.

CHAPTER XII.

KONDIVTE CAVES.

The Kondivtê caves, situated about eight miles south from the Kaṇheri group and about three from Karlâ station, near the village of Maroli, and not far from the Jogeśvari Brahmanical Caves, have been described with as much detail as they seem to merit in *The Cave Temples* (p. 360 ff.), but the plan of the whole group given in pl. xlii. will render that account more intelligible.

Beginning at the south end of the east side of the hill, the first is a very small cave with two square pillars in front of the verandah. The room within has a small recess in the back and a door in the right end into the verandah of No. 2. The next has a hall about 15 ft. wide by 23 ft. deep, with an altar at the back, and over it in a panel sunk in the wall is a rude bas-relief of a dâgoba. On the wall above are eight mortice-holes disposed in a semicircle, and three larger ones on each side, as if for some covering. The verandah in front has four square pillars with necks similar to those of Nos. 67 and 72 at Kaṇheri. They have bases and stand on a basement carved with rail pattern in front, and are surmounted by a frieze ornamented with Chaitya windows. Behind them are four large

[1] No. 39 of West's copies.
[2] Nos. 38, 40, and 41 of West's copies.
[3] West's No. 44, Stevenson's No. 13, and Bird's No. 14.
[4] If complete pillars they would have sixteen sides.

holes in the floor connected below. Close to this is No. 3—a small room 11½ ft. by 6, with two square pillars in front

No. 4 is a hall 36 ft. wide by 24½ ft. deep, with a bench round three sides, three doors, and two windows. In each side is a chamber about 19 ft. by 7 ft., with two octagonal pillars in front and three cells behind. In the back wall of the hall is also a small shrine, with two pillars in front, but it is perhaps later than the cave. The verandah is supported by four octagonal pillars.

No. 5 is much ruined, but seems to have consisted of three rooms behind one another. No. 6 consists of four cells, two of them with stone benches; No. 7 of two rooms opening into a common verandah, the second of them having three small irregular cells opening from it; and No. 8 is a single cell on a higher level than the next, with the remains of a bench at the back. All these are more or less ruined.

No. 9 is the only Chaitya cave in the series, and has been described in *The Cave Temples*.[1] The sculpture on the right wall, drawn in pl. xlii, fig. 1, has been added at a much later date than that of the original excavation. It is much defaced, but consists entirely of the usual Mahâyâna sculptures of Buddha seated on the lotus, supported by Nâgas and attended on his right by Padmapâṇi as one of the *chauri*-bearers, while the other was probably Vajrapâṇi. The details are rather better executed than in other examples, and may belong to the seventh century. Over one of the grated windows of the shrine is an inscription in rudely formed characters. Several letters are partially obliterated and uncertain; what can be read indicates that it records a benefaction by a Brâhman of the Gautama-gotra, an inhabitant of Pachikâmayi.[2] On the surface of the hill almost vertically above the dâgoba in this cave is the foundation of another, which has been a structural one.

No. 12 has three cells at the back of the hall, in two of which are stone beds. No. 13 is the largest in the group and the only one with pillars in the hall. The verandah is 23 ft. by 9 ft. and has two square pillars in front, but the roof extends some 10 or 12 ft. beyond them. The hall, into which are three doors, is nearly 29 ft. wide by 28 ft. deep, and has four octagonal columns disposed in a square, with plain circular bases and capitals of the Elephanta or Dheḍwâḍâ type. These stand on a platform raised a few inches above the surrounding floor. This hall has three cells in each wall; the central one in the back, having been the shrine, still contains the *âsana* or seat for it, and has a neatly carved doorway. The cell to the right of the shrine also contains a bench.[3] No. 14 consists of one cell behind another; and No. 15, the last in this range, is similar, but with a small verandah in front and much ruined.

The four on the west side of the hill, just behind the last, are very similar. The third from the north end (No. 17) has two side cells and a shrine with a seat for the image in the back, and a neat doorway with pilasters and mouldings drawn in fig. 2, pl. xliii. Between it and the last is a dâgoba carved in the rock in low relief. The two pillars of the verandah of the fourth are much of the style of those of the unfinished Chaitya cave at Kaṇheri, but more clumsy.

---

[1] P. 360 and p. 41 n.

[2] No. 60 in West's series, *Jour. Bom. B. R. A. Soc.*, vol. vi, p. 13. The sense given in the text is due to Dr. Bühler; the name Pachikâmayi, however, is doubtful.

[3] There was an inscription in about thirteen lines of very small letters, above a recessed seat on the right hand of the entrance to this cave, but it is so faint and obliterated that nothing can be made of it.

CHAPTER XIII.

PALÆOGRAPHY.

PALÆOGRAPHY, or the study of the gradual modification of alphabets in the course of time, is necessarily dependent, in the first place, on documents of approximately known dates. But when we have, in this way, arrived at a knowledge of the times when different changes of the forms of letters took place, we may apply this knowledge to inscriptions of unknown date, in order to determine, from a comparison of the styles of their alphabets, the ages to which they respectively belong. As applied to Indian inscriptions, Comparative Palæography has as yet made but little progress towards scientific accuracy, and much has still to be done before we can use the characters of different inscriptions with full confidence as a safe guide to chronology. Still its leading principles are understood, and the alphabetical characters of inscriptions, when carefully examined and compared, lend their aid to that of architectural style, and the two together often help to supply fairly accurate indications of the relative ages of different monuments.

Prinsep's table of the "Modifications of the Sanskrit Alphabet from 543 B.C. to 1200 A.D.," which was published in the *Journal of the Asiatic Society of Bengal* for March 1838,[1] represented the forms of the letters in ten alphabets, but after excluding the modern Devanâgarî, old Burmese Pâli, old Tibetan, and two mediæval alphabets, the ancient alphabets represented were only five:—(1) The alphabet of the Asoka inscriptions, which he entitled "Fifth century B.C."[2] (2) An alphabet of "uncertain" date collected from the Pâli inscriptions on the Western Cave Temples. (3) One founded on the Rudradâman inscription, which he erroneously styled "Third century B.C., Sanskrit inscription of Aśoka, Junâgaḍh."[3] (4) From Valabhi and Gurjara copper plates, which he called "Second century A.D.—Gujarat dated plates." And (5) the alphabet of the Allahabad Gupta inscription, "Fifth century, A.D."

The table was reproduced in Thomas's edition of Prinsep's *Antiquities*,[4] and in a later page (p. 52) Mr. Thomas gave another table of alphabets containing also the same five, described respectively as from—(1) "Aśoka's Edicts—3d century B.C.;" (2) "Western Caves;" (3) "Sâh inscription (Girnâr);" (4) "Gupta inscription (Allahabad);" and (5) "Valabhî plates (Gujarat),"—thus rectifying the dates and correctly placing the Valabhî plates after the Gupta inscriptions. To these were added a sixth alphabet derived from the Vakâṭaka plates of Śivani,[5] which he calls the "Nerbudda alphabet," and a seventh—the "Kistna" alphabet, derived from a portion of an inscription found by General Colin Mackenzie at Amarâvati—but probably of as late a date as the eighth century A.D., and taken from an eye-copy not representing the shapes of the letters very accurately.[6] The designation of "Kistna alphabet" given to this latter was by no means appropriate. Prinsep uses this name on his original plate,

[1] Vol. vii. p. 276, illustrating his remarks on the Pâli alphabet, vol. vi. pp. 467 ff. and vii. pp. 271 ff.

[2] He assigns as his reason for this—that he supposes the alphabet used in these edicts was the same as "that in which their sacred books had been written by the contemporaries of Buddha himself, who died in the year 543 B.C.," *ibid.*, p. 275; *Essays* by Thomas, vol. ii. p. 39.

[3] Prinsep mistook this Kshatrapa inscription for a genuine Maurya one from the name of Chandragupta occurring in it: *J. A. S. B.*, vol. vii. p. 275, or *Essays*, vol. ii. p. 38.

[4] Vol. ii. p. 41.

[5] *J. A. S. B.*, vol. v. p. 726; conf. *As. Res.*, vol. xv. p. 507.

[6] Conf. Sewell's *Report on Amarâvati*, pl. iv. and p. 63. The slab is now in the British Museum.

from which Mr. Thomas copied both additional alphabets, but in his account of it he calls it the Ândhra character.[1] The other alphabets added by Mr. Thomas were avowedly modern ones. His table was reproduced by Professor Monier Williams in the second edition of his *Sanskrit Grammar*, and again partially revised by Mr. Thomas and printed in Mr. Hope's *Inscriptions in Dharwar and Mysore* (1866).

Mr. Prinsep's attempt, however, was not really the *first* to tabulate the early forms of an Indian alphabet; for as early as 1828 Dr. B. G. Babington had given comparative tables both of the old Sanskṛit and Tamil alphabets from the inscriptions at Mâmallaipura.[2] In 1833 Mr. (now Sir) Walter Elliot, then of the Madras Civil Service, had published an elaborate comparative table of the older forms of the Kaṇṇaḍa alphabet in forty folio pages, in which many of the characters are identical with those of the early northern alphabets. This, again, was followed in 1837 by Captain H. Harkness's *Ancient and Modern Alphabets of the Popular Hindu Languages of the Southern Peninsula of India*, in which he tabulated the Devanâgarî, Grantha, Telugu, Karṇâṭaka, Malayalma and Tamil, with variations or old forms. For the Karṇâṭaka he availed himself of Sir W. Elliot's tables. But as he says the compilation was made "many years before publication," it was scarcely up to date when it appeared. Most of the early forms of the letters of the northern alphabets, however, are represented in it.

These tables are the only systematic attempts made previous to Dr. Burnell's to show the modifications of the Indian alphabet, and their meagreness has left room for hasty and unjustifiable conclusions on the part of amateurs in palæography.

They were principally founded too—not on facsimiles, then difficult of attainment—but on "eye-copies," whereby letters were liable to variations from the normal forms, easily understood by those who have had much practice in the copying of such inscriptions: for in many of these the same letter is formed with some slight variation of size, slant, curve, or proportion in some part or another, almost as often as it is repeated, and the hand of the copyist, in spite of himself, tends to a set form. Fortunately Prinsep's copyists, especially Captain Kittoe, were remarkably accurate and painstaking, and saved him from serious mistakes. It would have been impossible, however, at that date and in his circumstances, to have represented the early alphabets with perfect accuracy. For his second alphabet,—palæographically perhaps the most important in the series,—he had not even the materials on which to base an alphabet of one age, but drew the letters of it from copies of such inscriptions from Nânâghâṭ, Kârlê, Kanheri, Ajaṇṭâ, &c., as were supplied to him. Nor do we find any fault with him for this: his object seems to have been simply to present outlines of the varying types of alphabets to students who, like himself, were still struggling with the first epigraphical difficulties—the obsolete forms of the letters in which these old inscriptions were expressed—and not to attempt to exhibit the palæographic development of the alphabet.

---

[1] *J. A. S. B.*, vol. vi, pp. 219, 220, and pl. xiii at p. 222. If any alphabet, however, should be designated "Ândhra," it should be that used in the inscriptions of the Ândhra dynasty at Nânâghâṭ, Kârlê, Nâsik, and Kaṇheri, or that used by them on their coins,—not one like this, employed long after the dynasty was extinct. Nor is "Kistna" an appropriate epithet, for in the Vengi and early Eastern Chalukya inscriptions we have earlier types of the character from the same district.

[2] *Trans. R. As. Soc.*, vol. ii, plates xiii. xv. xvii. and xviii., and pp. 264–269. Colonel C. Mackenzie, at a still earlier date in all probability, had acquired a knowledge of the old alphabet used on the Amarâvati marbles from his paṇḍits. There are among his MSS. copies of inscriptions in early characters, and even translations of some of them.

For South-Indian Palæography Dr. A. C. Burnell did a splendid service by the preparation of his work on that subject (published in 1874), which he has since greatly enlarged and corrected in a second edition (1878). There are now ample materials, published and unpublished, for a similar work relating to Peninsular India from the Kṛishṇâ river to the Vindhya hills, that is, for the Dekhan, Koṅkaṇ and Gujarât.[1] The adequate illustration and discussion of so large a range of epigraphy, however, must be a work of much labour and care. Meanwhile, it seems desirable to supply some chart, however meagre, of the palæography of this great province, representing the characters used in the numerous inscriptions, especially those in the Cave Temples, from the age of Asoka, 250 B.C., till the end of the eighth century, when the old type of alphabet, founded on the Pâli or Mauryan, was disappearing, the Devanâgarî taking its place over the northern portions of this area, and the Canarese in the south. This is what has been attempted in the accompanying plate, No. v.

On tabulating the alphabets of different inscriptions, much of the apparent divergency of style among them disappears from the forms to be finally compared, in order to decide as to their relative ages. But in the consideration of all the elements that may help to indicate the chronological position of an inscription, the attached vowels and the compound letters form an important element. A comparison of inscriptions of the same age will show that, with certain points of agreement in the way in which the vowels are attached, their forms were subject to considerable variety of treatment, dependent on provincial or even personal manipulative taste. And a somewhat similar diversity seems also to have prevailed with respect to the lengths of the dependent stems of letters like *a*, *ka*, *ra*, and the form of the lower turn of the line. If we compare the large and beautiful inscription of Ushavadâta, the son-in-law of Nahapâṇa, at Nâsik,[2] with those of the same reign at Kârlê[3] and Junnar, and these again with that of Rudradâman at Girnâr[4]—all engraved probably within the same century—we shall be struck with the differences of style, which, most probably, are mainly due to the skill and taste of the official writers or engravers. That something is also due to locality seems to be indicated by the differences between the alphabets of the Gupta inscriptions at Allahabad and Kahaun and that at Junâgaḍh. The northern examples have many forms not found in the Junâgaḍh one, which scarcely differs from the alphabet of the earlier Valabhî plates. The form of *pha* is the only one in it that could be said to be copied from the northern inscriptions. The later alphabets from different parts of the peninsula show further marks of local divergences: thus the Vâkâṭaka and Chhatisgaḍh inscriptions are clearly marked off from the more westerly Valabhî ones, and both differ from the southern or Chalukya types, while even the eastern and western Chalukya alphabets early began to develop differences.

To develop fully all the details of the alphabets, it would be necessary not only to tabulate symmetrically, as Dr. Burnell has done, the consonants—both separately and combined with the different vowels—but also the varieties of each consonant and a large number at least of their compounds.

---

[1] A third volume might deal with the palæography of Hindustan and the Panjâb, and include even Nepâl, for which the excellent collection of Pandit Bhagwânlâl Indrâjî (published in the *Indian Antiquary*, vol. ix, pp. 163 ff.) supplies large and important material.

[2] See Prinsep's *Essays*, vol. ii, pp. 47, 48.

[3] Kârlê and Nâsik are each within fifty miles of Junnar.

[4] See note 4, p. 37, *ante*.

INDIAN ALPHABETS from B.C. 250 to A.D. 800.

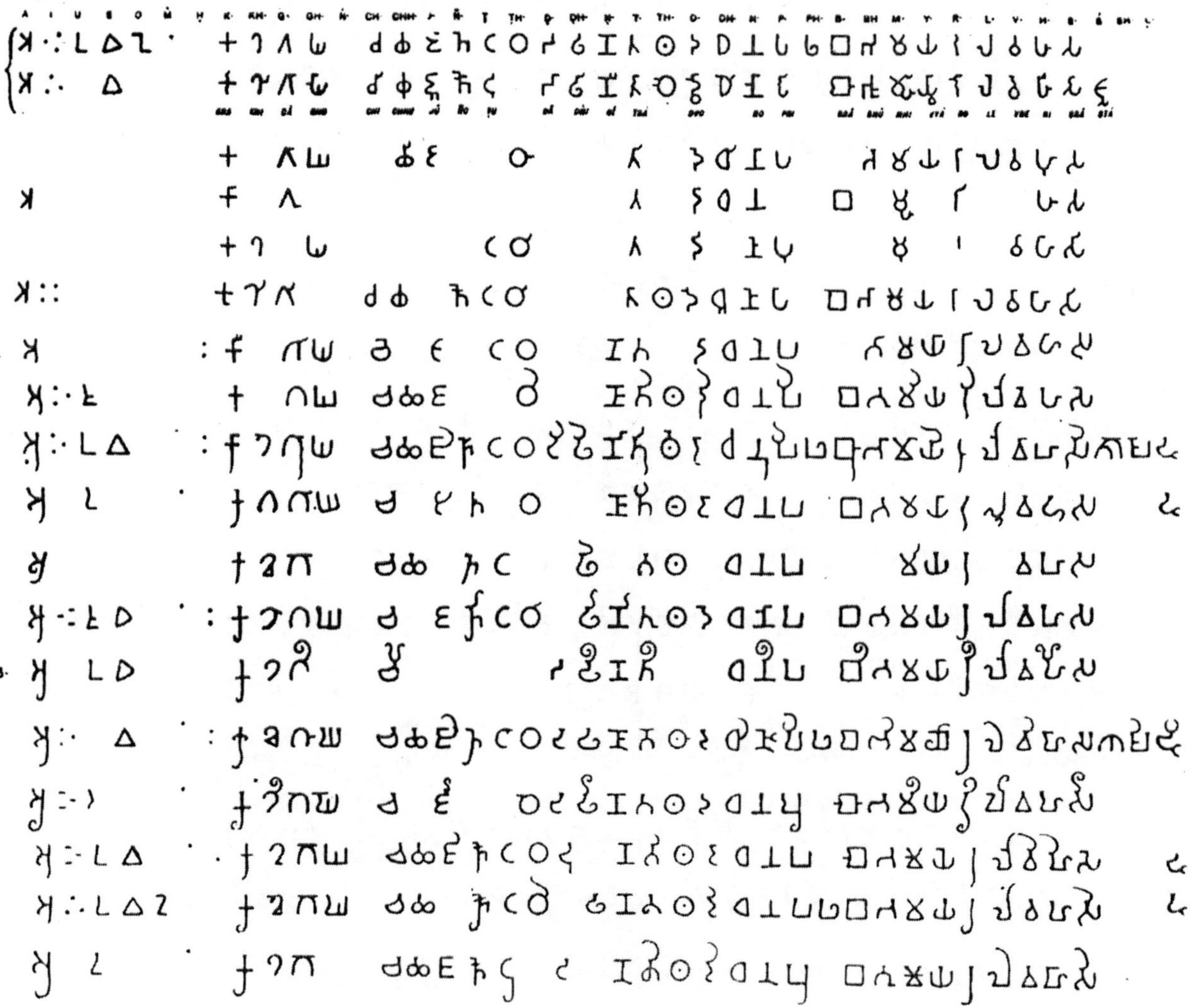

MAURYA
1. GIRNAR, 250 B.C.

2. PITALKHORA.

3. KOLHAPUR.

4. AJANTA, CAVE X.

ANDHRA
5. NANAGHAT.

6. NASIK, CHAITYA &c.

7. KARLE CHAITYA.

KSHATRAPA
8 NASIK, CAVE VIII.

KSHATRAPA
9. KARLE.

KSHATRAPA
10. JUNNAR.

11. JUNNAR— *various*.

12. JUNNAR, INS. NO. 3.

KSHATRAPA
13. GIRNAR, S. 78.

14. KUDA CAVES.

ANDHRA
15. NASIK, CAVE III.

ANDHRA
16. KARLE.

17. BANAVASI.

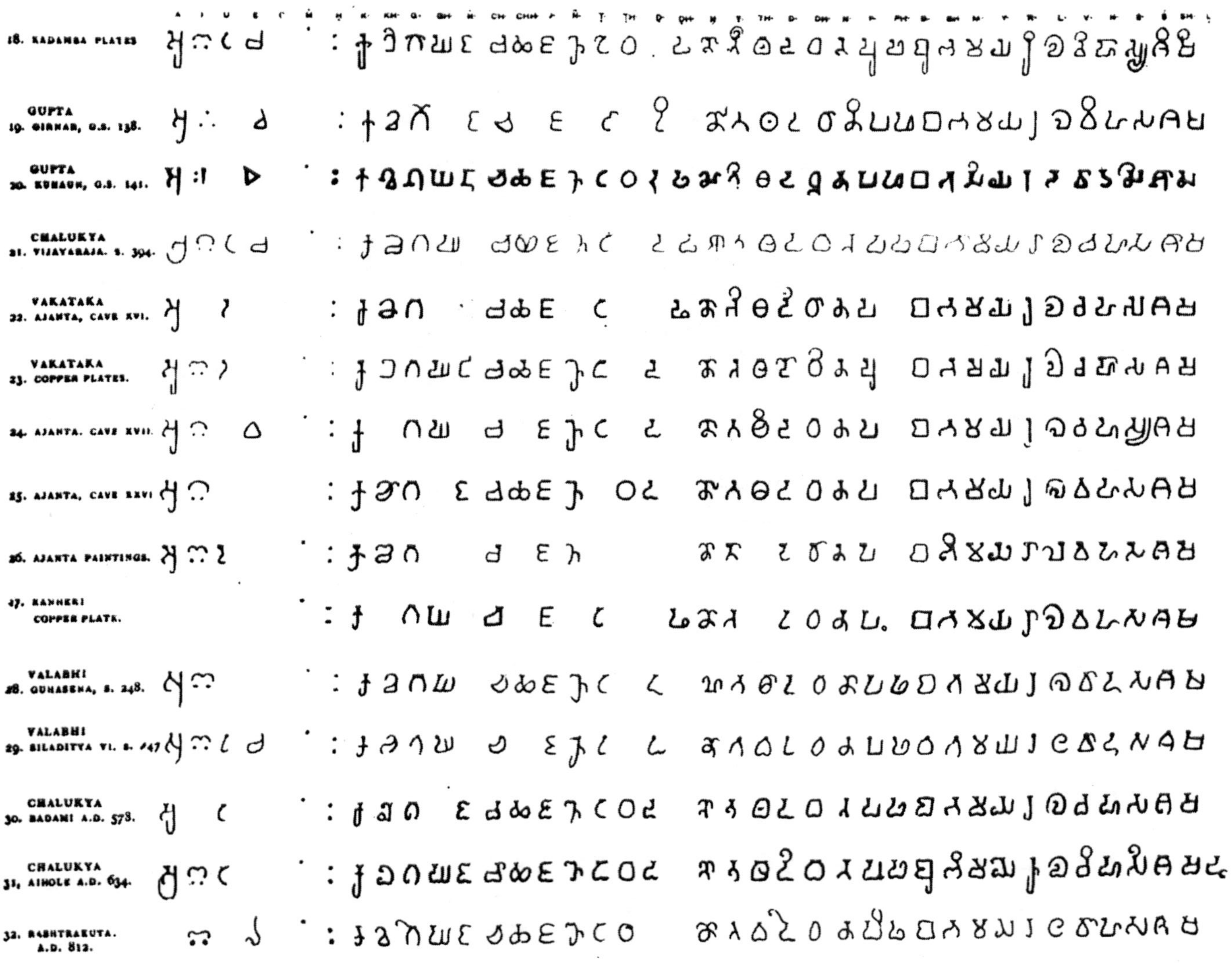

J. Burgess, 1880. *W. Griggs, Photo-lith.*

In the accompanying plates no such amplified representation has been attempted, but the alphabets are carefully reproduced from the original inscriptions, and, to save space, vowels have been attached, as in the inscriptions, to numbers of the consonants, and a few illustrative compounds have been inserted. In only two cases in the whole series have I been obliged to use copies; in all the others, impressions, rubbings, or photographs have been employed. But for the Skandagupta inscription at Girnâr, I had only a tracing; the original is cut on a very rough and uneven or bulged surface, unsuitable for taking a good impression. The other exception is the Kaṇheri copper plate, which was retained by the late Dr. J. Bird, and is now not to be traced;[1] for it we have only the lithograph in his *Historical Researches*, which is obviously faulty, but may be accepted as on the whole fairly representing the general outlines of the letters.

The following are the alphabets represented in the accompanying plate (pl. v):—

1. The Maurya alphabet, or that of the Aśoka inscription at the foot of Mount Girnâr. To this two lines have been given,—the first showing the simple letters (except *jha*, which occurs so rarely that it has been omitted throughout), and the second line, presenting varieties of form either alone or in combination with vowels and other consonants. The forms of *kra*, *trâ*, *prâ*, &c., in which the wavy vertical line represents the *-ra*,[2] will be noted among these.

2. The alphabet of the Pitalkhorâ Cave inscriptions. These are all short ones, and supply in all only nineteen different letters—*ka, gâ, gha, chhi, ja, thâ, ti, de, dhi, ṅâ, pa, bha, mi, ya, râ, la, va, hu, sa.*

3. A relic box was found at Kolhâpur in 1877 having an inscription on the lid.[3] This also is a short inscription yielding only twelve different letters, but of a type closely resembling the two preceding—*a, kâ, gu, ta, dâ, dha, na, bha, mha, ri, ha, sa.*

4. The inscription of Vâsiṭhîputa on the front of Cave X. at Ajaṇṭâ. This too is distinctly of the Maurya type, as is also the short one on the similar Chaitya at Kondâne and a fragment at Beḍsâ. The agreement in the alphabet of the inscriptions on the three large Chaityas with open fronts is conclusive of the accuracy of the deduction made independently from their architecture, that these are the earliest Chaityas we have, and that they belong to one age. The inscription at Bedsâ is not on the Chaitya but on a cell, and the Chaitya must be as old as any of the vihâras—possibly older than the one where the inscription occurs, which is probably later than the small vihâra excavated in December 1879. The letters with which vowels are represented as combined in the inscription of Vâsiṭhîputa are—*ṭhi, di, no, pu, mu, vâ, hâ, si.*

5. The fragments that remain of the great inscription of Śâtakarni Vedisiri at Nânâghâṭ supply another early alphabet and an important series of numerals.[4] The letters here represented combined with vowels are—*ku, khi, gi, ño, ṭhi, tâ, de, dhâ, no, pâ, be, bhâ, mo, râ, le, vâ, hâ, si.*

6. The Nâsik Chaitya furnishes inscriptions of Hakusiri and others, and Cave XIV

---

1 It cannot be too much lamented that private individuals should hoard up such documents; they are almost invariably lost in the end. All Bird's and Wathen's, the Sâmangaḍh plates, and many others have thus disappeared within the last thirty years. Very few indeed have found their way either to the British Museum or the Royal Asiatic Society, where they would be preserved and be accessible to scholars.

2 The nature of these characters was first pointed out to me by Pandit Bhagwânlâl Indrâjî some years ago. M. Senart has independently noticed the same compounds, and was the first in Europe to direct attention to them in the *Jour. Asiatique*, Mai-Juin 1879, viime ser. t. xiii. p. 537; see also t. xiv. p. 311 ff.

3 *J. B. B. R. A. S.*, vol. xiv, p. 147 ff.; numerous Ândhra coins were found at the same time.

4 *Ind. Ant.*, vol. vi, p. 43 ff.

has also an early inscription. These two caves being the earliest at Nâsik, their inscriptions may be regarded as early Ândhra ones. The letters combined with vowels in this line are—*kî, gi, che, dâ, bhâ, mâ, yâ, râ, hâ.*

7. The Kârlê Chaitya Cave bears inscriptions of different ages, but those of the founder and some of the donors to its completion are taken as the basis of this alphabet. The letters given with vowels are—*â, thî, ṇâ, ti, di, pî, mi, rî, vâ, se.*

8. The beautiful Sanskṛit inscription of Ushavadâta in Cave VIII. at Nâsik has yielded the next, in which the combined letters are—*kâ, khe, grâ, jâ, ño, ḍî, ḍhî, rṇâ, tri, rthe, dâ, rdha, nu, pî, brâ, bhâ, mâ, yî, ru, lê, vâ, sî, śo, sho.*

9. From the inscription of Ushabhadâta at Kârle, with the combined letters—*gâ, ṇa, tî, dâ, lu.*

10. From the inscription of Ayama, minister of the Kshatrapa Nahapâṇa at Junnar, with the combined letters—*go, ḍhi, mi.*

11. This is formed from several inscriptions at Junnar, all apparently of about the same age. The combined letters are—*â, khâ, ñi, ṭha, ḍhi, ṇi, tu, de, no.*

12. From an inscription in five lines, outside a cave, in the scarp of Śivanêri Fort at Junnar, with rather peculiarly curved vowel *mâtras*, here exemplified in *gi, chî, ḍhi, ti, ni, bi, ya, ri, lê, pî.*

13. From the Sanskṛit Kshatrapa inscription of Rudradâman at Girnâr dated "in the 72nd year" (probably A.D. 150). This certainly represents an older form than the preceding, and perhaps earlier than No. 11. The combined letters represented are—*gâ, jâ, ṭa, ṇâ, to, thâ, dhi, nau, pî, bhi, yau, vi, shi, ṭî.*

14. From the Kuḍâ Caves. There are numerous inscriptions in these caves, probably of different ages, but a few of the best contain the same names, and are evidently closely related in age. The combined letters here are—*khi, ge, gho, ji, ṭhe, ḍhi, pra, bo, mi, ri, li, si.*

15. From the inscriptions of Gautamîputra in Cave III. at Nâsik. The combined letters given in this are—*go, ji, ño, ḍu, ti, dâ, be, me, ye, lê, vi, hi, se.*

16. From the inscriptions of Puḷumayi Vasishṭhîputra at Kârle. The combinations represented are—*khe, go, ño, ṭhi, di, si.*

17. From a short Pâli inscription discovered at Banavâsi, on the borders of Maisur, in March 1880. The combined letters here are—*go, ño, ṭu, ti, di, pra, bhu, mo, hâ, si.*

18. From Kadamba copper-plate grants in Sanskṛit—published by Mr. J. F. Fleet in the *Indian Antiquary* (vol. vii. pp. 33 ff.) This being the first alphabet from a copper-plate grant, it may be remarked that it presents certain fluencies of line that are wanting in those from inscriptions on stone. The combined letters here are—*khi, go, ṭe, ṇâ, tî, pra, bra, ri, vi, hâ, sya, śi, shi.*

19. From the Skandagupta inscription at Girnâr dated in the Guptakâla, 138.[1] The compounds represented are *go, ṭâ, ḍi, ṇâ, dhâ, ni, vi.*

---

[1] General Cunningham (*Arch. Surv. Reports*, vol. ix, p. 16 ff.) has adopted a hypothesis suggested by Dr. Bühler (*Ind. Ant.*, vol. vi, p. 80; vol. ix, p. 253) which places the initial date of the Gupta era in A.D. 195, an hypothesis which I felt disposed to employ in the *Cave Temples* (p. 191). The era supported by the inscription in the temple of Harasata at Verâval and by Albiruni, placing the commencement of the Valabhî Saṁvat in A.D. 319, belongs to a Valabhî era, probably dating from the destruction of that city by the Guptas when they conquered the Surâshtran peninsula. The Valabhî copper-plate grants, however, are dated in the Gupta era proper. It may have been owing to some jumbled account of the two eras that Albiruni was led to state that the Gupta and Valabhî eras were the same, and dated from the "destruction" of the Guptas. A curious corroboration

20. From the Kahaun inscription of Skandagupta dated 141 of the Guptakâla, but with a few letters supplied from the Allahabad inscription.[1] The compounds are—*ti, dhu, mi, vâ, si, śâ.*

21. From the Chalukya grant of Vijayarâja found at Khêḍâ in Gujarat, dated "Saṁvatsara 394,"[2]—perhaps Ś.S. 394. The compounds are—*ṇâ, bhâ, râ, li, śâ.*

22. From an inscription of the Vakâtakas at Ajantâ, Cave XVI.; the combined letters are—*ti, di, dhâ.*

23. From a copper-plate grant of the Vakâṭakas, found by Major Sczepanski in a ploughed field at Chamak, seven or eight miles south of Ilichpur, about 1868.[3] The combinations given are—*dâ, dhi, hâ.*

24. From the inscription on Cave No. XVII. at Ajaṇṭâ. The combined letters are—*thi, li,* and *sya.*

25. From the inscriptions on the façade of the Chaitya, Cave No. XXVI. at Ajaṇṭâ.

26. From painted inscriptions of Ajaṇṭâ, excluding however a fragment of an inscription in Cave X., which, with the painting on which it is, belongs to a much earlier date than any of the others. The combined letters are—*tâ, dhâ, bhi, râ.*

27. From Dr. Bird's lithographed copy of a copper plate found at Kanheri, dated in "the 245th year of the Trikutakas"—possibly of the Gupta era.

28. From Valabhî grants of Guhasena, "Sam 240–248," *i.e.*, of the Gupta era. The combined letters are—*thâ, nâ, lt, vâ.*

29. From a Valabhî grant of Śîlâditya VI. Dhruvabhaṭa, Sam. 447. This and No. 28 represent the variation due to a difference of two centuries of age.

30. From the Chalukya inscription of Maṅgaliśa at Bâdâmi, dated Śaka 500, A.D. 579.

31. From the inscription of Pulikêśi II. Satyâśraya, at Aihole, dated Śaka 556, A.D. 634.[4] The combined letters are—*châ, di, bu, bhi, ru, li, vi, sî.*

32. From a Râshṭrakûṭa copper-plate grant of Karka Suvarnavarsha, in the British Museum, dated Śaka 734, A.D. 812. The combined letters given are—*ge, de, pi, vâ.*

Between the last two a blank of nearly 180 years is unrepresented (except by No. 29), —not from lack of materials, but because the above are sufficient for our purpose.

Nor are these thirty-two alphabets arranged in chronological order except in a general way. Thus the very early ones are placed first with that of the Aśoka inscription at Girnâr at their head, and the dated ones of A.D. 579, 634, and 812 are placed last. The Valabhî types of the times of Guhasena and Śîlâditya VI. are placed together, though the interval

---

of the placing the commencement of the Guptakâla in the end of the second century has recently turned up. I-tsing, a Chinese writer, in the end of the seventh century, speaking of a Buddhist pilgrim to India named Hwui Lun, says, "In recent times a king named Jih-kwan (or 'sun-army') built a new temple" near the Bodhi tree, and that at Nalanda were the remains of a "temple built by Sri Gupta Mahârâja for the use of priests from China—about 500 years ago or so." Jih-kwan is a translation of Âditya-sena; and from a Nepâl inscription (*Ind. Ant.*, vol. ix. p. 181) we learn that Âditya-sena, king of Magadha, was the great-grandfather of Jayadêva of Nepâl, who was ruling in 760 A.D. This would place Âdityasena about 670–690 A.D. And as the Gupta reckoning would still be known in Hwui Lun and I-tsing's time, it was probably in the mind of the writer when he said Sri Gupta, the founder of the dynasty, lived 'about 500 years ago or so,' taking us back to about 190 or 200 A.D. as the commencement of the Guptakâla.

[1] *Ind. Ant.*, vol. x, p. 125.

[2] *Ind. Ant.*, vol. vii, p. 241 ff.

[3] *Notes on the Rock Temples of Ajanta, &c.*, p. 54 ff.

[4] See also copper-plate grant of Maṅgaliśa, *Ind. Ant.*, vol. vii, p. 161.

[5] See *Ind. Ant.*, vol. viii. p. 237 ff.; *Archæol. Sur.*, vol. iii, p. 129 ff.

between them is two centuries, and the second of them (No. 29) stands chronologically between Nos. 31 and 32, while the Kaṇheri copper plate should probably come between Nos. 28 and 30. Where exactly to place each of the Ajaṇṭâ alphabets may possibly be questioned, but it seems desirable, in the absence of dates, to arrange them and the Vakâṭaka copper plates together for purposes of comparison. Of those numbered 2 to 17, we have no direct means of fixing very approximately the ages: our best guide is the architectural style of the works with which some of them are associated, but for others we have not even this aid.

The inscription of Rudradâman mentions the 72d year, probably of the Śaka era (A.D. 150–1), and it is accepted as later than those of Nahapâṇa or his son-in-law Ushavadâta, but we have as yet no authorised data for arranging in their precise relative places the members of the Kshatrapa and Ândhra or Śâtavâhana dynasties.[1]

The inscription of Seṭh Bhûtapâla, who constructed the Kârle Chaitya, and those of Agnimitra and other donors of pillars, &c., in the temple, must be older than the two on the frieze over the doors, which were evidently inserted just where there was a fairly suitable surface. They record donations by Usabhadâta and Śri Puḷumayi, but which is the earliest can only be guessed at on the assumption that the first would select the smoothest and best surface. Now this bears Usabhadâta's inscription, which, however, is decidedly the more clumsily engraved of the two, and with nothing distinctively more archaic in the forms of the letters than in the other, except in the case of the *kha*, which is more like *ga* than the letter it here represents. But then at Nâsik we have three inscriptions of Ushavadâta (in Cave VIII.) dated in "the years 41 and 42," and at Junnar is one of Nahapâṇa's minister in "the year 46;" and at Nâsik are also three of Puḷumayi Vasishṭhîputra, and another at Kârle in one of the Vihâras. If Ushavadâta's inscription is badly carved at Kârle, it is compensated for by a large and beautifully regular one at Nâsik, unmatched by any other in execution, and still in excellent preservation. A careful comparison of all the inscriptions of Nahapâṇa and his son-in law Ushavadâta with those of Puḷumayi Vâsishṭhîputra seems to indicate that the former precede the latter, but by what period is difficult to conjecture: little more than half a century might possibly bridge the interval, or it might be a much wider one.

Besides the inscriptions cut in stone on caves, rocks, and buildings, the grants on copper plates (*tâmrapaṭṭa* or (*tâmra-śâsana*), so numerous in India, are of nearly equal palæographic importance, and seven of the alphabets here given are derived from these documents. In the *Vishṇusûtra* (iii. 82) it is laid down as an aphorism, "To those upon whom the king has bestowed (land) he must give a document destined for the information of a future ruler, which must be written upon a piece of (cotton) cloth, or a copper plate, and must contain the names of his (three) immediate ancestors, a declaration of the extent of the land, and an imprecation against him who should appropriate the donation to himself, and should be signed with his own seal." Such grants we know have been in use from very early times. Fah-Hian (cir. 400–414 A.D.) speaks of those granted to Bauddha Vihâras[2] long before his time, and we possess numbers of Brahmanical grants dating from about the beginning of the fifth century downwards. The copper plates of the Valabhî, Gurjara, and early Chalukya dynasties are the best known. They generally give the genealogy of the donor from the rise or first notable prince of the race, and frequently with references to their contests with

---

[1] See *ante*, p. 37, Note 4.

[2] Beal's *Buddh. Pilgr.*, p. 55.

neighbouring princes, thus supplying fragments of information of the highest historical importance.

Now we must not forget that, in comparing inscriptions on copper with those on stone, the greater freedom and rapidity with which the letters are traced out in the metal must often give them a somewhat different appearance from those cut so much more slowly in stone. Besides having less body, the letters in copper have rounder and freer turns and more wavy lines.

From the signatures on the Kâvi and Umetâ plates of Jayabhaṭa and Dadda, Dr. Bühler has shown[1] that as early as the first half of the fifth century, a form of old Devanâgari was probably in use "for the purposes of everyday life." Hence it would appear that for royal grants and inscriptions a more antique form of alphabet long continued in use, side by side with old Devanâgarî, just as 'Gothic' or 'ecclesiastical' type has continued to be used to some extent among Western nations. As an index of age it must therefore be received with great caution.

How these old alphabets were preserved we do not know; whether, as is most probable, by court scribes (*diviras*) writing out the grants in the traditional character for the mason (*siletâ*) or engraver (*kansâr*) to copy letter by letter; or whether professional engravers kept specimen copies of the old alphabets, which they had learned to employ, often with skill and freedom, in engrossing on copper. The fact, however, that forged grants are either in alphabets bearing only clumsy resemblances to those of the period to which they profess to belong, or else are in letters of a much later type, would seem to indicate that ability to use the conventional alphabets was confined to a few experts, probably court servants. It is evident, however, that the conservatism aimed at was imperfect, and that in spite of it a slow but distinct departure from the old forms took place, which may be useful in determining, at least generally, the comparative age of different inscriptions.

Dr. Bühler in his remarks on the Umetâ plates[2] has pointed out that the curious mistake of ड (apparently *nd*) for ढ *vd* is not really a substitution of the letter *na* for *va*, but of the current or literary form of *va* for its earlier or inscriptional representation. And from this he inferred that the *kansâr* had before him the current form, and in this case substituted it for the antique one; but it is quite probable that the *kârkun* who drew out the fair copy for the *kansâr's* use made the mistake. He now suggests:—1. That the inscriptions being engraved by *kansârs* and *siletâs*, who, as a rule, are illiterate men only able to copy '*namunds*,' it is highly probable that the grants were written out in the courts by the *kârkuns* in the old alphabets and copied exactly as they stood. 2. The law-books are very particular in recommending that the *kârkuns* employed in courts should know all kinds of writing (*lipi*), and there was a regular writer caste, the old *diviras* or *Kâyasthas*. 3. He refers to the Lunâvâḍâ grant of Śîlâditya V.[3] in proof that the *kansâr* copied from a manuscript written in the old character; for there we have in one line (plate ii., line 4) *ranukiraṇa*, and in the line below *na ja pa*, where we ought to have had—*ratnakiraṇa*, and in line 5, just below, *na* bhu*ja pa*, but the *bhu* is wanting; and he thinks the mistake can have arisen only from the *tna* of line 4 in the copy having run into the *bhu* of the line below, and the *kansâr*, not knowing that two distinct signs were

---

[1] *Ind. Ant.*, vol. v, p. 113.
[2] *Ind. Ant.*, vol. vii, p. 62.
[3] *Ind. Ant.*, vol. vi, p. 20, and second plate, lines 4 and 5.

intended, combined them into one. If so, the letters in different lines on the plates must be in precisely the same relative positions as in the copy: in fact, the plates must be a facsimile of the original copy.[1]

To what extent local varieties of pattern alphabets prevailed may yet be investigated. The two Gupta alphabets are of the same reign, yet they differ most markedly. The Girnâr inscription in the letters *ṇa, la, ha, sa*, as in the others, follows the forms in the early Valabhî plates and other inscriptions of Western India, whilst the northern alphabet adopts other forms; in the case of *pha* only is there any distinct copying of what may be regarded as the northern form at that age. We might infer from this that the engraver, being a Gujarâtî, used his own archaic alphabet, in which he either had the peculiar form of *pha* used also in the north, or, being a letter of but rare occurrence, he borrowed it from some northerner. On the other hand, a comparison of the Râthoḍ or Râshṭrakûṭa plates from Gujarât and the Dekhan seems to indicate a copying, if not from some model alphabet, at least of the later plates from the earlier, so that the alphabet of A.D. 812 (No. 32) bears a strong resemblance to the Umetâ plates of Dadda Praśântaraga,[2] another of Ś. 417,[3] and other very early plates of the same family. But we have also old Nâgarî alphabets in grants of Dantidurga, Ś. 675, and Govinda Prabhûtavarsha, Ś. 730.

The letter *ḷa* () occurs in the Kshatrapa, Ândhra, and Chalukya inscriptions in a form which, from its resemblance to some of the early forms of *ḍa* (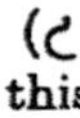), has been sometimes misread for that letter. It is curious to note in connection with this, that in the *Veda* the letter *ḷa* has frequently been used for *ḍa*, and seems to have been pronounced nearly in the same way.[4] The letter *śa* occurs first in the Nahapâṇa inscriptions at Nâsik and then in the Rudradâman one at Girnâr in allied forms, which seem to have afterwards disappeared. In the second of these the form is nearly the same as in the Kâlsi inscription of Aśoka and closely allied to that on the Kanishka coins, which form M. Senart holds to be used in the Kâlsi inscription 'only as a form parallel and simply equivalent to *sa*,' but it seems to have been derived from the Baktrian-Pâli , which was distinctly a cerebral.[5] The older form at Nâsik is a closely allied one, viz., .

The letter *kha* occurs in many of the older inscriptions as  or some slightly modified form of it, but in the Kâlsi inscription of Aśoka it has a loop below just as in the Gupta, Valabhî, and Chalukya inscriptions. It has no loop in the Nahapâṇa inscription at Nâsik, but it has in the one at Junnar; and in that at Kârle, as already noted, it is formed with two equal legs like the contemporary form of *ga*.[6] In one of the Ândhra inscriptions at Nâsik it is formed .

---

[1] This may seem difficult to conceive, unless we suppose that the Kârkun had scratched the letters on the plates for the Kansâr to cut. Dr. Bühler, however, supposes that the plates were made of the size of the material on which the grants were written, and the Kansârs got over the difficulty with the holes by making the letters of the lines in which they occurred smaller. I do not think the facts we as yet possess are sufficient to justify the hypothesis that the lines were always made to agree precisely with the copy supplied. But from the larger size generally of the Gujarat and northern plates, and the smaller size of the southern ones, it seems probable the plates were made to contain on each side a page of the copy. And, as Dr. Bühler suggests, birch bark was apparently used in Gujarât and the north, and palm leaves in the south, hence the northern plates are the size of ordinary birch bark leaves, and the southern ones of *tâlapattras* (see Burnell, *S. Ind. Pal.*, second ed. pp. 84, 85).

[2] *Ind. Ant.*, vol. vii, p. 61 f.

[3] Not yet published.

[4] See Max Müller's *Ṛig-Veda Sanhita*, vol. i, p. 44.

[5] *Jour. Asiatique*, vii, ser. tom. xv, pp. 319 ff.; but see Thomas's remarks in Prinsep's *Essays*, vol. ii, p. 159.

[6] Prinsep remarks generally that "the *kh* seems formed from the *g* rather than the *k*."—*J. A. S. B.*, vol. vi, p. 475; *Essays*, vol. ii, p. 9.

The vowel *i* is represented in most of the earlier inscriptions by three dots, but in one of those of Puḷumâvi at Kârle it is indicated by the sign ;[1] in the Girnâr Gupta inscription it is written as in the adjoining Aśoka and Kshatrapa inscription by the three dots, but in the Kahauṅ Gupta inscription it appears as . A single or double curve over two dots in a horizontal line continued long in use, but yielded to the symbol in the early Devanâgarî inscriptions.

The Mauryan forms of *ga, cha, chha, ta, pa, bha, ma, ra,* and *va* and *ha* undergo a distinct change after the date of the Nânâghâṭ and Ajaṇṭâ Cave X. inscriptions. The earlier alphabets have many letters of what may be called 'square' forms, which somewhat later assumed rounded ones; but, on the other hand, letters in the Mauryan alphabet like *pa, pha, ma, la, va, ha,* which had curved forms, took angular or 'square' ones, while *gha* and *ḍa* were probably written even from Aśoka's time indifferently in a round and square form. In the case of the *ḍa* we have the evidence of the round *ḍha*, which must have been formed from a letter like .

The inscriptions on the Kârle Chaitya and Nâsik caves stand between and connect the earlier ones with the next ten alphabets, before which, or about the fourth century, a marked change had passed over both the alphabet and the language of inscriptions. Pâli ceases to be used[2] except in small private donative labels, and Sanskrit is used by Buddhists equally with Brahmans. The letters lose their square forms and assume shapes more suitable for cursive writing; *i* is now written as a double curve over two dots rather than by three dots only; another form of *e* besides the triangle is introduced; *ṇa* and *na* assume curved forms that can be made with a single movement of the pen; *śa* and *sha* appear in every inscription; and *la* appears in some inscriptions under the new form . Most of the letters have now distinct 'heads' or serifs.

The Pâli inscriptions have never hitherto been interpreted in any systematic and scientific way. Various attempts have been made by Prinsep, Stevenson, Bhâu Dâjî and others to decipher and translate such of them as they could obtain copies of; but the copies were in many instances incorrect, and Pâli scholarship was, till very lately, still in its infancy. Thanks to the labours of Childers, Fausböll, Trenckner, Kuhn, Pischel, Senart, Bühler, Oldenberg, and others, we are now no longer left to conjecture as to the correct translation of documents in this language. The only real difficulty now in the way of reading the inscriptions on the Caves is the dilapidated state in which many of them are found. The action of the vicissitudes of the climate in the course of a thousand or even two thousand years, has doubtless utterly destroyed many—leaving not a trace behind, and many others have been reduced to mere fragments. The condition of such as are left renders them exceedingly difficult to copy with perfect accuracy. Indeed all "eye-copies" hitherto made, even by the most painstaking copyists, contain errors, and it is only by purely mechanical processes that errors can be most successfully avoided.

---

[1] Curiously enough, the Vaṭṭeḷuttu *i* in the Jewish and Syrian Christian grants is represented by two slight variations of the same form. See Burnell, *S. Ind. Palæog.*, pl. xvii., and *Ind. Ant.*, vol. i, p. 229 and plate.

[2] As noticed *ante* p. 19, the inscriptions of the Hînayâna sect were in Pâli; but when the Mahâyâna sect rose to influence, its followers adopted Sanskrit for their literary language. Thus the literature of the southern Buddhists, of Ceylon, Burma, &c., belonging to the first sect, is in Pâli, while that of the Nepâlese, who follow the Mahâyâna, is in Sanskrit, and the Bauddha scriptures of China and Tibet are translations from the Sanskrit. Dr. Bühler points out that there are one or two compounds in a Nâsik inscription (No. 14) which can hardly be explained except on the supposition that it was first written in Sanskrit and then translated into Pâli; and this was perhaps generally done in compliment to the followers of the Hînayâna school.

CHAPTER XIV.

INSCRIPTIONS.

THE inscriptions in the Bauddha rock-temples early attracted the attention of Mr. J. Prinsep, and he made tentative versions of such as he was able to obtain copies of. Dr. J. Bird, of Bombay, was commissioned by Sir C. Malcolm to visit and describe the various groups, and thus had ample opportunities of copying them, while Mr. Orlebar, Dr. J. Wilson, and others also helped him in this work, and a large number of inscriptions were lithographed in his "Historical Researches" (pl. xxxvi. to liii.) But Bird's ignorance of the language and his wild theories about the esoteric doctrines of the Buddhists rendered his work valueless. Lieutenant Brett's copies of many of the inscriptions were submitted to Dr. Stevenson, and a considerable advance was made by him in their translation.[1] The Messrs. West, during many years in Western India, collected very careful eye-copies of all the cave inscriptions then known, of which those from Kaṇheri and Nâsik[2] were published. The latter of these were made the basis of Professor Râmkṛishṇa G. Bhandarkar's careful and scholarly Sanskṛit and English annotated translations of the Nâsik inscriptions.[3] Between 1862 and his death in 1874 Dr. Bhau Dâji collected anew many inscriptions, and translated a few of them, especially those of Ajaṇṭâ.[4]

The first systematic attempt to collect and render the bulk of them into English was made by Pandit Bhagwânlâl Indrâji and myself in 1879-80,[5] and the following readings and versions are mainly reproduced from that collection, but revised, with those from the Nâsik cave temples and others added, by the kind assistance of Dr. G. Bühler, C.I.E.

I. BHAJA INSCRIPTIONS.

1. The oldest inscription at Bhâjâ is in the vihâra, No. XVII. (pl. xliv, 1). It reads—

Nâdasavasa Nâyasa
Bhogavatasa gâbho dânaṁ [||]

—"By Nâdasava a Nâya of Bhogavati (?), the gift of a cell."

The letters of this inscription are of so early a form that we can hardly err in referring them to a period considerably anterior to the Christian era.

On the sixth, seventh, eighth and ninth dâgobas, if not on others also, there have been short inscriptions. 2. That on the sixth begins, like several inscriptions at Junnar and elsewhere, with the sign *svastika*, and reads—

Theranaṁ bhayanta-Saṁghadinânam [||]

—"Of the Thera (or Sthavira), the reverend Saṁghadina."

3. The next has also a single line, introduced by a rude figure of the *triśûla*, and, though much weatherworn, appears to read—

Therânâṁ bhayaṁta-Aṁpikiṇakânaṁ thûpo [||]

—"The stûpa of the Sthavira the reverend Aṁpikiṇaka (*or* Ahikiṇaka)."

---

[1] *Jour. Bom. Br. R. As. Soc.*, vol. v, pp. 1 ff., 35 ff., and 151 ff.
[2] *J. B. B. R. A. S.*, vol. vi, pp. 1 ff., and vol. vii, pp. 37 ff.
[3] *Trans. Orient. Cong.*, 1874, pp. 306 ff.
[4] *J. B. B. R. A. S.*, vol. vii, pp. 53 ff.
[5] *Inscriptions from the Cave Temples of Western India* (Bombay, 1881).

4. On the eighth, also much weatherworn, we seem to have—

Therânaṁ bhaṅaṁta Dhamagirinâṁ thûpa [||]

—"The stûpa of the Sthavira the reverend[1] Dhamagiri."

These three inscriptions are on the bases of the dâgobas, the fourth is on the dome of the ninth one, and is still more obliterated, but, like the rest, it records its being the *thûbho* of some one.

5. On the capital of one of the three in the back row, under the rock, an inscription has been commenced, but only the words *Therânaṁ bhayaṁta* have been carved, filling the front of one of the thin members of the abacus,—the name of the Thero, which should have been in the next member below, has not been added.

6. In Cave VI., over the door of one of the cells in the back, is a short inscription not very clearly made out, but apparently reading—

Bâdhayâ hâlikajayâyâ dânaṁ [||]

—"The gift of Bâdhâ the ploughman's wife."

7. One more inscription, but in much later characters, stands over two rock-cisterns between Caves XIV. and XVII., and reads—

Mahârathisa Kosikîputasa
Viṇhudatasa deyadhama podhi [||]

—"The meritorious gift (*or* benefaction) of a cistern by Viṇhudata the Mahârathi, son of the Kosikî (*or* Kauśika mother)."

II. Kondane Inscription.

The only inscription at Kondâṇe is the short one on the right side of the front of the Chaitya beside the sculptured head (pl. xliv).[2] It is in the Maurya style of letters, and reads—

Kaṇhasa aṁtevâsinâ Bala(lu?)kena kataṁ [||][3]

—"Made by Balaka, the pupil of Kaṇha (or Kṛishṇa)."

III. Pitalkhora Inscriptions.

1. On one of the pillars in the Chaitya is the following short inscription, in pure Maurya characters, in three lines (pl. xliv, No. 1)—

Patiṭhâṇâ Mitadêvasa
Gâdhikasakulasa
[*thab*]o dâna[ṁ]

—"A pillar, the gift of Mitradeva of the Gâdhi family, from Pratishṭhâna" (Paiṭhâṇ)

2. The other reads—

Patiṭhânâ Saghakasa pu-
tâna ṭhabo dânaṁ [||]

—"A pillar, the gift of the sons of Saṁghaka, from Patithâna."[4]

---

[1] Here the usual title of respect, *bhadamta*, spelt *bhayamta* in the preceding and following, is presented under the form of *bhaṅaṁta*. The final syllable of the line may have been °*po*.

[2] See p. 9, woodcut No. 9.

[3] There are apparently two anusvâras in the inscription, which are here disregarded; we might read it *Kaṁṇhasa aṁtevâsinâ Baṁlukena kataṁ*, but as the anusvâras after the fourth and last aksharas are after and not above the letters, it is probable that the additional two which are *above* are only holes in the stone.

[4] These two inscriptions were translated by Dr. G. Bühler, C.I.E.;—*Cave-Temple Inscriptions*, p. 39.

The Patiṭhâṇa (Sans. Pratishṭhâna) of these inscriptions is doubtless Paiṭhâṇ on the Godâvarî, about sixty-five miles to the southwards. Had the façade been left, we might possibly have there discovered the king's name.

In the adjoining vihâra the first and second inscriptions read only—

(3) . . . . trasa Magilasa dânaṁ [‖]
(4) . . Râjave . . . . . sa . . .

5. A third, however, reads—

Râjavejasa Vachhîputasa Magilasa dâ[*nam*]

—"Gift of the royal physician Magila (or Mṛigila), the son of the Vâchhî (*or* mother of the Vatsa family)."

A fourth and fifth read respectively—

(6) Râjavejasa Vachhîputasa [*Ma*]gilasa dahutu Datâya dâna[ṁ] [‖]
And, (7) Râjavejasa Vacchî[*putasa Ma*]gilasa putasa Datakasa dâna[ṁ] [‖]

"Gift of Dattâ, daughter of the royal physician Magila, the son of the Vâchhî (or Vâtsî mother);" and "Gift of Dattaka, son of the royal physician Magîla, the son of the Vâtsî (mother)." [1]

IV. Kuda Inscriptions (Plates xlv, xlvi).

No. 1 (pl. xlv). At the left side of the door of the cave a large piece of the wall is broken away, carrying with it two or three letters and parts of others. It reads—

Mahâbhojîya Sadageriya Vijayâya putasa Mahâbhojasa Maṁdavasa Khaṁdapâlitasa lekhakasa
Sulasadataputasa Utaradatâputasa cha Sivabhûtisa saha bhayâya Naṁdâya deyadhammaṁ [*leṇaṁ* ‖]

—"This cave is the meritorious gift of Sivabhûti, the son of Sulasadata and Utaradatâ, and writer to Mahâbhoja Mandava Khandapâlita, son of the Mahâbhojî Sadagerî Vijayâ—together with his (Sivabhûti's) wife Naṁdâ." [2]

No. 2. From what remains of this inscription, the first line ending in *-bhûtisa* suggests that it may have been the work of the same Sivabhûti as is mentioned in Cave I.; the other line ends in *lenaṁ*, "a dwelling or cave."

No. 3. The inscription in Cave V. is cut on a rough surface, and so weatherworn as to be undecipherable. In the second line seem to be the words—

poḍhio be 2 deyadhamaṁ.

—". . . . . . . the meritorious gift of two (2) cisterns."

Inscription No. 4 reads—

Sidhaṁ Therâ(*ṇam Bhadamta*) S[iva]da-
taṇa a(*tevâsino*) pava(*ḍa*)ta-
sa go â (*ḍa*)ma leṇaṁ
sâtimita
yâ ya

All we can learn from this is that one of the donors was an ascetic and disciple of the Thera Sivadata; the other was Sâtimitâ, a female.

---

[1] The vihâra inscriptions were translated by Paṇḍit Bhagwânlâl Indrâji; see *Cave-Temple Inscriptions*, p. 40.

[2] See *Cave-Temple Inscriptions*, p. 4; and Prof. H. Jacobi, *Ind. Ant.*, vol. vii, p. 253; Stevenson's No. 5 *Jour. Bom. B. R. A. Soc.*, vol. v, p. 171.

The surface on which is inscription No. 5 [1] in Cave V. is decaying, but only two or three letters are much injured. It reads—

Siddhaṁ Therâṇaṁ bhadata Pâ[Sâ]timitâna Bhadaṁta
Âgimita[tâ](na) cha bhâgiṇeyiya pâva-
yitikâya Nâganikâya duhutaya pâva-
yitikâya Padumaṁnikâya deyadhaṁmaṁ
leṇaṁ poḍhî cha sahâ atevâsiniya Bodhiya
saha cha ativâsiniya Asâlhamitâya [‖]

—"Hail! A cave and cistern, the meritorious gift of the female ascetic (*or* nun) Padumanikâ, daughter of Nâganikâ the ascetic, the sister's daughter of the Thera Bhadanta Sâtimita and Bhadanta Âgimita, and of her female disciples Bodhî and Asâlhamitâ.

Inscription No. 6 [2] reads—

Mahâbhojiya Sâḍageriya Vijayâya
Mahâbhojasa Maṁdavasa Khaṁdapâlitasa upajîvinaṁ
Sulasadatasa Utaradatâya cha putânaṁ bhâtûnaṁ lekha-
kâ Sivabhûtimhâ kaneṭhasa Sivamasa deyadhaṁmaṁ lenaṁ
saha bhayâya Vijayâya putânaṁ cha sa Sulasadatasa Siva-
pâlitasa Sivadatasa Sapilása cha selarupakamaṁ duhutûnaṁ
sa Sapâya Sivapâlitâya Sivádatâya Sulaśadatâya cha thaṁbhâ

—"The meritorious gift of a *Leṇa* by Sivama, the youngest, after the writer Sivabhûti, among the brothers, sons of Sulasadata and Utaradatâ, and servants of the Mahâbhoja Maṅdava Khaṅdapâlita, the son of Mahâbhojî Sâḍagerî Vijayâ; and the rock sculpture (or statues—*selarûpakamaṁ*) by his (*Sivama's*) wife Vijayâ, and sons Sulasadata, Sivapâlita, Sivadata, and Sapila; and the pillars by his daughters (*-in-law*) Sapâ, Sivapalitâ, Sivadatâ. and Sulasadatâ."

Inscription No. 7 [3] is in four lines and four letters, faintly cut, but legible. This and the next three are in Sanskrit and of much later date than the others—

Deyadharmoyaṁ Śâkyopâ-
sika[kâ] Vyâghra[ghri]kâyâ yad atra
puṇya[ṁ] tadbhavatu mâtâpitṛipû-
rvvaṅgamaṁ kṛitvâ sarvvasatvânâ[ṁ] anuttari[ra]jñâ-
nâvâpa[pta]ya[ye ‖]

—"This is the meritorious gift of the female Śâkya worshipper (*upâsikâ*) Vyâghrakâ: may the benefit of it be for the attainment of supreme knowledge, first by her father and mother, and next (*after them*) by the whole sentient world."

No. 8—

Deyadharmmoyaṁ Sâkyabhikshusa . .
sya yad atra punyaṁ tad bhavatu mâtâ[*pitṛipûrva*]
ṅgamaṁ kri[kṛi]tvâ sarvvasatvânâ[*ṁ anuttarajñânâvâptaye*]

—"This is the meritorious gift of the Śâkya mendicant . . . . may the merit of it be for the attainment of supreme knowledge, first by his father and mother, and then by the whole sentient world."

---

[1] *Ind. Ant.*, vol. vii, p. 254; *Cave-Temple Inscriptions*, No. 5, p. 6; Stevenson's No. 8, *J. B. B. R. A. S.*, vol. v, p. 173.

[2] *Ind. Ant.*, vol. vii, pp. 254, 255; *Cave-Temple Inscriptions*, No. 9, p. 9; Stevenson's No. 9, *J. B. B. R. A. S.*, vol. v, pp. 173, 174.

[3] *Cave-Temple Inscriptions*, No. 7, p. 8.

[4] Tigress; *Śâkyupâsika* is properly a devout Buddhist laic.

No. 9—

Deyadharmmoyam Sâkyabhikshu[ksho]-
rbuddhasigha[simha]sya mâtâpitṛi-
purvvaṅgamam kṛitvâ bhaṭâka[rka]cham[cha] ya
datra puṇyam tad bhavatu sarvvasatvâ-
nâm anuttarajñânâvâptaye [||]

—"This meritorious gift of the Śâkya mendicant Buddhasimha—may its merit be for the attainment of supreme knowledge by his father, mother, and Bhaṭârka, and then by the whole sentient world."

No. 10, also in Sanskrit, reads—

(1) Deyadharmmoyam Sâkyabhikshoḥ
Samghadevasya atra cha
Chemdinakhetra[m] badhvâ dî-
pamûlya Buddhasya
dattam [||]

(2) yo lopaye[t]
pa[m]chamahâpâ
takaba[sam]yukto bhave[t] ||

—"This (*image*) is the meritorious gift of the Śâkya-bhikshu Saṅghadeva, and the Chenḍina field is given for the expense of lights to Buddha. Whoever cuts off (*this*) is guilty of the five great sins."[1]

No. 11[2]—

Mâmakavejiyasa vejasa Isirakhitupâsaka-
sa putasa vejasa Somadevasa deyadhammam leṇam
putasa cha sa Nâgasa Isirakhitasa Sivaghosasa cha
duhutuya cha Isipâlitâya Pusâya Dhammâya Sapâya cha [||]

—"The meritorious gift of a cave by the physician Somadeva, the son of the Mâmakavejiya[3] physician and worshipper, Isirakhita (Ṛishirakshita), and his (*Somadeva's*) sons Nâga, Isirakhita, and Sivaghosa, and daughters Isipâlitâ, Pusâ, Dhammâ, and Sapâ."

No. 12—

Mamdavânam parusa[si ?]vama-
sa pa[pu]tasa Kumârasa
Madavasa deyadhama [||]

—"The meritorious gift of the Maṅdava Kumâra, son of Sivama, the chief of the Maṁdavas (?)."

No. 13[5]—

Ayitilu upâsakasa Bammhanasa bhayâya Bhayilâya Bammaniya chetiyagharo deyadhammam [||]

—"The benefaction of a Chêtiyaghara by Bhayilâ, a Brâhmaṇî, wife of Ayitilu, a Brahman lay worshipper."

No. 14.[6] Some two or three of the letters are doubtful, but it may be read—

Mâlâkâmsa Vadhukasa putasa ma(â)lâkârasa Sivapiri(? pâli)tasa deyadhamma leṇam [||]

—"The benefaction of a cave by Sivapirita (? Śivapâlita), a gardener, son of the gardener Vadhuka."

No. 15 is so damaged that it yields only the words *Mahâbhoja bâ*[likâya] in the first line, and *Mamdaviya I-* in the second.

---

[1] Here we get the style of the copper-plate grants of the same age.

[2] *Cave-Temple Inscriptions*, No. 13, p. 12; *Ind. Ant.*, vol. vii, p. 255; Stevenson's No. 6, *u. s.*, p. 172.

[3] This word is left untranslated; the Pandit suggests that it may mean a member of some family or class of physicians.

[4] In Sanskrit these names are Ṛishipâlitâ, Pushyâ, Dharmâ, and Sarpâ.

[5] *Cave-Temple Inscriptions*, No. 15, p. 14; Stevenson's No. 1, *u. s.*, p. 170.

[6] *Cave-Temple Inscriptions*, No. 16, p. 14; Stevenson's No. 2, *u. s.*, p. 170.

No. 16 has at the commencement a rough conventional representation of a lion. It is mutilated, but may be read—

Râjamachasa Hâlasa [*duhu*]-
tâya Goyaṁmâyâ [*leṇaṁ*]

—"The (*cave*) of Goyaṁmâ (Gautamâ), the daughter of Hâla the royal minister."

No. 17 [1]—

Mahâbhoyasa Sâḍakarasa Sudaṁsaṇasa duhutuya Vijayanikâya deyadhaṁmaṁ lena [‖]

—"The meritorious gift of a cave by Vijayanikâ,[2] daughter of the Mahâbhoya Sâḍakara Sudaṁsaṇa."

No. 18 [3]—

Karahâkaḍakasa lohavâṇiyiyasa mahikasa
deyadhaṁmaṁ leṇaṁ [‖]

—"The meritorious gift of a cave by Mahika of Karahâkaḍa,[4] an ironmonger."

No. 19, partly illegible—

Gahapatino Vasulasa
seṭhino sanâ[*napoḍhi*]

—"Of the householder Vasula, a merchant—a bathing (tank)."

Another short inscription in two lines and a few letters, in an exposed recess, is so weatherworn that it has not been read.

No. 20 [5] (pl. xlvi)—

Mahâbhoje Maṁdave Kochhipute Velidate Ahilasa putasa Aanagachhakasa Râmadatasa deya-
dhama chetiyagharo uyarako cha bhayâva Velîdatâva deyadhaṁmaṁ uyarako [‖]

—"The meritorious gift of a Chêtiyaghara and cell by Râmadata the Adhagachhaka,[6] the son of Ahila,[7] when Velidata, son of the Kochhî (*or* Kautsî mother), was Mahâbhoja Mandava; and by his wife, Velîdatâ. the meritorious gift of a cell."

No. 21. Only the last line is now distinct, and some parts of letters in the preceding.

sa . sâ . . . . [*n*]hu . . .
savaṁ cha aṁtivâsiniya Bodhiya [‖]

The name Veṇhuyâ (Vishṇukâ) was probably[8] in the first line. The second reads—"and all, of the female disciple Bodhî."

No. 22 [9]—

Sidham therâṇa bhayata
Vijayâṇa âtivâsiṇiya
pavaïtikaya sapilâya
deyadhaṁmaṁ leṇaṁ saha sâ-
lohitâhi Veṇhuyâhi sa[ha] cha
âtivâsiṇiya Bodhiya

—"Hail! The meritorious gift of a dwelling-cave by the nun Sapilâ, the female disciple of the Thera the reverend Vijaya, with her venerable kinswoman Veṇhuyâ, and her disciple Bodhî."

---

1 *Cave-Temple Inscriptions*, No. 19, p. 15; Stevenson's No. 3, *u. s.*, p. 170.

2 Apparently the same as Vijayâ in Nos. 1 and 5.

3 *Cave-Temple Inscriptions*, No. 20; Stevenson's No. 4, *u. s.*, p. 171.

4 Karahâkaḍa or Karahâkaṭa is Karâḍh in the Sâtârâ district. Lat. 17° 15′ N., long. 74° 12′ E.

5 See *Ind. Ant.*, vol. vii, p. 256.

6 *Adhagachhaka*, Sans. *Ardhagachhaka*, is the name of a religious sect or division.

7 "Ahila" is perhaps a diminutive from the Sanskrit *ahi*, "snake," and equivalent to "Sapila" (Sarpila) in No. 6.

8 See next inscription.

9 *Cave-Temple Inscriptions*, No. 25, p. 18; Jacobi, *Ind. Ant.*, vol. vii, p. 256.

No. 23.[1] This is weatherworn and broken.

Mâlâkârasa Mugudâ[*sasa*] de-
yadhamma poḍhi [||]

—"The meritorious gift of a cistern by the gardener Mugudâ[sa]."

No. 24. The early portion of this is much obliterated.

Koṭa . . . . svâmiputasa gaha[pu]tiṇo sathavâhasa Nâgasa leṇaṁ deyadhamma [||]

—"The meritorious gift of a cave by Nâga, the householder and trader . . . . . son of . . . svâmi . . ."

No. 25—

Seṭhiṇo Vasulaṇaka-
sa deyadhammaṁ leṇa [||]

—"The meritorious gift of a cave by the merchant Vasulaṇaka."

No. 26 records the gift of a cistern by the same individual.

Sethiṇo Vasulaṇakasa
deyadhamma poḍhi [||]

No. 27—

Sathavâhasa Vehamitasa bitiyikaya Sivadatâya Pu-
saṇakamâtuya deyadhamaṁ leṇaṁ [||]

—"The meritorious gift of a cave by Sivadatâ, the mother of Pusaṇaka, and wife of the trader Vehamita (*or* Vedamitra)."

No. 28 is much weatherworn and indistinct.

Saṭhavâhasa Acha[la]
dâsasa
Asâḷamitasa [le]ṇa[ṁ] deyadhamma saha
[ta]sa patho (?) deya (?)

—"The meritorious gift of a cave from Asâḷamita, son of the trader Achaladâsa, and a path (?)"

V. Inscriptions at Mahad, Kol, and Karadh (Pl. XLVI).

No. 1, at Mahâd—

[1.] Sidhaṁ Kumârasa Kâṇabhoäsa Vheṇupâlitasa
[2.] [e]sa leṇa chetiëghara ovarakâ cha aṭha 8 vi[ti]kamaṁ niyû-
[3.] taṁ le[ṇa]sa cha ubhato pasesu poḍhiyo be 2 leṇasa
[4.] alugaṇake patho cha dato etasa cha kumârasa deya-
[5.] dhamaṁ [||]

—"Success! Prince Kâṇabhoä Vheṇupâlita's Leṇa, Chetiyaghara and eight (8) cells; this much is allotted; and two (2) cisterns, on each side of the leṇa, also a path connected with the leṇa, are presented. It is a meritorious gift of that prince."

No. 2, at Mahâd—

[1.] Sidham gahapatisa seṭhisa Saṁgharakhita saputasa Vi . . . .
[2.] Vâdasiriya deyadhammaṁ leṇaṁ chetiakoḍhi pâ . . . . . .
[3.] chhetâni yâni leṇasa peṭhâ gorâva . . naṁ . . . . . .
[4.] ti chhetehi kare tato chetiasa gadha . . . .
[5.] aṭha 8 bhatakaṁmâṇikâ aṭha 8 koḍhipura . . . .
[6.] kâraṇakâraṇe cha leṇasa savenâ ka . . . .

---

[1] *Cave-Temple Inscriptions*, No 26, p. 18; *Ind. Ant.*, vol. vii, pp. 256, 257.

This fragment records the dedication of a cave and of a *Chetiyakodhi*, together with an endowment of land for the worship of Buddha. The donor's name may be Vâdasiri (l. 2), but seems to belong to a female. In the first line are the names of the Gṛihapati and Seṭh Saṁgharakshita and the first syllable of his son's name, Vi- . . . . Vâdasiri was probably his wife.

No. 3, at Kol—

[1.] Gahapatiputasa seṭhisa
[2.] Saṁgharakhitasa deyadhamaṁ lena[ṁ ‖]

—"A cave—the religious gift of Seṭh Saṅgharakhita, son of Gahapati."

No. 4, at Kol—

[1.] . . . upâsakasa duhutuya Dhamasiriya Sivadatasa bitiyakâya
[2.] leṇa deyadhama [‖]

—"A cave, the meritorious gift of Dhamasiri (Dharmaśrî), daughter of the lay worshipper . . . [1] (*and*) wife of Sivadata (Śivadatta)."

No. 5, at Kol—

Âghâakasâ-gâmikiyasa Sivadatasa leṇa deyadhama [‖]

—"A cave, the meritorious gift of Sivadata, an inhabitant of the village of Âghâakasâ (Âghâtakarsha ?)."

No. 6, at Karâḍh, is much effaced, and has been in rudely-cut letters, like those of Kol.

G[o]p[â]laputasa Saṁgha-
m[i]tarasa leṇa deyadhama [‖]

—"The meritorious gift of a cave by Saṅghamitra, the son of Gopâla (?)."

VI. Bedsa Inscriptions (Pl. xlvii).

No. 1. The first here reads—

Nâsikato Ânadasa seṭhisa putasa Pusaṇakasa dânaṁ [‖]

—"The gift of Pushyaṇaka, son of Śeṭh Ânanda, from Nâsik." [2]

No. 2. The second is on the rock behind a dâgoba, a short distance from the Chaitya, much weatherworn, [3] and the commencement of both lines lost [4] —

. . . ya Gobhûtinaṁ âraṇakâna peḍapâtikânaṁ Mârakuḍavâsinâ thupo
. . . . [*aṁte*]vâsinâ bhatâsâḷa[]ha]mitena kârita [‖]

—"The stûpa of . . . Gobhûti, a hermit [5] living in the forest [*and*] mendicant who dwelt on Mârakuḍa [6] [Mârakûṭa]: caused to be made by his pupil, the devoted Asâḷamita [Ashâḍhamitra]."

---

[1] I am unable to make out the name satisfactorily; it looks like Kharud or Kharad.

[2] See Dr. Bird's mislection and absurd version in *J. B. B. R. A. S.*, vol. i, p. 440.

[3] See *Cave-Temple Inscriptions*, p. 26; the version here given is Dr. G. Bühler's.

[4] The letters lost in the first line are probably [*âchari*]ya, "the teacher."

[5] The literary Pâli form is *âraññako* (Sans. *âraṇyaka*), an eremite.

[6] *Mârakuḍa*, Sans. *Mârakûṭa*, "the devil's peak," was probably the ancient name of the hill in which the Bedsâ caves are excavated.

No. 3[1] is cut on the rock over a cistern near the Chaitya cave—

Mahâbhoyabâlikâya ma[hâ]devi-
ya mahârathiniya Sâmadinikâya
[*de*]yadhama Âpadevaṇakasa bitiyikâya [||]

—"The meritorious gift of Sâmadinikâ the Mahâdêvî (princess), the Mahârathinî, daughter of the Mahâbhoya and wife of Âpadêvaṇaka."

VII. Earliest Karle Inscriptions.

No. 1 (pl. xlvii), in the great Chaitya Cave—

Vejayamtito seṭhiṇâ Bhutapâlenâ selagharaṁ pariniṭhapitaṁ Jabudipamhi utama [||]

—"Seṭh Bhûtapâla from Vejayantî has established a rock-mansion—the most excellent in Jambudvîpa (India).

No. 2, on the lion-pillar—

Mahârathisa Gotiputrasa Agimitraṇakasa sihathabho dânaṁ [||]

—"The gift of a lion-pillar by the Mahârathi Agnimitraṇaka, the son of Goti."

No. 3[2]—

Therânaṁ bhayaṁta-Indadevasa hathi cha puvâ do hathinaṁ cha uparimâ hethimâ cha veyikâ dânaṁ [||]

—"[*Three*] Elephants,[3] as well as, above and below, in front of the first two elephants a [*rail pattern*] moulding, the gift of the Thera, the venerable Indadeva [Indradeva]."

No. 4—

Dhenukâkaṭâ gaṁdhikasa Sihadatasa dânaṁ gharamuga [||]

—"The gift of a door by Sihadata, a perfumer,[4] from Dhenukâkaṭa."

No. 5—

Gahatasa Mahâdeva-
ṇakasa mâtu Bhâyilâyâ dânaṁ [||]

—"The gift of Bhâyilâ [Bhrâjilâ], the mother of Mahâdevaṇaka, a householder."

No. 6—

Dheṇukâkaṭeṇa va[ḍha]kinâ Ṣâmi[la]
ṇa Veṇuvâsaputeṇa gharasa
mughaṁ kataṁ dâre mu . . dhuka [||]

—"Sâmila [Śyâmila], son of Veṇuvâsa, a carpenter, a native of Dheṇukâkaṭa, made the doorway; on the door . ."

No. 7—

Dheṇukâkâṭâ Yavanasa Sihadhayâna thaṁbho dâna

—"The gift of a pillar by Sihadhaya, a Yavana from Dheṇukâkaṭa."

---

[1] See *Cave-Temple Inscriptions*, p. 27; conf. Bird, *J. Bom. B. R. As. Soc.*, vol. i, p. 441.

[2] *Cave-Temple Inscriptions*, p. 29.

[3] *Hathi* in this inscription must stand for *hathî*, and like the Sanskrit *hastinaḥ*, means "three elephants. *Veyika*, which, as well as *vedikâ* and *vetikâ* in other Buddhist inscriptions, stands for Sanskrit *vedikâ*, does not mean "altar, dais, &c.," but bands or string-courses carved with the rail pattern; conf. *Mahâvanso*, 228.

[4] *Gharamugha*, Sanskrit *grihamukha*, "a façade," implies also the architrave and sculpture round the door, with the arch over it. *Gandhika*, literally "a dealer in perfumes," applied also to a druggist.

No. 8 [1]—

Sopâraka bhayatâna Dhamutara[ri]-
yâna sa[mâ]nathasa therasa [A]-
tulasa [a]ṁtevâsisa bhâna-
kasa Nadipatisa Sâtimitasa
saha . . . tiya thabho dâna[ṁ] mu [‖]

—"A pillar, the gift of **Sâtimita** [Svâtimitra] from **Sopâraka**, the husband of **Nadi** [Nandî], a preacher [*and*] pupil of the Thera **Atula**, (?) the . . of the venerable **Dhamutariya** [Dharmottarîya] [2] school."

No. 9.

This inscription is, as stated above, the improved version of No. 8.

Sopâraka bhayaṁtânaṁ Dhamutariyâna bhâṇa-
kasa Sâtimitasa
sasariro thabho dânaṁ

—"A pillar containing a relic, [3] the gift of **Sâtimita** [Svâtimitra], a preacher of the venerable **Dhamutariyas** [Dharmottarîya school], from **Sopâraka**.

No. 10 (pl. xlvii)—

[1.] Dhenukâkaṭâ **[2.] Dhaṁmayavanasa**

—"Of Dhamma (Dharma), a Yavana from **Dhenukâkaṭa**."

No. 11 (pl. xlviii)—

[1.] Dhenukâkaṭa Usabhadataputasa Mitade-
[2.] vaṇakasa thabho dânaṁ [‖]

—"The gift of a pillar by **Mitadevaṇaka** [Mitradevaṇaka], son of Usabhadata [Ṛishabhadatta] from **Dhenukâkaṭa**."

No. 12—

Asâḍhamitâye bhikhuṇi[ye] . . .

—"of **Asâḍhamitâ**, a nun . . "

Nos. 13 and 14, identical—

Bhadasamasa bhikhusa deyadhama mithûna

—"Gift of a pair by the mendicant (or Bhikshu) Bhadasama (Bhadraśarman)."

No. 15—

. . . [sa]maṇâya mâtuya dânaṁ veyikâ [‖]

—". . . . the gift of a *vêdikâ* [rail-moulding] by the mother of . . . . Samaṇâ [a Śramaṇâ].

No. 16—

Koḍiya bhikhuṇiya Ghuṇikamâta veyikâ daṇa Nadikena ka[ta ‖]

—"The gift of a *vêdikâ* by the nun Koḍî, mother of Ghuṇika; made by Nadika [Nandika]."

---

[1] For Pandit Bhagwânlâl's reading and version see *Cave-Temple Inscriptions*, p. 31. The inscription is much obliterated, probably intentionally, to substitute the next for it (see No. 9), and the words *samânathasa* (l. 2) and *atulasa* (2, 3) are by no means certain. I am unable to explain the former, though I suspect that it denotes some spiritual office, held by the Thera in the Dharmottarîya school; possibly it may be a mistake for *samaṇanâthasa*, "the lord of the monks" or abbot. *Bhâṇaka* apparently corresponds to the Pâli *bhâṇaka*, "a preacher," and probably means that Svâtimitra recited and expounded the texts of the Dharmottariyas. The Jains have a similar title *vâchaka*, "a reader," sometimes applied to their Yatis. I am unable to make out the last word, beginning with *mu*, but the last letter is not *lasi*, as Pandit Bhagwanlâl reads it.

[2] See *Ind. Ant.*, vol. ix, pp. 300, 302; Vassilief, *Le Bouddisme*, p. 230.

[3] There is a hole or receptacle cut for the purpose of holding the relic mentioned in the inscription, in the centre of a lotus carved on the front of the pillar, just where the inscription ends.

No. 17 [1] (pl. xlviii)—

Sidha Pavaïtasa Budharakhitasa deyadhamam [||]

—"Hail! The meritorious gift of the ascetic Budharakhita."

No. 18—

[1.] . . . [*savachhare?*] 5 hemâtâṇa pakhe . . . [etâ]ya puvâya dha[bha]yata
[2.] . . . . hiṇâm atevâsiniṇa leṇa bhagine . . . sâvikâṇa sadigâ
[3.] . . . . ghasu kâle pavaïtâṇa saṁghâya bu . . . . . cha deyadhama
[4.] . . . . parivâreṇa upaya . . . . .
[5.] . . . . atevâsinihi Usabhâë . . . .

This is so mutilated as to render translation impossible: it seems to mean that in the 5th year, in the hemanta (winter) season of some raja's reign, possibly Puḷumâyi, a female disciple of some Bhadanta gave the cave; and a sister's daughter, a Srâvikâ or laic, gave a cistern to the saṁgha or assembly of ascetics. With the donor the names of some other relations have been associated, and Usabhâ (or Ṛishabhâ) a female disciple.

No. 19. Inscription at Śailarwadi—

[1.] Sidham Dheṇukâkaḍe vâthavasa
[2.] hálakiyasa kuḍubikasa Usabha-
[3.] ṇakasa kuḍubiṇiya Siäguta-
[4.] ṇikaya deyadhaṁma leṇa saha pute-
[5.] ṇa Naṁdagahapatinâ saho

—"Success! The meritorious gift of a cave, by Siagutaṇikâ, wife of Usabhaṇaka [Ṛishabhaṇaka], a Kunbi and ploughman, residing in Dheṇukâkaḍa, together with her son Nanda, a householder, with—[2]"

VIII. Junnar Inscriptions.

Several of the Junnar inscriptions are of very early date, and the whole of them perhaps range from 150 B.C. to 150 or 200 A.D., but none are of much later date.

1. The first inscription here is damaged from a part of the wall on which it is having been broken away, carrying off the first portions of each of the two lines. What is left is clear and distinct (pl. xlviii), and reads [3]—

. . . . thabhutinakasa
. . . . poḍhi châ deyadhama [||]

—"The benefaction of a cistern and (*probably* of a cave) by (*some person whose name ended in*) -thabhutinaka.[4]

Inscription No. 2 (p. 27 above) reads—

Mudhakiyasa Malasa Golikiyasa Ânadasa beṇa janâna deyadhama upaṭhâṇa [||]

—"The meritorious gift of a reception-room, by the two men, the Mudhakiya Mala and the Golakiya Ânada."

Here *Mudhakiya* (Sans. *Mûrdhakîya*) means "belonging to the Mûrdhaka caste" or (according to the *Śabdaratna—Pet. Dict.*, s. v.) to the Kshatriyas. *Mala* (Sans. *Malla*)

[1] For the other Kârle inscriptions see Nos. 6 17.

[2] The inscription stops short here.

[3] These inscriptions were translated in the *Cave-Temple Inscriptions*, pp. 41, 42; but have now been revised and re-edited by Dr. Bühler.

[4] The termination *-bhutinaka* corresponds with the Sanskrit *-bhûti*.—G. B.

"the wrestler," is a suitable name for a soldier. *Ânada, i.e., Ânanda*, belonged apparently to the Gauḷî or herdsman caste.

Inscription No. 3 [1] reads thus—

Apaguriyâna Savagirîyâsasa putasa Patîbadhakasa Giribhûtisa sakhuyârusa leṇa poḍhi cha [*de*]yadhamaṁ etasa cha leṇasa podhiya cha nakare cha bhikhuni upasayo[ya]sa Dhaṁmutariyâna akhaya nivi ka[kâ] [*hâ*]paṇâni . . . . . . eto lôṇasa chîvarikâ kâhâpako[ṇa] sodasa poḍhiya chîva . . . . [*e . mata*]cha bisahasatâ payogâ torivaḍhi sahasavaḍha dhaṇa . upayyasa . . . . . . yo upasayo nagare giribhûtisa bitiyikâyi[ya] Sivapâ[*li*]tanikâ[*ya* ||]

—"A cave and a cistern, the meritorious gift of Patîbadhaka Giribhûti Sakhuyâru,[2] son of Savagiriyâsa of the Apaguriyas; and for this cave and the cistern and the nunnery of the Dhaṁmutariyas in the town, a perpetual endowment of . . kârshâpaṇas (*has been given*) . . . . the nunnery of Sivapâlitanikâ, wife of Giribhûti, in the town."

Apaguriya seems to be a clan or the name of the inhabitants of some district. *Dhaṁmutariyas* (*i.e.*, Dharmottarîyas) are one of the ancient Bauddha schools[3] founded in the third century after the Nirvâṇa. The mutilated passages in lines 3 and 4 apparently contained provisions regarding the distribution of the interest accruing from the endowment.

Inscription No. 4 (pl. xlix), in the Chaitya cave in the scarp of Śivaneri, reads—

Vîrasenakasa gahapatipamughasa
dhaṁmanigamasa deyadhaṁmaṁ chetiyagharo
niyuto savalokahitasukhâya [||]

—"The meritorious gift of Vîraseṇaka, a chief householder and upright merchant—a Chaityagṛiha, dedicated for the welfare and happiness of the whole world."

No. 5 reads—

Yavanasa Irilasa Gatâna deyadhama be poḍhiyo [||]

—"The meritorious gift of two cisterns by the Yavana Irila of the Gatâ (*country*)."[4]

Inscription No. 6, so far as legible, reads—

Apaguriyâna Savagiriyâsaputasa Patibadhakasa [*Gi*]ribhûtisa [*saha*] bhayâya Sivapâlanikâya
deyadhama poḍhi leṇa cha etasa akhayanivi . . . .

—"A cave and a cistern, the meritorious gift of Patibadhaka Giribhûti, son of Savagiriyâsa of the Apaguriyas, with his wife Sivapâlanikâ: for this a permanent endowment . . . ."

---

[1] This was not translated in the *Cave-Temple Inscriptions*. It is No. 15 of Lieutenant Brett's series, and is divided into Nos. 8 and 9 of Dr. Stevenson's series, *J. B. B. R. A. S.*, vol. v, p. 163 f.; and it is No. 6 of those copied by Colonel Sykes, *J. R. A. S.*, vol. iv, p. 287 f.; but from so defective copies, there was no possibility of making translations of any value. It is here partly translated for the first time by Dr. Bühler.

[2] I am unable to explain the terms *patîbadhaka* and *sakhuyâru*.—G. B.

[3] One of the schools of the Sthavira division;—Vassilief, *Le Bouddisme*, pp. 230, 253; *Ind. Ant.*, vol. ix, pp. 300, 302.

[4] *Gatâna*, which is also found in No. 8, after the name of a Yavana, is a genitive plural. Its base, *Gata*, corresponds with the Sans. *Garta*, which is the name of a district (a part of Trigarta or Kângra) in the Panjâb; hence, Gatâna may be translated "of the Garta country" or "of the Gartas." It is intelligible how a Yavana might have his home in the Panjâb, where Greeks and Persians resided from early times. Conf. Lassen, *Pentap. Ind.*, p. 52; Wilson, *Vishṇu Pur.*, p. 193; Cunningham, *Arch. Rep.*, vol. v, pp. 148 ff.; and *Ind. Ant.*, vol. ix, p. 252.

Inscription No. 7 [1] (pl. xlix) reads—

Ugâha-upâsakasa putasa
Isipâlitasa sapa[pu]takasa dânaṁ [||]

—"The gift of Isipâlita, the son of Ugâha, an Upâsaka (*or* laic), with his sons."

No. 8,[2] in Cave 67 on Sivaneri hill, reads—

Yavaṇasa
Chiṭasa Gatânaṁ
bhojaṇamaṭapo
deyadhama saghe [||]

—"The meritorious gift of a refectory for the community (Saṁgha) by the Yavana Chiṭa (Chaitra) of the Gatas (*or* of the Gatâ [3] country)."

No. 9 [4]—

Ugâhaputasa Isipâlitasa saparivârasa chetiyagharo dânaṁ [||]

—"The gift of a Chetiyaghara by Isipâlita (Ṛishipâlita), son of Ugâha (Udgrâha), with his family."

No. 10 [5] reads—

Dhaṁññikaseṇiya satagabhaṁ pôdhi cha deyadhamaṁ [||]

—"The meritorious gift of a seven-celled (*cave*) and cistern by the guild of corn-dealers."

No. 11,[6] on the Chaitya cave at Gaṇeśa Leṇâ, reads—

Kaliañasa Heraṇikaputasa Sulasadatasa ekapurisasa chetiyagharo niyuto deyadhama [||]

—"A Chaityagṛiha, dedicated as a meritorious gift by the distinguished Sulasâdatta, son of Hairaṇyaka of Kalyâṇa." [7]

No. 12 [8]—

Kapila-upâsakasa natuno Tâpasa-upâsakasa
putasa Ânadasa deyadhaṁmaṁ chetiyagharo niyuto [||]

—"The meritorious gift of a Chaityagṛiha given by Ânada (Ânanda), son of Tâpasa the Upâsaka, and grandson of Kapila the Upâsaka." [9]

No. 13,[10] in two lines, about 3½ feet in length, begins and ends with the *swastika* symbol, and reads—

卐 Kaliañakasa Kuḷiraputasa suvaṇa-
kârasa Saghakasa poḍhi deyadhaṁmaṁ [||] 卐

—"The meritorious gift of the goldsmith Saṁghaka, son of Kuḷira (Sans. Kulîra) of Kalyâṇâ."

---

[1] This is No. 32 in the *Cave-Temple Inscriptions*, p. 55.

[2] *Cave-Temple Inscriptions*, No. 33.

[3] Compare inscription 5.

[4] *Cave-Temple Inscriptions*, No. 34, p. 55.

[5] *Cave-Temple Inscriptions*, No. 31, p. 54.

[6] *Cave-Temple Inscriptions*, No. 30, p. 54.

[7] This was first translated by Dr. Stevenson, *J. B. B. R. As. Soc.*, vol. v, p. 161; and again by Dr. Kern in Weber's *Indische Studien*, Bd. xiv, § 396, *Ind. Ant.*, vol. vi, p. 40. A Sulasâdatta is also mentioned in two of the Kuḍâ inscriptions. Sulasâ is one of the *jaganmâtaraḥ*, or mothers of the world, with the Jainas; see Jacobi, *Ind. Ant.*, vol. ix, p. 28; *Cave Temples*, p. 209.

[8] *Ind. Ant.*, vol. vi. p. 35; and *Cave-Temple Inscriptions*, No. 29, p. 53.

[9] This is substantially Dr. Kern's translation;—Weber's *Indische Studien*, Bd. xiv, S. 393.

[10] *Cave-Temple Inscriptions*, No. 28, p. 53.

No. 14 [1] is in three lines about 2 feet 9 inches long, and also begins with the *swastika* symbol. It reads—

> 卐 Isimulasâmino bhaya-
> Nadabâlikâya Nâḍaka-Torikasa
> Lachhinika[kâ]ya deyadhama poḍhi [||]

—"The meritorious gift of a cistern by Lachhinikâ (Lakshmî), wife of Torika the Naḍika (by caste, and) Nadabâlikâ, wife of Isimulasâmi (Ṛishimûlasvâmi)."

No. 15 [2] (pl. xlix) reads—

> Sâmarupâsakasa putasa
> Sivabhûtisa deyadhama leṇaṁ
> Kapichite saṁghasa niyutaṁ ka(?)

—"The meritorious gift of a *leṇa* by Sivabhûti, the son of Sâmara (Śyâmala), the Upâsaka, dedicated to the Saṁgha at Kapichita." [3]

No. 16 [4] (pl. l) reads—

> Yavanasa Chaṁdânaṁ deyadhama gabhadâ(ra)

—"The meritorious gift of a hall-front by Chanda the Yavana."

The name Chandra, used here in the *plural majestatis*, is Hindu; yet he is called a Yavana or Westerner.

What can be read of No. 17 [5] is—

> Gaṇâchariyânaṁ therâna bha-
> yaṁta-Sulasânaṁ Tevijâ-
> naṁ aṁtevâsinaṁ therâna
> bhayaṁta Chetiyasânaṁ Tevi-
> jânaṁ naṁdanakanavaka
> . . . . . . aṁ kothalakâ
> . . . . . . cha gahapati
> . . . . . . natuno Nadaṇaka
> aya . . . . . . ! . . . . . .
> deyadhama.

—"The Âchârya of the Gaṇa, the venerable (*thera*) and reverend (*bhayaṁta*) Tevija [6] Sulasa; his disciple, the Thera Bhayanta Chetiyasa, a Tevija . . . . and householder . . . his grandson Nandaṇaka . . . . the meritorious gift."

Curiously enough, No. 18 [7] stops short before completing the sentence. It reads—

> Sayiti-gahapatiputasa gahapatisa Sivadâsasa
> bitiyikâya cha sahâ parivâ

—"Of the householder Sivadâsa, son of the householder Sayiti, and his wife, with all his relatives. . . ."

---

1 *Ind. Ant.*, vol. vi, p. 35; *Cave-Temple Inscriptions*, No. 27, p. 52.

2 *Ind. Ant.*, vol. vi, p. 35; *Cave-Temple Inscriptions*, No. 26, p. 52.

3 Kapichita is probably the old name of the monastic establishment in the Leṇâdri Hill.

4 *Cave-Temple Inscriptions*, No. 7, p. 43.

5 *Cave-Temple Inscriptions*, No. 22, p. 50.

6 Sana *Traividya*, "Knowing the Tripiṭaka;" Fausböll, however, translates it, "masters of the three Vedas,"—*Sutta-Nipata*, pp. 98, 110, 117 (v. 63), 189. It appears also to have been adopted by the Buddhists as an epithet of Arahats,—Rhys Davids' *Buddhist Suttas*, p. 162.—J.B.

7 *Cave-Temple Inscriptions*, No. 21, p. 50.

Inscription No. 19[1] has the short middle line inserted in smaller letters and reads—

Bhârukachhakânaṁ Laṁkuḍiyânaṁ bhâtûṇam
Asasamasa putâṇa
Budhamitasa Budharakhitasa cha bigabhaṁ deyadhaṁmaṁ [||]

—"A double-roomed house, a meritorious gift by the brothers Buddhamita and Buddharakhita, Lankuḍiyas, sons of Asasama (Aśvaśarman), inhabitants of Bhârukachha (Bharoch)."

The following inscriptions (Nos. 20–30[2]) are in the large unfinished Chaitya cave, near where the Mânmoḍi Hill bends round to the south.

No. 20 (pl. l) is on the left end of the back wall of the verandah just above the level of the door, faintly cut out on a rough surface—

Game Puvânadesu nivatanâni
panarasa 15 palapasa
deyadhama apajîtesu ga-
ne payogo ka[kâ]hâpaṇanâ[ṇâna ||]

—"Fifteen, 15 *nivartanas* in the village of Puvânadâ, the meritorious gift of Palapa. With the company of the Apajîtas[3] (*rests*) the investment of the *Kârshâpanas*."[4]

Nos. 21, 22, 23, are three short inscriptions on two large octagonal pillars in front of the Chaitya; they are in well-cut letters, but no translation of them can be offered, as the language is neither Pâli nor Sanskrit.

No. 24 is in distinct letters on the left wall of the large recess over the door, on the same level with the arched window—

Koṇâchike seṇiya
uvasako Âḍuthuma
Sako || Vaḍâlikâyaṁ
Karajamula nivataṇâ
ni visa || Kaṭaputake
vaḍamule nivata-
ṇâni[*na*]va

—"By Âḍuthuma the Śaka, an Upâsaka of the guild of the Koṇâchikas[5] (*a gift of*) 20 *nivartanas* in Vaḍâlikâ, near the Karanja tree, and in Kataputaka, 9 *nivartanas* near the banyan tree."

No. 25 is close to No. 24, on the left of the arched window, and is cut on a rough surface. Many of the letters, especially in the lower lines, are very uncertain—

Mahâveje game Jâbabhati
udeseṇa nivataṇâni shaṇuvisa
sidhagaṇe[6] Aparâjite-
su satâni[7] selasa
Mânamukaḍasa purato

---

[1] *Cave-Temple Inscriptions*, No. 20, p. 49.

[2] *Cave-Temple Inscriptions*, Nos. 9–19, pp. 44, *seqq.*

[3] Possibly the *gaṇa* of the Apajîtas mentioned here is the same as the Siddhagaṇa of the Aparâjitas who are the trustees in No. 23; if so, *gaṇa* may be taken in the sense of "school;" by "the *kârshâpanas*" the income from the field must be meant.

[4] Translated by Professor G. Bühler, C.I.E.

[5] It is doubtful if the first part of this translation is correct; neither *Âḍuthuma* nor *Koṇâchika* are known words.

[6] *Sidhagaṇa*, "assembly of saints," may be a name of the assembly or school of the Aparâjitas.

[7] *Satâni* corresponds with the Sanskrit *saktâni*, "entrusted."

talakavâdake nivata-
ṇâni tiṇi ‖ nagarasa-
. . . ka . sela ude
seṇa nivataṇani ve [‖]

—"In the village of Mahâveja, in the direction of the Jâbabhati (*i.e.*, *Jambu-plantation*), twenty-six *nivartanas* entrusted to the holy assembly (?) of the Aparâjitas; in front of Mount Mânamukaḍa three *nivartanas*. The town . . . . . . towards the mountain . . . *nivartanas.*"

Mânamukada (Sans. Mânamukuṭa, "Crown of pride,") appears to be the old name of the Mânamoḍa Hill, in which the cave is.

No. 26 (pl. 1) is on the left side of the front arch round the window in eight short lines of two or three letters each, reading together—

Âbikâbhati nivataṇâni dve Vâhata-Vacheḍukasa esa [‖]

—"Two *nivartanas* (*near*) the mango plantation—this (*is the gift*) of Vâhata Vacheḍuka."

No. 27 is along the right side of the arch in three lines—

Seniye ne[va]sakare[su]
mâse pâönaduke ‖
kâsâ[sa]kâresu seniya pâ[do]se[ma]

—"With the guild of bambu-workers, monthly, one and three-quarters, and the guild of braziers a quarter . . . ."

No. 28. On the back of the recess to the right of the window, much damaged towards the end—

Game Valâhakesu kara-
jabhati udeseṇa nivata-
ṇâni bârasa ‖ Gâma-Se-
urakesu nivataṇâni
. . . .

—"In the village of Valâhakâ (*in the direction*) of the Karanja plantation[1] two *nivartanas*. In the village Seüraka . . *nivartanas.*"

No. 29. To the right of the preceding; many of the letters are doubtful—

Âvarile Vasarikha-
ḍake nivataṇâni cha-
târi ‖ . . . . . .
avarila . . . . .
ke nivataṇâni . . .
eta . . . . . .
avarile[la] jipu . u .
ka udeseṇa nivata-
ṇâni aṭha ‖ gama[me] ko-
ḍakesu nivataṇâni
. . bâra deya . . .

—"In Upper[2] Vasarikhaḍa, four *nivartanas* . . . Upper . . . . *nivartanas* . . . . In the direction of Upper Jipu . . uka, eight *nivartanas*. In the village of Koḍaka, twelve *nivartanas*, a meritorious gift."[3]

[1] The *karaja* is a timber tree, the Pongamia Glabra.—J. B.

[2] The translation of *âvarila* or *avarila* is not certain. The vocable corresponds, however, with Mahârâshṭhrî *avarilla*, which, according to Hemachandra, ii. 166, means "upper" (garment); see also *Pâiyalachhî*, s. v.

[3] By Dr. G. Bühler.

No. 30 is on the rough surface of a quadrantal moulding over the door, and many of the letters are very uncertain.[1] It seems to consist of a number of donations at different places, similar to those already given.

No. 31 [2] (pl. li) is much defaced, but the intent of it is pretty clear—

. . . . [*ga*]hapatipu[*tânaṁ*] bhâtûṇaṁ dâṇa ka-
. . . . sacha pa[*cha*]gabhaṁ deyadhaṁmaṁ [||]

—"A five-celled (*house*) . . . the meritorious gift of the brothers . . . . sons of the . . . a householder."

No. 33 [3] (pl. li)—

Sivasama putasa Sivabhûtino deyadhama poḍhi [||]

—"The meritorious gift of a cistern by Śivabhûti, son of Sivasama (Śivaśarman)."

No. 34 [4] (pl. li). Only a fragment at the beginning of the three long lines of which this inscription consisted is left, reading—

Sidhaṁ upâsakasa negama . . .
Satamala putasa . . . .
. . puta Virabhuti . . . .

The only other Junnar inscription (No. 32) is given below as No. 11 of the next section.

IX. Nasik, Karle, and Junnar Inscriptions of Nahapana and the Andhras.

Arranging the inscriptions in chronological order, we take first one over a window in the small vihâra cave at Nâsik, No. XIV [5] As Professor Bhâṇḍârkar pointed out, the letters are of a much older type than those of the other Nâsik inscriptions. They belong, in fact, to the times of the last Mauryas or the earliest Śuṅgas, in the beginning of the second century B.C.

No. 1 (pl. li) Nâsik (West, No. 6)—

Sâdavâhanakula-Kanhe râjini [6] Nâsikakena
Samaṇena [7] mahâmâteṇa leṇa kârita [||]

—"When Kṛishṇa of the Sâtavâhana race was king, the Mahâmâtra Samaṇa resident at Nâsik made (*this*) cave."

No. 2 Nâsik (West, No. 8)—

This inscription shows nearly pure Maurya characters, and is, if not the oldest of the series, certainly not later than that of Râjâ Kṛishṇa—

Nâsikakanaṁ Dhaṁbhikagâmasa dânaṁ[||]

—"The gift of Dhaṁbhikagâma, of the inhabitants of Nâsika."

---

[1] This is given as Nos. 23 and 24 of Dr. Stevenson's *Jo. Bom. B. R. As. Soc.*, vol. v, p. 168, and plates; Dr. Bird gives the fifth line of it as No. 7, *Histor. Res.*, pl. xlix.

[2] *Cave-Temple Inscriptions*, No. 8, p. 44.

[3] *Cave-Temple Inscriptions*, No. 24, p. 51; *Ind. Ant.*, vol. vi, p. 40.

[4] *Cave-Temple Inscriptions*, No. 23, p. 51.

[5] *Cave Temples*, p. 275. As mentioned elsewhere, these translations of the Nâsik inscriptions have been prepared by Professor G. Bühler, C.I.E.

[6] *Kanhe râjini* is the locative absolute; see also Kuḍâ insc. No. 20, and *Ind. Ant.*, vol. vii, p. 256.

[7] *Samaṇena* is not quite certain, as a large flaw runs aslant between the first and second letters, and has given the first a curious shape. As the space between the letters is large, a letter may have been lost.

No. 3 (pl. li) Nâsik (West, No. 7)—

Benacha . . . ni . e . . . yâva Nadâsiriyâva cha veikâ yakho cha kâritâ[||]

—"A rail-pattern ledge and Yaksha were caused to be made by . . . . and by Nadâsiriyâ"[1] . . . . .

No. 4 (pl. li) Nâsik (West, Nos. 9 and 10)—

(1.) Râvâmacha Arahalayasa Chalisâlaṇakasa[2] duhutuya Mahâhakusi-
(2.) [3]ri[yâ]yaya Bhaṭapâlikâya râyâmachasa Agiyataṇakasa Bhaḍâkârika-
(3.) yasa bhâriyâya Kapaṇaṇakaṃâtuya chetiyagharaṁ pavate
(4.) Tiraṇhumi niṭhapâpita[||]

—"A Chaityagṛiha has been established on Mount Trirasmi (Tiraṇhu) by Mahâhakusiriyâ Bhaṭapâlikâ, daughter of the royal minister, Arahalaya Chalisâlaṇaka, wife of the royal minister, Agiyataṇaka Bhaḍâkârikaya (*and*) mother of Kapaṇaṇaka."[4]

No. 5 (pl. lii) Nâsik (West, No. 17), An inscription of Ṛishabhadatta—

(1.) Siddham râjñaḥ Kshaharâtasya Kshatrapasya Nahapânasya jâmâtrâ Dînîkaputreṇa Ushavadâtena trigośatasahasradena nadyâ bârṇâsâyâṁ suvarṇadânatîrthakareṇa devatâbhyaḥ brâhmaṇebhyaś cha shoḍaśagrâmadena anuvarsha brâhmaṇaśatasâhasrîbhojâpayitrâ[5]

(2.) Prabhâse puṇyatîrthe brâhmaṇebhyaḥ ashṭabhâryâpradena Bharukachhe Daśapure Govardhane Śorpârage cha chatuśâlâvasadhapratiśrayapradena ârâmatadâga-udapânakareṇa Ibâ-Pârâdâ-Damaṇa-Tâpî-Karabeṇâ-Dâhanukâ nâvâ puṇyatarakareṇa etâsâṁ cha nadînâṁ ubhato tîraṁ sabhâ-[6]

(3.) prapâkareṇa Piṁdîtakâvaḍe Govardhane Suvarṇamukhe Śorpârage cha Râmatîrthe Charakaparshabyhaḥ grâma Nânaṁgole dvâtrîśatanâḷigeramûlasahasradena Govardhane Triraśmishu parvateshu dharmâtmanâ idaṁ leṇa kâritaṁ imâ cha podhiyo[|]bhaṭârakâ añâtiyâ cha gatosmi varshâratuṁ mâlayehi rudhaṁ Utamabhadraṁ mochayituṁ[7]

(4.) te cha mâlayâ pranâdeneva apayâtâ Utamabhadrakânâṁ cha kshatriyânaṁ sarve parigrahâ kritâ tatosmi gato Poksharâni tatra cha mayâ abhiseko krito tîṇi gosahasrâni datâni gâmo cha[|] data chânena kshetra brâhmaṇasa Vârâhiputrasa Aśvibhûtisa hathe kiṇitâ mûlena kâhâpaṇasahasrehi chatuhi 4000 ya sapitusatakanagarasîmâya utarâparâya diśâya eto mama lene vasa-

(5.) tâna châtudîsasa bhikhusaghasa mukhâhâro bhavisati[||]

"Success! The son-in-law of the Kshaharâta king, Kshatrapa Nahapâna, Dînîka's son, charitable Ṛishabhadatta (Ushavadâta),—who has given (*as alms*) three hundred thousand cows—who by a gift of gold established a tîrtha on the river Bârṇâsâ[8]—who gave sixteen villages to the gods Brâhmaṇas—who annually causes to be fed one hundred thousand

---

[1] *Nadâsiriyâ* corresponds to Sanskrit *Nandâśrîkâ*. Regarding the instr. gen. in *âva* for *âya* (see Kuḍâ inscriptions, No. 20; compare also *Puḷumavi* (No. 17) for *Puḷumâyi*.

[2] Possibly *Chalisilaṇakasa*.

[3] The first letter may also be read, *râ*; the second, which looks like *râ*, is certainly mutilated.

[4] I connect *Mahâhakusiriyâya* with the male proper name, *Hakusiri*, which is found in the Nânâghâṭ inscriptions. The last syllables represent °*śrîkâ*. *Bhaṭapâlikâ* seems to correspond to Sanskrit *bhartṛipâlikâ*. The explanation of the other names is very doubtful.

[5] Read *nadyâṁ*; *anuvarshaṁ*.

[6] Read *chatuḥśâlâvasatha*; *taḍâgodapâna*; °*Dâhanukânâṁ*.

[7] Read *parshadbhyaḥ*; *leṇaṁ*. The *a* of *aṇâtiyâ* stands below the line, and is a correction which only causes confusion. It ought to be either *bhaṭârakâñâtiyâ* or *bhaṭâraka añâtiyâ*, i.e., *bhaṭârakâjñaptyâ*. There is an empty space between *mâlaye* and *hi*, but no letters have been lost. The text, as shown above, gives perfectly good sense.

[8] It would seem that Ṛishabhadatta gave money to build the flights of steps leading to the bathing-place (*tîrtha*) on the Bârṇâsâ. The latter word, which corresponds with the Sanskrit Parṇâśâ and the modern Banâs, is the name of several rivers in Western India. One Baṇâs, which comes from Mount Âbû, falls into the gulf of Kachh; another Baṇâs is a tributary of the Chambal; a third in Revâ is a tributary of the Sôn. The former river can hardly be meant, as it rarely contains any water except during the rains.

Brâhmaṇas—who has given wives to eight Brâhmaṇas at the holy tîrtha of Prabhâsa—who has given, at Bharukachha, Daśapura, Govardhana and Sorpâraga,[1] quadrangular rest-houses—who has made gardens. tanks and drinking fountains—who has established, for the sake of spiritual merit, ferries, with boats on the rivers Ibâ, Pârâdâ, Damaṇa, Tâpî, Karabeṇâ and Dâhanukâ,[2] and has erected, on both banks of these rivers, rest-houses (*for travellers*) and places for the (*gratuitous*) distribution of water—who has given, in the village of Nânaṁgola, one thousand as the price of thirty-two cocoanut trees (*destined*) for (*the benefit of*) the Charaka congregations at Pîṁḍîtâvaḍa, Govardana, Suvarṇamukha, and at Râmatîrtha near Sorpâraga,[3]—has caused this cave and these cisterns to be made on Mount Triraśmi, in (*the district of*) Govardhana.

And by order of the supreme lord I went in the rainy season to liberate the Uttamabhadra chief[4] who was besieged by the Mâlayas, and those Mâlayas fled before the roar (*of my army*) as it were, and they were all made dependants of the Uttamabhadra warriors. Afterwards I went to the Pushkaras (Poksharas[5]), and I bathed there, and gave three thousand cows and a village.

And a field was given by him, bought for the sum of four thousand (4000) *kârshâpaṇas* from the Brâhmaṇa Aśvibhûti, the son of the wife of the Vârâha gotra, which (*field*) lies to the north-west of the boundaries of the town belonging to my own father. From that the community of monks from the four quarters, who live in my cave, will obtain their provisions."[6]

---

[1] *Prabhâsa* is Somnâth Pâṭhan or Pattan in Kâṭhiâvâḍ (Soraṭh); Bharukachha is Bharûch; Govardhana is at present a village near Nâsik; Sorpâraga, *alias* Sûrpâraka, is Supârâ near Basin (Vasai) in the Thâṇa Collectorate (see *Ind. Ant.*, vol. i, p. 321, and Bhâṇḍârkar, *Tr. Or. Cong*, 1874, p. 328). A Daśapura lay in Râjputânâ, north of the Chambal (see Mallinâtha and Wilson on *Meghadûta*, vs. 48). Wilson is, however, wrong in identifying the town with Rintambor, which in Sanskrit is known as Raṇastambhapura. The expression "quadrangular rest-houses" exactly fits the Dharmaśâlâs or Serâis built on the native plan, as the rooms or sheds for the accommodation of travellers invariably run along the four sides of a spacious court, leaving just space enough in the front for an arched entrance. I do not think that more than one kind of buildings is intended by the whole compound *chatuḥśâlâvasathapratiśraya*, lit. "shelter by the means of quadrangular buildings."

[2] Tâpî is the Taptî, near Surat; Pârâdâ is the Pâraḍî or Pâr river, in the Surat Zilla; Damaṇa is the Damaṇgangâ, which joins the sea near the Portuguese colony of Damaṇ (Damân); Dâhanukâ is probably the creek south of Dahanu in the Thâṇâ Collectorate. Ibâ may possibly be the Ambikâ river near Jalâlpur in the Surat Collectorate. The *sabhâs*, or "rest-houses," erected on the banks of these rivers, were probably roofed sheds, intended to shelter travellers waiting for the boat from the sun and the rain, such as we often find near fords in the present day.

[3] *Nâḷigera* is clearly the Sanskrit *nâlikera*, a cocoanut tree. Cocoanut trees are valuable property, not only on account of their fruit, but on account of the palm-wine which is drawn from them; and if the coin whose name is left out after "one thousand" was a small one, the price paid by Rishabhadatta was not too high. The object of the gift seems to have been to distribute annually the income accruing from the trees to the Charaka congregations at the four places mentioned. It is difficult to determine what these Charaka congregations were. Though *parshad*, "congregation," is the technical term for an "assembly of learned Brâhmaṇas convened for a special purpose," it has also the same meaning as *charaṇa*, and means "a Brahmanical school studying under one teacher." *Charaka* has also two meanings; it is both the proper name of a Vedic school, and a general term for a Brahmanical student. The recipients of the gift, therefore, may have been either "congregations of students" or "assemblies of Brâhmaṇas studying the *Charaka śâkhâ*." Regarding *Râmatîrtha*, see Bhâṇḍârkar, loc. cit., note 3.

[4] The expedition which the first postscript mentions must have followed immediately after the gift of the cave had been made. The Mâlayas are, no doubt, the inhabitants of the Malaya hills in Southern India. In the same direction the home of the Uttamabhadras must be sought. *Uttamabhadraḥ* (sing.) denotes the chief of the clan, just as *Panchâlaḥ* the king of the Panchâlâḥ.

[5] *Pokharâṇi* is probably a corruption of Pushkarâṇi. The famous *tîrtha* of Pokhar near Ajmir, where there are three sacred tanks, is probably meant, but there are other sacred lakes of the same name.

[6] The name of the Brâhmaṇa from whom the field mentioned in the second postscript was bought is doubtful Aśribhûti (Professor Bhâṇḍârkar's reading) is possible, but the name then gives no sense. With *supitusataka*, "belonging to my own father," compare *amasataka* in No. 14, l. 3.

No. 6. Karle No. 19 (pl. li).

The inscription is badly injured and carelessly written. But it can be restored and explained, with the help of the Nâsik inscription No. 5, where Ṛishabhadatta enumerates and more fully describes his various benefactions in very bad Sanskrit.

[1.] Sidhaṁ Raṇo Khaharâtasa khatapasa Nahapânasa jâma[mâ]ta ra[râ] Dinikapûtena Usabhadâtena tini-
[2.] ga[go]satasahasadeṇa ṇadiyâ Baṇâsâyâ suvaṇara[ti]thakareṇa [devâna] Bra[brâ]hmaṇâna cha solasagâ-
[3.] madena Pâbhâse pûñatithe Brâhmaṇâṇa aṭhe[ṭha] bhâryâpa[deṇa] [a]n[u]vâsaṁ pitu satasâhasi[bho]-
[4.] japayita[tâ] Valûrakesu leṇavâsâ[si]na pavajitânaṁ châtudisasa saghasa
[5.] yapaṇatha gâmo Karajiko dato sa[vâ]na [va]savasitâna-

"Success! The son-in-law of the Khaharâta king Kshatrapa Nahapâna Dinika's son, Usabhadâta [Ṛishabhadatta], who gave three hundred thousand cows, who founded by (a gift of) gold a Tîrtha on the Baṇâsâ [Parṇâśâ] river, who gave to gods and Brâhmaṇas sixteen villages, who gave at the holy Tîrtha of Pâbhâsa [Prabhâsa[1]] wives to eight Brâhmaṇas, who annually causes to be fed one huudred thousand Brâhmaṇas for the sake of his father, has given for their support the village of Karajika to the community of ascetics from the four quarters, living in the cave at Valûraka [*i.e.*] to all dwelling there during the rainy season."

No. 7 (pl. liii). Nâsik, No. 6A (West, No. 14)—An inscription of Ṛishabhadatta—

(1.) [Sidhaṁ raño Kshaharâ]tasa kshatrapasa Nahapânasa jâmâ-
(2.) [tu Dînîkaputrasa] Śakasa Ushavadâtasa netyakesu
(3.) [. . . . . Śorpâra]ge Vechimñe Dâhanûkânagare Kekâpure
(4.) [. . . . Bharuka]chhe Anugâmimhi Ujeniya Sâkhâya
(5.) [. . . . . . bha]ga[vaṁ]to brâhmaṇâ bhujate satasâha-
(6.) [rî . . . .] brâhmaṇâna gavâṁ satasa-
(7.) [hasra . . . . . . bhagava]tâ[ṁ] d[e]v[â]na brâhmaṇânaṁ cha datâ
(8.) [. . . . .] chetrasudhe panarasa Kshaharâ-
(9.) [ta . . . .] gavâ[ṁ] śatasahasradena Usha-
(10.) [vadâtena . . . . ha . . .] nadîya Banâsâya da-
(11.) [. . . . .] suvaṇâtitha cheñayate tasa[2]

1, 2. "[Success!] At the daily rites of the Śaka[3] Ushavadâta (Ṛishabhadatta), the son-in-law of [the Kshaharâ]ta [king] the kshatrapa Nahapâna [and the son of Dinîka].
3. . . . . at [Śorpâra]ga, Vechimña, Dâhanûkânagara,[4] Kekâpura.
4. . . . . at [Bharuka]chha, Anugâmi, Ujjain, Sâkhâ.[5]
5. . . . . worshipful Brâhmaṇas, one hundred thousand dine.
6. . . . . to the worshipful Brâhmanas one hundred thousand cows.

---

[1] Valûrakâ (nom. pl.) appears to be the ancient name of Kârle.

[2] As the restitution of the first two lines can be made with tolerable certainty, it appears that seven to eleven *aksharas* have been lost at the beginning of each line. A comparison of the fragments with Nâsik No. 5 permits us to restore a few of the names of towns, and shows that the contents of the inscription probably were as follows:—l. 1, 2, description of the donor; l. 3–5, the annual feeding of one hundred thousand Brâhmaṇas in various towns; l. 6, gift of one hundred thousand cows; l. 7, gift of sixteen villages to gods and Brâhmaṇas; l. 8, 9, a date and another gift of cows; l. 10, 11, the establishment of a *tîrtha* on the Baṇâs

[3] Considering the great probability of the restoration of the first two lines, it seems to me almost certain that *Sakasa* is a complete word, and that Ṛishabhadatta calls himself here a Śaka.

[4] Dâhanûkânagara is, of course, the modern Dâhanu in the Thânâ Zillâ.

[5] A town called Sâkhâ is mentioned in the apocryphal *Romakasiddhânta* (*Oxford Cat.*, p. 339A).

7. . . . . to the worshipful gods and Brâhmaṇas have been given [sixteen villages].

8. . . . . on the fifteenth of the bright half of Chaitra the Kshaharâ[ta].

9. . . . . Ushavadâta (Rishabhadatta), who gave one hundred thousand cows.

10. . . . . on the river Baṇâs . . . . .

11. . . . . through gold a *tîrtha* . . . .

No. 8 (pl. liii). Nâsik. No. 6B—

(1.) . . . . [bha]gavatâ[ṁ] brâhmaṇâ
(2.) . . . . do sahaśa 2000
(3.) . . . . mâsiyaṁ tithe
(4.) . . . . he (?) yâna ja .

No. 9 (pl. lii). Nâsik, No. 7.[1]—An inscription of Rishabhadatta, dated in the year 42—

(1.) Sidhaṁ vase 42 vesâkhamâse raño Kshanarâtasa kshatrapasa Nahapânasa jâmâtarâ Dînîkapûtrena Ushavadâtena saṁghasa châtudisasasa ima leṇa niyâtitaṁ[|]data chanena akshaya nivi kâhâpaṇasahasrâ-
(2.) ni triṇi 3000 saṁghasa châtudisasa ye imasmiṁ leṇe vasâtâna[2] bhavisati chivarika kuśaṇamûle cha ete cha kâhâpaṇâ prayutâ Govadhanavâthavâsu śreṇîsu kolikanikâye 2000 vadhi paḍikaśata aparakolikanikâ-
(3.) ye 1000 vadhi pâyunapaḍikaśata[|]ete cha kâhâpaṇâ apaḍidâtavâ vadhibhojâ[3][|] eto chivarika sahasrâni be 2000 ve paḍike sate eto mama lene vasavuthâna bhikhunaṁ vîsâya ekîkasa chívarika bârasaka ya sahasra prayutaṁ pâyunapaḍike śato ato kusaṇa-
(4.) mûla[|] Kâpurâhâre cha gâme Chikhalapadre datâni nâḷigerâna mûla sahasrâni aṭhâ 8000 [|] eta cha sarva srâvita nigamasabhâya nibadha cha phalakavâre charitrato ti [|] bhûyonena dataṁ vase 41 kâtikaśudhe panarasa puvâkavase 45
(5ᵃ.) panarasa niyutaṁ devânaṁ brâhmaṇânaṁ cha karshapaṇasahasraṇi sattari 70,000 paṁchatriśakasuvaṇakṛitâdina suvarṇasahasranaṁ mûla [|]
(5ᵇ.) phalakavâre charitrato ti [||][4]

"Success! In the year 42, in the month of Vaiśâkha, Rishabhadatta (Ushavadâta), the son-in-law of the Kshaharâta king, Kshatrapa Nahapâna, (*and*) son of Dînîka, gave this cave to the community of monks from the four points of the horizon. Moreover, he gave a perpetual endowment (*of*) three thousand, 3000, *kârshâpaṇas*, which will serve the community (*of monks*) from the four points of the horizon, living in this cave, (*to defray*) the expenditure for clothes, and (*to pay*) the price of *kuśaṇa*.[5] And these *kârshâpaṇas* have been deposited with the mercantile companies dwelling in Govardhana, (*viz.*) with (*one*) guild of weavers 2000 (*at an*) interest of one hundred *kârshâpaṇas*,[6] with another guild of weavers 1000 (*at an*) interest of seventy-five *kârshâpaṇas*. And these *kârshâpaṇas* shall not be repaid by him who pays the interest. Out of the two thousand, 2000, which (*have been invested*)

[1] This inscription corresponds with Nos. 16 and 18 of Professor Bhâṇḍârkar, who took its left and right hand portions for two separate documents, because they stand on two different walls.

[2] L. 2. Read *vasatâna*.

[3] L. 3. Read *vuḍhibhâjâ*.

[4] Line 5ᵇ gives nothing but a repetition of the last three words of the chief inscription (l. 4), and seems unconnected with the second postscript.

[5] *Kuśaṇa*, or *kusaṇa*, as the reading is in l. 3, corresponds exactly to the Vedic *kṛiśana*, which is translated by "gold or pearls." It cannot have that sense here, as some comparatively cheap article for the use of the monks must be intended. *Chîvarika* does not mean the same as *chîvara*, "a monk's mantle or clothing," as Prof. Bhâṇḍârkar thinks, but is an adjective meaning "sufficient for clothes," and may be translated by "the price or expense for clothes."

[6] Regarding *paḍika* see Prof. Bhâṇḍârkar, loc. cit. p. 331.

at (*an interest of*) one hundred ***kârshâpaṇas*** a piece of twelve[1] (*as*) expense for clothes (*shall be paid*) to each of the twenty monks keeping the ***vasso***[2] in my cave. Out of the thousand invested at (*an interest of*) seventy-five ***kârshâpaṇas*** the price of ***kusaṇa*** (***shall be paid***). And in the village of Chhikhalapadra, (***situated***) in the district of **Kâpura**, eight thousand, 8000, have been given as the price for cocoanut-trees. And all this has been proclaimed in the guildhall and has been written on boards according to custom.[3] Further, he has given on the 15th of the bright half of **Kârtika**, in the year 41.[4] . . . ."

No. 10 (pl. lii). **Nâsik**, Nos. 8 and 9 (West, 16A and 20)—Two identical inscriptions of **Dakshamitrâ, Ṛishabhadatta's wife**—

(1.) Sidhaṁ raño Kshaharâtasa kshatrapasa Nahapânasa dhi-
(2.) tu Dînîkaputrasa Ushavadâtasa kuḍuṁbiniya Dakhamitâya
(3.) deyadhaṁmaṁ ovarako [‖]

—"Success! An inner cell, the meritorious gift of **Dakshamitrâ**, wife of **Dînîka's** son Ṛishabhadatta, and daughter of the king the **Kshaharâta** kshatrapa Nahapâna."

No. 11. **Junnar**, No. 32[5] (pl. liv)—

This inscription is[6] in the fourth excavation on the eastern side of **Mânmoḍi** Hill. It is in three lines about 4 feet long. The first few letters in each line are considerably decayed and faint. It reads—

[*Raño*]mahâkhatapasa sâminahapânasa
[*Â*]mâtyasa Vachhasagotasa Ayamasa
[*de*]yadhama cha [*po?*] ḍhi maṭapo cha puñathaya vase 46 kato

—"The meritorious gift of a maṇḍapa and cistern by Ayama of the Vatsa-gotra, prime minister to the king, the great Satrap, the Lord Nahapâna, made for merit, in the year 46."

No. 12 (pl. liii). **Nâsik**, No. 10 (West, No. 15)—Dated in the year 9 of the **Âbhîra** king, **Îśvarasena**—

(1.) Sidhaṁ râjñaḥ . . rîputrasya Śivadattâbhîraputrasya
(2.) Abhîrasy[e]śvarasenasya[7] savatsare navame [9]
(3.) [gi]mhapakhe chothe 4 divas[e] trayodaś[e] 13 [e]-
(4.) [tâ]yâ puvâya Śakâgnivarmmaṇaḥ duhitrâ gaṇâpaka-
(5.) [sya] Rebhilasya bhâryayâ gaṇâpakasya Viśvavarmasya
(6.) gâśakânikâyâ[8] upâsikâya Vishnudatâyâ sarvasatvahi-

---

[1] *Bârasaka(ṁ)*, which corresponds to Sanskrit *dvâdaśakam*, must mean here "a piece or sum of twelve." What the twelve coins were is not said; but they cannot be *kârshâpaṇas*, as the whole interest amounted to one hundred kârshâpanas only, and each of the twenty monks could only get five. The correctness of this interpretation of *bârasaka* is proved by the parallel passages of the Kaṇheri inscriptions quoted by Prof. Bhâṇḍârkar. No. 39 has *chivarika dâtava solasaka*, and No. 44, *dâtava chivarika soḍasaka*, "a piece of sixteen," is to be given (as) the expense for robes, while the other inscriptions say that a *bârasaka* is to be given.

[2] "Keeping the *vasso*," *i.e.*, residing there during the rainy season, as is prescribed for Brahmanical and Bauddha ascetics.

[3] *Nigamasabhâya*, "in the guildhall," may also be translated "in the assembly of the traders." I take *vâra* in *phalakavâre*, "on boards," in the sense of "number or multitude." For another explanation, see Bhâṇḍârkar, loc. cit. The *ti* which follows after *charitrato* corresponds to Sanskrit *iti*, and indicates that the chief inscription is finished.

[4] I am unable to make out the exact meaning of the second postscript. It contains another date, "the year 45," and appears to record a large donation of 70,000 *kârshâpaṇas* made to gods and Brâhmaṇas.

[5] Vide *ante*, p. 98.

[6] *Cave-Temple Inscriptions*, No. 25, p. 51.

[7] L. 2. The first syllable after *abhîrasya* is doubtlessly *śva*, hence it becomes necessary to write *abhîrasyeśvara-senasya*. Îśvarasena is a not uncommon name for a warrior or king. The beginning of the stroke for the *e* is visible.

[8] L. 6. The reading *gâśakânikâyâ* makes no sense. Professor Bhâṇḍârkar's emendation—*bhrâtṛikanyakâyâ*—seems probable.

(7.) tasukhârtha Triraśmiparvata vihârav[â]stavyasya châtudiśa[ya]
(8.) bhikhusaghasya gilinabheshajârtham akshayanivî prayuktâ . va . na . .[1]
(9.) vy[â]su Sugatâgatâsu śreṇishu yata[ḥ] kularikaśreṇyâ haste k[â]rshâpaṇa-
(10.) sahasra[ṁ] 1000 deuyatrikaśreṇyâ[ṁ] sahasrâni dve [2000 . . . . . sre]-
(11.) ṇyâ[ṁ] śatâni pancha 500 tilapishakaśreṇyâ[ṁ] śatâ . . . . .
(12.) ete cha k[â]rshâpanâ [chatâ]lopa . . oha . . . . . .
(13.) . . . . sya mâsa . . . . sarva[ṁ] rakshati Vishn[udatâ] . . . .

—"Success! On the thirteenth, 13th, day of the fourth, 4th, fortnight of the ninth [9th] year of the Âbhîra king Îśvarasena, son of the Âbhîra Śivadatta, (*and*) born of the queen of the . . . ra family;—on the above [*mentioned day*] the lay-worshipper Vishṇudattâ, daughter of the Śaka Agnivarman, wife of the *Gaṇâpaka*[2] Rebhila (*and*) niece of the *Gaṇâpaka* Viśvavarman, placed for the good and happiness of all creatures, (*and especially*) to provide medicine for the sick of the community of monks residing in the monastery on Mount Triraśmi, a perpetual endowment with the Bauddha (?) companies dwelling in [Govardhana], viz.,[3] in the hands of the guild of the Kularikas[4] one thousand, 1000, *kârshâpaṇas*, with the guild of the Deuyatrikas (?) two hundred . . with the guild of the . . . . five hundred, 500, with the guild of the oil-millers . . . hundred. And these *kârshâpaṇas* . . . . Vishṇ[udattâ] protects all . . . ."

No. 13 (pl. liii). Nâsik. No. 11A (West, 25A). An inscription of Gautamîputra Sâtakarṇi[5]—

(1) Sidhaṁ[6] senâye vejayatiye vijayakhadhâvârâ Govadhanasa Benâkaṭakâ Svâmi Gotamiputo Sirisadakaṇi

(2) ânapayati Govadhane amacha Viṇhupâlitaṁ gâme Aparakakhaḍiya ya khetaṁ ajakâlakiyaṁ Usabhadatena[7] bhûtaṁ nivatane

(3) satâni be 200 eta amhakheta nivatanasatâṁni be 200 imesa pavajitâna Tekirasinâ[8] vitarâma etasa chasa khetasa parihâra

(4) vitarâma apavesaṁ anomasaṁ aloṇakhâdaka araṭhasavinayika[9] savajâtapârihârika cha etahi na parihârehi parihartlhi

---

[1] L. 8. Read *gilâna*°. The break at the end of the line may possibly be filled in the following manner: [*go*]va[*rdha*]na[*vâsta*].

[2] *Gaṇâpaka* means "protector or leader of a *gaṇa*," which consists of three *gulmas* or battalions, and may be taken as an equivalent of colonel or brigadier-general.

[3] *Yataḥ*, literally "out of which" perpetual endowment.

[4] Possibly *kularika* may contain a corruption of *kulâla*, "potter."

[5] My readings and interpretation differ in many points from Professor Bhâṇḍârkar's.

[6] The transcript follows the text in the use of the *anusvâra* and the long vowels, which are not regularly marked.

[7] Perhaps *Usabhadâtena*.

[8] Perhaps *Tekârasinâ*; I can find no explanation for this, nor any other reading that may be adopted. If, however, we might write *Terasikâna*, and to assume that the *kâ* had been accidentally misplaced, the word would exactly correspond with the Mahârâshṭra-Prâkrit *Terassikâṇam* (Sans. *Trairaśmikânâm*), "of those living on Triraśmi." As the Sanskrit inscriptions (Nos. 5, 12) show, the hill in which the caves are excavated was called Triraśmi, and with Professor Bhâṇḍârkar, I believe that Puḷumâyi's *Tiraṇhu* and *Teraṇhuka* (see below, No. 14, l. 9) are derived from that Sanskrit word, though the *u* is irregular. The *sa* which follows *cha* is purely pleonastic, just as in Pâli *sache*, "if," and similar words.

[9] These two compounds are left untranslated. The term *alavaṇaklinnakreṇibanaka* in the Ilichpur and Seoni grants of Pravarasena II., seems to be connected with the first, and perhaps refers to an exemption from the salt tax; but I am unable to find the correct Sanskrit expression. The second word, I think, refers to a tax on carriages and horses. I believe it to stand for *arathâśvavinayikam*, and to mean literally "exempt from that which refers to chariots and the training of horses;" but the question is, whether the villagers usually had to pay for their own chariots and horses or for those of the king. *Etaiḥ* is the correct equivalent of *etehi na*, which corresponds with the Jaina Mahârâshṭra *etehi ṇam*: the particle *ṇaṁ* stands, as the Jains say, simply *vâkyâlaṁkâre* (Jacobi, *Kalpasûtra*, index, s. v.)

(5) eta chasa kheta parihâre cha nibadho [1] lihi aviyeṇa ânataṁ [2] amachena Sivagutena chheto mahâsâmiyehi uparakhito

(6) datâ paṭikâ savachhare 14 vasa pa[khe] 2 divase 1 Tâpasena kaṭâ [||]

"Success! From Benâkaṭaka in the Govardhana (*district*), the victorious camp of the army that is protected by Indra (*Vijayanta*),[3] the lord, the illustrious Sâtakarṇi, the son of the queen of the Gautama race, issues (*these*) orders to Vishṇupâlita (Viṇhupâlita), the minister in (*charge of*) Govardhana: 'We give that field of ours, (*measuring*) two hundred, 200, Nivartanas, (*and situated*) in the village of Aparakakhaḍi (Western-Kakhadi), which hitherto Ṛishabhadatta (Usabhadata) has enjoyed, (*viz.*) two hundred, 200, *Nivartanas*, to those Tekirasi (Terasika? living on the Tirassi or Trirasmi hill) ascetics. Moreover, we grant immunity (*from interference and taxation*) for this field; (viz.) it shall not be entered (*by royal officers*), nor be meddled with (*by them*) . . . . and possess immunities of all kinds. Moreover, with respect to this field and with respect to this immunity, a charter has been drawn up, which has been approved of by the minister, Śivagupta (Sivaguta), who received (*our*) verbal orders (*to that effect*), and which is preserved by the great lords.[4] A document,[5] prepared by Tâpasa on the first day of the second fortnight of the rainy season of the year 14, has been given (*to the donees*).'"

No. 14 (pl. liii). Nâsik, No. 11B (West, 25B). An inscription published by Śyâmaka, official at Govardhana, by order of Sâtakarṇi Gautamîputra and his mother, Queen Balaśri Gautamî.

This grant is written immediately in continuation of the preceding, and the form of it is very peculiar, as Śyâmaka has apparently given the words of the order (ll. 7 ffg.) exactly as he received them from the donors. It is supplementary to No. 11A, as it makes over a second field to the donees of the former grant, because the field in Aparakakhadî was no longer cultivated and the village had been deserted by its inhabitants.

(6) Siddham Govadhane amachasa Samakasa [6] deyo râjaṇito

---

[1] I admit that it is possible to take *nibadho lihi* as a corruption of *nibaddhâ lipiḥ*, and that the explanation of *lihi* by *alekhi* may be objected to. Still I think the masculines, *chhato* and *uparakhito*, require us to read *nibandho*, which also occurs below, l. 13.

[2] Read *âṇata*. The translation of *aviyeṇa âṇata* by Sans. *mukhâjñâjñaptu**, may be justified from Hemachandra, *Deśîkosha*, I. 10, who explains *anaṁ* by *uktam*, "spoken." The *mukhâjñâ*, "verbal orders," of the king are frequently quoted in land grants. *Chato*, the meaning of which is clear from the varia lectio, *mata*, "approved of," in the next inscription, corresponds to Sanskrit *kshânta*, which may have that meaning (see *Pet. W.*, s. v., *ksham*; and Childers, *Pâli Dict.*, s. v., *kham*).

[3] The beginning of this inscription closely corresponds with that of many Valabhî grants and other documents of the same class, which are dated from a "victorious camp" (*vijayaskandhâvâra*) where the king stopped during his progress. In this case Sâtakarṇi had pitched at Benâkaṭaka—literally "the town, royal residence, or village on the Benâ river"—which belonged to the district of Govardhana or Govadhanâhâra, as inscription No. 18 has it. Perhaps the Benâ intended may be the Benagaṅgâ in the Central Provinces; but as the name is a common one for rivers, it may be one nearer to Nâsik. The army is called *vejayati*, which I take to stand for *vejayantî*, and to be derived from Vijayanta, a name of Indra. Possibly the word may, however, be connected with the name of the famous town, Vaijayantî (Prakrit Vejayantî), the Byzantion of the Greeks, which was situated in the Koṅkaṇ, and doubtless formed part of the Ândhra dominions. If that were the case, the adjective might be translated by "recruited at or lying in garrison at Vaijayantî."

[4] The great lords, *mahâsâmiyâ* (*mahâsvâmikâḥ*), must be the officials in charge of the records.

[5] *Paṭikâ* (*paṭṭikâ*), which I translate by "document," is of course the copper plate or cloth which the donees received. As the old grants were written both on copper and on cloth, I prefer a general word

[6] Read *sâmakasa* in accordance with *sâmako* in the next line, and the etymology, *śyâmaka*

(7) raño Gotamiputasa Sâtakaṇisa mahâdeviya cha jîvasutâya râjamâtuya vachanena Govadhane Sâmako âroga vatavo tato eva [1]

(8) vatavo etha amhehi pavate Tiraṇhumhi amhadhamadâne leṇe pativasatâna pavajitâna bhikhûna gâme Kakhaḍisu puva khetaṁ data ta cha khege [2]

(9) va [3] kaṁsate so cha gâmo na vasati eva sati yaṁ dâni etha nagarasîme râjakaṁ khetaṁ amasatakaṁ tato etesa pavajitâna bhikhûna Teranhukânaṁ dada(*ma*)

(10) khetasa nivataṇasatam 100 [4] tasa cha khetasa parihâra vitarâma apâvesa anomasa aloṇakhâdaka araṭhasavinayika savajâtapârihârika

(11) etehi na parihârehi pariheretha eta chasa kheta parihâra cha etha nibadhâ laṭha aviyena âṇatapaṭihârakhiya [5] Loṭâya matâ lekhe savachhare 24

(12) [*va*]sâna pakhe 4 divase pachame 5 Pujitinâ kaṭâ nibadho nibadho saṁvâchhare [6] 24 gimhâṇa pakhe 2 divase 10 [||]

"Success! A gift which proceeds from the king (*made over*) by Syâmaka (Sâmaka), the minister in (*charge of*) Govardhana.[7] 'By order of the King Sâtakarṇi, the son of the queen of the Gautama race, of the Great Queen, the queen-mother whose son is living, —Śyâmaka in (*charge of*) Govardhana shall be asked about his health,[8] and be afterwards addressed as follows:—We have formerly [9] given a field in the village of Kakhaḍî to the ascetics (*and*) mendicants who live here on the mount Triraśmi (Tiraṇhu) in the cave that is our meritorious gift; and that field is not (*now*) tilled, and that village is no (*longer*) inhabited. As it is so, therefore we give to those ascetics (*and*) mendicants who live on Triraśmi (Tiraṇhu) one hundred, 100, *nivartanas* of a royal field which (*is*) here within the boundaries of the town,[10] and belongs to us. Moreover, we grant for that field immunity (*from interference and taxation, viz.*): it shall not be entered nor meddled with (*by royal officers*) . . . . and be endowed with immunities of all kinds. It has been exempted by these exemptions. And with respect to this field, and with respect to this exemption, a charter has been drawn up [11] (*which has been*) approved of by Loṭâ, the chief lady-in-waiting [12] (*to the Queen-Mother*), who received oral instructions (*regarding this*

---

[1] The three last letters of the line are slightly damaged, especially the *e*; but the reading is not doubtful.

[2] The last letter of the line is misshaped: *taṁ* must be read for *ge*.

[3] This letter is not quite distinct; it most closely resembles *va*, but the sense requires *na*; possibly the cross line is due to a vein or flaw in the rock.

[4] The stroke after Ɔ, the sign for hundred, gives 101, which does not agree with the word preceding: possibly it only indicates that *e* has been left out before *tasa*.

[5] Read *paṭihârarakhiya*, corresponding to Sans. *pratihârarakshî*; *Vikramâṅkacharita*, ix. 7, and *passim*.

[6] Read *saṁvachhare*.

[7] I take *deyo* as the subject of the sentence, for *deyam*, and *râjaṇito*, i.e., *râjaṇiṁto*, for the present participle of the root *ṇî* = *niri* or *niryâ*; *ṇiṁto* is a common form in Mahârâshṭra-Prâkṛit.

[8] Literally, "shall be addressed (*the question if he has*) freedom from disease." This formula is prescribed in the law-books as a polite form of address to Śûdras (*e.g.*, *Âpastamba*, I. 4, 14, 29). Śyâmaka probably belonged to that caste. The form is equivalent to the modern official superscription, *Sâlâmat sâthe*, "after compliments."

[9] *I.e.*, in the year 14, as above.

[10] Possibly Nâsika is meant.

[11] Like Professor R. G. Bhândârkar, but with hesitation, I take *nibadhâ* for the past participle passive; but I am unwilling to correct *laṭha* to *lipi* as he proposes; we may here have an untraced Deśî word, *leṭha* or *laṭha*, meaning "charter" or *śâsana*. The *Deśîkosha*, vii. 28, gives *leso* for "written," and there seems to have been a root *les* or *lis*, meaning to write or compose.

[12] The appearance of a "chief lady-in-waiting" in a grant is unusual, though females appear as *dûtakas* on some Valabhî grants (*Ind. Ant.*, vol. vii, p. 76). The field here granted belonged to the Queen-Mother, and she gave her instructions about the deed to her waiting-woman, who got the grant drawn up by a Kârkun, or writer, in the royal office, and the king's name was inserted to signify his approval of his mother's act, and to secure the immunities which none but the sovereign could grant.

grant), and it has been done in writing by Pujiti[1] on the fifth, 5th, day of the 4th fortnight of the rainy season[2] of the year 24. The charter was drawn up on the 10th day of the 2nd fortnight of the hot season of the year 24.'"

No. 15 (pl. liv). Nâsik, No. 12 (West, No. 3). An inscription dated in the 2nd year of Puḷumâyi—

Sidhaṁ raño Vâsiṭhiputasa Sâmisiri-Pulu-
mâisa saṁvachhare 2 hemaṁtâ [*ṇaṁ*] pakhe 4 divase 8
etiya puvâya [*ku*]ṭuṁbikeṇa Dhaṇameṇa iṇa
kâritaṁ saha [*mâtâ*]pituhi saha . . .
. . ina

"Success! On the 8th day of the 4th fortnight of winter, in the 2nd year of the king, the lord, the illustrious Puḷumâi, the son of the queen of the Vâsishṭha race! On the above-(*mentioned day*) the husbandman Dhaṇama, together with his (*mother*) and father, and together with . . . . made . . . . "

No. 16 (pl. liv). Nâsik, No. 13 (West, No. 27)—

Sidhaṁ raño Vâsaṭhiputasa Siri-Puḷumayisa savachhare chhathe 6 gimapakhe pachame 5 divase 1[3]. po . hi . ti . â

"Success! On the 1st day of the fifth, 5, fortnight of the hot season, in the sixth, 6, year of the king, the illustrious Puḷumâyi, the son of the queen of the Vâsishṭha race . . . ."

No. 17. Karle inscription,[4] No. 20 (pl. liv), from the great Chaitya Cave at Kârlê, on the front of the sill of the great arched window, to the left of the main door, dated in the 7th year of Pulumâyi :—

Raño Vasiṭhiputasa Sâmisiri[-*Puḷumayisa*[5]] savachhare satame 7 gimhapakhe pachame 5
divase pathame 1 [|] etâya puvâya Okhaḷakiyânaṁ Mahârathịsa[6] Kosikiputasa Mitadevasa putena
[*ma*]hârathinâ Vâsiṭhiputena Somadevena gâmo dato Valurakâsaṁghasa[7] [|] Valûrakalenana[8] sakarukarosa deya-
meyo [||]

"On the 1st day, 1, of the fifth, 5, fortnight of the hot season, in the seventh, 7, year of the king, the lord, the illustrious Puḷumâyi, the son of the queen of the Vâsishṭha race. On the above (*day*) the Mahârathi[9] of the Okhaḷakiyas,[10] Somadeva—born of the

---

[1] Pujiti is the stonemason or engraver who incised or *did* the grant in writing.

[2] Several months later than the following date. This is due to the delay in transmitting the orders to Śyâmaka, and getting them engraved.

[3] The letters after this are half effaced and uncertain excepting *hi*.

[4] This has also been translated by Pandit Bhagwânlâl Indrâji, *Inscriptions from the Cave Temples*, p. 34.

[5] There seems to be no doubt about this restoration, as the *i* and *sa* are still perceptible.

[6] The *thi* of this word is not quite distinct, and might perhaps be read *ṭhi*.

[7] Perhaps we should read *Valûrakasaṁghasa ;* the *û* is quite distinct in the repetition of the name.

[8] Read *Valûrakalenânaṁ*. *Sakarukarosa* is, doubtless, a misspelling of *sakârukâraṁ*, *i.e.*, *saṁskârakârya*.

[9] I leave *Mahârathi* untranslated, because I take it to be a title. The word is, probably, closely connected with the old Sanskrit *mahâratha*, "a great warrior," and stands to it in the same relation as *surûpin* to *surûpa ;* but when a person dating his grant by the regnal year of an Andhra king is called the *Mahârathi* of a certain tribe or people, as in this case, it is evident that the word has a technical meaning, and characterises the person indicated as a feudatory or official of the Andhras. The meaning of the term is probably allied to that of *Mahâbhoja* or *Mahâsâmanta*. At all events, M. Garrez's conjecture (*Jour. Asiat.*, ser. vi, tom. xx, p. 203), that it is equivalent to "a Marâṭha," is shown by this inscription to be untenable.

[10] The termination, *-iya*, *i.e.*, *-îya*, frequently means "living in," and it might be expected that Okhalaka was the name of a country. It may be noted that, according to the *Kshitîśavaṁśâvali*, there was a district called Ukhaḍa (see *Pet. Dict.*, s. v.), and possibly Okhaḷaka may be the same.

wife of the Vâsishṭha race (*and*) son of the Mahârathi Mitadeva (Mitradeva), born of the wife of the Kauśika race—gave a village to the community (*of monks*) at Valûraka.[1] This gift (*has been made*) in order to keep the caves at Valûraka in repair."

18. Nasik, No. 14[2] (pl. lii)—

(1.) Siddham raño Vâsiṭhiputasa[3] Siri-Puḷumâyisa[4] saṁvachhare ekunavîse 19 gimhâna pakhe bitîye 2 divase terase 13 râjaraño Gotamîputasa[3] Himavata-Meru-

(2.) Madarapavatasamasârasa Asika-Asaka-Muḷaka-Suraṭha-Kukurâparaṁta[5]-Anupa-Vidabha-Âkarâvatirâjasa[6] Vijhachhavata-Parivâta-Sayha Kaṇhagiri-Macha-Siriṭana[7]-Malaya-Mahida—

(3.) Seṭagiri[8]-Chakorapavatapatisa savarâjalokamaṁḍalapatigahîtasâsanasa divasakarakaravibodhitakamalavimalasadisavadanasa tisamudatoyapîtavâhanasa paṭipuṇachadamaḍalasasirîka-

(4.) piyadasanasa varavâraṇavikamachâruvikamasa bhujagapatibhogapînavaṭavipuladîghasuda[ra]bhujasa abhayodakadânakilinanibhayakarasa avipanamâtususûsâkasa suvibhatativagadesakâlasa

(5.) porajananivisesasamasukhadukhasa Khatiyadapamânamadanasa Saka-Yavana-Palhavanisûdanasa dhamopajitakaraviniyogakarasa kitâparâdhe pi satujane apâṇahisâruchisa dijâvarakuṭubavivadha-[9]

(6.) nasa Khakharâtavaṁsaniravasesakarasa Sâtavâhanakulayasapatiṭhâpanakarasa savamaṁḍalâbhivâditacha[ra]ṇasa vinivatitachâtuvaṇasakarasa anekasamarâvajitasatusaghasa aparâjitavijayapatâkasatujanadupadhasasanîya-

(7.) puravarasa kulapurisaparaparâgatavipularâjasadasa âgamâna nilayasa sapurisâna asayasa sirîya adhiṭhânasa upachârâna pabhavasa ekakusasa[10] ekadhanudharasa ekabamhaṇasa Râma-

(8.) Kesavâjuna-Bhîmasenatulaparâkamasa chhaṇaghanusavaśamâjakârakasa[11] Nabhâga - Nahusa - Janamejaya-Sakara-Yayâti-Râmâbarîsasamatejasa aparimitam akhayam achitam abhuta[12] Pavana-Garuḷa-Sidha-Yakha-Rakhasa-Vijâdhara-Bhûta-Gadhava-Châraṇa

(9.) Chada-Divâkara-Nakhata-Gahavichiṇasamarasirasi jitaripusaghasa nagavarakhadhâ[13] gaganatalam abhivigâdhasa kulavipulasirikarasa Siri-Sâtakaṇisa mâtuya mahâdeviya Gotamiya Balasirîya[14] sachavachanadânakhamâhisâniratâya tapadamani-

---

[1] Valûraka is evidently the name of the monastic establishment at Kârle; it occurs also in the inscription of Usabhadata, on the other side of the door from this.

[2] West's No. 26, first 10½ lines; *Trans. Or. Cong.*, 1874, pp. 306 *seqq.*

[3] See my remarks in Cunningham's *Bharhut Stûpa*, p. 128.

[4] Professor Bhândârkar reads *Puḍumâyisa*, and in other words assigns to 𑀴 the value of *ḍha*, e.g. in *muḍhaka*, l. 2. The correctness of my reading is no longer doubtful; see Dr. Burgess' Table, plate v.

[5] Kukura, *i.e.* Kukkura, is not Kiu-she-lo of Hiwen Thsang, as Professor Bhâṇḍârkar supposes, as the latter regularly corresponds to Gujjara. The *Trikâṇḍaśesha* gives Kukkura as a synonym for Daśârha, a Yâdava tribe.

[6] Âkarâvati,—see Pandit Bhagwânlâl in *Ind. Ant.*, vol. viii, p. 260.

[7] For Viṁjhachhavata, and is a correct translation of the Sanskrit *Vindhyarkshavat—i.e.*, Vindhya and Ṛikshavat—the latter is the Uxentos of the ancients, a part of the Vindhya range near the Narmadâ. Parivâta may be read Parichâta, but I prefer the first as equivalent to Paripâtra, which I take to be the correct form for Pariyâtra, the north-western Vindhyas. Siriṭana cannot stand for Śrîstana, but may be the equivalent of Śrîparvata.

[8] Seṭagiri cannot be Śreshṭagiri, but possibly Śvetagiri, a hill on the Coromandel coast (*Mackenzie Coll.*, vol. i, p. 88).

[9] I take the compound *dijâvara°* to stand for *dvijâś châvarâś cha*, while Professor Bhândârkar makes it *dvijavara°*.

[10] Professor Bhâṇḍârkar correctly emends this as *ekakusalasa*.

[11] I read *chhaṇaghanu°* instead of *chhaṇayanu*, the signs for *gha* and *ya* being very similar. The Sanskṛit is *kshaṇaghanotsavasamâjakârakasya kshaṇeshu ghanân utsavân samâjaṁś cha kârayatîti kshaṇetyâdi tasya.*

[12] I translate these words by *aparimitam akshayam achintyam adbhutaṁ*, and take them as adverbs modifying *jita°* in l. 9. They may also be taken with *vichiṇa°*, which need not be altered as Professor Bhândârkar proposes; it is the regular representative of vichîrṇa, past part. pass. of *vichar*. *Yuddhaṁ vichar* simply means "to fight a battle" (*Pet. Dict.*, s. v. *char + vi*). The passage seems to mean that Wind, Sun, Moon, and other celestial beings, assisted the king in a great battle.

[13] I translate this by *nagavaraskandhât* and take the ablative as ablativus comparationis, which occasionally appears in Sanskrit with the positive instead of the comparative. The phrase seems to mean "of him who, from his majestic greatness and fame, is loftier than the highest mountain."

[14] Balaśrî is the real name of the queen.

(10) yamopavâsataparâya râjarisivadhûsadam akhilam anuvidhîyamânâya kârita deyadhama [kelâsa]pa[vata]sikharasadise Tiraṇhupavatasikhare vimâ[na]varanivisesamahiḍhîka[1] leṇa eta cha leṇa mahâdevî mahârâjamâtâ mahârâjap[i]tâmahî dadâti nikâyasa bhadâvaniyâna bhikhusaghasa

(11.) etasa cha leṇasa chitanânimita mahâdevîya ayakâya sevakâmo piyakâmo cha ṇa[tâ . . . . dakhiṇâ] paṭhisaro pitupatiyo dhamasetusa dadâti gâmaṁ Tiraṇhupavatasa aparadakhiṇapase pisâchipadakaṁ savajâtabhoganiraṭhi [||][2]

"Success! On the thirteenth (13) day of the second (2) fortnight of the hot season in the nineteenth (19) year of the illustrious Puḷumâyi, the son of the queen of the Vâsishṭha family! The great queen Balaśrî, of the Gautama family, who takes delight in truthfulness, liberality, forgiveness, and abstention from injuring creatures, who is intent on practising austerities, self-control, self-imposed restraint and fasts, who regulates her (*behaviour*) entirely in accordance with the (*meaning of her*) title, 'the consort of a royal sage,' who is the mother of the king of kings, the illustrious Sâtakaṇi, (*surnamed*) Gotamîputa (i.e., *the son of the queen of the Gautama race*), of him whose firmness resembled (*that of*) Mount Himavat, Mount Meru, and the Mandara mountain—of (*him who was*) the king of Asika, Asaka, Muḷaka, Surâshṭra, Kukura, Aparânta, Anûpa, Vidarbha, Âkara, Avanti—of him who was the lord of the mountains Vindhya, Ṛikshavat, Pâripâtra, Sahya, Krishnagiri, Macha, Siritana, Malaya, Mahendra, Seṭagiri and Chakora—of him whose orders were obeyed by the multitude of all kings—of him whose face was similar to and pure like a lotus that has opened itself at the rays of the sun—of him whose army drank the water of three oceans—of him whose appearance was agreeable and radiant like the orb of the full moon—of him whose gait was beautiful (*and majestic*) as the gait of an excellent elephant—of him whose arms were long, broad, round, and fat like the folds of the king of serpents—of him whose fearless hand was (always) moist with (*libations of*) water (*poured out*) in giving promises of safety—of him who never disobeyed his mother—of him who properly distinguished the places and times (*fit*) for (*the attainment*) of the three objects (*of human*) life (*dharma*, *artha*, and *kâma*)—of him who fully shared the joys and sufferings of the citizens (*of his realm*)—of him who humbled the pride and arrogance of the Kshatriyas—of him who destroyed the Śakas, Yavanas, and Pahlavas—of him who properly expended the taxes which he levied in accordance with the sacred law—of him who took no pleasure in destroying the life even of offending enemies—of him who made the families of twice-born and low-caste people prosper—of him who entirely destroyed the Khakharâta (Kshaharâta) race—of him who restored the fame of the Sâtavâhana race—of him whose feet were saluted (with prostrations) by all provinces—of him who prevented the mixing of the four castes (varṇa)—of him who conquered his enemies in many battles—of him whose banner of victory was never vanquished, and whose excellent capital was difficult to assail for his foes—of him who bore many royal titles descended to him from a (*long*) line of ancestors—

---

[1] *Kelâsapavata°* is a pretty certain restoration, as the letter *e*, the top of *la*, the greater part of *sa* and *pa* are visible. *Mahiḍhîka* stands for S. *Maharddhika*, Pali *Mahiddhika*. I do not think it has the technical Buddhistic meaning here.

[2] In line 11 *chitanâ* stands, with the usual omission of the anusvâra, for *chintana°*, and apparently means "the taking care of" or "keeping in repair." The word used for it in the next inscription is *paṭisamtharaṇa*. Half the *ta* of *ṇatâ* is visible and the reading certain. The donor is of course Puḷumâyi. Before *paṭhisaro* we may safely supply *dakhiṇâ*. For the other lost letters, probably four, I venture to suggest *Puḷumâyi*, though with some doubt. I take *pitupatiyo* for *pitṛipatnyoḥ*. The third letter of *Pisâchipadakaṁ* is doubtful; if my reading is correct, the name corresponds to *Piśâchîpadraka*, "the site of the she-goblin." I take *savajâtabhoganiraṭhi* as a sentence by itself, and translate it by the Sanskrit *sarvajâtabhoganirasanam*. Strictly the equivalent of *niraṭhi* would be *nirastiḥ*, which, however, is not found in the dictionaries.

of him who was an abode of traditional lore—of him who was the protector of good men—of him who was the dwelling-place of Fortune—of him who was the source of all politeness—of him who alone was clever—of him who alone (*deserved the name of*) an archer—of him who alone (*deserved the name of*) a hero—of him who alone (*was worthy the name of*) a Brâhmaṇa—of him whose prowess was equal to that of Râma, Keśava, Arjuna, and Bhîmasena—of him who on festive days caused to be made much merrymaking and many joyous assemblies—of him whose lustre was equal to (*that of*) Nabhâga, Nahusha, Janamejaya, Sagara, Yayâti, and Ambarîsha—of him who in wondrous, unthinkable, imperishable, and immeasurable wise conquered a crowd of foes (*standing*) in the foremost ranks in a battle fought by Pavana, Garuḍa, the Siddhas, the Yakshas, Râkshasas, the Vidyâdharas, the Bhûtas, the Gandharvas, the Moon, the Sun, the Constellations, and the Planets—of him who dives deeper into the sky than the shoulder of the most excellent mountain—who made the prosperity of his race great—caused to be prepared as a meritorious gift, on the top of Mount Tiraṇhu (Triraśmi), that resembles a peak of [*Mount Kailâsa*], a cave, equal in perfection to a most excellent palace. And the great queen, mother and grandmother of a great king,[1] gives that cave to the community of the Bhadâvanîyas[2] . . . . . . a fraternity of monks. And in order to allow this cave to be (*duly*) taken care of, (*her*) grandson . . . the lord of the [Dakhiṇâ]patha (Dekhan), who is desirous to serve and (to do what is) agreeable to the venerable great queen, gives the village of Pisâchipadaka, (*situated*) south-west of Mount Tiraṇhu (Triraśmi), (*intending it*) as a bridge of merit for his father (*and his father's*) wife. The abandonment of all enjoyments accruing (*to us out of this village has been decreed*)."

The pedigree of the family in this inscription stands thus :—

+ married to Balaśrî of the Gautama gotra

Gautamîputra Sâtakarṇi married + of the Vâsishṭha gotra

Vâsishṭhîputra Puḷumâyi.

No. 19. Nâsik, No. 15—An inscription of Puḷumâyi dated saṁvat 22.

This inscription is a postscript to the last (Nâsik 14, pl. lii), and informs us that the village assigned by Puḷumâyi in his 19th year for the repairs of the Queen's Cave was exchanged, three years later, for what reason is not stated, for another one.

The document is highly interesting, both on philological and palæographical grounds. It contains a number of rare Deśî words, and is written in characters which show traces of a current hand, differing from the usual stiff "cave-alphabet." But these characteristics, as well as its slightly mutilated state, the small size of the letters, and the slovenliness of the stonemason's work, make its translation a task of great difficulty, in spite of the assistance which the three analogous edicts, Nâsik Nos. 11A and 11B (p. 104) and Kârle No. 19 (p. 101), as well as the *Deśîkosha*, afford.

(11b.) Siddhaṁ navanarasvâmî Vâsiṭhîputo Siri-Puḷumavi ânapayati Govadhane amacha.

(12.) Sivakhadila ya amhepa[3] sava 19 gi pa 2 diva 13 Dhanakaṭa samaneni ya etha pate[4] Tira[ṇhumhi] . . . .

---

[1] From this Professor Bhâṇḍârkar argues that Gautamîputra Sâtakarṇi was alive when the grant was made; but this is a mistake. The inscription is dated in the reign of Puḷumâyi, and the epithets here applied to Gautamî Balaśrî indicate her special claim to veneration, whether both her son and grandson or only one were alive.

[2] The Bhadrâyanîyas, a branch of the Mahâsthaviras. *Ind. Ant.*. vol. ix, p. 300.

[3] Read *amhehi;* the beginning of the curve of the *i* is still visible.

[4] Read *pavate.*

. . . na dhavâsetisa[1] leṇasa paṭisatharaṇe akhaya[nîvî]hetu etha Govadhanâhâre dakhiṇamage gâmo Sadasanâ[2] bhikhuhi devileṇavasehi[3] nikâyena Bhadâyaniyena patikhaya datâ etasa dânagâmasa Suda sanâna parivaṭake etha Govadhanâhâre puvama[ge]

(13a.) gâmo Samalipada dadima etata[4] maha airakana[5] odena dhamasetusa leṇasa paṭisatharaṇe akhayaniviheta[6] gâma Sâmalipada ta [. . bhi]khuhi leṇa[vâsehi nikâ]y[e]na Bhadâyanayahi[7] patikhaya uyapaya etasa cha gâmasa Sama[li]padasa bhikhuhalaparihâra

(14.) [8]vitarâma apâlasa[9] anomasa aloṇakhâdaka araṭhasavinavika savajâtapârihârika cha etehi na parihareni pariharîhi eta cha gâma Samalapada parihâre ṇa[10] eṭha nibadha la[11] . . . mi gâmasa cha Sudasanâna vinibakârehi aṇatâ[12] mahâsenapatinâ Medhunana . . . . nâ chhato paṭikâ vâsakehi

(13b.) (hathi chhatâ datâ hi ṇa)[13] sava 22 gi pa diva 7 . sâ . kanena katâ Govadhanavathavana phesakaye V[i]ṅhupâlana sâmivananânata[14] nama bhagatasa[15] patipatapasa jinavarasa budhasa [||]

"Success! The new Nara,[16] the lord, the illustrious Puḷumâyi (Puḷumavi), born of the queen of the Vâsishṭha race, addresses (*these*) orders to Śivaskandila, the minister in (*charge of*) Govardhana;[17] 'On the 13th day of the 2d fortnight of the hot season in the year 19, we gave the village of Sudarśana,[18] (*which is situated*) here in the southern subdivision of the district of Govardhana, as a perpetual endowment for the repairs of the cave (*which is*) a "bridge of merit" for the . . . . (*and has been excavated*) here in the mount Triraśmi, to be administered[19] by the monks of Dhanakaṭaka,[20] the ascetics living in the Queen's Cave, of the school of the Bhadrâyanîyas. In exchange for this gift-village, we have (*now*) given the village of Śâlmalipadra,[21] (*which is situated*) here in the eastern subdivision of the district of Govardhana. This same village of Śâlmalipadra, (*which is*) to be a perpetual endowment for the repairs of the cave (*that is*) "a bridge of merit," has

---

1 Read *dhamasetusa*. 2 Read *Sudasanâ*. 3 Probably *leṇâvâsehi* is to be read.

4 Perhaps *eta cha* is to be read 5 Read *airakena*.

6 Read °*hetu*. 7 Read *Bhadâyaniyehi*.

8 A comparison of Nos. 13 and 14 above shows that line 14 is to be read after the first half of line 13, and that the second half of line 13 concludes the inscription.

9 Read *apâvesa*. 10 Read *cha*. 11 Probably *laṭha* to be read, as in No. 25a.

12 Read *âṇata*. 13 The words in parentheses are uncertain.

14 Read *sâmivachanâ*°. 15 Read *bhagavatasa*; °*patâpasa*.

16 As Nara is a name of Arjuna, and Inscription No. 26 shows that the Andhras compared themselves to the heroes of the *Mahâbhârata*, I think it probable that *navanara*, "the new Nara or Arjuna," is one of Puḷumâyi's *birudas*. In later times various kings assumed the same title. For other possible explanations see Bhâṇḍârkar, *Tr. Or. Cong.*, 1874, p. 318.

17 The whole portion of the inscription down to *katâ*, l. 14, which has been enclosed by hyphens, is introduced by the untranslated *ya*, *yat*, "that," which follows *âṇapayati*, "issues (*these*) orders."

18 Sudasanâ, the name of the village given in the year 19, stands, as is often the case with village-names of the cave inscriptions, in the plural. It corresponds to Sanskrit Sudarśana, "the lovely or fair one," and must be another name for Piśâchîpadra, which is mentioned in No. 16. The term *maga*, "subdivision," means literally "path" (*mârga*), and has probably the same technical meaning as its synonym *pathaka*, which, in the Valabhî, Solankî, and other inscriptions, means "a subdivision of an *âhâra* district or ziliâ," *i.e.*, a tâlukâ or pargana.

19 *Paṭikhaya*, "to be administered," may either be the neuter of the part. fut. pass. of *kshi*, "to govern," with the prefix *prati* (compare *pratikshaya*, "a watchman") or the gen. dat. of *pratîkshâ*, "the looking after." In the former case it would stand for *paṭikhayaṁ*, in the latter for *paṭikhâya*. The neglect of the vowel-marks and of the anusvâra, which is so common in these inscriptions, makes it difficult to come to a definite conclusion regarding the explanation.

20 As *dhanakaṭasamanehi* stands before the lacuna, and *bhikhuhi* a long way from it after the lacuna, it is not certain that the two instrumentals belong together. If my way of construing be correct, it may be inferred that the inmates of the Queen's Cave came originally from a monastery in the Andhra capital. Regarding Dhanakataka, see Bhâṇḍârkar, *loc. cit.*, p. 349, and *ante*, p. 37.

21 *Samalipada* corresponds to Sanskrit Śâlmalipadra and means "the site of the cotton tree."

been made over by the warm-hearted Mahâaïraka[1] to be administered by the mendicants of the school of the Bhadrâyanîyas, living in the cave. And for this village of Śâlmalipadra we grant the immunity (*from taxation and interference suitable*) for a *bhikhuhala*,[2] (viz.,) it is not to be entered nor meddled with (*by royal officers*) . . . . and to be endowed with immunities of all kinds. We exempt it with these exemptions.[3] And with respect to this village of Śâlmalipadra and to (*this*) exemption, a charter has been drawn up, which has been approved of by the commander-in-chief Medhuna (?) . . . who received orders from the . . . . . of the village of Sudarśana. (*And*) a document[4] . . . . which was executed by . . . . on the 7th day of the . . fortnight of the hot season of the year 22 was given (*to the donees*).' Viṇhupâlana[5] (*has been*) appointed by the order of the lord to the charge of the inhabitants of Govardhana. Adoration to the divine Buddha, the best of Jinas, who has attained the glory of Arhatship."[6]

No. 20. Karle, No. 21 (pl. liv)—

This inscription is badly mutilated, and what remains is half obliterated. If, nevertheless, I have attempted to translate the fragments, and believe that the readings and my rendering are tolerably certain, the circumstance which encourages me is that this document is very similar to the three Nâsik inscriptions, No. 14, No. 11A, and 11B, which also contain land grants made in favour of Bauddha mendicants. This resemblance permits us, also, to confidently assign our inscription to one of the two *Andhra* kings who caused the three Nâsik edicts to be incised, *i.e.*, either to *Gautamîputra Sâtakarṇi* or to *Vâsishṭhîputra Puḷumâyi*.

[1.] . . . . [ânâpayati] mâmâ[le] amacha pa . ga . . masu etha lenasa valurakasa vâṭhavâna

[2.] pavajitâna bhikhuna nikâyasa mahâsagh[i]yâna yapanaya etha mâmâlâhâre utaramaga[ge] gâma[me] karajake[su] . . .

[3.] bhikhuhala dadama [|] etesa gâma[me] karajake[su] bhikhuhaladeya papahi [|] etasa cha sa.

[4.] gâmasa karajakâna bhikhuhalaparihâra vitarâma a[pa]vesa . . . . pârihârika cha [|] etehi na parihârehi parihariha[7] [|] ete chasa gâm[e] karajake[su]

[5.] bhikhuhalaparihâre[cha] etha nibadho[lehi] aviyena ânata . . . . to vijayathasâtâre[8] dato ṭhe rañâ paṭikâ sava 1 [4 ?]

[6.] vâ pa 4 diva 1 sivakhadagutena kaṭâ [||]

---

[1] *Mahaaïrak(e)na*, "the Mahaaïraka," must refer to Puḷumâyi. Hemachandra, *Deśîkosha*, i. 16, gives *aïro* in the sense of "an official," *e.g.*, "the lord of a village." Here it may either be a special title; or *aïraka*, which corresponds to the Pâli *ayiraka*, and Sans. *âryaka* (Bhâṇḍârkar, *loc. cit.*, p. 318) may mean simply "the venerable one." *Odena* is the instr. of *oda*, which appears as a varia lectio for *olla*, Sanskrit *ârdra*, "warm-hearted, affectionate," in Hâla's *Gâthâkosha* (see Weber, *Hâla*, index s. v.) and in the Uriya *odâ*.

[2] Regarding *bhikhuhala*, see the remarks on Kârle Inscription No. 19.

[3] *Parihariṁhi*, "we exempt," I am inclined to take as a corruption of *parihariṁhe*, first pers. plur. âtm. In Karle No. 19 we have *parihariha* in its stead.

[4] The name of the commander-in-chief is, of course, corrupt. I am unable to explain *vinibakârehi* or to translate the doubtful words between *paṭikâ* and *datâ*. I think the former term refers again to the king. The general sense of the phrase following *paṭikâ*, "a document," is, I think, certain from No. 11A and Karle No. 19.

[5] *Viṇhupâlana* is probably a mistake for *Viṇhupâlita*, Vishṇupâlita. The translation of *phesakaye* by "to the charge" is based on Hem. *Deś.* vi, 87, where *pheso* is stated to mean *sadbhâva*, "kindness." I think Vishṇu pâlita must have been Śivaskandila's successor, and have been sent after the edict was first issued and before it was engraved.

[6] If *pati*, which corresponds to Pali *patti* (Sanskrit *prâpti*), might mean (as Childers, *Pali Dict.*, s. v., suspects) *nirvâṇa* or "final liberation," that sense would be more suitable.

[7] Read *parihariṁha*.

[8] Read *vijayakhadhâvâre datâthi*.

"[*King*] . . . . addresses [*these*] commands to . . . . the minister in [*charge of*] Mâmâla . . . . we have given for the support of the mendicant friars of the school of the Mahâsaghiyas [Mahâsamghikas][1] who live here in the Valuraka [Valûraka] cave, a *bhikhuhala*[2] here in the village of Karajaka[3] [*which is situated*] in the northern division of the Âhâra [*Zillâ of*] Mâmâla.[4] To them the gift of a *bhikhuhala* in the village of Karajaka has been granted. And we grant for this village of Karajaka the exemption [*from taxes and interference suitable*] for a *bhikhuhala* [viz., *that*] it shall not be entered [*by royal officers*] . . . . and be endowed with immunities [*of all kinds*]. By [*granting*] these immunities we exempt it [*from interference by the revenue officers*]. With respect to this village of Karajaka and with respect to this exemption a deed has here been drawn up by . . . . . . who received verbal orders [*to that effect*] . . . . and a written grant has been given by the king in his victorious camp on the first day of the fourth fortnight of the rainy season in the year 1 [4 ?] [*which has been*] prepared by Sivakhadaguta [Śivaskandhagupta]."

No. 21. Kârlê, No. 22 (pl. liv)—An inscription dated in the 24th year of Puḷumâyi.[5]

(1.) Siddha raṇo Vasiṭhiputasa Siri-Puḷimâvisa savachhare chatuvise 24 hematâna pakhe tatiye 3 divase bi-

(2.) tiye 2 upâsakasa Harapharaṇasa Setapharaṇaputtasya Sovasakasya Abulâmâvâthavasya ima deyadhama maṭapo

(3.) navagabha mahâsaghiyâna parigahe saghe châtudise dina mâtapituna pûjâ[6] savasatâna hitasughasthataya [|] ekatise[7] sa-

(4.) vachhare niṭhito saheta cha me puna Budharakhitena Mâtarakhiâ[8] upâsikâya Budharakhitasa mâtu[9] deyadhama pâṭho ano [||]

—"Success! On the second (2d) day of the third (3d) fortnight of winter, in the twenty-fourth (24th) year of the king, the illustrious Puḷimâvi, the son of the queen of the Vâsishṭha race, this meritorious gift, a hall, has been given to the adherents of the Mahâsaṅghika (*school*), the community (*of monks*) living in the four quarters (*of the world*), by the lay worshipper Harapharaṇa, son of Setapharaṇa,[10] a Sovasaka,[11] living in

---

[1] One of the most ancient divisions of the Bauddhas (conf. *Mahâvaṁso*, v, 4; *Ind. Ant.*, vol. ix, pp. 300, 301; Vassilief, *Bouddisme*, p. 225).

[2] Literally, "a mendicant-plough;" the precise technical meaning of this term is unknown to me, but as the village is also allowed the immunities (*parihâra*) usually granted for *dharmadâna* land, it would seem that the royal share of the produce was made over to the Bauddha mendicants.

[3] This is probably identical with the Karajika which, according to No. 13, Ṛishabhadatta, the son-in-law of Nahapâna, gave to the community at Valûraka. If this be so, we have in this grant one of the effects of the destruction of the Kshaharâta dynasty, of which Gautamîputra boasts in Nasik No. 16.

[4] The term *âhâra*, as we know from the Valabhî grants, corresponds exactly to the modern "Zillâ or Collectorate." The name *Mâmâla* is evidently the ancient form of the modern *Mâvaḷ* (Mâul); the change of medial *ma* to *va* is common in Marâṭhî. *Mâvaḷ* being still the name of the tract along the Sahyâdri or Ghâṭ range, fully corresponds with the position of the ancient *Mâmâla*. We have thus another proof that the lapse of two thousand years has not changed much in the geographical names of Western India and its territorial divisions.

[5] *Cave-Temple Inscriptions*, pp. 36, 37. The spelling, grammar, and execution of this inscription are execrable; but it is epigraphically interesting. Notice, *e.g.*, the form of *i* in *ima*, which recurs on the coins of the Satrap Îśvaradatta and in the Gupta and other later inscriptions.

[6] Read *pûjâya*.

[7] *Ekatise* is not quite certain, as the *ti* has been damaged or badly engraved.

[8] Probably we should read *Mâturakhiâa*, i.e. *Mâtṛirakshitâyâḥ*.

[9] Read *mâtûya*.

[10] As remarked in *Cave-Temple Inscriptions*, these two names are foreign and probably Persian, the former corresponding with the Græco-Persian 'Ὀρσφέρνης or 'Ὀλοφέρνης; and the latter with Σατα... My friend Professor Nöldeke informs me that the termination *-pharaṇa* probably contains the N. Persian *frana* "lord," and that *Seta* may be a corruption of O Persian *kshata*, N. Persian *shîd*. The name of the town Abulâmâ is also foreign.

[11] *Sovasaka* is probably the Sanskrit *Sauvarshaka*, "belonging to the Suvarsha or Kâsyapiya school," a branch of the Sarvâstivadins (Vassilief, *Bouddisme*, p. 231; *Ind. Ant.*, vol. ix, p. 302).

Abulâmâ, in honour of his parents and for the welfare and happiness of all living creatures. In the thirty-first year (*of the same king*) was completed a second passage (?), the meritorious gift of **Mâtarakhi[t]â**, a lay worshipper, the mother of Budharakhita, (*and*) associated with me and with Budharakhita." [1]

No. 22. Nâsik, No. 16 (pl. lv)—An inscription dated in **Srîyajña Sâtakarṇi's** seventh year—

(1.) Sidhaṁ raño Gotamiputasa Sâmi-Siriyaña-Sâtakaṇisa savachhare sâtame 7 hematâṇa pakhe tatiye 3
(2.) divase paṭhame Kosikasa mahâsenâpatisa Bhavagopasa bharijâya mahâsenâpatiniya Vâsuya leṇa
(3.) bopakiyatisujamâṇasa payavesitasa mâne [2] bahukâṇi varisâṇi ukute payavasâne nito châtudi-
(4.) sasa bhikhusaghasa âvâso dato ti[||]

—"Success! On the first day of the third (3rd) fortnight of winter in the seventh (7th) year of the king, the lord **Śrîyajña Śâtakarṇi**, born of the queen of the **Gautama** race, *mahâsenâpatinî* **Vâsu**, the wife of the commander-in-chief, **Bhavagopa** of the **Kauśika** family, completed (*this*) cave after [3] . . . . had been destroyed for many years, and gave (*it as*) a dwelling to the community of ascetics from the four quarters."

X. Nasik Inscriptions of Private Individuals (Plate lv).

1. Nâsik, No. 17 (West, No. 1)—

(1.) Sidhaṁ Sakasa Dâmachikasa lekhakasa Vudhikasa
(2.) Vishṇudataputasa Daśapuravâthavasa leṇa po-
(3.) ḍhiyo cha do 2 ato ekâ poḍhi yâ apara[dhâ] [4] sa me mâtâ-
(4.) [pi]taro udisa [||]

—"Success! (*The gift*) of **Vudhika**, the writer of the **Śaka Dâmachika**, [5] and son of **Vishṇudattâ**, an inhabitant of **Daśapura**—a cave and two, 2, cisterns; of these one cistern which (*lies*) to the west (*is*) for the benefit of my parents."

2. Nâsik, No. 18 (West, No. 2)—

(1.) Sidhaṁ Sakaśa Dâmachikasa
(2.) leghakasa Vudhikasa podhi [||]

—"Success! A cistern, (the gift) of **Vudhika**, the writer of the Saka Ḍâmachika."

3. Nâsik, No. 19 (West, No. 4)—

(1.) Sidhaṁ Otarâhasa Daṁtâmitiyakasa Yoṇakasa Dhaṁmadevaputasa Îdâgnidatasa dhaṁmâtmanâ
(2.) ima leṇaṁ pavate Tiraṁṇhumhi khânitaṁ abbhaṁtaraṁ cha leṇasa chetiyagharo poṁdhiyo cha mâtâpi-
(3.) taro udisa [|] ima leṇaṁ kâritaṁ savabudhapûjâya châtudiśasa bhikhûsaṁghasa niyâtitaṁ sa-
(4.) ha putena Dhaṁmarakhitena [||]

---

[1] The construction of the last sentence is very ungrammatical: *saheta cha me puna Budharakhitena* seems to stand for *mayâ cha Buddharakshitena cha sahitâyâḥ*, and the case termination *sahita* to have been left out, as it is above in *pâḍâ* and below in *mâtu*. The translation of *pâtho* by "passage" I have borrowed from Pandit Bhagwânlâl, though I am not satisfied with it.

[2] L. 3. Possibly we should read *tiajamânasa payavasitasamane*.

[3] The words "*bopkaiyati—mâne*" have been left untranslated, as they are to me unintelligible. *Ukute*—I take to stand for *utkrite*, and the construction to be that of a loc. absolute.

[4] L. 3. The *dhâ* in *uparadhâ* is half obliterated. Possibly *aparato* ought to be read. Read *sd me*, &c.

[5] In the absence of all certainty about the meaning of the word *Dâmachikasa*, it is also possible to take it differently, and to assume that it describes Vudhika as a member of some particular clan of Sakas. Compare also Bhandârkar, loc. cit., p. 344. Regarding Daśapura, see note to No. 13.

—"Success! The righteous Yavana Indrâgnidatta, son of Dharmadeva, a native of the northern country (*and*) inhabitant of Daṁtâmitrî,[1] caused this cave to be excavated on Mount Triraśmi (Tiranhu), and inside the cave a Chaityagṛiha and (*three*) cisterns, for the sake of his parents. This cave, caused to be made for the worship of all Buddhas, has been made over to the community of monks from the four points of the horizon (*by him*), together with his son Dharmarakshita (Dhaṁmarakhita)."

4. Nâsik, No. 20 (West, No. 12)—

(1.) Velidataputasa nekamasa Râmaṇakasa
(2.) Chhâkalepakiyasa lenaṁ deyadhaṁmaṁ châtudi-
(3.) sasa bhikhusaṁghasa niyâtitaṁ [|] data cha-
(4.) nena akhaya nivi kâhâpana sata 100
(5.) saghasa hathe eto vasavuthasa pavaïtasa chivari-
(6.) kaṁ dâtavaṁ bârasakaṁ [||]

—"The merchant Râmaṇaka, a Chhâkalepakîya,[2] the son of Velidata, made over to the community of monks from the four points of the horizon a cave as a meritorious gift. Moreover, he gave a perpetual endowment (*of*) one hundred, 100, *kârshâpaṇas* into the hand of the community. Out of that a piece of twelve shall be given to an ascetic keeping the vasso (*to defray*) the expenditure for a garment."

5. Nâsik, No. 21 (West, No. 13)—

Sidhaṁ Sivamitalekhakaputasa
Râmaṁṇakasa leṇaṁ deyadhaṁmaṁ[||]

—"Success! A cave, the meritorious gift of Râmaṇaka, son of the writer Śivamitra."

6. Nâsik, No. 22 (West, No. 21)—

(1.) Chetika[3] upâsakiyasa Mûgûdâsasa saparivârasa leṇa deyadhama [|] etasa lenasa Bodhiguta
(2.) upâsakasa putena Dhamanadinâ data kheta apariliya Kaṇhahiniya[|] eto khetâto chivarika pavaïta-
(3.) sa [||]

—"A cave, the meritorious gift of Mûgûdâsa, who belongs to the lay-worshippers of the Chaitikas, and of his family. Dharmanandin, the son of the lay-worshipper Bodhigupta, has given a field in Western Kaṇhahini for this cave. Out of (*the income from*) that field the expenditure for a garment for an ascetic (*is to be defrayed*)."

7. Nâsik, No. 23 (West, No. 22)—

Dâsakasa Mugudâsasa saparivârasa leṇa deyadhama [||]

—"A cave, the meritorious gift of the fisherman Mugudâsa, and of his family."

---

[1] For the explanation of the geographical terms see *ante* p. 38, and Professor Bhâṇḍârkar's note, *Tr. Or Congr.*, p. 345. It may, however, be observed that the Sanskrit name of the town is not necessarily Dattâmitrî. The Prakrit form Daṁtâmitıyakasa rather points to "Dântâmitri, (the town) by which, or of him whose foes are subdued or restrained."

[2] *Chhâkalepakiya* stands for *Chhâgalepakîya*, just as *nekamasa* for *negamasa*. The former word may mean, as Professor Bhâṇḍârkar thinks, "an inhabitant of Chhâgalepaka."

[3] The *Chetikas*, in Sanskrit *Chaitikas*, are a subdivision of the Mahâsaṁghika school. Mugudâsa apparently attended the *bhâṇa* of some monk of the school, or, to use a modern phrase, "sat under a Chaitika." Compare Vassilief, *Bauddisme*, p. 228.

8. Nâsik, No. 24 (West, No. 24)—

(1.) Sidhaṁ Viragahapatisa nyegamasa[1] lena
(2.) deyadhama [|] kuṭuṁbiṇiya chasa Naṁdasarâya ovarako [|] duhutu-
(3.) ya chasa Purisadatâva ovârakâ [|] eva leṇaṁ chatugabhaṁ
(4.) ṇiyuta bhikhusaṁghasa châtudisasa niyâchitaṁ [||]

—"Success! A cave, the meritorious gift of the merchant Vîragṛihapati; and one cell, (*the gift*) of his wife Nandaśrî; and (*three*) cells, (*the gift*) of his daughter Purushadattâ. Thus a cave containing four cells has been dedicated and made over to the community of monks from the four points of the horizon."

9. Nâsik, No. 25, pl. lv (West, No. 5[2])—

(1.) Deyadharmmoyaṁ upâsi-
(2.) kâyâ Mammâyâ layanaṁ [||]

—"The meritorious gift of the lay-worshipper Mammâ,[3] a cave."

XI. Ajanta Inscriptions.

No. 1 (pl. lvi). The letters of this inscription[4] closely resemble the Maurya alphabet, and are not of later age than the first half of the second century B.C.

Vasiṭhiputasa Kaṭa-
hâdino gharamukha
dânaṁ

—"A façade, the gift of Katahâdi, the son of the wife of the Vâsishṭha family."

No. 2. This is partially defaced, and possibly very corrupt (pl. lvi). Paṇḍit Bhagwânlâl reads it—

Thânako deyadhamaṁ
Ghanâmadaḍasa vanija[*sa*]
sauvavarako saupâ[*satho*]

With the additions in italics he translates it—

"The meritorious gift of a dwelling with cells (*apavaraka*), and a hall (*upaśraya*), by the merchant Ghanâmadaḍa."[5]

Chammak Copperplate Grant.

The following grant of the Vâkâṭaka king, Pravarasena II., was discovered about 1868 in a ploughed field at Chammak, some seven or eight miles south of Ilichpur. A transcript of it was prepared by Pandit Bhagwânlâl Indrâji, and published in India in 1879.[6] It is incised on

[1] The group in the beginning of *nyegamasa* is really *yne*, but intended to be read as above. *Ye* for *e* is caused by the peculiar pronunciation of the diphthong, which, at present too, often sounds as if it were preceded by the semivowel. *Sa* in *chasa* is purely pleonastic (see No. 2, note). *Niyâchitaṁ* may be a corruption of *niyâtitaṁ*, or a misspelling.

[2] This inscription is not earlier than the end of the fifth or the sixth century A.D., and its characters belong to the northern or central group of alphabets. The form of the *na* shows that it has nothing to do with the southern group.

[3] *Mammâ* probably is a corruption of Mahimâ, just as *Mammaṭa* is of Mahimabhaṭṭa.

[4] *Cave-Temple Inscriptions*, p. 67.

[5] This name is utterly corrupt.

[6] *Notes on the Buddha Rock-Temples of Ajaṇṭa*, p. 54, seqq. The plates were obtained by Major H. Szczepanski and forwarded by him to the late Dr. J. Wilson of Bombay, by whom they were lent to the late Mr. Bhâu Dâjî.

seven plates measuring 3·6 inches by 7·5, and on an average about an eighth of an inch thick each. They are hung on a ring about 3¾ inches outside diameter, formed of copper rod ⅛ inch thick, the ends of which overlap and have been hammered together, but not welded. On this is hung a seal 2·8 inches diameter and about 3/16 thick, slightly convex in front from the hammering-in of a small ring or "eye" by which to run it upon he larger ring. The first and last plates are inscribed on the inner sides only. The execution of the inscription is good, though the engraver has left out a few syllables, and it has been fairly well preserved. The alphabet resembles that of the Seonî grant,[1] and of the Ajaṇṭâ inscription (No. 3) of the same dynasty. The little sunk square at the top of the letters,[2] so characteristic of the Vâkâṭaka and Chhatisgaḍh alphabets, is a marked feature of the Ilichpur grant. To judge from the style of the letters, the document belongs to the first half of the fifth century A.D.

The language is not very grammatical Sanskṛit. Half a dozen bad grammatical mistakes occur in the middle of it, and towards the end, in the list of names, the use of the case endings is scant and irregular. The spelling is sometimes faulty, *e.g.* in *sakliptopakliptaḥ* (IV*a*, 3), and the Sandhi rules receive little attention. The omissions and mistakes, however, can be nearly all corrected by the help of the Seonî plates, which were engraved only a few months earlier, and copied from the same model. Down to III*a*, l. 4, the text of both grants is almost literally the same.

In translating the Seonî grant, Prinsep's Pandits have unfortunately done their task in a very slovenly manner, and press of work seems to have prevented the illustrious epigraphist from checking them. This circumstance, as well as the fact that very unsatisfactory attempts have been made to harmonise the information respecting the Vâkâṭakas furnished by the Ajaṇṭâ inscription in Cave XVI. with the statements of the two grants, induce me to present a short summary of the historical facts known about these Vâkâṭakas.

Vâkâṭaka—a word which unfortunately does not admit of an etymological explanation —is both the name of a country and of the Râjpût tribe governing it. In the latter sense it is used in the frequently recurring phrase of the two grants, "the great king of the Vâkâṭakas" (*vâkâṭakânâm mahârâja*), in the epithet "the ornament or chief of the Vâkâṭakas" given to Pravarasena II. on the seal of the two grants, and in the expression "the banner of the Vâkâṭaka race" (*vâkâṭakavaṁśaketu*)—Ajaṇṭâ inscr. l. 3. It denotes a place in the compound *Pavarajja-Vâkâṭaka*, the name of a village to the north of Brahmapûra, mentioned in the Seonî grant. The position of the kingdom of the Vâkâṭakas is fixed partly by the sites where the two grants have been found and partly by geographical names mentioned in the inscriptions. The Ilichpur grant was found seven or eight miles south of Ilichpur in the northern corner of the Berars. It is quite clear that the modern village of Chammak is the representative of the ancient Charmâṅka, conveyed by the *S'âsana* "to one thousand Brâhmaṇas of various schools and families." For, according to the strict laws of the ancient Prâkṛits, Charmâṅka would become Chammaṅka, to which the present name comes very near. The identification of the village of Charmâṅka permits us to infer that the Ilichpur district corresponds with the province (*râshṭra*) of Bhojakaṭa, and that the river Madhu, on which Charmâṅka lay, is one of the tributaries of the Pûrṇâ. In the case of the second grant which was found at Seonî, half-way between Nâgpur and Jabalpur, I am not in a position to identify, on the maps at my disposal, any of the villages named. But the

---

[1] *Jour. As. Soc. Beng.*, vol. v, p. 729, *seq.*

[2] This seems to have been cut out with a small chisel, and the copper raised from it in very many cases lies over part of the upright stroke of the letter, rendering it very difficult to obtain a satisfactory facsimile.—J. B.

document contains an allusion to the Beṇâgaṅgâ (Waingaṅga on the maps), which, flowing southwards, falls into the Paingaṅgâ. It is found in the word which Prinsep's Pandits have read *Erṇâkâryyaratâge*,[1] and have failed to explain. The facsimile gives very plainly *Berṇâkârpparabhâge*, "in the portion called *Berṇâkârppara*." It is possible that the reading is correct, but as *bhâga* is not often used for a territorial division, I should prefer to change it to *bhoga*, which like *bhukti* may denote an Inâmî district or a Zilla, and in the *Koshas* is given as an equivalent of *râjya*. *Kârppara*, which is evidently a Taddhita formation derived from *karpara*, "a skull," "Udumbara tree," &c., can have various meanings. Perhaps the whole compound might be literally translated, "in the district on the Berṇâ where the Udumbara trees grow." But, however this may be, the word Berṇâ occurs, and can refer only to the Beṇâgaṅga. Under these circumstances, General Cunningham's proposal[2] to fix the boundaries of the kingdom of the Vâkâṭakas, approximately between the Mahâdeva hills on the north, the Godâvarî on the south, the Ajaṇṭâ hills on the west, and the sources of the Mahânadî on the east, may be accepted. The Ilichpur grant giyes the name of the capital as Pravarapura, evidently so called in honour of one of the two Pravarasenas. General Cunningham[3] feels certain that the modern Bhâṇdak must have been the ancient capital of the Vâkâṭakas, and seems inclined to derive the former name from the latter. If Bhândak is correctly spelt with an initial *Bh*, it cannot have any etymological connection with Vâkâṭaka. But, in case it could be shown that Bândak is the correct form, or that Bhândak had another, more ancient name, the identification might perhaps stand.

According to the two land grants, the pedigree of the Vâkâṭaka kings is as follows:—

1. Pravarasena I.
   |
   Gautamîputra, married to a daughter of the great king, Bhavanâga Bhâraśiva.
   |
2. Rudrasena I.
   |
3. Prithivîsheṇa.
   |
4. Rudrasena II., married to Prabhâvatiguptâ, daughter of the great k. of kings Devagupta.
   |
5. Pravarasena II.

The whole dynasty belonged to the Vishṇuvṛiddha gotra. According to Baudhâyana's *Gotrapravaranirṇaya*,[4] the Vishṇuvṛiddhas are a subdivision of the Bharadvâjas, and a Brahmanical family. It does not, however, necessarily follow that the Vâkâṭakas were Brâhmaṇas. For, according to the *S'rauta-Sûtras* and the compilations on gotras, it was the practice of royal families to be affiliated to the Vedic gotra of their domestic chaplain.

As regards the history of the individual princes, we learn regarding Pravarasena I. that he offered a good many Śrauta sacrifices. The fact that *Aśvamedhas* or horse-sacrifices were among their number, and the title *samrâj*, "universal king," which he assumes, shows conclusively that he was independent and did not owe allegiance to a paramount power. His reign was probably a long one, as he survived his son. If I am right in assigning the two land grants, on epigraphic evidence, to the middle of the fifth century A.D., Pravarasena I. must have ascended the throne about 300 A.D.; for, as Pravarasena II. is the fifth descendant of the first king, and twenty-five to twenty-six years is the duration of an Indian generation, the interval between the two Pravarasenas is 125 to 130 years.

Pravarasena's son, Gautamîputra, died, as already stated, before his father; for the

---

[1] Seonî grant, pl. iiia, l. 1–2.
[2] *Archæological Reports*, vol. ix. p. 123.
[3] *Archæological Reports*, vol. ix, p. 124.
[4] Weber, *Cat. Berl. MSS.*, p. 60.

fact that he receives no title of any kind, and that he is only incidentally mentioned in the paragraph referring to his son, shows that he did not actually rule. The name given to him is not his real proper name, but a metronymic, which designates him as the child of a wife of Pravarasena I., who belorged to the Gautama gotra. General Cunningham has published[1] my remarks on the use of metronymics by the ancient princes of India, and has given his adhesion to my explanation, which is based on the observation of the practice still prevailing among the Râjpûts. Gautamîputra, it appears, made a great marriage, and obtained the daughter of the Bhâraśiva king, Bhavanâga, for his wife. The epithets applied to the Bhâraśiva clan give a punning explanation of the name, which is derived from their having carried Siva's emblem as a load (*bhâra*) on their shoulders, and show that their seat lay to the north of the Vâkâṭakas, on the Ganges (Bhâgîrathî). Possibly the Bhârasivas are the same as the Bhâr Râjpûts.

Regarding Rudrasena I. nothing is stated except that he was an ardent devotee of the Lord Mahâbhairava, or, in other words, a Saiva who worshipped Śiva in his form as Bhairava. This reticence, and the circumstance that the preceding and following reigns were long ones, make it probable that he sat on the throne for a short time only. His reign probably fell between 340–350 A.D.

About Rudrasena's son, Pṛithivîsheṇa, who also was a worshipper of Śiva (*atyanta-mâheśvara*), the grants say that "his treasures, means of government, and line increased during a hundred years, and that he had sons and grandsons." The correct explanation of this phrase seems to be that he ruled for a long time, and saw his sons and grandsons grow up. The expression "a hundred years" need not, of course, be taken literally. His reign probably lasted up to the end of the fourth century, or from about 350–400.

Prithivîsheṇa's son, Rudrasena II., seems to have forsaken the creed of his fore-fathers, and to have chosen Vishṇu as his *ishṭadevatâ*; for the grants say that "he obtained great prosperity through the favour of divine Chakrapâṇi." He was married to Prabhâvatîguptâ, the daughter of the great king of kings, Devagupta. The title given to Devagupta shows that he must have been a greater man than the Vâkâṭaka king. It is, unfortunately, hopeless to speculate at present on the question where his dominions lay. I would only warn against the assumption that every ancient king whose name ends in *gupta* must necessarily be a member of the so-called Gupta dynasty which ruled in the third and fourth centuries over a great part of Central and Western India. Rudrasena II. probably reigned for a few years only, and his end may be placed about 410–415 A.D.

His son, Pravarasena II., again returned to the Śaiva creed, as he receives the epithet *paramamâheśvara*, and is said to have been a prince worthy of the Kṛitayuga, "through the favour of Śambhu." Both the grants are dated in his eighteenth year, the Seoni one in the month of Phâlguna (February–March), and the Ilichpur grant in Jyeshṭha (May–June). In the former the Senâpati is Bâppadêva,[2] and in the latter, Khatravarman. It seems to me improbable that Pravarasena, in the course of a few months, had two different commanders-in-chief; and I think the term *senâpati* rather denotes here the commander of the troops in the district in which the village granted lay, and should be rendered by "military governor." As Charmânka (Chammak) was situated in the province of Bhojakaṭa and Brahmapûra in Karanjaviratata, two different persons would naturally be employed.

---

[1] See *Barahut*, p. 129.

[2] So the lithograph; the transcript gives, erroneously, *Nâpyadeva*, and the translation, Bappadeva.

Transcript.

Plate I.

[1.] Om̃ Om̃ svasti Pravarapurâd agnishṭomâptoryyâmokthyashoḍaśyâtirâttra-
[2.] vâjapeyabṛihaspatisavasâdyaskrachaturaśvamedhayâjinaḥ
[3.] Vishṇuvṛiddhasagotrasya samrâ[jo] Vâkâṭakânâm̃ mahârâja-Srî-Pravarasenasya [1]
[4.] sûnoḥ sûnoh atyantasvâmimahâbhairavabhaktasya ansa[am̃sa]bhârasannivesi- [2]
[5.] taśivaliṅgodvahanaśivasuparitushṭasamutpâditarâjava[m̃]śâ-

Plate II.—First Side.

[6.] nâm parâkramâdhigatabhâgîratthyâmalajalamûrddhnâ[rddhâ]bhishiktânân daśâ-
[7.] śvamedhâvabhṛithasnâtânâm bhâraśivânâm̃ mahârâja-śrî-Bhavanâgadau-
[8.] hitrasya Gautamîputrasya putrasya Vâkâṭakânâm̃ mahârâja-śrî-Rudrase-
[9.] nasya sûnor atyatna[nta]mâheśvarasya satyârjjavakâruṇyaśauryyavikramana-
[10.] yavinayamâhâtmyâdhi[dhî]matva[Hva]hâ[pâ]trâgatabhaktitvadharmmavijayitva-

Plate II.—Second Side.

[11.] manonairmmâ[rmma]lyâdiguṇais samupetasya varshaśatam abhivarddhamânakośa-
[12.] daṇḍasâdhanasantânaputtrapauttrinah Yudhishṭhiravṛitner[tter] Vvâkâṭakâ-
[13.] nâm̃ mahârâja-śrî-Pṛithivi[vî]sheṇasya sûnor bbhagavataś chakrapâṇeḥ prasâ-
[14.] dopârjjitaśrîsamudayasya Vâkâṭakânâm̃ mahârâja-Srî-Rudrasena-
[15.] sûnor mmahârâjâdhirâja-Srî-Devaguptasutâyâm̃ Prabhâva-

Plate III.—First Side.

[16.] tîguptâyâm utpannasya sambhoḥ prasâdadhṛitikârttayugasya
[17.] Vâkâṭakânâm paramamâheśvaramahârâja-Srî-Pravarasenasya vachanâ[t]
[18.] Bhojakaṭarâjye Madhunadîtaṭe Charmmâṅkanâmagrâmaḥ râjamânikabhûmi-
[19.] sahasrair ashṭâbhiḥ 8000 śatrughnarâjaputra-Koṇḍarâjavijñâ[jña]ptyâ nânâgo-
[20.] tracharaṇebhyo brâhmaṇebhyaḥ sahasrâya dattaḥ

Plate III.—Second Side.

[21.] yatosmatsantakâ[ḥ]sarvvâdhyakshâdhiyoganiyuktâ âjñâsañcha[ñchâ]rikulaputrâdhikṛitâ
[22.] bhaṭâchchhâ[śchhâ]trâścha viśrutapûrvvayâjñayâjñâpayitavyâ viditam astu vo yathe- [3]
[23.] hâsmâkam manodharmmâyurbbalavijayaiśvaryyavivṛiddhaye ihâmutra hitâ-
[24.] rttham âtmânugrahâya vaijai[jayi]ke dharmmasthâne apûrvvadatyâ udakapûrvva-
[25.] matiṣrishṭaḥ athâsyochitâm̃ pûrvvarâjânumatâm̃ châturvvaidyagrâmama-
[26.] ryyâdânvi[mvi]tarâmas tad yathâ akaradâyî abhaṭachhchhâ[chchhâ]trapraveśya[ḥ]

Plate IV.—First Side.

[27.] apâram̃paragobalibardda[ḥ] apushpakshirasandoha[ḥ] avarâ-
[28.] sanavarmmâṅgâra[ḥ] aravaṇaklinnakreṇibanakaḥ sarvvaveshṭipari-[4]
[29.] hâraparirhṛi[rihṛi]taḥ sanidhis sopanidhiḥ sakli[klṛi]ptopakli[klṛi]ptaḥ
[30.] âchandrâdityakâlîyaḥ putrapautra[trâ]nugamakaḥ bhuja[ñja]tâm̃ na ke-
[31.] nachid vyâghâtam̃[taḥ] karttavyas sarvvakriyâbhis sa[m̃]rakshitavyah para[ri]varddhayi-
[32.] tav[vy]aś cha yaś châ[śche]yam̃[dam̃] śâsanam agaṇayamâno svalpa[pâ]m api (pa)ribâdhâ-

---

[1] In line 3 the second and third aksharas are battered and the third illegible: with the lithograph of the Seonî plate I read *Vishṇuvṛiddha;* Prinsep's transcript has *Vishṇurudra.*

[2] In line 4 the plate reads apparently *asabhâra°*, but the reading given is confirmed by the *varia lectio* of the Seonî lithograph, *ansasannivesita°*.

[3] In line 22, in '*pûrvvayâ*' the *pû* has first been made *mu* and then corrected as far as practicable.

[4] L. 28. The Seonî lithograph has *alivanatlinvakrenidhanataḥ*, which is as corrupt as *alavaṇa°*.

Plate IV.—Second Side.

[33]. ṅkuryyât kârayitâ vâ tasya brâhmaṇair vveditasya sadaṇḍanigrahaṁ kuryyâ-
[34.] maḥ asmiṁś cha dharmmâvarakaraṇe atîtânekarâjadatna[tta]sañchintana-
[35.] paripâlanaṁ kṛitapuṇyânukîrttanaparihârârtthaṁ na kîrttayâmaḥ
[36.] vyâsagîtau châtra ślokau pramâṇî[ṇî]karttavyau svadattâm paradattâṁ
[37]. vvâ yo hareta vasundharâṁ gavâṁ śatasahasrasya hantu-

Plate V.—First Side.

[38.] rharati dushkṛitaṁ shashtiṁ varshasahasrâni[ṇi] svargge modati bhû-
[39.] midaḥ âchchhettâ chânumantâ cha tâny eva narake vased itiś[ti] śâsana-
[40.] sthitiś cheyaṁ Brâhmaṇair Îśvaraiś chânupâlanîyâ tad yathâ râjñâṁ sa-
[41.] ptâṅge râjye addrohapravṛintâ[ttâ]nâṁ brahmaghnachôrapâradârikarâjâ-
[42.] pathyakâriprabhṛitînâṁ saṅgrâma[ma]kurvvatâṁ anyagrâmeshv ana-

Plate V.—Second Side.

[43.] para[râ]ddhânâṁ âchandrâdityakâlîyaḥ atonyathâ kurvvatâm anumoda[di]tâ[ta]vyô
[44.] râjñaḥ bhûmichchhedaṁ kurvvatah asteyam iti prâ[pra]tigrâhiṇaś châtra
[45.] vâraniyuttâ[ktâ]ḥ Śâṭyâyanaḥ Gaṇâryyaḥ Vâtsya-Devâryyaḥ Bhâradvâja-
[46.] Kumâraśarmmâryya[ḥ] Pâraśaryya-guhaśarmmâ Kâśyapa-Devâryyaḥ Maheśvarâ-
[47.] Mâtrâryyaḥ Kauṇḍiṇya-Rudrâryya[ḥ] Somâryya[ḥ] Hariśarmmâryyaryya[ḥ].[1]

Plate VI.—First Side.

[48.] Bhâradvâja-Kumâraśarmmâryya[ḥ] Kauṇḍiṇya-Mâtriśarmmâ Varaśarmmâ
[49.] Goṇḍaśarmmâ Nâgaśarmmâ Bhâradvâ[ja]-Śântiśarmmâ Rudraśarmmâ Vâtsya[syâ]ḥ
[50.] Bhojakadevâryya[ḥ] Maghaśarmmâ Devaśarmmâ Bhâradvâja-Mokshaśarmmâ
[51.] [Nâ]gaśarmmâ Revatiśarmmâ Dharmmâryya[ḥ] Bhâradvâja-Śarmmâryya[ḥ] [2]
[52.] Nandanâryya[ḥ] Mûlaśarmmâ Îśvaraśarmmâ Varaśarmmâ

Plate VI.—Second Side.

[53.] Vâtsya-Skandâryya Bhâradvâja-Bappâryya Dharmmâryya Âtreya-Skandâryya
[54.] Gautama-Somaśarmmâryya Bhatṛiśarmmâryya Rudraśa(*rmmâ*)ryya Maghâryya Mâtṛi-
[55.] śarmmâryya Îśvaraśarmmâryya Gautamasagotra-Mâtṛiśarmmâ-
[56.] ryya Kauṇḍiṇya-Devaśarmmâryya Varaśarmmâryya Rohâryya

Plate VII.

[57.] Gautamasagotra-Svâmide(vâ)ryya Revatîśarmmâryya
[58.] Jyeshṭhaśarmmâryya Śâṇḍilya-Kumâraśarmmâryya Svâtiśarmmâ-
[59.] ryya Śâṭyâyaṇa[na]-Koṇḍâryyaprabhṛitayaḥ senâpatau
[60.] Khatravarmmaṇi saṁvatsareshṭâdaśe 18 Jyeshṭhamâsaśukla-
[61.] pakshe trayodaśyâm śâsanaṁ likhitam iti

On the Seal.

Vâkâṭakalalâmasya
kkramaprâptanṛipaśriyaḥ
râjñaḥ Pravarasenasya
śâsanaṁ ripuśâsanaṁ

---

[1] L. 47. Delete the last *ryya*.
[2] L. 51. First letter obliterated.

Translation.

Oṁ, Oṁ,[1] hail; from Pravarapura! [2] By command of the illustrious Pravarasena, the great king of the Vâkâṭakas, the ardent devotee of Maheśvara, who, through the possession of Śambhu's favour, is (*a ruler*) worthy of the Kṛitayuga, who was born of Prabhâvatîguptâ, the daughter of the great king of kings Devagupta, (*and who is*) [3] the son of the illustrious Rudrasena, the great king of the Vâkâṭakas, who gained great prosperity through the favour of the divine Chakrapâṇi, (*and who was*) the[4] son of the illustrious Pṛithivîsheṇa, the great king of the Vâkâṭakas, who behaved like Yudhishṭhira,[5] whose treasure, means of government, and line increased during a hundred years, and who had sons and grandsons, who was gifted with such excellent qualities as truthfulness, uprightness, mercy, heroism, bravery, political wisdom, modesty, high-mindedness,[6] intelligence, devotedness to worthy men and guests, ability of making righteous conquests, and purity of mind, who was an ardent devotee of Maheśvara (*and*) the son of the illustrious Rudrasena, the great king of the Vâkâṭakas, (*who was*) the son[7] of Gautamîputra (and) the daughter's son of Bhavanâga, the great king of the Bhâraśivas—who bathed after the celebration of ten horse-sacrifices, whose heads were sprinkled with the pure water of the Bhâgîrathî, obtained by their valour,[8] and whose royal line was produced by Śiva, exceedingly pleased with their carrying in procession his liṅga, that had been placed as a burden on their shoulders—who (viz., Rudrasena) was exceedingly devoted to the Lord Mahâbhairava, (*and who was*)[9] the son's son

---

[1] Though the two first signs look like *dṛishṭaṁ* or *dṛiptaṁ*, I think they cannot be read otherwise than I have done. For an anusvâra is visible above either of the two syllables. There are, further, among the numerous varieties of the letter *o*, some which are similar to those here employed. Finally, it is a practice not uncommon on Sanskrit inscriptions, to place two Oṁkâras at the head, and to use a different form for each (see *e.g.* the facsimile of the Ignodâ śâsana, *Ind. Ant.*, vol. v, p. 56). The beginning of the Seonî plates (*J. R. A. S. Beng.*, vol. v, p. 729) is, according to Prinsep's facsimile, *O, Om, siddham*. The two small makâras are so-called *arddhamakâras*, and mark, as is usual in the Gupta and other old inscriptions, the vowelless, final *m*.

[2] The peculiar construction of the text makes it necessary to give the description of the last king first. The corresponding Sanskrit passage occurs pl. iii*a*. l. 2, and those who wish to control the translation have to go backwards from that point.

[3] Prinsep's transliteration and translation of the Seonî plates give *sthâne*, "in the place of," for *sûnoḥ*, "the son of." But the facsimile has the latter reading (plate ii*b*. l. 2).

[4] Prinsep again reads and translates *sthâne*. His lithograph (pl. ii*b*. l. 1) reads *sûno bhagavata°*, omitting the *r* above *bha*.

[5] The compound *abhivardhamânakoshadaṇḍasâdhanasantânaputrapautriṇaḥ* consists of two adjectives, which both refer to the king, *abhivardhamânakoshadaṇḍasâdhanasantâna* and *putrapautrin*. It is possible to take *daṇḍasâdhana*, which I have assumed to be a tatpurusha compound as a dvandva. Prinsep's transcript gives wrongly *santata* for *santâna*, while his lithograph has *santana*.

[6] It is worthy of note that the Seonî plates have exactly the same mistakes as ours. The copy reads *mâhâtmyadhimatvahâtrâgatabhaktitva*, which the transcript erroneously renders by *mâhâtmyâdhimakhanotragatabhaktitva*. I have given my corrections above. *Pâtra*, which I substitute for *hâtra*, means "a worthy person," and especially "a Brâhmaṇa worthy to receive gifts." The compound *pâtrâgatabhaktitva* may either be translated "devotedness to worthy guests," or as has been done above. To offer hospitality to distinguished Brâhmaṇas is a duty of kings which the Smṛitis inculcate repeatedly (see *e.g. Âpastamba Dharmasûtra*, ii. 10 25. 4, 8–9).

[7] Prinsep's transcript of the Seonî plates omits by mistake the end of pl. ii*a*. l. 1, and the whole of l. 2. His translation is one series of mistakes.

[8] The correctness of the translation of the beginning of the compound, *aṁsabhârasanniveśitaśivaliṅgodvahanaśivasuparitushṭasamutpâditarâjavaṁśânâm*, is attested by the various reading of the lithograph of the Seonî plates, *ansa-(aṁsa-)sanniveśita*. Prinsep's transcript gives wrongly, *indusannibhaśita* and *śivasya paritushṭa*.

[9] Prinsep's transcript gives wrongly, *sthâṇesthâne*.

[1] of the illustrious Pravarasena, the great king of the Vâkâṭakas, a universal ruler, who belonged to the Vishṇuvṛiddha *gotra*, and offered an Agnishṭoma sacrifice, an Âptoryâma, an Ukthya, a Shoḍaśin, an Âtirâtra, a Vâjapeya, a Bṛihaspatisava, a Sâdyaskra, and four horse-sacrifices;[2]—at the request of Prince Kondarâja, the destroyer of his foes, the village called Charmmânka, in the kingdom of Bhojakata, on the bank of the river Madhu, (*and containing*) eight thousand (8000) *bhûmis*,[3] measured by the royal measuring-rod, has been given to one thousand Brâhmaṇas belonging to various families and schools.

Wherefore[4] our obedient noblemen and officers who are appointed to the office of general overseers, (*our*) soldiers and umbrella-bearers, should be given the (*following*) order, preceded by (*the word*) *viśruta*[5] (famous):—

"Be it known to you that, in order to increase our spiritual merit, life, strength, conquests, and rule, for the sake of our welfare in this and the next world, (*in fact*) in order to benefit ourselves, (*the above-mentioned village*) has been given, at our victorious Office of Justice,[6] as a new donation, (*the act of giving*) being preceded by a libation of water."

Now (*as*) appropriate for this (*village*), we grant the charter of a village inhabited by Brâhmaṇas versed in the four Vedas, such as has been approved of by former kings. That is as follows:—"(*The village*) shall be free from taxes, it shall not be entered by soldiers or parasol-bearers . . ., it shall not furnish flowers and milk . . . ., it shall be free from all obligation of furnishing forced labour, it is granted with[7] the right of treasure-trove and of (*keeping unclaimed*) deposits . . . . . ., it (*has been granted*) for as long a time as the moon and sun endure, and shall descend to the sons and grandsons (*of the donees*). Nobody shall cause hindrance to them while they enjoy it. It shall be protected by all means, and be made to prosper. And him who, disregarding this edict, even slightly annoys (*the donees*) or causes them to be annoyed, we will fine and punish, if he is denounced by the Brâhmana (*proprietors*)."

"And in this document,[8] which procures at least spiritual merit, we do not mention the care and protection bestowed (*by us*) on grants made by various former kings, in order to avoid boasting of meritorious actions performed (*by us*)."

---

[1] Prinsep's transcript gives wrongly *ukta* for *ukthya*, *vishṇurudra* for *vishṇuvṛiddha*, and *kâṭarkânâm* for *vâkâṭakânâm*.

[2] For analogous cases of grants being made at the request of a third person, a feudal baron, see inscr. from Nepal No. 9 (*Ind. Ant.*, vol. ix, p. 172).

[3] *Bhûmi* must here be a technical term, and denote a particular measure of land.

[4] *Asmatsantakâ*[*ḥ*] simply means "our." *Santaka* is a Prakritic derivative from *sat*, pres. part. of *as*, "to be," which is common in Pâli; see Childers' *Dict.*, s. v. *Chhâttra*, "umbrella-bearer," includes probably the whole host of menial servants attached to the court.

[5] I am unable to refer to any passage where the title *viśruta* is given to Râjpûts. For Brâhmanas the title *vichakshaṇa*, "learned," is prescribed.

[6] *Dharmasthâna* is, more accurately speaking, not only the Ministry of Justice, but the office where all business relating to justice, spiritual matters, and charities is transacted.

[7] The right of treasure-trove is guaranteed to learned Brâhmaṇas by the *Smṛiti* (see *e.g. Vasishṭha*, III. 14). According to the *Smṛiti*, deposits, the owner of which cannot be found, go, like all unclaimed property, to the king. From the above passage it would appear that kings usually relinquished this right in Agrahâras.

[8] I take *karaṇa* in the sense of "document," and suppose that the king means to say that if the grant does not produce the many rewards enumerated above, it will at least procure spiritual merit. The Seoni plates have a *varia lectio*: *dharmâdhikaraṇe*, which may possibly mean, "in this court of justice (where we give this edict.)." The rest of the phrase is there mutilated, the words *kîrtanaparihârârtham na* having been left out by mistake.

"And with respect to this matter, two verses, sung by Vyâsa, must be acknowledged as authoritative :—

(1.) 'He who resumes land given by himself,' &c.

(2.) 'The giver of land rejoices,' &c.

"And the conditions (*of*) this (*charter*) must be observed both by the Brâhmaṇas and by the (*future*) rulers (*of the country*). That is as follows :—[1] 'The king shall allow (*the village to be held*) by the (*Brâhmaṇas*) as long as moon and sun endure, if they do not commit treason against (*his*) government, which consists of seven essential parts, and if they are not guilty of offences (*e.g.*) of slaying Brâhmaṇas, committing theft, adultery, or acts prejudicial to the king, (*or*) engage in frays with other villages : if the king takes the land from those who act otherwise, (*he will*) not (*be guilty of*) theft.'

"And the donees appointed here for the occasion (*are*) :—Gaṇârya a Śâṭyâyana, Devârya a Vâtsya, Kumâraśarmârya a Bhâradvâja. Guhaśarman a Pâraśarya, Devârya Maheśvara Mâtrârya (*three*) Kâśyapas, Rudrârya, Somârya (*and*) Harisarmârya, (*three*) Kauṇḍinyas, Kumâraśarmârya a Bhâradvâja, Mâtṛiśarman, Varaśarman, Goṇḍaśarman, Nâgaśarman, (*four*) Kauṇḍinyas, Sântiśarman (*and*) Rudraśarman (*two*) Bhâradvâjas, Bhojakadevârya, Maghaśarman and Devaśarman, (*three*) Vâtsyas, Mokshaśarman, Nâgasarman, Revatîśarman, (*and*) Dharmârya (*four*) Bhâradvâjas, Śarmârya, Nandanârya, Mûlaśarman, Îśvaraśarman (*and*) Varaśarman (*five*) Bhâradvâjas, Skandârya a Vâtsya, Bappârya (*and*) Dharmârya (*two*) Bhâradvâjas, Skandârya an Atreya, Somaśarmârya, Bhartṛiśarmârya, Rudraśarmârya, Maghârya, Mâtṛisarmârya (*and*) Îśvaraśarmârya (*six*) Gautamas, Mâtriśarmârya of the Gotama family, Devaśarmârya, Varaśarmârya and Rohârya (*three*) Kauṇḍinyas, Svâmidevârya, Revatîśarmârya and Jyeshṭhaśarmârya of the Gautama family, Kumâraśarmârya (*and*) Svâtisarmârya (*two*) Sâṇḍilyas, Koṇḍârya a Sâṭyâyana, and so forth."

This edict has been written while Khatravarman was commander-in-chief (*senâpati*) in the eighteenth (18) year on the thirteenth day of the bright half of the month Jyeshṭha.

Seal.

An order of King Pravarasena, who is the ornament of the Vâkâṭaka (*race*), and has obtained his royal dignity by inheritance, is an order (*even*) for his enemies.

No. 3. The inscription (pl. lvii) in Cave XVI. has already been transliterated and translated by Paṇḍit Bhagwânlâl Indrâji,[2] who, with great care and pains, prepared beautiful facsimiles of it and the other inscriptions. The following transcript does not much differ from his, who, as usually, has done his work very well. Some of his emendations have also been adopted.

(1.) udîrṇṇalokatrayadoshavahni-nirvvâpaṇâ . . . . [|] . . . . ti praṇamya pûrvvâm pravakshye kshitipânupûrvvî[m || 1 ||]

---

[1] The text, as it stands, gives no sense, and it seems that the words have been transposed through a mistake of the copyist. I correct and arrange them as follows :—*râjñâ saptânge râjye adrohapravṛittânâm* [*a*]*brahmaghnachorapâradârikarâjâpathyakâriprabhṛitînâm samgrâma*[*m a*]*kurvatâm anyagrâmeshvanaparâddhânâm âchandrâdityakâliyomimoditavyaḥ | atoanyathâ kurvatâm râjño bhûmichchhedam kurvatosteyam iti* ||. Regarding the seven essential parts (*anga*) of the kingdom, see *Vishṇu*, III. 33. *Anyagrâmeshu*, which I have construed with *samgrâmam akurvatâm*, may also be taken with *anaparâddhânâm*.

[2] *Cave-Temple Inscriptions*, p. 69.

(2.) mahâvimarddeshv abhivṛiddhaśaktiḥ kruddhas surair apy anivâryya[*vîryaḥ* |] . . . . . . ṇadânaśaktiḥ dvijapḥ prakâso bhuvi Vindhyaśa[*ktiḥ* || 2 ||]

(3.) purandaropendrasamaprabhâvaḥ svabâhuvîryyâ[*rji*]ta[*sarvalokaḥ* |] . . . . kânâṁ babhûva Vâkâṭakavaṁśake[*tuḥ* || 3 ||]

(4.) raṇe [*sva*]haryyutthitareṇujâla-sañchchhâditârkka . . . . [|] . . . . narâtîn kṛitvâbhivâdapravaṇâ[ṁ]ś chakâra [|| 4 ||]

(5.) [*vini*]*rjitâri*[*s sura*]râjakâryyaś-chakâra puṇyeshu paraṁ praya[*tnam* |] . . . . [|| 5 ||] [*ari*]narendramaulivinyastamaṇikiraṇâlîḍhakramâmbujaḥ [|][1]

(6.) Pravarasenas tasya putrobhûd vikasannavendîvarekshaṇa[ḥ || 6 ||] ravimayûkhada . . . . [||] [*dra*]senah Pravarasenasya jitasarvvasenas suto bhavat [|| 7 ||]

(7.) . . . . pârtthivendrasya praśa[śâ]sa dharmmeṇa medinî[*m* |] Kuntalendra[ṁ] vi[*jitya*] . [*Pṛi*]thivî[*shenaḥ*] . . . . [|| 8 ||] Pravarase[*nas ta*]sya putrobhût pravarorjjitodâraśâsanaḥ [|] pravara

(8.) . . . . [|| 9 ||] . . . . yâtmaja . ma . . . . [|] . . . . . . [*ma*]-vâpya râjyam ashṭâbdako yaḥ praśaśâsa samya[k || 10 ||]

(9.) tasyâ[*tmajo*]bhûn naradeva . . . . bhuvi Devasenaḥ [|] yasyopabhogair lalitair vvi . . . devarâjasya . . . . bhûḥ [|| 11 ||] puṇyânubhâvât kshitipasya [*tasya*]

(10.) . . . . [|] . . . . . yaguṇâdhivâso - . . . kośo bhuvi Hastibhojaḥ [|| 12 ||] pra . . . . ḥ pṛithupînavakshâṣ-saroruhâkshaḥ kshapi-

(11.) . . . . [|] . . . . -diggandhahastipratimo babhûva [|| 13 ||] hito vinîtaḥ praṇaya . . . -manonukûlonuvidhânavarttî[|]niratyaya

(12.) . . . . kaścha[|| 14 ||] ta[*thai*]va loka suhitâśayatvât-sukhena[2] samya[*kpa*]ripâlanena [|] . . . mâteva sakheva nityaṁ-priyobhigamyaś cha babhûva

(13.) . .[|| 15 ||] . . . . [|] svasthas samâveśya sa tatra râjâ-[*sasa*]ñja bhogeshu yatheshṭacheshṭaḥ [|| 16 ||] atha tasya suto babhû

(14.) [*varâjâ*]- . . . . [|] hari[*râma*]harasmare[va]kântir-Harisheṇo[3] harivikkramapratâpaḥ[|| 17 ||] sa Kuntalâvanti-Kaliṅga-Kosala-Trikûṭa-Lâṭândhra-

(15.) . . . . . . [|] . . . . pi svanirdeśa . . . . . . [|| 18 ||] prathito bhuvi Hastibhojasûnus-sachivas tasya mahîpater bbabhûva [|] sakalakshiti-

(16.) . . . . [|| 19 ||] . . . jeshṭa sthiradhîrachetâs-tyâgakshamaudâryyaguṇair upeta[*ḥ* |] dharmmeṇa dharmmapravaṇaś śaśâsa-deśam yaśaḥpuṇyaguṇâśu

(17.) . . [|| 20] . . . . -. prati puṇyopachayaṁ paraṁ chakâra [|] yata ûrddhvam adas sahâya-dharmmâ-parito lokagurau chakâra kârâ . [|| 21 ||] âyurvvayovittasakhâṇi

(18.) . . . . lâni [|] u[*ddiśya*] mâtâpitarâv udâraṁ-nyavîviśad veśma yatîndra[*sevyam* || 22 ||] sajalâmbuda . . . ddhitâgre-bhujagendrâdv yushite mahîdharendre [|]

(19.) . . . . śrîpatinâ śarâ nikuñje [|| 23 ||] gavâkshaniryyûhasuvîthivedikâ-[*su*]rendrakanyâ-pratimâdyalaṁkṛitam [|] manoharastambhavibhaṅga-

(20.) [*meduraṁ*] . . . . . -[*uddhu*]rachaityamandira[ṁ|| 24 ||] ma . . . . . talasannivishṭa-vi . . . . . mano[*bhi*]-râmaṁ [|] . . . . ñchâmvumahânidhâna[ṁ]-nâgendraveśmâdibhira

(21.) . . . . [|| 25 ||] . . . . samaraṇâ . . . . [|] grîshmârkkasya cha kiraṇopatâ[*pa*]-ta[*ptaṁ*]-sarvartuprathitasukhopabhogayoga[ṁ || 26 ||]

---

1 Unfortunately, it has not been possible to determine accurately the metre of the very important verses 6–9 (ll. 5–7), which have baffled Bhagwânlâl Pandit also They look like *Mâtrâchhandas*, allied to the *Vaitâlîya*, with fourteen to sixteen mâtrâs in each pada; but they do not agree with any of the varieties noticed by the known writers on metrics; the new readings and restorations, therefore, remain uncertain. From the extent of the lacuna between *pravarase* and *sya* in vs. 9*a* (l. 7), it seems impossible that only one syllable should have been lost; two are required to fill it, and these were probably *nas ta*. The reading—*pravarasenas tasya*—thus obtained, recommends itself, because Pravarasena's son, Rudrasena, has already been mentioned in l. 6, and because the Seoni and Ilichpur plates name two Pravarasenas, and the correction thus brings this inscription into accord in this respect with the plates. Of the name of the son of Pravarasena I. mentioned in vs. 7, *-drasena* is left, and we may safely restore it as Rudrasena, as in the grants. In vs. 8 (l. 7) the first legible word is *pârthivendrasya*, "of the best of princes," and suggests that *tanayas tasya*, "the son of that," should be supplied before it; and as Rudrasena's son was Pṛithivîsheṇa, and in the middle of the lacuna in vs. 8 *pra* or *pṛi* is faintly visible, and after it *thivî*, it seems highly probable that Pṛithivîsheṇa's name had been here.

2 The reading violates the metre; perhaps *loke suhitâ°* or *lokeshu hitâ°* should be read.

3 Sl. 17. Read *°smarendrakântir.*

(22.) . . . . [su]rendramandirâṇâ[ṁ]-ruchiman[ma]ndarakanda . . . . [|] . . . . ha[ṁ]-yathepsita . [|| 27] asama[prati]rochane girer-vaka

(23.) . . . . . . sramâ . kâ . [|] laya . . . . [|| 28 ||] . . . . yasya janena nâma-prîtiprasâdavikachapraṇayena chakre [|] [e]ta

(24.) . . . . layanaṁ surendramauli-[prabho]pachita . . . . hâya [|| 29 ||] nivedya saṅghâya . . . . gya-sabandhuvarggas sa Varâhadevaḥ [|] nṛidevasaukhyâny anubhûya

(25.) . . . . . śâstâ Sugatapraśastaḥ [|| 30 ||] sândrâmbhodabhujangabhoga . . . . . ma . . . . nna-manaś śilâlakapilair yyâvat karair bhâsvaraḥ [1] [|] tâvach chhe

(26.) . . . . sevyatâm antarmmaṇḍaparatna[m e]tad amalaṁ ratnatrayodbhâvita[ṁ || 31 ||] vividhalayanasânus sevyamâno mahadbhir girir aya

(27.) . . . . ddhya [|] yad api cha samastavyastadoshaprahâṇâ [d] [vi]śatu padam aśokaṁ nirjvaraṁ śântam âryya [ṁ || 32 ||]

1.[2] "Having adored [*Buddha who taught*] . . . . the extinction of the high rising flames of the three worlds' sins, I will declare the ancient succession of kings.

2. "There was a famous twice-born man on earth [*named*] Vindhyaśakti, whose strength grew in great battles—whose valour, when he was angered, could not be overcome even by the gods . . . . . mighty in gifts.

3. "He whose majesty was equal to that of Indra and of Upendra (*Vishṇu*), who by the valour of his arm gained [*the whole world*], became the banner of the Vâkâṭaka race . . . .

4. "He, covering in battle the sun with the dust-clouds raised by his horses' hoofs, making his enemies . . . . caused them to become prone to salute.

5. "Having conquered his enemies, living like the king of gods, he strenuously exerted himself to (*gain*) spiritual merit . . . .

6. "His son was Pravarasena, whose lotus-feet were kissed by the rays from the gems on the heads of [*hostile*] princes, and whose eyes resembled fresh opening lotuses.

7. "The rays of the sun . . . . Pravarasena's son was [*Ru*]drasena, who conquered all armies.

8. "[The son] of [that] king, [*Pṛi*]thivî[*sheṇa*] . . . . [*having conquered*] the lord of Kuntala, righteously ruled the earth.

9. "His excellent son was P . varasena, who gained exalted rule . . . .

10. "[*His*] son . . . . [*was*] . . . . who, having obtained the kingdom when eight years of age, ruled well.

11. "His son was . . king . . . . . . on earth Devasena, through whose lovely enjoyments . . . . of the king of gods . . . . . .

12. "Through the greatness of the spiritual merit of [*that*] king, Hastibhoja . . . . the abode of . . . virtues, a treasury of . . . . . on earth [*became his minister*].

13. ". . . broad and stout of chest, lotus-eyed, ... he resembled a scent-elephant [*guarding*] a point of the horizon.

14. "Good, modest . . . . agreeable, obedient . . . .

15. "Likewise, as, owing to his desire for the good of the world (?), he well and happily protected it, he was . . always dear and accessible like . . . . . a mother, like a friend.

---

[1] Read *karair bhâskaraḥ* (Bhagwânlâl).

[2] Metres:—ll. 1, 2. Upajâti. 3. Upendravajra. 4. Upajâti. 5. Upajâti or Upendravajra. 6–9. Metre doubtful. 10. Upajâti or Upendravajra. 11. Upendravajra. 12. Indravajra. 13. Upajâti. 14, 15. Upendravajra.

16.[1] ". . . . . The king, being at ease, and having installed [*him*], there attached himself to enjoyments according to his heart's desire.

17. "Then his son became [*king*] . . . . Harishena, who in beauty resembled Hari, Râma, Hara, Cupid, and Indra, who was brave like a lion.

18. "He [*conquered*] Kuntala, Avanti, Kaliṅga, Kosala, Trikûta, Lâṭa, Andhra . . . .

19. "The son of Hastibhoja, famous on earth, became the minister of that king. The whole earth . . . .

20. "Beloved by . . . ., of staid and tranquil mind, endowed with the virtues of liberality, patience, and generosity, intent on justice, he ruled righteously [*excelling by*] glory, spiritual merit, and great qualities.

21. "For . . . . he laid up a very great store of merit, after which he, to whom the sacred law is a helper to gain the other world, made a prison (?) all around for the teacher of the world.

22. "Life, age, wealth . . . . For the sake of his parents he built a splendid house to be inhabited by the best of ascetics.

23. "On the best of mountains, the top of which [*is covered*] with water-bearing clouds, and which is inhabited by serpent-lords . . . .

24. "Adorned with windows, spires, beautiful terraces, ledges, statues of the nymphs of Indra and the like, [*supported*] by lovely pillars and stairs . . . . a lofty Chaitya-building.

25. ". . . . . placed on the ground . . . . lovely . . . . a storehouse of . . . . . with dwellings of Nâgas and the like . . . .

26. ". . . . . and warmed by the heat of the rays of the summer sun, affording the enjoyment of comfort at all seasons.

27. ". . . . . of the palaces of the lords of the gods, [*standing in the*] ravines of the brilliant mount Mandara . . . .

28. "On the exceedingly brilliant . . . . of the . . mountain . . . .

29. "That cave clothed in the brilliance of Indra's crown, which the joyous and pleased people affectionately called . . . .

30. "Having presented [*the cave*] to the community of monks . . . . . that Varâhadeva, together with the crowd of his relatives, having enjoyed the happiness of a king . . . . a ruler, praised by Sugata.

31. "As long as [*the earth rests*] on the . . . . . folds of the serpent, [*and*] the sun shines with rays yellow like red arsenic, so long may this pure [*cave*], which internally contains a gem-like hall, and which was made for the sake of the three gems [*Buddha, Dharma, Sangha*], be enjoyed . . . .

32. "[*May*] this mountain, which possesses various caves and summits, which is inhabited by great . . . . May also the world, by renouncing all its manifold sins, enter that state which is free from sorrow and pain, that is tranquil and worthy."

---

[1] Metres :—*ll.* 16. Upajâti. 17. Aupachchhandasika. 18. Vaṁśasthâ. 19. Aupachchhandasika. 20. Indravajra. 21. Aupachchhandasika. 22. Upajâti. 23. Aupachchhandasika. 24. Vaṁśasthâ. 25. Upajâti. 26. Praharshiṇî. 27, 28. Aupachchhandasika. 29. Vasantatilaka. 30. Upendravajra. 31. Śârdûlavikrîḍita.

Remarks.

Mr. Bhâû Dâjî, in 1863,[1] was the first to give a tolerably accurate facsimile and transcript of the inscription on Cave XVI., as well as of the other Ajaṇṭâ inscriptions. In his opinion,[2] Vindhyaśakti was the first prince of the Vâkâṭaka race, and was probably identical with the chief of the Kailakila Yavanas[3] mentioned in the *Purâṇas.*[4] Among other speculations, Pravîra (according to him, Pravara), whom the *Vâyupurâṇa* makes the son of Vindhyaśakti, was the same as Pravarasena II. The remarks prefixed to Paṇḍit Bhagwânlâl Indrâji's improved transcript and translation,[5] are much more correct and free from the extravagances which disfigured Mr. Bhâû Dâjî's speculations.

Owing to the fragmentary state of the Ajaṇṭâ inscription, it is impossible to say whether one or more names may not have been lost in the four lines (ll. 2–5), or whether they contained the eulogy of Vindhyaśakti alone, and that the words, *Pravarasenas tasya putrobhût,* "his son was Pravarasena," may mean that the latter was Vindhyaśakti's son. The chief discrepancy, however, between the *Vaṁśâvali* or genealogy in this inscription and in the Seonî and Chammak grants, is that it makes Pravarasena II. the son of Pṛithivîsheṇa, while the grants insert Rudrasena II. between them. But as the Ajaṇṭâ inscription dates three reigns, or about eighty years, later than the grants, and was issued, not by the king himself, but by a minister, while even the grants say little about Rudrasena II., whose reign was probably a short one, the omission may be excused, or explained as omitted purposely. The two genealogies may be represented thus :—

Ajaṇṭâ Inscription.			*Land Grants.*
1. Vindhyaśakti,	cir. A.D.	285–310	
2. Pravarasena I., son (?),	„	310–345	Pravarasena I.
3. (Ru)drasena I., son,	„	345–360	Rudrasena I., grandson.
4. Pṛithivîsheṇa, son,	„	360–410	Pṛithivîsheṇa, son.
5. *Omitted.*	„	410–420	Rudrasena II., son.
6. Pravarasena II., son,	„	420–450	Pravarasena II., son.
7. ———— son,	„	450–475	
8. Devasena, son,	„	475–500	
9. Harisheṇa, son,	„	500–520	

No. 4. The subjoined transcript has been prepared from the new facsimile (pl. lvi), and does not differ much from Pandit Bhagwânlâl's.[6] The translation differs, however, a good deal from the earlier ones, and the differences somewhat affect the historical interpretation of the document.

Pandit Bhagwânlâl is probably right in assuming that the Harisheṇa mentioned in l. 21 is the Vâkâṭaka prince whose name occurs in Ajaṇṭâ No. 3, and that the Vâkâṭakas were the lords paramount whom these rulers obeyed. The characters belong to the

---

[1] *Jour. Bom. B. R. As. Soc.*, vol. vii, pp. 53–74.

[2] *Ibid.*, p. 66.

[3] The Ajaṇṭâ inscription (v. 2) distinctly states that the Vâkâṭaka Vindhyaśakti was a "distinguished Ârya" (*dvijaḥ prakâśaḥ*), while the Kailakila, according to the *Purâṇas*, was a foreigner—not necessarily a Greek. Not a single name in the Kailakila dynasty agrees with those of the Vâkâṭakas; and all the MSS. of the *Vâyu*, consulted by Prof. H. H. Wilson, Dr. Hall, and myself, give the name Pravîra, not Pravara.

[4] *Vishṇu-Purâṇa* (ed. Hall), vol. iv, pp. 209–211.

[5] See *Cave-Temple Inscriptions*, pp. 69, *seqq.*

[6] *Cave-Temple Inscriptions*, p. 73, *seq.*

Northern, or rather the central group of alphabets. With the Southern alphabets they have nothing to do, as is evident from the forms of *ta* and *na* used here. The inscription probably belongs to the end of the fifth or the beginning of the sixth century A D.

The *Vaṁśâvali* is as follows :—

1. Dhṛitarâshtra
2. Harisâmba
3. Saurisâmba
4. Upendragupta
5. Kâcha I.
6. Bhikshudâsa
7. Nîladâsa
8. Kâcha II.
9. Kṛishṇadâsa

10. * *not known* — Ravisâmba

The names show that the family deity of the dynasty was Vishṇu-Kṛishṇa. The first prince began, probably, to reign about 250 A.D.

[1.] . . . . mâ[vanim]-praṇamya vidyâtrayapâraga[m] munim [|] vihâradâtur vyavadâtakarmaṇo guṇâbhidhânopanayaḥ karishyate ||

[2.] . . . . ne[na]-labdhâtmabhâvasya narâdhipasya [|] dhṛitâtapatrasya babhûva putras-sitatapatro Dhṛitarâshṭrasaṁjñaḥ [||]

[3.] . . . . sya râjño-Harisâmbomburuhendukântavaktraḥ [|] nṛipates tanayo babhûva tasy[â] py amalaśrî[ḥ] kshitipâlaśaurisâmba[ḥ ||]

[4.] . . . . [śa]-prithukîrttir dyutimân Upendraguptaḥ [|] samabhûd ava . s suto[1] tha tasya-kshitipaḥ Kâcha iti prakâśanâmâ [||]

[5.] . . . . [d-bhu]vi kîrttinyasanâya Bhikshudâsaḥ [|] pracitho bhuvi Nîladâsanâmâ-nṛipatis tasya suto narâdhipasya ||

[6.] . . . . -prathitaḥ Kâcha iti pradîptakîrttiḥ [|] nṛipater atha tasya Kṛishṇadâsaḥ-kulavaṁśa-dyutivarddhano babhûva ||

[7.] . . . . -[sta]nayâ chandrakarâvadâtaveshâ. [|] abhavat paripûrṇachandravaktrâ-vinayâchâra-vibhûshaṇâ [Su]chandrâ ||

[8.] . . . . dyotakarîm avâpa[|] tasyâñ cha tasyâmburuhâyatâkshâv-uttaptachâmîkara-kântar[û]pau [||]

[9.] . . . . -[pradyu]mnasâmbapratimau kumârau[|] ekâdhipatyaṁ prathamovatâraṁ[2]-daddhre dvitîyo Ravisâmbasaṁjñâm[||]

[10.] . . . . samaśmakâdi[bhiḥ |] . nu tâbhyâm abhibhûya bhûyasâ-rarâjatuś chandradivâkarâv iva ||

[11.] . . . . [|] vivṛiddhasauhârdda[yaśa]ḥpratânayos-sadânukûlyena sukhaṁ vijahr[usho]ḥ [||][3]

[12.] . . . . vair apy anivâryyaśâsanaḥ [|] purâkṛitodbhâvitabhîmavikramaḥ-kanîyasi pra-[syata.] . . tâśaniḥ ||

[13.] . . . . vadhairyyâ . . . . . . jaḥ [|] achityasaṁjñaḥ sachivas tataḥ paraṁ-vyavîvig dhat puṇyamahâmahîruham ||

---

[1] L. 4. Pandit Bhagwânlâl, who has seen the original inscription, says that *avanas suto* or *agajas suto* may be read. The facsimile has *ava*, the last letter is illegible.

[2] L. 9. Read *ekâdhipatyam prathamo babhâra*, as the sense requires. The *va* is very indistinct, and may be intended for *ba*. *Ta* and *ba* are hardly to be distinguished in this inscription.

[3] L. 11. The *u* stroke attached to the *hr* is very faint, and of the *sho* only *o* distinctly visible. But the reading is certain, as sense and grammar require the form *vijahrushoḥ*, the gen. loc. part. perfect act. *vijahrivas*.

[14.] . . . . tatosham [|] bhûyaśśrutatyâgadayâpramoda-maitrîkshamâvîryya-dhiyas sisheve ||

[15.] . . . . [na]rendrân[|] praśastavṛittân suviśuddhavṛitto-vṛittena samyakshu-bhitonuchakre [1] ||

[16.] . . . . chakâra [|] artthikasyârtthijanas tathaiva-kîrtti[ṁ] [2] kṛitârtthaḥ pratha-yâṁ babhûva ||

[17.] . . . . sa . . bhiplutâkshân [|] amûmuchad vittavisarggaśaktyâ-putrâdhicheshṭân karuṇâbhimṛishṭaḥ ||

[18.] . . . . [ye]na putravat [|] anûchivâṁsopi hi yasya hṛidgatâṁ-vidanraṿadhyâśa-[ya]śuddhisampadam ||

[19.] . . . . karâṇi sadyaḥ [|] sarvvajñabhâvapraṇidhânasiddhiḥ-satyâbhidhânâbhi-bhavâd apeyuḥ ||

[20.] . . . . cha . . yogaḥ [|] yaśoṁ[śu]bhiś [3] chandramarîchiśubhraiḥ-jjagat samagra-[ṁ vi]malañ chakâra ||

[21.] . . . . vadanâravindachandre [|] paripâlayati kshitîndrachandre-Harisheṇe hitakâriṇi prajânâm ||

[22.] . . . . tyadbhutapuṇyarâśi[ḥ |] [chak]r[e] bhuva [4] stûpavihârabhûshâ-dânodayaiś chârtthi[ja]napramodam [||]

[23.] . . . . nâ . . nâ[da]vadbhi[ḥ |] . . . . hadbhir-a . . . . ma . sahyapâde ||

[24.] . . . . gâmbhîryyaguṇair upetam [|] niveśitântarmunirâjachaityam-ekâśmakaṁ maṇḍaparatnam etat ||

[25.] . . . . vipulaṁ visṛijya [|] achîkarach chaityam[ahî]nakalpam-alpâtmabhiḥ kalpanayâpy aśakyam ||

[26.] . . . . nayanâbhirâmam [|] nyavîviśat svâdulaghuprasanna-śîtaprakâmâmbuma-hânidhânam ||

[27.] . . . . nnetramanobhirâmâm [|] anyâ[ṁ]gadeśesya diśi pratîchyâm-achîkarad gan-dhakuṭîm udârâm ||

[28.] . . . . ddhitâyodyatasarvvakarmmaṇa [5] [|] munîndranâthapraṇidhânasiddhaye-bhavantv abhîshṭâ bhuvi sarvvasampadaḥ ||

[29.] . . . . praṇayena maṇḍapa[ḥ |] karotu tâvat kuśalodayaṁ satâṁ-nihanti yâvad ravir aṁśubhis tamaḥ || Oṁ

1. ". . . . . . Having adored the ascetic who completely knows the three sciences [*Piṭakas*], I will set forth a description of the donor of the *Vihâra* whose deeds are pure.

2. ". . . . . to the king who had obtained existence through . . . . and who wore a parasol [*over his head*], a son named Dhṛitarâshṭra was born, who possessed a white parasol.

3. "[*The son*] . . . . . of that king was Harisâmba, whose face was lovely as a lotus, and the moon. Again, the offspring of that king was king Śaurisâmba, possessed of spotless beauty.

4. "[*His son was*][6] . . . . resplendent Upendragupta of wide-spread fame. To him was born a . . . son, whose famous name was king Kâcha.

---

[1] L. 15. Read *samyakkshubhito.*

[2] L. 16. Read *kîrttim*, as an object to *prathayâm babhûva* is required. In *tathaiva* the second letter is not quite plain.

[3] L. 20. *yaśomśubhiḥ* looks like *yaśombubhiḥ*, as Paṇḍit Bhagwânlâl reads. But the resemblance is caused only by the loss of the left-hand vertical stroke of the *śa*.

[4] L. 22. Read *chakre bhuvam* . . . . *bhûshâm.*

[5] L. 28. Read *°sarvvakarmaṇâm.*

[6] The relation of Upendragupta to Saurisâmba, and that of Bhikshulâsa to Kâcha, is, of course, not certain.

5. "[*From him was descended*] . . . . . in order to deposit his fame on earth, Bhikshudâsa. The son of that ruler was called Nîladâsa, famous on earth.

6. "[*His son was*] . . . . he who is known as Kâcha, of brilliant fame. Then Kṛishṇadâsa became the increaser of the splendour of that king's race and line.

7. "[*His wife*] was Suchandrâ,[1] the daughter of . . . ., clad in garments pure as the moon's rays, whose face resembled the full moon, whose ornaments were modesty and virtuous conduct.

8. ". . . . . obtained . . . . causing brilliancy . . . On her he [*begat*] two lotus-eyed, almond-eyed [*sons*], with bodies lovely like burnished gold.

9. ". . . . . two princes resembling Pradyumna and Sâmba. The elder one bore the office of sole ruler, the second bore the appellation, Ravisâmba.

10. ". . . . . [*with* or *by*] Aśmaka and others . . . having conquered with very great . . . they shone like sun and moon.

11. ". . . . ., while those two whose creeper-like friendship and glory had grown very much, were living always in concord and happiness,

12. "The thunderbolt of . . . . whose decree is not to be evaded even by . . . . . and whose dread strength is produced by deeds done in former existences, was hurled on the younger one.[2]

13. ". . . . . Afterwards a minister, called Achitya, made the great tree of spiritual merit grow.

14. ". . . . . he worshipped those who possess great learning, liberality, mercy, contentment, friendship, patience, heroism and wisdom.[3]

15. ". . . . . Greatly moved by [*their*] conduct, he whose own conduct was very pure imitated the princes whose conduct is praised.[4]

16. "He made . . . ., and likewise needy men whose wants were satisfied, spread the fame of him who . . . .

17. ". . . . . by the power of an expenditure of wealth, he who was touched by compassion freed those who were struggling with cares for their sons, and those whose eyes were overflowing . . . .

18. "By whom as by a son . . . . the store of purity of whose heart even learned men.[5] . . . .

19.[6] ". . . . .

---

[1] The restoration of the queen's name, Suchandrâ, is suggested by the following considerations:—Firstly, a short syllable has been lost before *chandrâ*, and the three syllables together form a separate word; secondly, Suchandra is a not unusual name for males and females; thirdly, the verse contains two puns on *chandrâ*, whence it is probable that the word occurred in the queen's name.

[2] The meaning of the verse is that the younger brother perished suddenly by an accident or died of a disease.

[3] This and the following verses refer, in my opinion, solely to the minister, the donor of the vihâra. The persons whom he worshipped or served are the Bauddha monks

[4] Greatly moved by (*their*) conduct, *i.e.*, by the piety of the monks, "he imitated the princes," *i.e.*, he showed princely liberality.

[5] Though the latter part of the verse is almost completely preserved, it seems impossible to accept the text as correct. In the transcript the words have been given exactly according to the facsimile. It seems that some mistake of the engraver or poet is concealed in *vidanravadhyâśaya*°. The sense seems to be that even learned men, *i.e.*, those acquainted with the sacred law, had to acknowledge the minister's purity of heart.

[6] The general sense of the verse seems to be that misfortunes fled (*apeyuḥ*) from the pious minister being overcome by his supplications (*praṇidhâna*) addressed to Buddha (*sarvajñabhâva*). I do not risk a translation, as there seems to be a corruption in °*siddhiḥ*, which, as it stands, interrupts the construction.

20. ". . . . . He purified the whole world by the light of his fame, which was resplendent like the rays of the moon.

21. " While [*that*] moon-among princes, Harisheṇa, who did what was good for his subjects, ruled . . . .

22. ". . . . . he who possessed a prodigious store of merit adorned the earth with *stûpas* and *vihâras*, and gave great joy to the needy by lavish liberality.

23. ". . . . .

24. ". . . . . this monolithic, gem-like hall, in which a *Chaitya* of the king of ascetics has been placed, and which is endowed with the excellent qualities of depth and . . . . . .

25. ". . . . . having expended much [*money*], he caused to be built a perfect *Chaitya*, [*the beauty of*] which cannot be imagined by little-souled men.

26. ". . . . . he placed [*in it*] a great reservoir, charming to the eyes, [*which is filled*] with sweet, pure, clear, cool, and copious water.

27. ". . . . . On the other side of his [Buddha's ?] body, towards the west, he caused to be built a beautiful *gandhakuṭî*, pleasing to the eye.

28. ". . . . . may all desired success on earth attend those who, with all their acts, strive for the welfare of those [*monks*], in fulfilment of the prayers to the lord of Munis.

29. ". . . . . may [*this*] hall, [*given*] out of affection, so long increase the comfort of the saints, as the sun chases the darkness away with his rays."

No. 5. A fragment on a pilaster in Cave XX.[1] (pl. lviii)—

[1.] [*deyadharmmo*]ya[ṁ] maṇḍapa . .
[2.] . . . pautrasya Kṛi . . .
[3.] . putrasya Upendra . . . .
[4.] . sya dharmma haga . . . .
[5.] trasya jayatâṁ . . . . .
[6.] lyakalapri . . . . . .
[7.] mochâsakasya . . . . . .
[8.] nvâmika . . . .
[9.] puṇya(ṁ) tadbha[*vatu mâtṛipitṛi*]
[10.] [*pûrvaṁ*] gamânâṁ sa[*kalasattvânâm utta*]
[11.] [*rajñâ*]nâv[â]p[*taye*].[2]

According to this transcript, the inscription recorded the donation of a "hall," *maṇḍapa*, by Upendra or Upendra[*gupta*], whose father and grandfather were named. The father's name may have been Kṛi[*shṇa*] or Kṛi[*shṇadâsa*].

No. 6 (pl. lviii). The subjoined transcript agrees almost exactly with Pandit Bhagwânlâl's, most of whose restorations have also been accepted. The translation, on the other hand, differs considerably from his.

The characters in which the inscription is written belong to the central group of alphabets. They differ from the southern types of the Chalukya, Kâdamba, and other

---

[1] *Cave-Temple Inscriptions*, pp. 76, 77.

[2] Pandit Bhagwânlâl's restoration of lines 1 and 9–11 seems to be correct, but his readings in lines 2, 3, and 6 certainly do not agree with the facsimile.

inscriptions in the forms of *na* and *ta*, which resemble those used in the Valabhî and Gurjara śâsanas. They come very close to the inscriptions in Caves XVI. and XVII., and probably belong to the latter half of the sixth or beginning of the seventh century A.D.

The language is faulty and ungrammatical Sanskrit, containing a number of peculiar Buddhistic phrases. It is such as might be expected to be written by a Bauddha Âchârya (vs. 19) who, like the Jaina Yatis of our days, possessed only a superficial knowledge of the Brahmanical idiom. According to the inscription, the person who ordered Cave XXVI. to be excavated, and provided the funds for the work, was a monk called Buddhabhadra (vs. 13). His agents were the monk Dharmadatta and his own pupil Bhadrabandhu (?), who superintended the actual work. Buddhabhadra seems to have been no common monk (vs. 7). The nature of the work which he performed clearly indicates that he possessed considerable wealth. His friendship with the minister of the king of Aśmaka, in whose honour the cave was excavated, and the epithet "*abhijanopapanna*" (vs. 16), which seems to mean that he was of noble family, indicate, too, that he was more than a common begging friar. Perhaps we shall not err, if we assume that he occupied a position analogous to that of a Jaina Śrîpûj and was the spiritual head of some Bauddha sect. The fact that he mentions "his striving for the welfare of the people" (vs. 16), and "his having taken upon himself the care of the people," may be adduced in support of this view.

It is at present impossible to trace the two ministers of the Aśmaka king, Bhavvirâja and Devarâja, who held office one after another. But the Sthavira Achala, who is mentioned (vs. 6) as one of the former builders of Vihâras, is known from Hiwen Thsang's *Mémoires* (tom. ii. p. 152). It is stated there that the Arhat, 'O-che-lo, a native of Western India, traced his mother (who had died, but had been born again as a woman) to a village in Mahârâshṭra, converted her to Buddhism, and, touched by the kindness he had received from her who had born and nursed him, and thinking with emotion of the acts in her former life, caused a convent to be built (on the eastern frontier of the kingdom of Mahârâshṭra) in order to thank her for her great benefits. M. St. Julien transliterates 'O-che-lo by Âchâra, but that is certainly a mistake, as Achala comes much closer to the Chinese sounds. Moreover, the epithet *kṛitakṛityenâpi satâ*, "though his desires were fulfilled," which is applied to Sthavira Achala, seems directly to refer to the story of 'O-che-lo's finding and converting his mother. If the identification of our Achala with Hiwen Thsang's 'O-che-lo be accepted, the conjecture that Hiwen Thsang meant to describe Ajaṇṭâ[1] in his account of the monastery on the eastern frontier of Mahârâshṭra gains in probability.

[1.] jayati lokahitâvahitodyato- . . . . . sukhântakaraḥ paramârthavi[t |] trividhanirmmalasarvvaguṇodayo-mu-[shitabhiḥ] karuṇâmalachandrika[ḥ || | ||]

[2.] puṇar api maraṇâdi yena samya[2] . . . ivam ajarâmaradharmmatâ cha labdhâ [|] śivam abhayam anâlayaṁ gatopi-praśamapuraṁ jagatâṁ karoti chârttha[ṁ || 2 ||]

[3.] tato namaskâraguṇâbhidhâna[ṁ]-bhavaty avandhyaṁ vipulaṁ mahârtthaṁ [|] pradattam ekaṁ kusumaṁ cha yatra-svarggâpavarggâkhyaphalasya hetu[ḥ || 3 ||]

---

[1] *Cave-Temples*, p. 282; Cunningham (*Geography*, pp. 555, 556) suggests that Ajaṇṭâ might be meant, but prefers to change "eastern" into "western" frontier, and identify the monastery referred to with Kaṇheri. The Aśmakas are mentioned by Varâha Mihira, *Bṛihat Saṁhita*, ix. 18, xi. 55, xvi. 11, xvii. 15, xxxii. 15; in xiv. 22 he places them in the north-west; and, in a note on this verse, Dr. Kern identifies them with the Assekanoi of the Greeks.—J. B.

[2] L. 2. The sign after *samya* is not clear. Pandit Bhagwânlâl reads it as *kshi*, which, in my opinion, is impossible. I believe that it is meant for *gji*, and that the phrase must be read *samyag-jitam*, instead of *samyag-jivam*.

[4.] ata iha vidushâ Tathâgateshu-prathitaguṇâdhikalokavatsaleshu [|] kṛitam anusaratâ janena kâryyâ-dravakaruṇâḥṛidayeshv atî-

[5.] va bhakti[ḥ] || [4 ||] devâ nirastavijayâs savipattikatvâch-chhâpena Śaṁbhur api kâcharalochanobhût || Kṛishṇovaśopi vaśam âpatitontakasya-tasmâj jayaṁti

[6.] Sugatâ bhayavipramuktâḥ || [5 ||] Sthavirâchalena muninâ śâsanam udbhâvayaṁkṛitajñena [1] [|] kṛitakṛityenâpi satâ śailagṛihaṁ kâritaṁ śâstuḥ || [6 ||]·

[7.] prâg eva ḃodhisattvair bhavasukhakâmaiś cha mokshakâmaiś cha [|] saṁvidyamânavibhavaiḥ kathaṁ na kâryyâ bhave kîrttiḥ || [7 ||] yâvat kîrttir loke tâvat svargge-

[8.] shu modati cha dehî[|]chandrârkkakâlakalpâ kâryyâ kîrttir mahîdhreshu || [8 ||] anekajanmântarabaddhasauhṛidaṁ-sthiraṁ kṛitajñaṁ sudhiyaṁ vipaśchitam [|]

[9.] surâsurâchâryyamateshu kovidaṁ-mahânubhâvâśmakarâjamantriṇam || [9 ||] lokajñam ekântasamantabhadraṁ-sarvvârtthinâm artthakaraṁ suvâcham [|] guṇonnataṁ praśraya-

[10.] nâmramûrttiṁ-khyâtiṁ [2] gataṁ sachcharitaiḥ pṛithivyâṁ || [10 ||] daṇdaśâdhyâni kâryyâṇi vyâyâmaikaraśâny api-yas sâdhayati sâmnaiva nṛipater mantṛipuṅgava[ḥ] || [11 ||] itthaṁ

[11.] bhûtosya putropi Devarâjo dhuraṁdharaḥ[|] pitaryy uparate yena padam unnâmita[ṁ] guṇaiḥ || [12 ||] taṁ Bhavvirâjam uddiśya mâtâpitaram eva cha[|] bhikshuṇâ Buddhabhadreṇa

[12.] kâritaḥ Sugatâlaya[ḥ || 13 ||] âgamya Dharmmadattañ cha bhikshuṁ sachchhishyam eva cha [|] Bhadrabudhum [3] idaṁ veśma tâbhyâṁ nishpâditaṁ cha me || [14 ||] yad atra puṇyaṁ tat teshâ[ṁ]

[13.] jagatâ[ṁ] cha bhavatv idaṁ [|] sarvvâmalaguṇavyâtamahâbodhiphalâptaye [4] || [15 ||] yo Buddhaśâsanagatiṁ samabuddhya jâto-bhikshur vvayasy abhinavebhijanopapanna[ḥ |]

[14.] bahuvrataḥ śîlaviśuddhachetâ-lokasya [mokshâ]ya kṛitâdhikâraḥ || [16 ||] na saṁsârâpannaṁ śubham api[tu k]iṁchich chhubhakaraṁ-vipâko divyo ·

[15.] . . . . châ niyamâ [|] [5] . . lokârtthâya prasṛitamana . puṇyamahato-[dhî]râṇâ[ṁ] bhavati sukha . .

[16.] na jagatâm ||[17 ||] . . . . valabhirnnânâṇḍaja- . . . [|] golâṅgûlaninâdapûritadare prâgbhâravi . . . .

[17.] yogîśvarâdhyâsite veśmedaṁ jana . . . janakabhûtyai . pratishṭhâpitaṁ || [18 ||] pûrvvâpi cheyam tenaiva dribddhâchâryyeṇa saugati [|] lokachi[ntâmu]pâdâya . . . .[|| 19 ||] [6]

1. "Victory to him who pays attention to and strives for the welfare of the people, who destroys . . . . . . comforts, who knows the highest aim [*of men*], in whom all the threefold spotless qualities have been developed, [*who has freed men from fear*], and who sheds the spotless radiance of mercy.

2. "He who completely conquered repeated deaths and the like [7] [*misfortunes*], and who obtained eternal youth and immortality does good to the world, though he has reached the happy, fearless, and houseless city of emancipation.

3. "For this cause, adoration and praise [*offered to him*] remains not without its reward, and yields great and abundant advantage; and if on that occasion [8] even one flower be offered, it becomes the cause of the reward called heaven and final liberation.

---

[1] L. 6. Read *udbhâvayat*, as Pandit Bhagwânlâl suggests.

[2] L. 10. Read *namramûrtiṁ*;—°*mantripuṅgavaḥ*.

[3] L. 12. The last ligature in the second name is uncertain. It looks like *dhdhum*. But Pandit Bhagwânlâl's emendation, *bhadrabandhum*, is probable.

[4] L. 13. Read *sarvvâmalaguṇavyâpta*°. Pandit Bhagwânlâl's reading, *dhyâta*°, is against the facsimile; °*vyâtta*° would also give sense.

[5] L. 15. Possibly *prasṛitamana*[*sâm*] *puṇyamahatâm* is to be read; Pandit Bhagwânlâl's restoration, *sukha*[*bhogâya*], cannot stand, as *na* is distinct before *jagatâm* (line 16).

[6] L. 17. Possibly *jana*[*sevitaṁ*] or *jana*[*saṁstutaṁ*] may have been the original reading; read *dṛiḍhâchâryeṇa*; it must remain doubtful if *saugati* or *saugatiṁ* is the correct reading. In the former case the word would have to be taken with *praśastiḥ*, which doubtlessly stood in the last pâda of the mutilated anushṭubh; in the latter it belongs to *lokachi*[*ntâṁ*].

[7] Repeated deaths and the like, *i.e.*, the repetition of births, sickness, old age.

[8] I take *yatra cha* to refer to *namaskâraguṇâbhidhânaṁ*, "adoration and praise."

4. "Therefore, a wise man who seeks rewards, must devoutly worship the Tathâgatas' reward, whose virtues are famous, who are exceedingly affectionate towards the people, and whose hearts melt with pity.[1]

5. "The Dêvas through being [*themselves*] subject to miseries have lost the power of conquering [*the misfortunes of others*]. In consequence of a curse, Śambhu even was afflicted with blinking eyes.[2] Kṛishṇa, though he obeyed no other man's sway, fell under the sway of Death. Therefore the Sugatas, who are freed from fear, are [*alone*] victorious.

6. "The ascetic Sthavira Achala, who glorified the faith and was grateful, caused to be built a mountain-dwelling for the Teacher, though his wishes were fulfilled.[3]

7. "How much more must not fame in this world be acquired by opulent Bodhisattvas, both by those who are desirous of mundane happiness and by those who desire final liberation?

8. "A corporeal being rejoices in heaven as long as his fame [*remains*] among men. Therefore it is meet to acquire in the mountains a fame which lasts as long as moon and sun endure.

9. "[*In honour of*] the minister of the high-minded Aśmaka king, who was bound to him by friendship during many births, who was firm, grateful, clever, wise, and learned in the opinions of the teachers of the gods and of the demons;[4]

10. "Who knew the world, was lucky in small and great affairs,[5] fulfilled the desires of all needy men, was eloquent, exalted by his virtues, [*but*] lowly through modesty, and gained fame on earth by his virtuous conduct;

11. "Who, being a most excellent minister of the king, settled[6] by peaceful means even the most tedious business, which is [*usually*] settled by severity [*only*] ——.

12. "His son, Devarâja, in like manner became a man of business [*in the king's service*], and, after his father's death, exalted his dignity by his virtues ——.

13. "In honour of that Bhavvirâja, and of his [*own*] parents,[7] the monk Buddhabhadra has caused a temple of Sugata to be erected.

14. "When I had recourse to the monk Dharmadatta, and [*my*] good pupil Bhadhrabandhu, those two constructed this temple for me.

15. "May the merit which is in this [*work*] procure for those three[8] and the world the reward of *mahâbodhi*, which is filled with all spotless qualities.

16. "He who, possessed of noble birth,[9] became, after he had perfectly learnt the path

---

1 *Dravakaruṇâhṛidayeshu* is bad Sanskṛit, though its meaning, "*karuṇâdravahṛidayeshu*," is plain.

2 I take *kâchara* with Bhagwânlâl for *kâ* + *chara*. The Petersburgh Dictionary translates it by "glassy," connecting it with *kâcha*.

3 I take *satâ* as pres. part. with *kṛitakṛityenâpi*, not as an adjective.

4 The construction is altogether ungrammatical. The accusatives in this verse are governed by *uddiśya*, "in honour of," which occurs in verse 13, though a parenthetic description of Bhavvirâja's son, Devarâja, intervenes in verse 12. The "opinions" are the treatises on polity by Bṛihaspati and Uśanas.

5 The phrase, *ekântasamantabhadram*, has probably a double sense, and means also, "who in some respects resembled [Buddha] Samantabhadra."

6 *Sâdhayati* means literally "settles;" but as we learn from verse 12 that Bhavvirâja was dead, it becomes necessary to translate it by "settled."

7 *Mâtâpitaram* is bad Sanskṛit for *mâtâpitarau*, and probably used only because the correct form did not fit the metre.

8 *Teshâm*, "those three," *i.e.*, Bhavvirâja and the donor's parents.

9 *Abhijanopapannah*, "possessed of noble birth," may possibly mean, "he who possessed a family," *i.e.*, had already children.

of Buddha's teaching, an ascetic in his youth, performed many religious observances, purified his mind by virtuous conduct, and strove for the final liberation of the people.

17. "No happiness obtained in the circle of births produces [*real*] happiness. . . . .

18. "This temple, which [*is praised by*] the people, has been erected for the welfare of [*my*] parents [*on the hill which is tuneful with the songs*] of various birds, whose caves resound with cries of Golângûla monkeys,[1] whose summit . . . ., which is inhabited by lords of Yogîs.

19. "And this Buddhistic [*inscription or eulogy*], given above, has been likewise composed by the Âchârya, after he had taken upon himself the care of the people . . . . ."

No. 7, under a statue outside Cave XXVI.—

[1.] Deyadharmoyaṁ Sâkyabhikshor bhadanta-Guṇâkarasya yad atra puṇyaṁ tad bhavatu mâtâpitaraṁ pûrvvaṅgamaṁ kritvâ

[2.] sarvasatvebhya anuttara jñânâvâptaye

—"The Śâkya-Bhikshu, the Badanta Guṇâkara's meritorious gift: may whatever merit is in this be for the attainment of supreme knowledge by all sentient beings, mother and father being first."

No. 8 (pl. lviii), under a similar statue opposite the last—

[1.] Oṁ deyadharmo[ya . . . . .

[2.] yad atra puṇyaṁ[*tadbhavatu*, &c.]

[3.] sarvvasatvânâma[*nuttarajñânâvâptaye ?*]

—"Hail! The meritorious gift . . . ." &c.

No. 9 (pl. lviii), under a small sculpture in the right aisle—

[1.] Deydharmoyaṁ Sâkya-

[2.] bhikshu-Saṁghamitrasya

—"The meritorious gift of the Śâkya-Bhikshu Saṅghamitra."

XII. Ajanta Painted Inscriptions.[2]

On plate lix specimens are given of the inscriptions painted on the frescoes in the Ajaṇṭâ Caves. The facsimiles indicate pretty clearly that the great majority of these inscriptions are of comparatively late date in the history of Indian Buddhism.

The first four are from the Chaitya cave No. IX. No. 1 is on the front wall inside, over the entrance and close to the head of a Bhikshu painted on the wall. It reads—

[*Deyadharmmo*]yaṁ Śâ(*kyabhiksho*)-
ssaṅghapri(*yasya*)
. . . . mâtâ

—"The meritorious gift of the Śâkya Bhikshu (or mendicant) Saṅghapriya . . . ."

No. 2 is on the first pillar on the left side of the nave, under a painted figure of a standing Buddha, in characters of about the sixth century—

Deyadharmmo upâsaka-Jasade-
vasya

—"The meritorious gift of the lay-worshipper Jasadêva."

[1] The Golângûla monkeys are the common "Langurs" with long tails and black faces. Langur seems to be a corruption of the Sanskṛit word.

[2] See *ante*, p. 45.

No. 3 is on a jamb attached to the first pillar, under the throne of a seated representation of Buddha, and in somewhat earlier letters than Nos. 1 and 2—

Deyadharmmoyaṁ Bhadanta-(*Dha*)rmasena(*sya*)

—"The meritorious gift of the reverend Dharmasena."

No. 4 is in Pâli, on the back wall of the cave under a painted dâgoba, in characters perhaps of the fifth century A.D., but only fragments of it are left, which read—

Deyadahama bha . . . sya ma . . . .

No. 5 is on the ninth pillar on the left side of the nave, under a standing Buddha—

Deyadharmmoyaṁ Sâkyabhikshor bhadanta-Bhadrase(*nasya?*)

—"The meritorious gift of the Sâkya mendicant, the reverend Bhadrasena."

No. 6 is in Cave X., on the left wall opposite the third pillar, and though only a fragment, the letters belong to the age of the carved inscriptions of the Andhra kings—

Bhagavasa yatipuvade(*va*) . . . ta yatipatisa yasa . . .

—"Of Bhagava (Buddha), first dêva of Yatis . . . master of Yatis . . ."

No 7 is on the same wall, further back, just below a portion of later painting, and is in characters of about the sixth century—

Âchârya . . . . . . Sachivasya
deyadharmmo yad atra puṇyaṁ tad bhavatu sarvvasa-
tvânâṁ duḥkhamochâ . . . . . .

—"The meritorious gift . . . Âchârya . . . of Sachiva: may the merit of this be for (*the release*) from miseries of all sentient beings."

No. 8 is on the sixth pillar on the right side of the nave in Cave X., at the feet of a standing figure of Buddha. The characters may be of about the fifth century—

Deyadharmmoyaṁ S'âkya-
bhikshor bhadaṁta Drâdha-
dharmmasya

—"This meritorious gift of the Śâkya mendicant Dridhadharma."

No. 9 is on the next pillar, below a similar figure—

Vipaśśi samyaksaṁbuddhaḥ Chetika(*ya*)rikasya

—"Vipaśśi,[1] the perfectly wise; (*the gift*) of Chetikayarika."

No. 10 is on the eighth pillar on the left side of the nave—

Bhadanta Sudattasya

—"Of the reverend Sudatta."

No. 11 is on the same pillar, under a seated figure of Buddha, and when complete has been identical with the last.

No. 12 is on the tenth (fifth standing) pillar on the same side, on the umbrella over a figure of Buddha—

Deyadharmmoyaṁ S'âkyabhikshor bhadaṁta-Saṁghaguptasya

—"This meritorious gift of the Śâkya mendicant, the reverend Saṅghagupta."

---

[1] Vipassi is the name of one of the five human Buddhas.

No. 13 is on the fifth pillar on the right side of Cave X., below a standing figure of Buddha—

Deyadharmmoyaṁ bhadanta-Śilabhadrasya mâtâ-
pitaramudi(*sya*).

—"This meritorious gift of the reverend Śilabhadra, in honour of father and mother."

Nos. 14 and 15 are in Cave XVI., below two seated figures of Buddha, painted on the left wall of the hall, in characters of about the sixth century A.D.

No. 14—

Deyadharmmoyaṁ Śâkyabhikshor bbhadanta Dâpukasya
yad atra puṇyaṁ tad bhavatu mâtâpitro[ḥ] sarvasatvânâñ châ-
nu[*tta*]rajñânâvâptaye

—"The meritorious gift of the Sâkya mendicant, the reverend Dâpuka: may whatever merit is in this be for the attainment of supreme knowledge by mother and father and all sentient beings."

No. 15—

Deyadharmmoyaṁ Śâkyabhikshor bbhadanta Dharmmadattasya yad atra (*puṇyaṁ*)
tad bhavatu mâtâpitros sarvvasatvânâñ chânuttarajñânâvâptaye.

This is identical with the preceding, except that the donor's name is Dharmadatta, who has another similar inscription under a third figure beside these.

There are also some fragments in Cave II., a few names on paintings in Cave XVII., and one fragment in Cave XXII.[1]

XIII. Ghaṭotkacha Cave Inscription.

The portion of this inscription[2] (pl. lx) which has been preserved gives the pedigree of Hastibhoja, who, according to v. 10 of this inscription and v. 12 of Ajaṇṭâ inscription No. 3, was the minister of the Vâkâṭaka king Devasena. He belonged to the Vallûras, apparently a subdivision of the Malabâr Brâhmaṇas. His ancestors were :—

1. Yajña[pati]; 2. Deva; 3. Soma; 4. Ravi, son of a Kshatriyâ wife and ruler of Malaya or Malabâr; 5. Pravara; 6. Śrî-Râma; 7. Kîrti.

The wording of v. 5 makes it probable that Deva also held the office of prime minister—it is not stated where. The obliterated portion of the document, doubtless, contained an account of Hastibhoja's descendants, among whom must have been the donor of the Gulwâḍâ cave.

[1.] Munir muntnâm amaromarâṇâ[ṁ]-gurur gurûṇâṁ pravaro varâṇâ[ṁ |]
jayaty anâbhogavibuddhabuddhir-Bbuddhâbhidh[âno] ni[dhi]r adbhutânâ[ṁ ||]
[2.] dharmmas tato dharmmavidâ praṇîtas-tathâ [ga]ṇaś châgryatamo gaṇânâ[ṁ |]
bhavanti yasmin nihitâ[ḥ] supâtre-kârâpakârâstanayâ py[u]dârâḥ[3] [||]
[3.] asti prakâśo diśi dakshiṇasyâ[ṁ]-Vallûranâmnâṁ dvijasattamânâṁ[|]
â brahmanas sa[ṁ]bhṛitapuṇyakîrttirttir-vaṁśo[4] mahîyân mahito mahadbhiḥ [||]

---

[1] For full details see *Cave-Temple Inscriptions*, pp. 80–88.

[2] *Cave-Temple Inscriptions*, pp. 88 *seqq.* The transcript, and still more the translation, differ in various points from Pandit Bhagwânlâl's.

[3] L. 2. Either °*nayâḥ pyudârâḥ* or °*nayâ hyudârâḥ* to be read.

[4] L. 3. Read °*puṇyakîrttir.*

[4.] tasminn abhûd âha[ta]lakshaṇânâṁ-dvijanmanâ[ṁ] [prâ]thamakalpikânâṁ [|]
bhṛigvatrigarggâ[ṅgi]ra[sâṁ] samâno-dvijarshabho Yajña[patiḥ] [1] prakâśaḥ [||]
[5.] tadâtmajo Deva ivâsa Devaḥ-kṛitî gṛihî nayavân [2] kriyâvân [|]
sarâjaka[ṁ] râshtraṁ upetya yas[min-dha]rmyâḥ kriyâ [nâ]tha iva prachakkre [||]
[6.] Somas tata[ḥ Soma ivâ]parobhû[t-sa] brâhmanakshatriyavaṁśajâsu [|]
[śru]tismṛitibhyâṁ vihitâ[rtha]kârî-dvayî[shu] bhâryyâsu ma[n]o dadhâra [||]
[7.] sa Kshatriyâyâ[ṁ] kulaśîlavatyâm-utpâdayâmâsa narendrachihnaṁ [|]
sutaṁ surûpaṁ Ravinâmadheyaṁ-kṛitâdhi[patyaṁ] Malaye samagro [||]
[8.] dvijâsu chânyâsu sutân udârân-sa[ma]stavedeshu samâptakâmâ[n |]
Vall[û]ranâmâ [3] diśi dakshiṇasyâm-adyâpi yeshâm vasati[r dvijânâṁ ||]
[9.] Raves sutobhût Pravarâbhidhâna[ḥ]-[Srî-Râ]manâmâtha babhûva tasmât [|]
tadâtmajaḥ Kîrttir abhût sukîrttir-bbabhûva ta[smâd] atha [Hastibhojaḥ ||]
[10.] [Vâ]kâṭake râjati Devasene-gunai[shikośo] bhuvi [Ha]stibhojaḥ [ ]
adyâpi . tasyâbhimana . . . . [||]|
[11.] dhîreshu dhîmatsu sahotthiteshu- . . . . guṇânviteshu [ ]
. . . [yaṁ] nṛipaterya . . . . [||]
[12.] yasyâsanârddha[ṁ] surasâ . . . .
[13.] atha devarâjasya †† [?] [4]
[14.] śaśikaradhavala [?]
[15.] atha guṇa [?] . . . .
[16.] tasyâtmajeshu . . . . . .
[17.] phale [makhilamila ?] . . . . . .
[18.] samyagvibhâvî [5] . . . . .

1. "Glory to him who is called Buddha, the ascetic among ascetics, the immortal among immortals, the teacher among teachers, the best among the good, a store of marvels, to him who obtained [*supreme*] wisdom by abstaining from fruition.

2. "Next [*glory to*] the Law which has been promulgated by him who knows the law, then [*glory to*] the Community [*of the ascetics*], the best of communities, placed in which, as in a beautiful vessel, even those who have sinned by committing murder, become exalted.[6]

3. "In the southern country there is an illustrious and very extensive race of most excellent Brâhmaṇas called Vallûras, that has accumulated religious merit and glory since Brahman's [*time*], and is worshipped by the great.

---

[1] L. 4. The conjecture *yajñapatiḥ* is probable, because the metre requires – ⏑ ⏑ – and only one name, *yajña-dharaḥ*, besides *yajñapatiḥ* fulfils this condition, but is little used.

[2] L. 5. P. Bhagwânlâl's conjecture, *gṛihastho*, fits the metre, but is impossible, as the î in *gṛihî* is quite plain.

[3] L. 8. Read *vallûranâmnâṁ*.

[4] Pandit Bhagwânlâl takes Devarâja to be a proper name, and conjectures that he was the minister of the Aśmaka king mentioned in Ajaṇṭâ Inscription No. 6, v. 12, and if so, the great grandson of Hastibhoja, and grandson of Varâhadeva (Ajaṇṭâ Ins., No. 3, v. 30); but I see no ground for these combinations.

[5] L. 18. The readings in lines 13, 14, and 17 are very doubtful, especially as the apparent readings do not fit the metre, which is Upajâti throughout the inscription.

[6] Verses 1 and 2 contain the usual salutation to Buddha, Dharma, and Saṁgha. The phrase *kârupakârâstanayâḥ* is very ambiguous, as it may be taken as one compound, consisting of *kârûpakâra* and *astanaya*, or as two words, *kârûpakârâḥ* and *tanayâḥ*, and as *kâra* may be interpreted "effort," or "a Yati," or "murder." If it is taken as a compound it may be literally translated by "those whose efforts are offences, and who thus cast aside good behaviour or prudence," or by "those who offend against ascetics, and thus," &c., or by "those whose offence is murder, and who thus," &c. If we adopt the second division, *tanayâḥ* means "sons," and *kâropakârâḥ* can again be taken in various ways. The poet, no doubt, intended to puzzle the reader. But, in any case, the general sense remains the same, and the half-verse is intended to assert that sinners are purified by joining the Buddhist Saṁgha.

4. "In that [*family*] was born famous Yajña[*pati*], a chief of twice-born men equal to Bhṛigu, Atri, Garga and Angiras, those Brâhmanas of ancient times who are noted for their good qualities.

5. "His son was Deva, similar to a god [*Deva*], a virtuous householder (?) . . . who possessed political wisdom and performed religious rites; under whom, when he had gained possession of the kingdom and of the king, lawful rites were performed, just as in the [*time of the*] Lord [*Buddha*]

6. "From him sprung Soma, a second moon [*soma*] as it were. He, following the precepts of the revelation and of the tradition, gave his heart to wives [*of*] two [*classes*], born in Brâhmaṇa and in Kshatriya families.

7. "Of a Kshatriyâ wife of high family and good conduct he begat a beautiful son, called Ravi, who bore [*on his body*] the marks of a king, and who ruled over the whole Malaya.[1]

8. "And by other wives of the twice-born [*i.e. Brâhmaṇa caste*] illustrious sons, who obtained their desires in [*studying*] all the Vedas, and who, called Vallûras, dwell even now in the southern country.

9. "The son of Ravi was he who is called Pravara; from him next sprung Śrî Râma. His son was Kîrti, of good repute [*kîrti*], and then from him was descended [*Hastibhoja*].

10. "When the Vâkâṭaka, Devasena, was king, Hastibhoja was on earth a treasure for those who desire good qualities . . . ."

---

[1] For the Hindu lawyer vv. 6, 7 have some interest, as they clearly show that the ancient custom, which allowed Brâhmaṇas to take wives of other castes, prevailed and was considered lawful up to the sixth century, though the compilers of the modern *Nibandhas*, such as Nîlakaṇṭha and Kamalâkara, who are as profoundly ignorant of the history of their country as Hindu schoolmen always are, declare that it is forbidden in the Kaliyuga, *i.e.* since 3101 B.C.

END OF VOL. IV.

1. SCULPTURE IN THE SMALL VIHARA.

FIG. 2

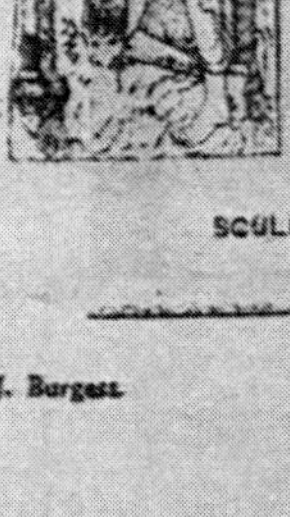

FIG. 3.

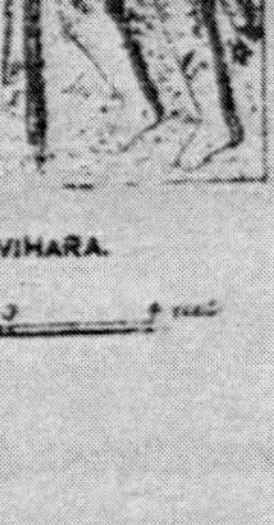

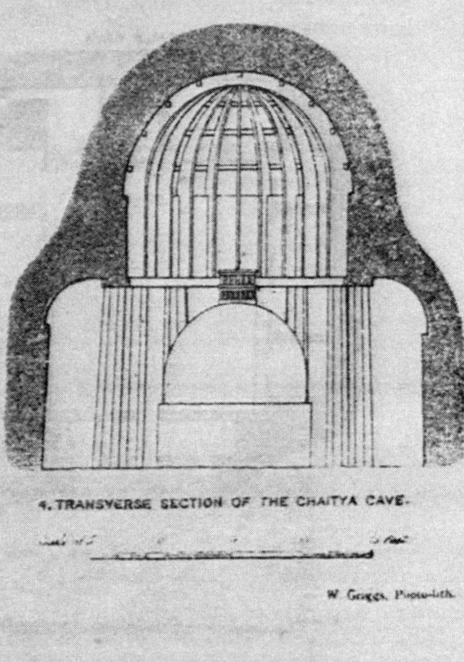

SCULPTURES IN THE SMALL VIHARA.

4. TRANSVERSE SECTION OF THE CHAITYA CAVE.

J. Burgess

W. Griggs, Photo-lith.

PLATE VII.

1. PITALKHORA VIHARA CELLS.

2. SECTION.

3. PLAN

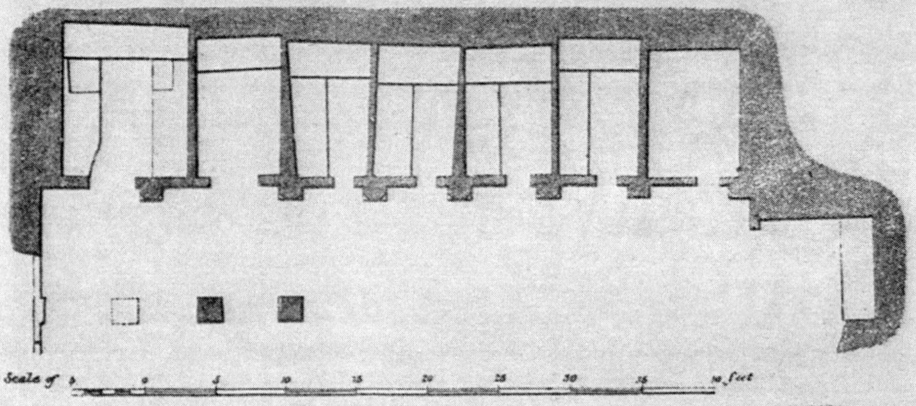

4. AMBIVALE CAVE.

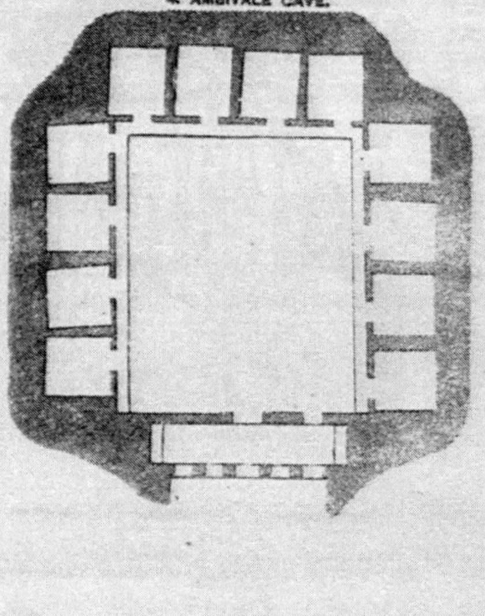

5. PILLAR
IN AMBIVALE CAVE.

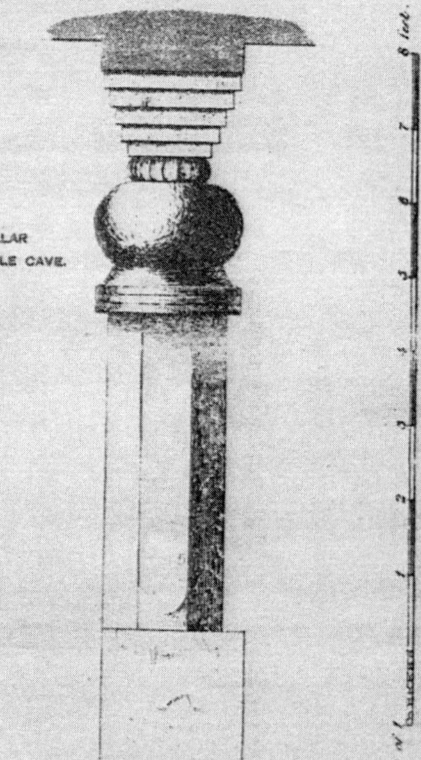

J. Burgess

H. Cousens, Del

KUDÂ CAVES. PLATE VIII.

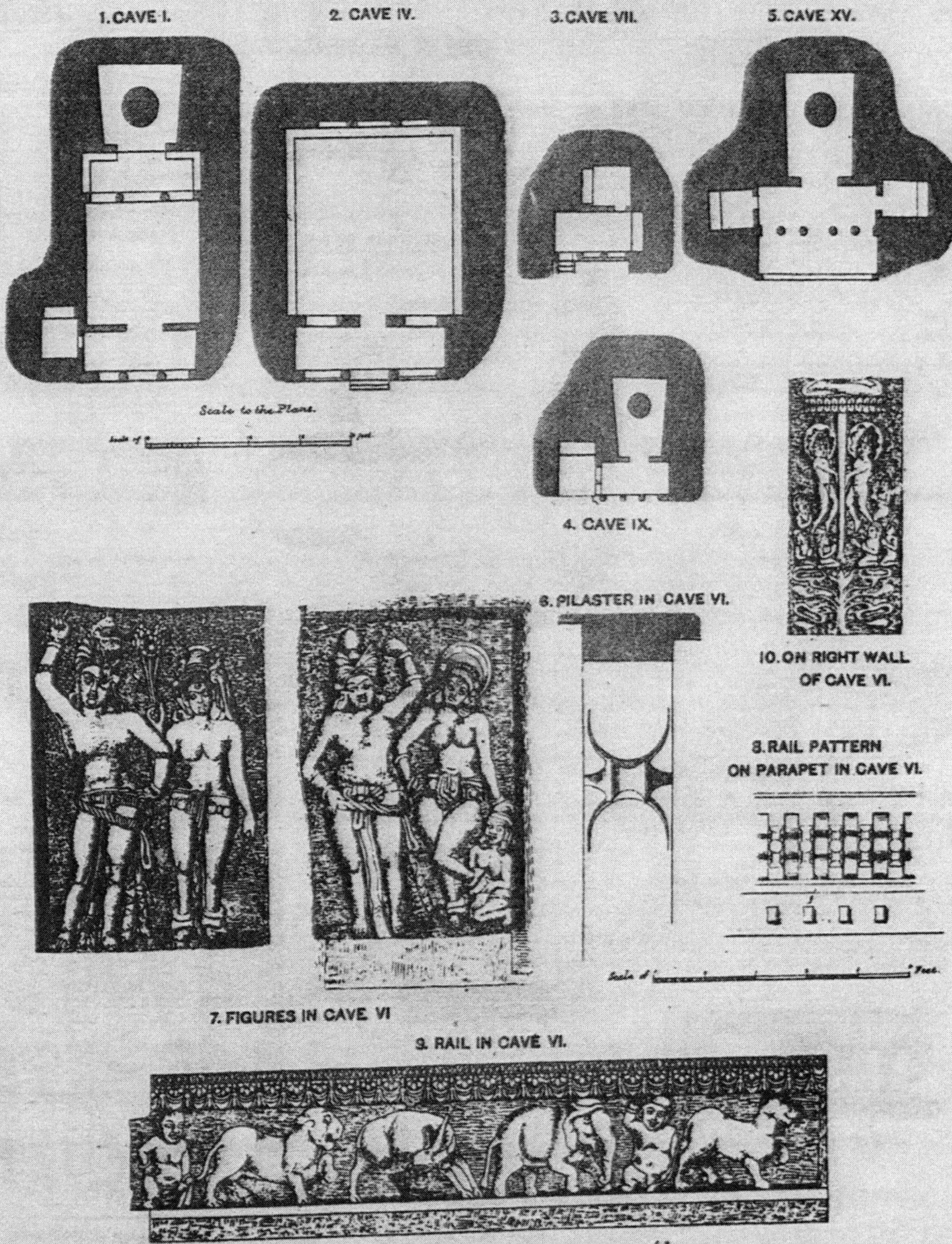

J. Burgess. W. Griggs. Photo-lith.

PLATE IX.

CAVES AT MAHÁD.

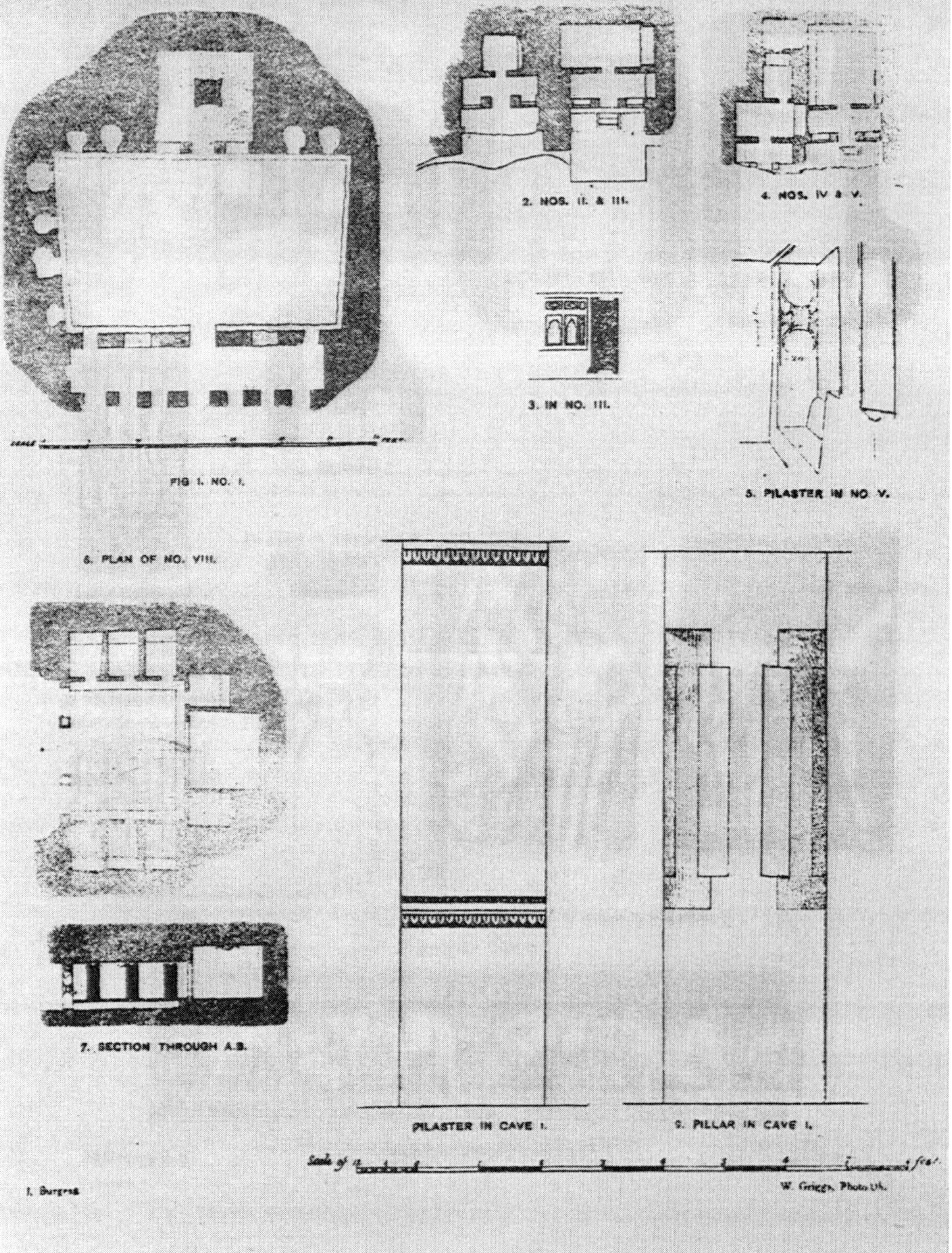

J. Burgess

W. Griggs, Photo-lith.

PLATE X

KARADH CAVES.

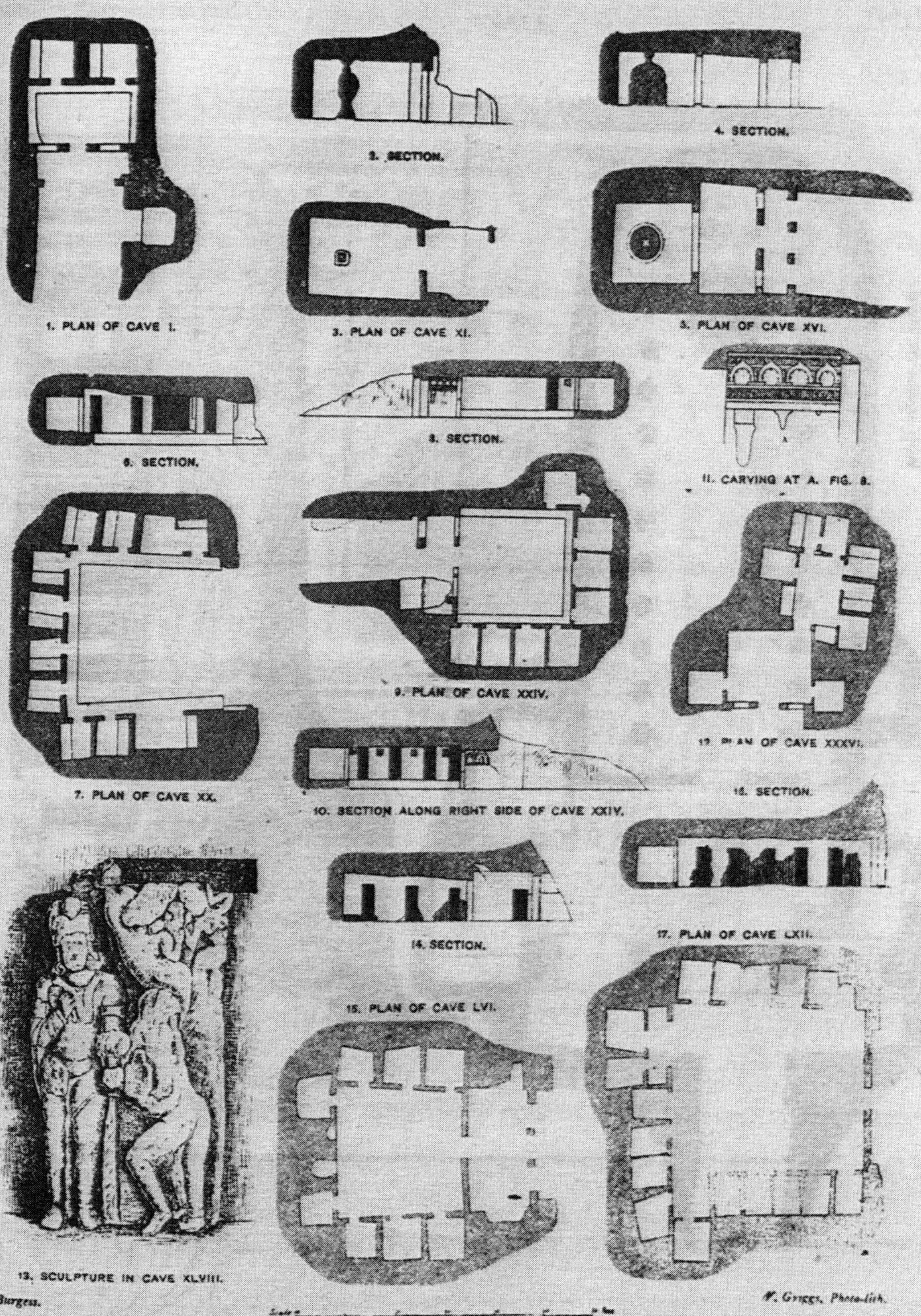

1. PLAN OF CAVE I.
2. SECTION.
3. PLAN OF CAVE XI.
4. SECTION.
5. PLAN OF CAVE XVI.
6. SECTION.
7. PLAN OF CAVE XX.
8. SECTION.
9. PLAN OF CAVE XXIV.
10. SECTION ALONG RIGHT SIDE OF CAVE XXIV.
11. CARVING AT A. FIG. 8.
12. PLAN OF CAVE XXXVI.
13. SCULPTURE IN CAVE XLVIII.
14. SECTION.
15. PLAN OF CAVE LVI.
16. SECTION.
17. PLAN OF CAVE LXII.

J. Burgess. W. Griggs, Photo-lith.

PLATE XI.

BEDSA.

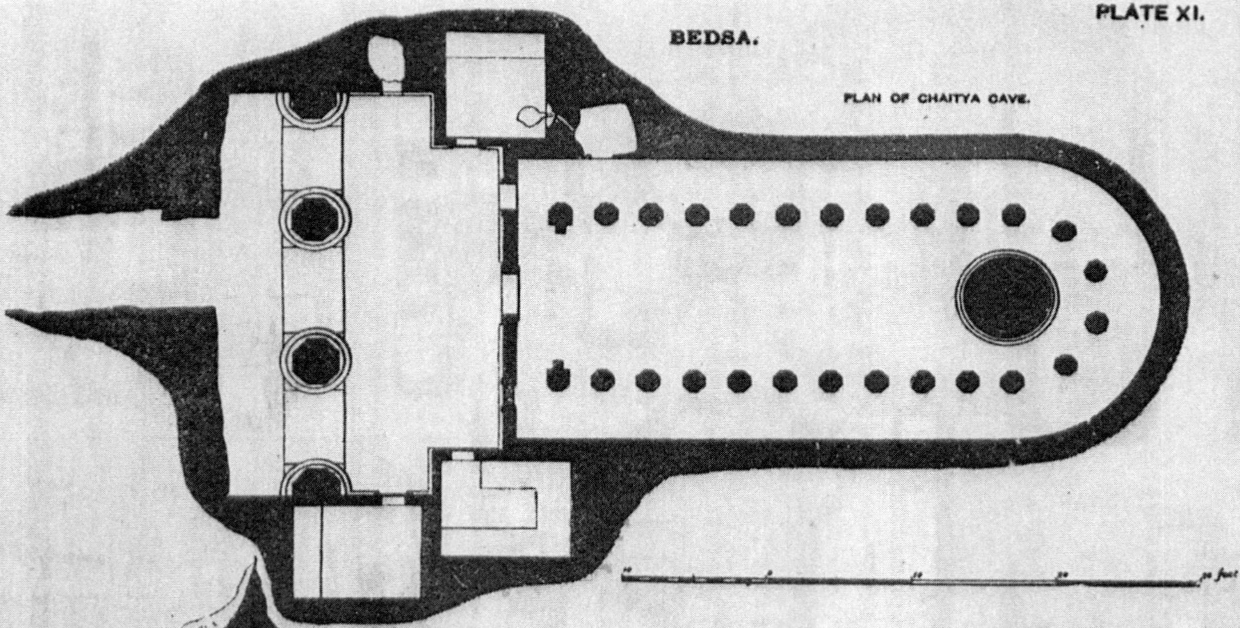

PLAN OF CHAITYA CAVE.

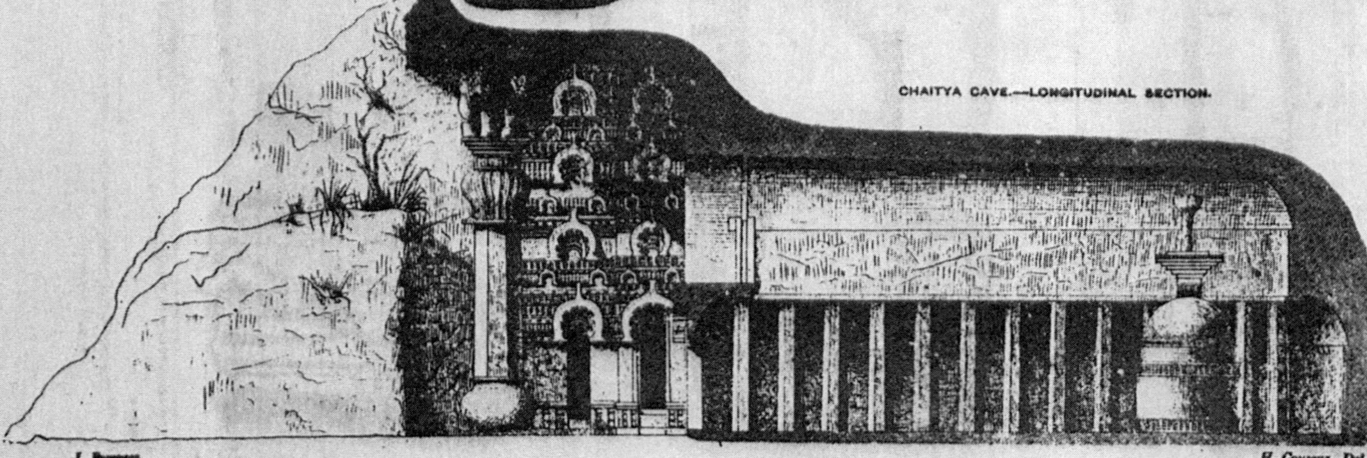

CHAITYA CAVE.—LONGITUDINAL SECTION.

J. Burgess.

H. Cousens, Del.

KÁRLÉ.

FAÇADE OF THE CHAITYA CAVE.

J. Burgess.

H. Cousens, del.

FIG. 1. COLUMN IN THE LEFT SIDE OF THE NAVE.

FIG 2. SCULPTURE IN THE LEFT END OF THE VERANDAH OF THE CHAITYA CAVE.

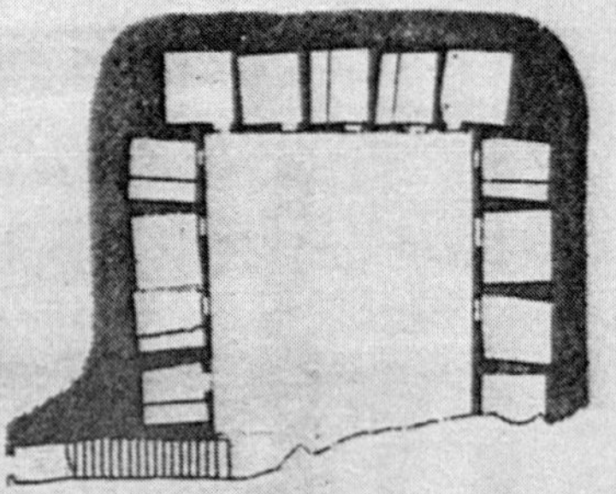

3. FIRST FLOOR OF VIHARA NO. I.

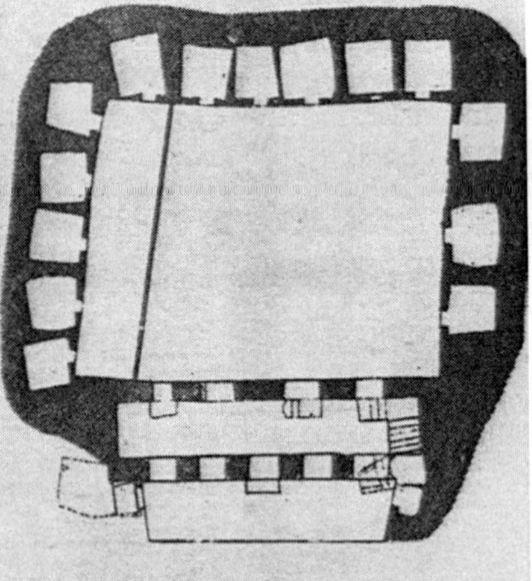

4. SECOND FLOOR OF VIHARA NO I.

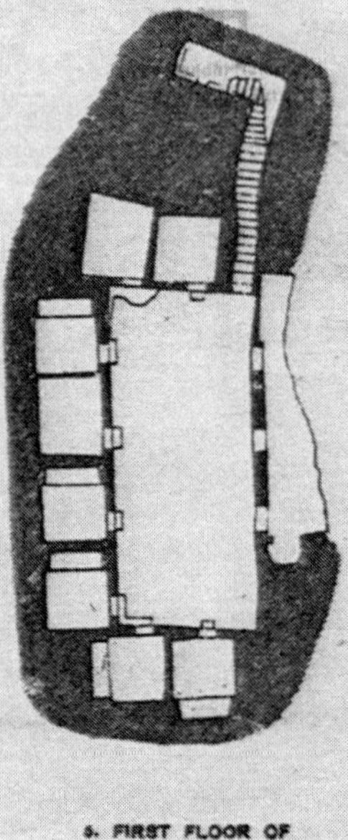

5. FIRST FLOOR OF VIHARA NO. II.

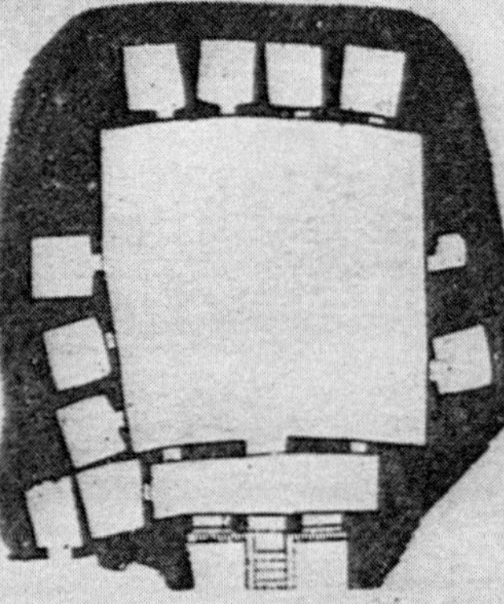

6. VIHARA SOUTH FROM THE CHAITYA CAVE.

J. Burgess.

PLATE XIV.

GENERAL PLAN OF THE CAVES OF
AJANTA.

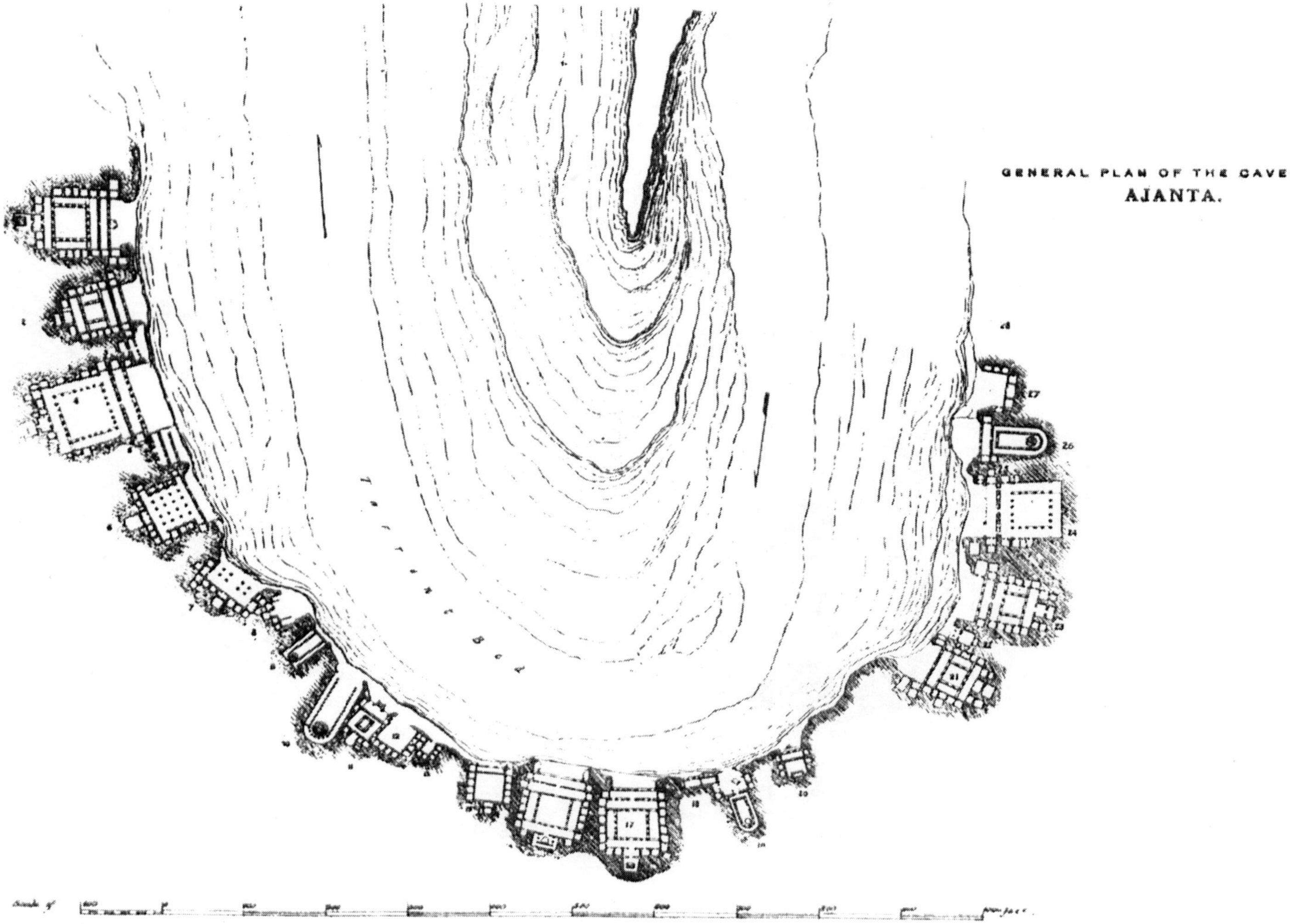

J. Burgess.

W. Griggs, Photo-lith.

AJANTA.

1. FRONT OF THE CHAITYA CAVE NO. X.

2. CAVE I. – RIGHT HAND DOOR.

J Barr sc.

W. Griggs, Photo-lith.

PLATE XVI.

AJANTA.

PAINTING FROM THE RIGHT WALL OF CAVE X.

Scale [illegible] of the original.

LEFT SECTION.

RIGHT SECTION.

J. Burgess. *W. Griggs, Photo-lith.* *H. Cousens, Del.*

PLATE XVII.

AJANTA.

TRANSVERSE SECTION.

FAÇADE OF CAVE IX.

J. Burgess. W. Griggs, Photo-lith.

Scale of 5 0 5 10 15 20 feet

PLATE XVIII.

AJANTA.

1. PILLAR IN CAVE 1. — 2. CAVE 1. RIGHT FRONT CORNER PILLAR. — 3. VERANDAH PILASTER, AT RIGHT END.

J. Burgess. W. Griggs, Photo-lith.

AJANTA.

HALL DOOR, CAVE I.

PLATE XIX.

J. Burgess.

H. Cousens, Del

PLATE XX

AJANTA.

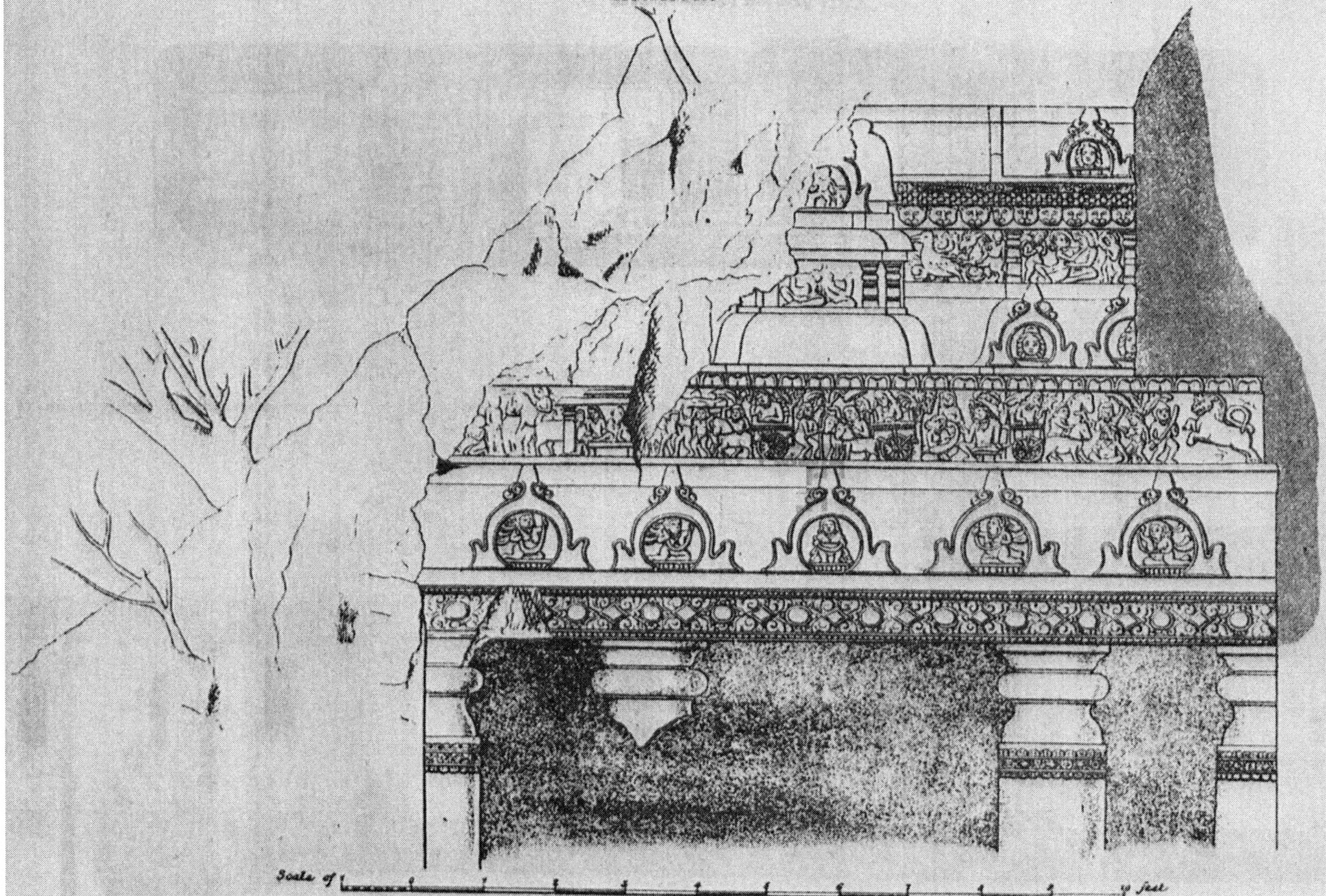

FRIEZE OVER THE FRONT OF THE LEFT HAND CHAPEL OF CAVE I

J. Burgess.

H. Cousens, Del.

AJANTA

PLATE XXI.

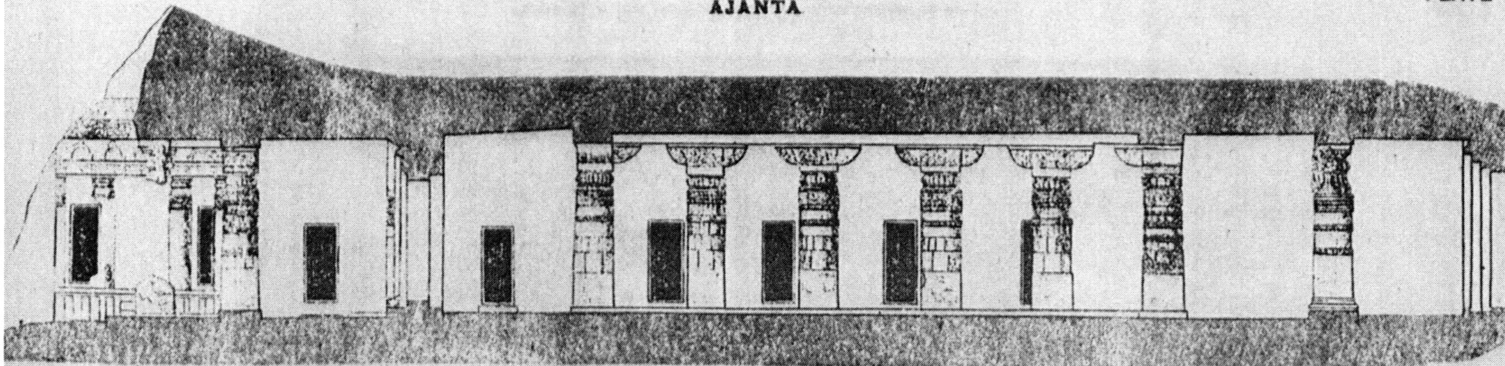

1. CAVE I.—LONGITUDINAL SECTION.

Scale of 10 0 10 20 30 40 50 Feet.

CAVE I.—SECTION CONTINUED.

J. Burgess. 2. CAVE II.—CROSS SECTION. H. Cousens, Del

PLATE XXII.

AJANTA.

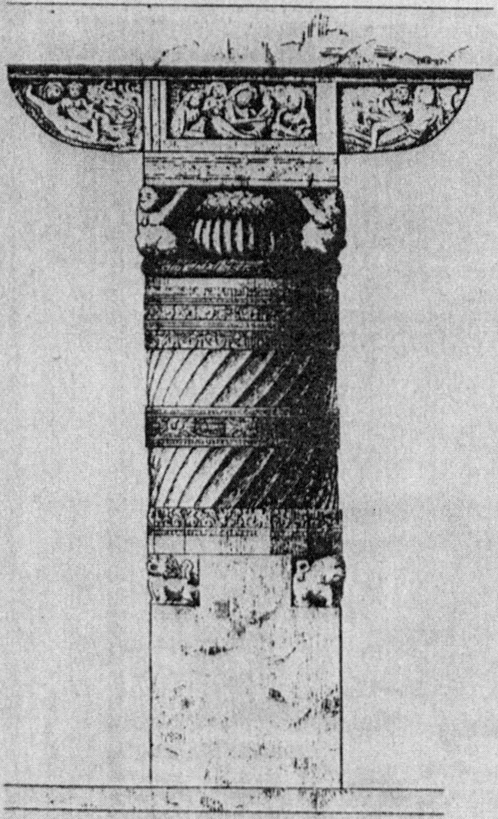

I CAVE II.—LEFT CORNER PILLAR IN HALL.

2. PILASTER AT LEFT END OF FRONT AISLE. OF CAVE II.

3. CAVE II.—PILLAR IN FRONT OF LEFT CHAPEL. IN THE VERANDAH.

Scale of 1 2 3 4 5 6 7 8 9 10 feet.

J. Burgess. W. Griggs, Photo-lith.

PLATE XXIII

AJANTA.

1. CAVE I.—HEAD OF SIDE DOOR.

2. CAVE II.—SCULPTURE IN THE LEFT BACK CHAPEL.

3. CAVE IV—
SCULPTURE TO RIGHT OF MAIN ENTRANCE.

4. WINDOW OF CAVE IV.

J. Burgess.

W. Griggs, Photo-lith.

HALL DOOR CAVE IV.

AJANTA.

DOOR OF CAVE V.

SECTION.

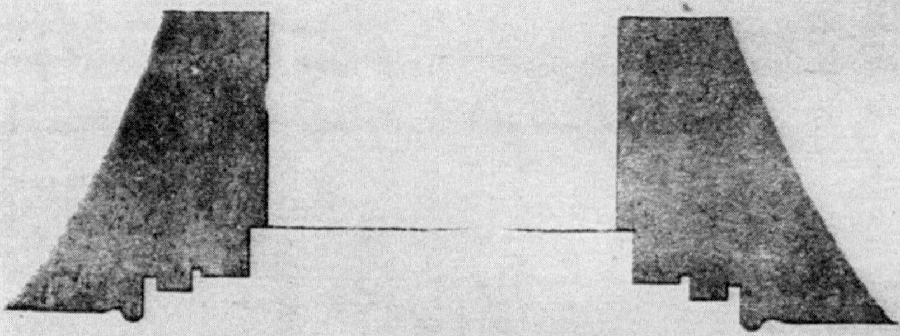

PLAN.

Scale of 1 0 1 2 3 4 5 6 7 8 feet

J. Burgess.

S. J. Pacheco, del.

PLATE XXVI.

AJANTA.

CAVE VI.-SECTION.

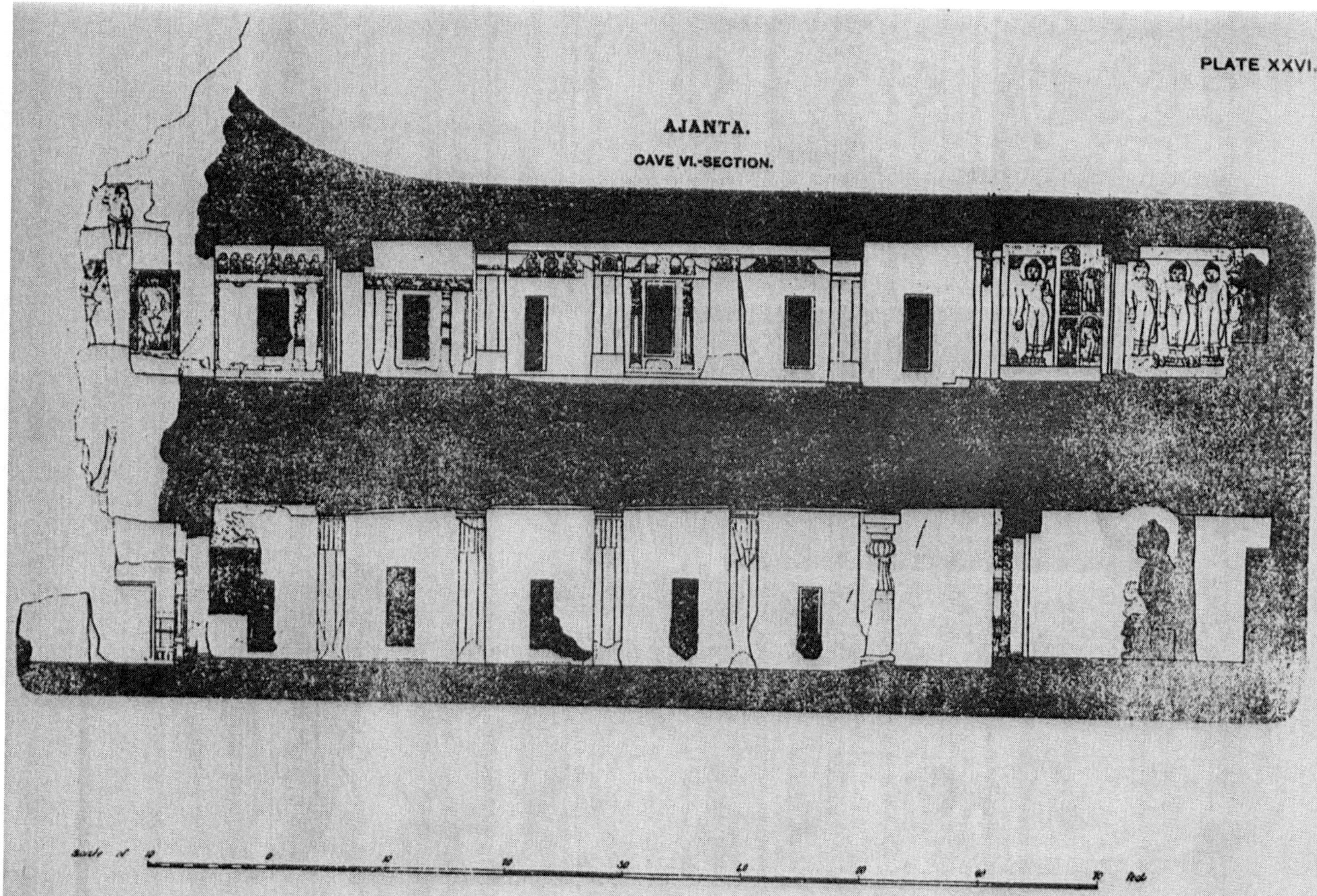

J. Burgess.

H. Cousens, Del.

AJANTA.

CAVE VII.—DOOR OF SHRINE.

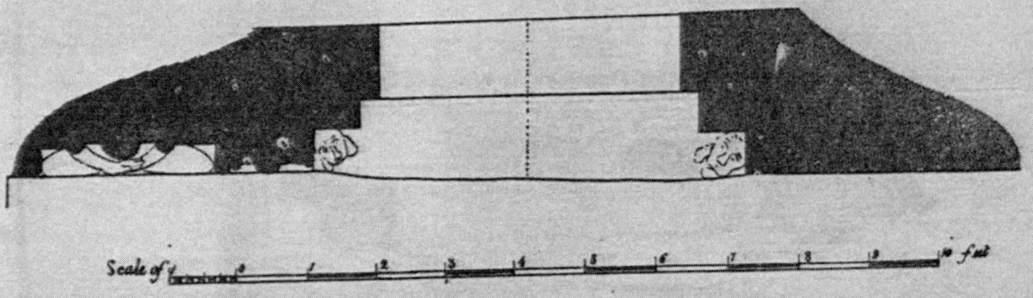

H. Cousens, Del.

J. Burgess.

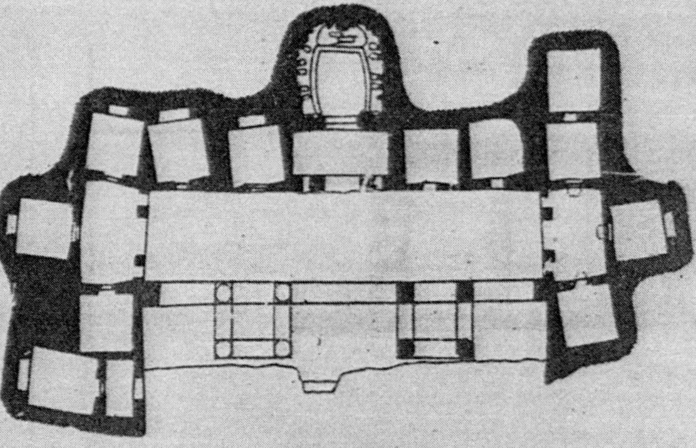

1. PLAN OF CAVE VII.

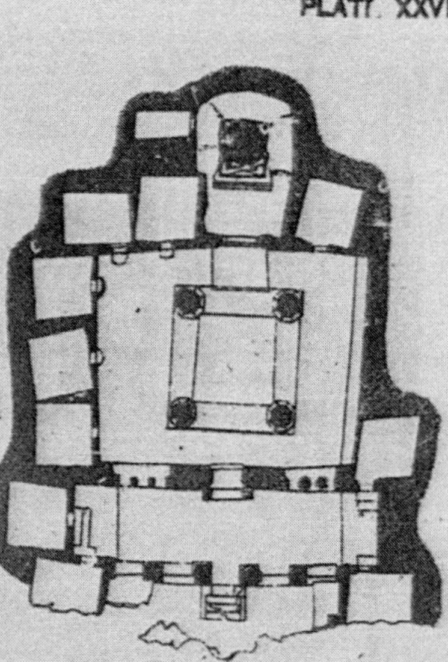

2. PLAN OF CAVE XI.

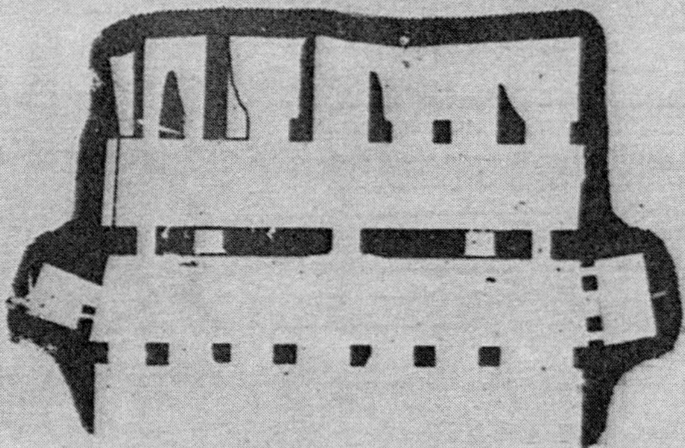

4. PLAN OF CAVE XIV.

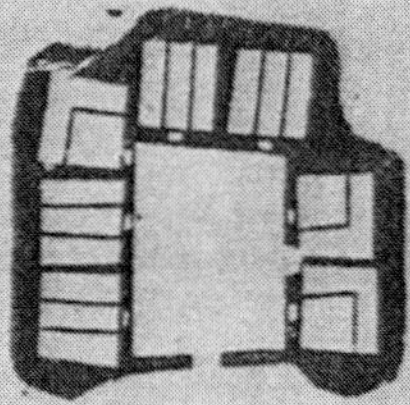

3. PLAN OF CAVE XIII.

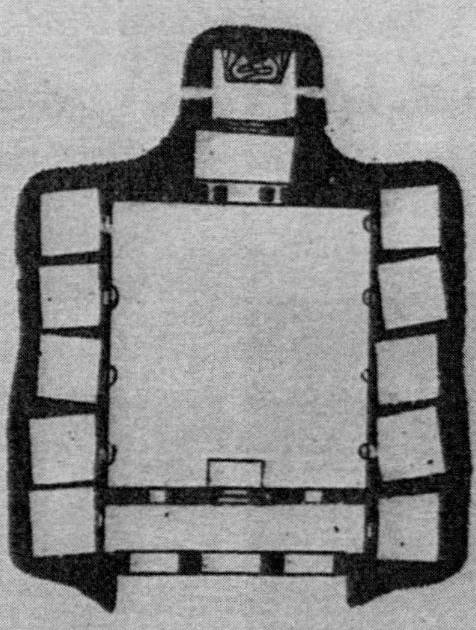

5. PLAN OF CAVE XV.

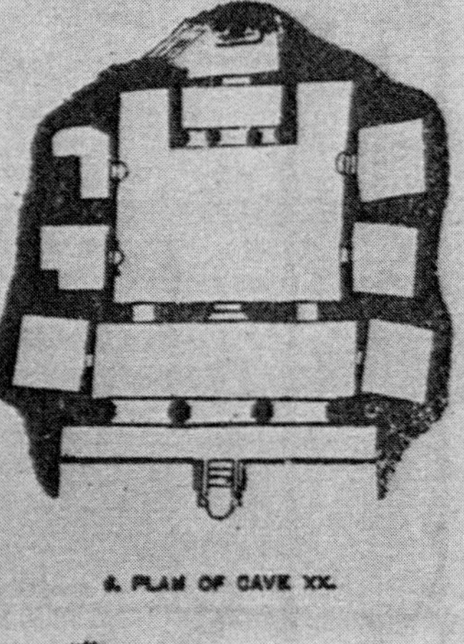

6. PLAN OF CAVE XX.

J. Burgess.

AJANTA.

PLATE XXIX.

FIG 1. DOORWAY OF CAVE XV.

2. CAVE XVI.—LEFT PILASTER IN THE VERANDAH.

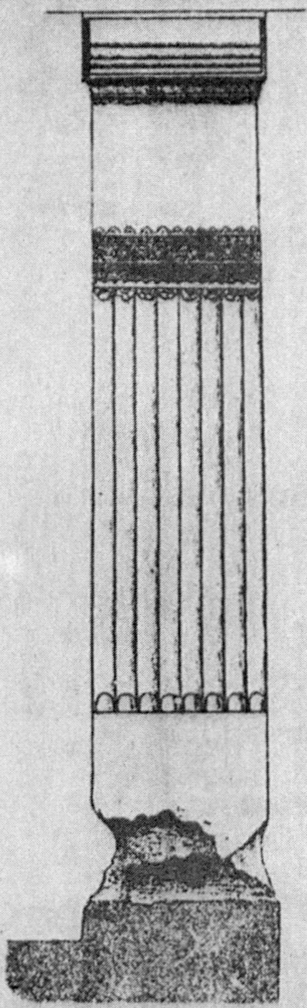

3. CAVE XVII.—PILLAR IN THE ANTECHAMBER.

Scale of 12 feet

J. Burgess. W. Griggs. Photo.-lith.

AJANTA.

FACADE OF THE CHAITA CAVE. No. XIX.

J. Burgess

W. Griggs, Photo-lith.

PLATE XXXI.

AJANTA.

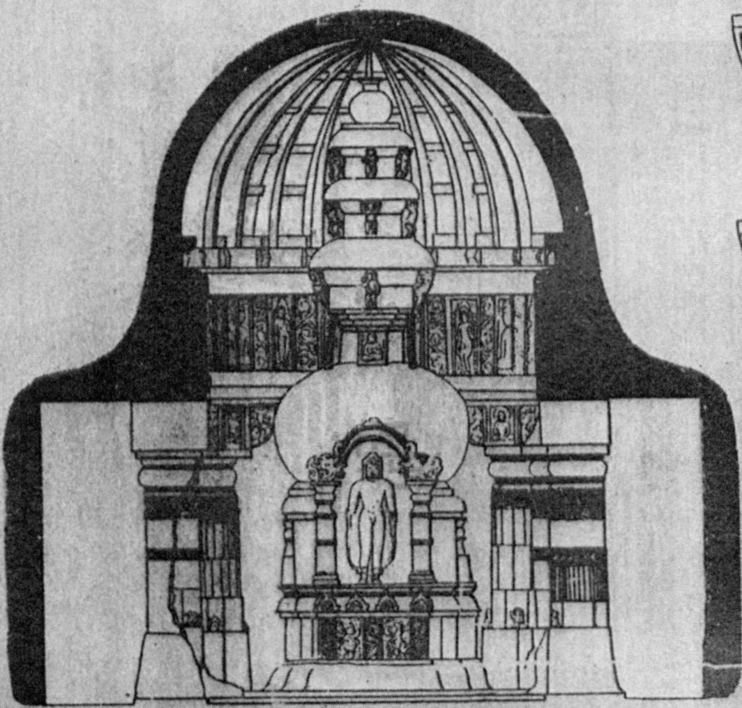

1. CAVE XIX.—TRANSVERSE SECTION.

Scale to Figs. 1 & 2.

2. SIDE VIEW AND PLAN OF DAGOBA.

3. CAPITALS OF TWO PILLARS BESIDE THE DAGOBA.

4. PANEL FROM THE TRIFORIUM.

Scale to 3 & 4.

J. Burgess

H. Cousens, Del.

AJANTA. PLATE XXXII.

1. DOORWAY OF CAVE XX.

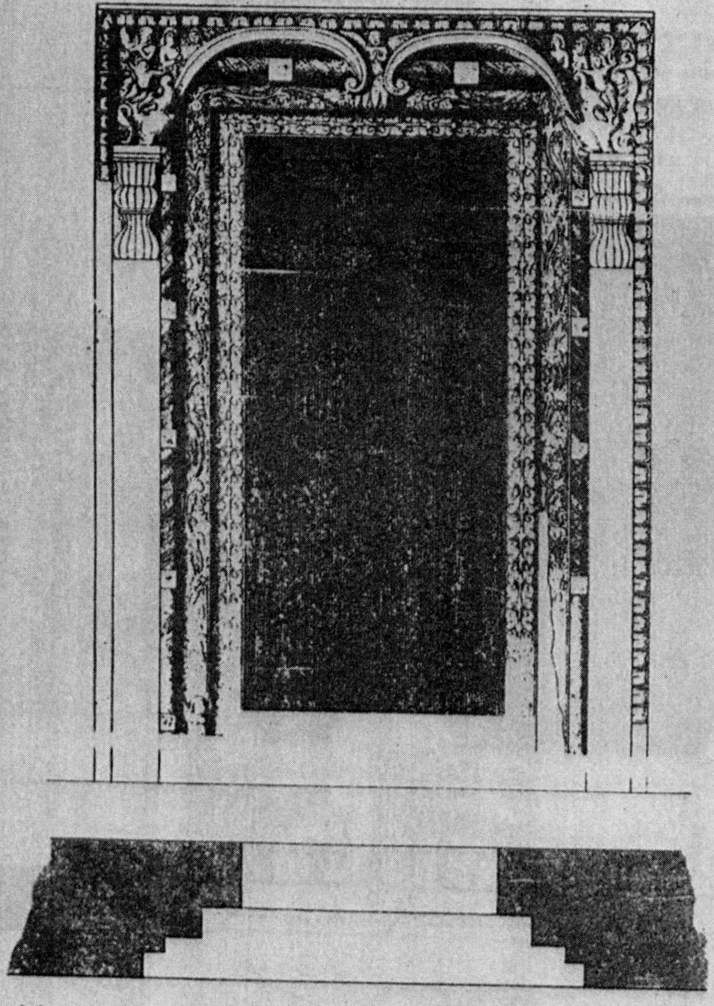

2. DOORWAY OF CAVE XXII.

J. Burgess. Scale of 1 2 1 3 3 4 5 6 7 8 feet S. J. Pacheco, del.

PLATE XXXIII

AJANTA.

1. CAVE XXI.—CHAPEL IN LEFT END OF THE VERANDAH.

2. CORNER PILLAR IN THE HALL.

Scale of 10 feet.

J. Burgess.

W. Griggs, Photo-lith.

AJANTA.

PLATE XXXIV.

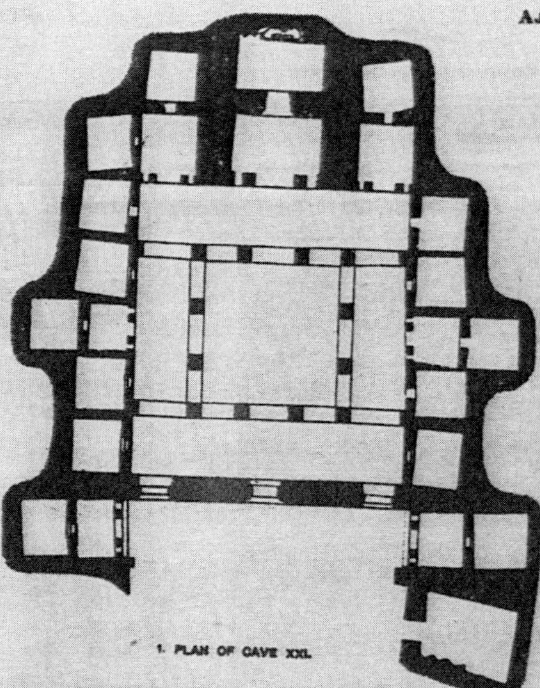

1. PLAN OF CAVE XXI.

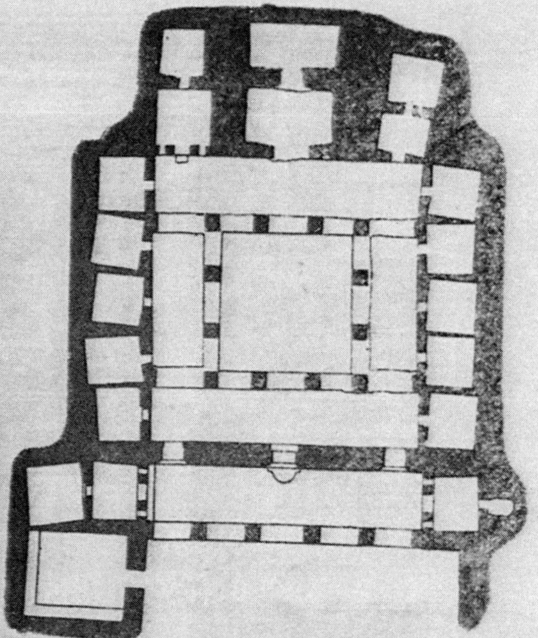

2. PLAN OF CAVE XXIII.

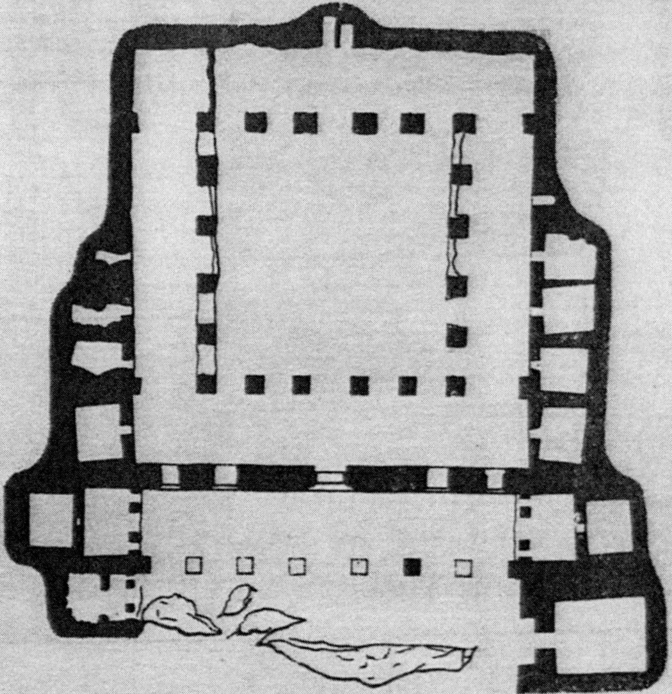

3. PLAN OF CAVE XXIV.

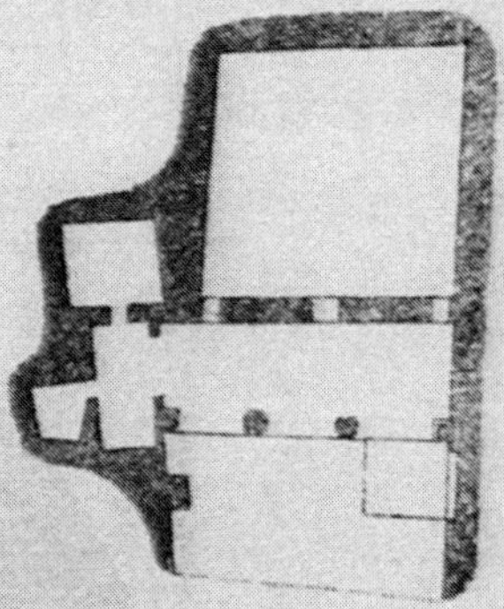

4. PLAN OF CAVE XXV.

J. Burgess.

AJANTA.

FRONT DOOR OF CAVE XXIV.

J. Burgess

AJANTA.

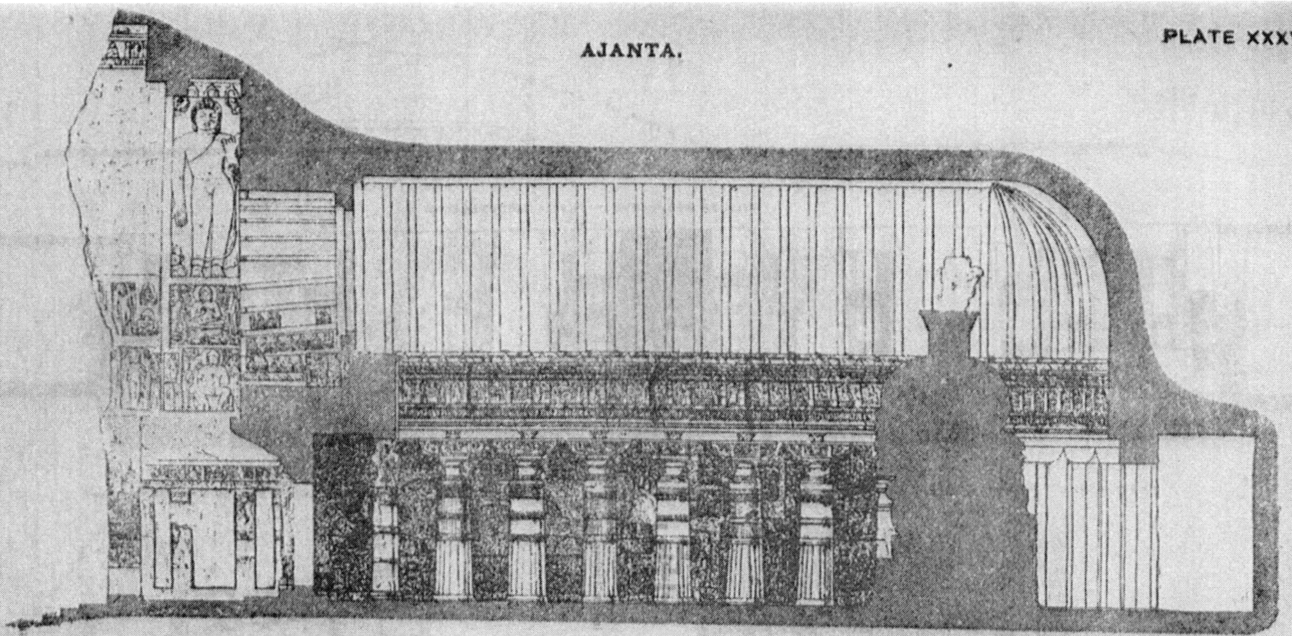

CAVE XXVI.—1. LONGITUDINAL SECTION.

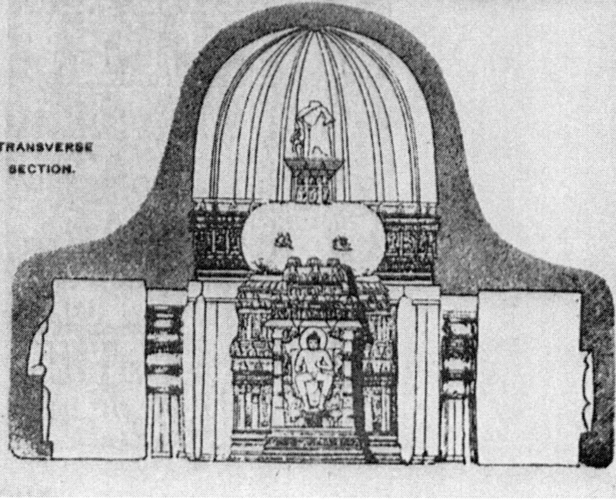

2. TRANSVERSE SECTION.

J. Burgess

AJANTA & GHATOTKACHH.

PLATE XXXVII.

1. CAVE XI.—SALIKA FIGURE BEFORE THE THRONE OF BUDDHA.

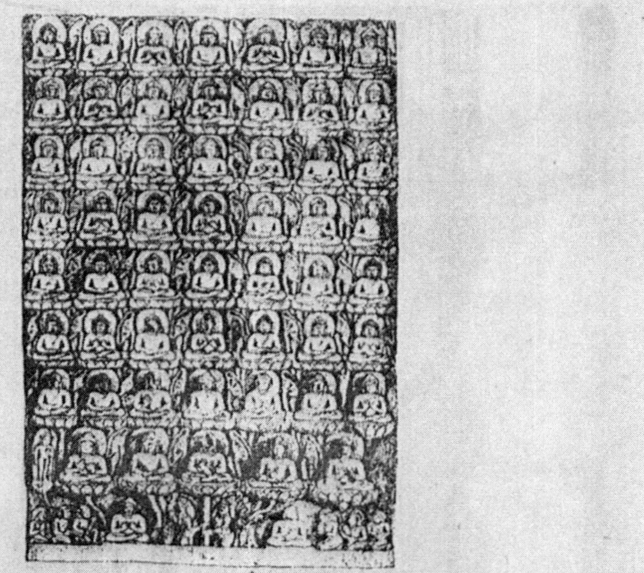

2. CAVE VII.—SCULPTURE ON THE RIGHT SIDE OF THE ANTECHAMBER.

3. GHATOTKACHH VIHARA—TRANSVERSE SECTION.

Scale of 5 0 5 10 15 20 25 30 35 40 45 50 55 60 65 70 75 feet.

J. Burgess.

W. Griggs, Photo-lith.

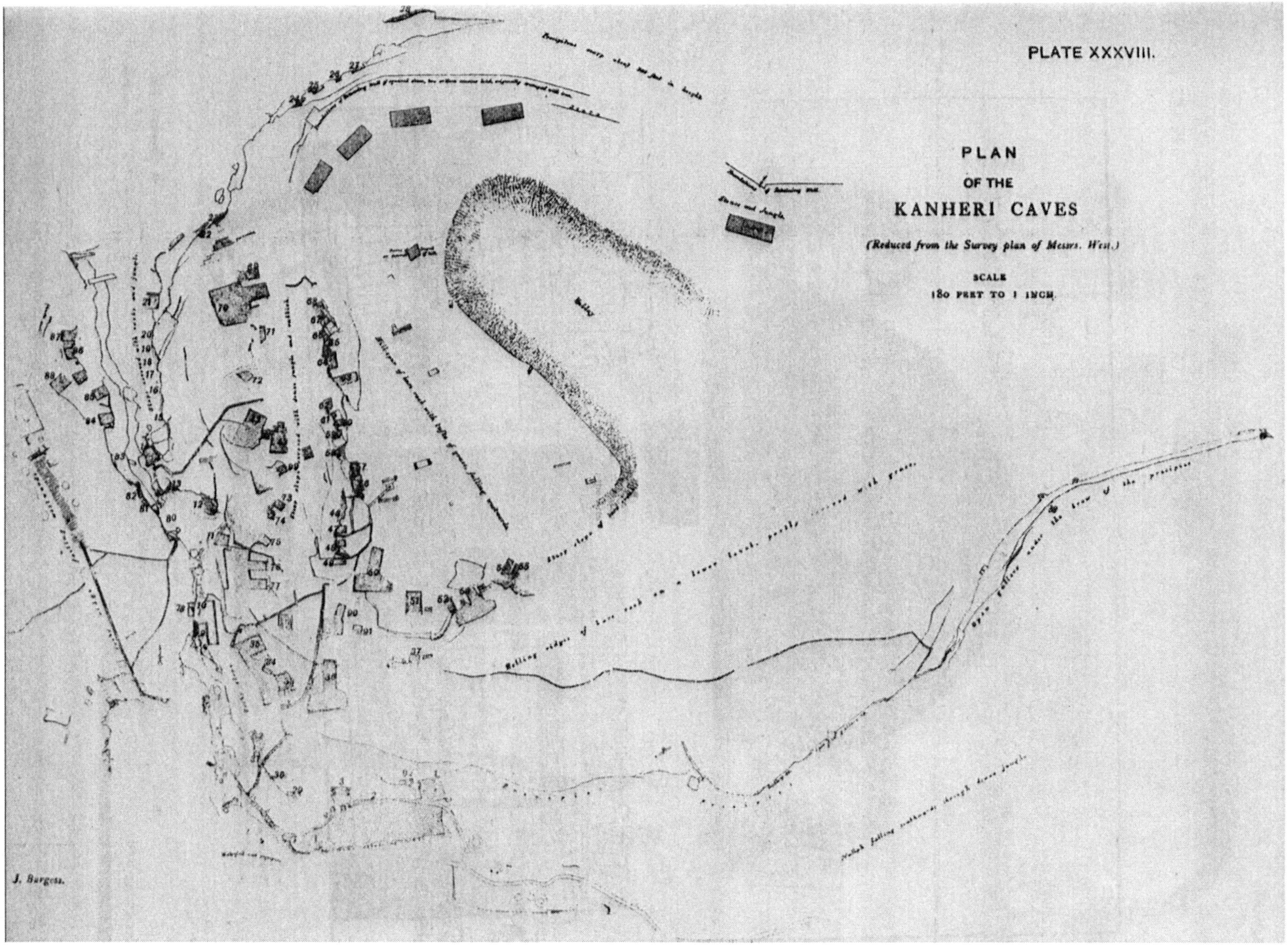

PLATE XXXVIII.

PLAN
OF THE
KANHERI CAVES

(Reduced from the Survey plan of Messrs. West.)

SCALE
180 FEET TO 1 INCH.

J. Burgess.

INNER FACADE OF THE CHAITYA CAVE.

Scale of 5 0 5 10 15 20 Feet.

J. Burgess. H. Cousens, Dd.

1. KANHERI CHAITYA CAVE—LONGITUDINAL SECTION.

HEADS FROM THE FAÇADE OF THE CHAITYA CAVE.

5. FACADE IN CAVE LI.

6. PILLAR IN CAVE X.

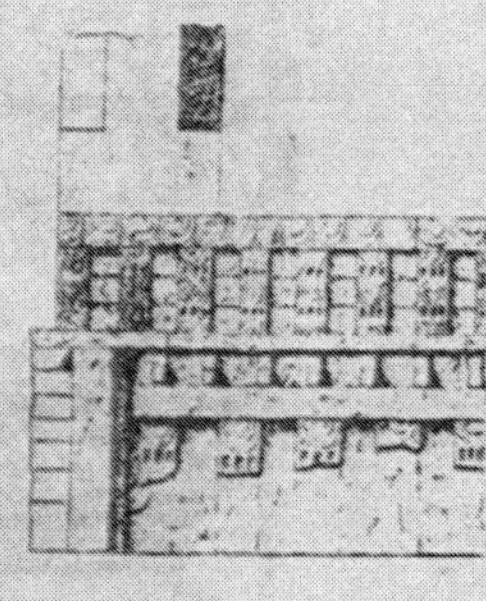

7. BASEMENT OF CAVE LI.

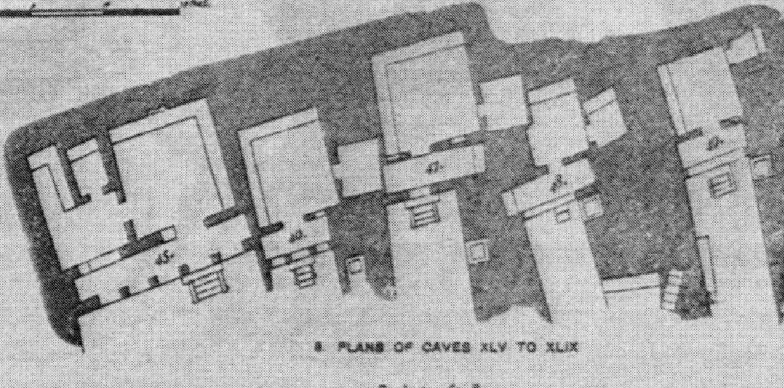

8. PLANS OF CAVES XLV TO XLIX

Scale to fig. 8.

J. Burgess W. Griggs, Photo-lith

PLATE XLI.

KANHERI.

CAPITALS OF COLUMNS IN THE CHAITYA CAVE.

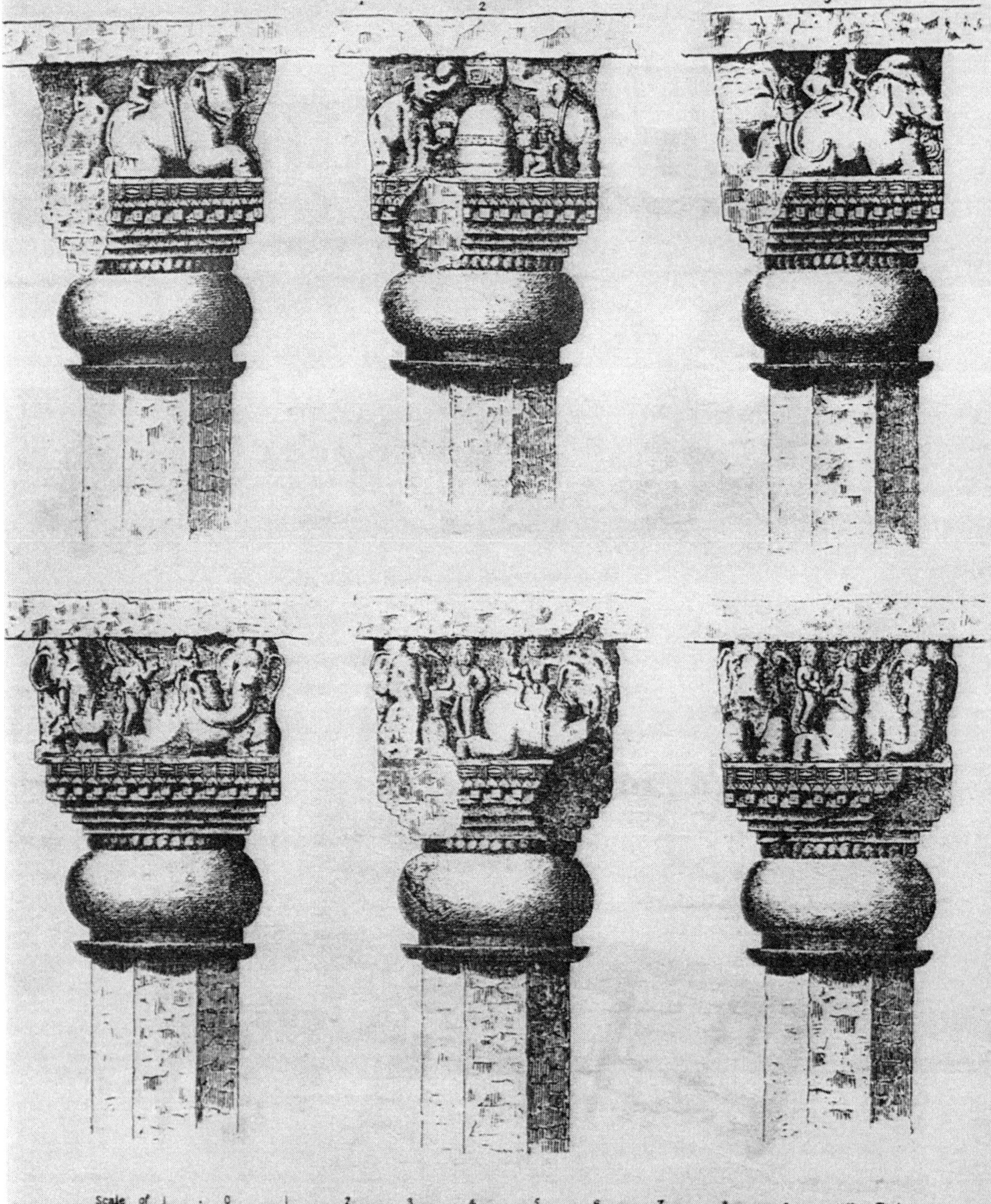

Scale of 0 1 2 3 4 5 6 7 8 9 10 Feet

J. Burgess. *W. Griggs, Photo-lith.*

PLATE XLII.

GENERAL PLAN
OF
KONDIVTE CAVES TEMPLES.

Scale of 100 0 100 200 300 400 500

J. Burgess.

H. Cousens, Del.

KONDIVTE

1 SCULPTURE ON RIGHT SIDE OF CHAITYA CAVE NO. IX.

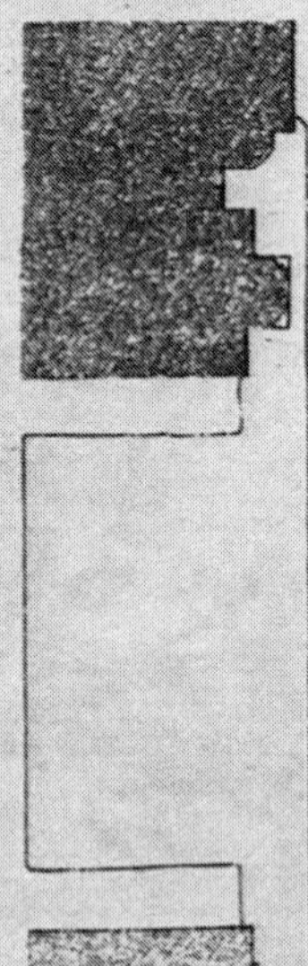

3 PLAN OF DOOR.

2. SHRINE DOOR OF CAVE XV

Scale of 1 2 3 4 5 6 7 8 Feet.

J. Burgess.

H. Cousens, Del.

BHAJA INSCRIPTIONS. PLATE XLIV.

Bhájá No. 1.

No. 3.

No. 2.

No. 4.

No. 5.

No. 6.

No. 7.

KONDANE INSCRIPTION

PITALKHORA INSCRIPTIONS.

No. 1.

No. 2.

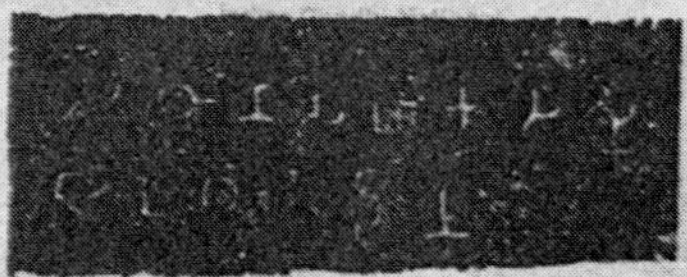

No. 3.

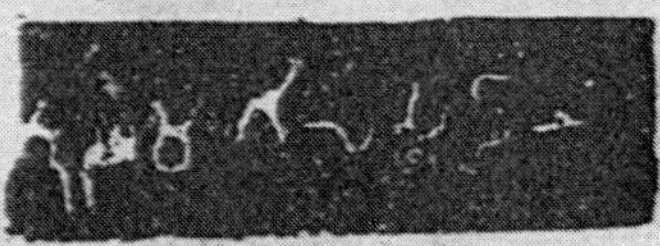

No. 4.

No. 5.

No. 6.

No. 7.

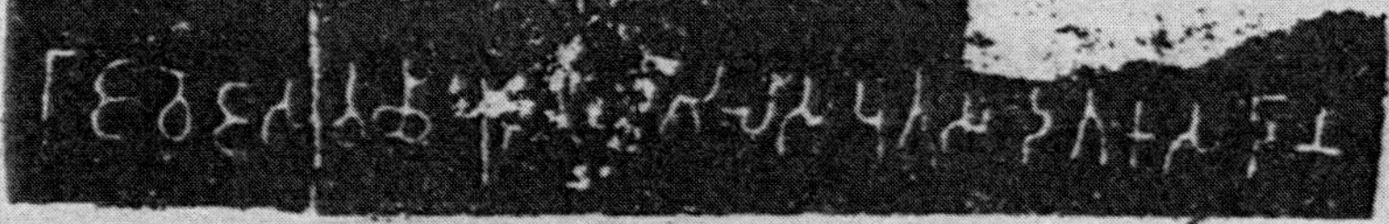

Pandit Bhagwanlal Indraji fecit.

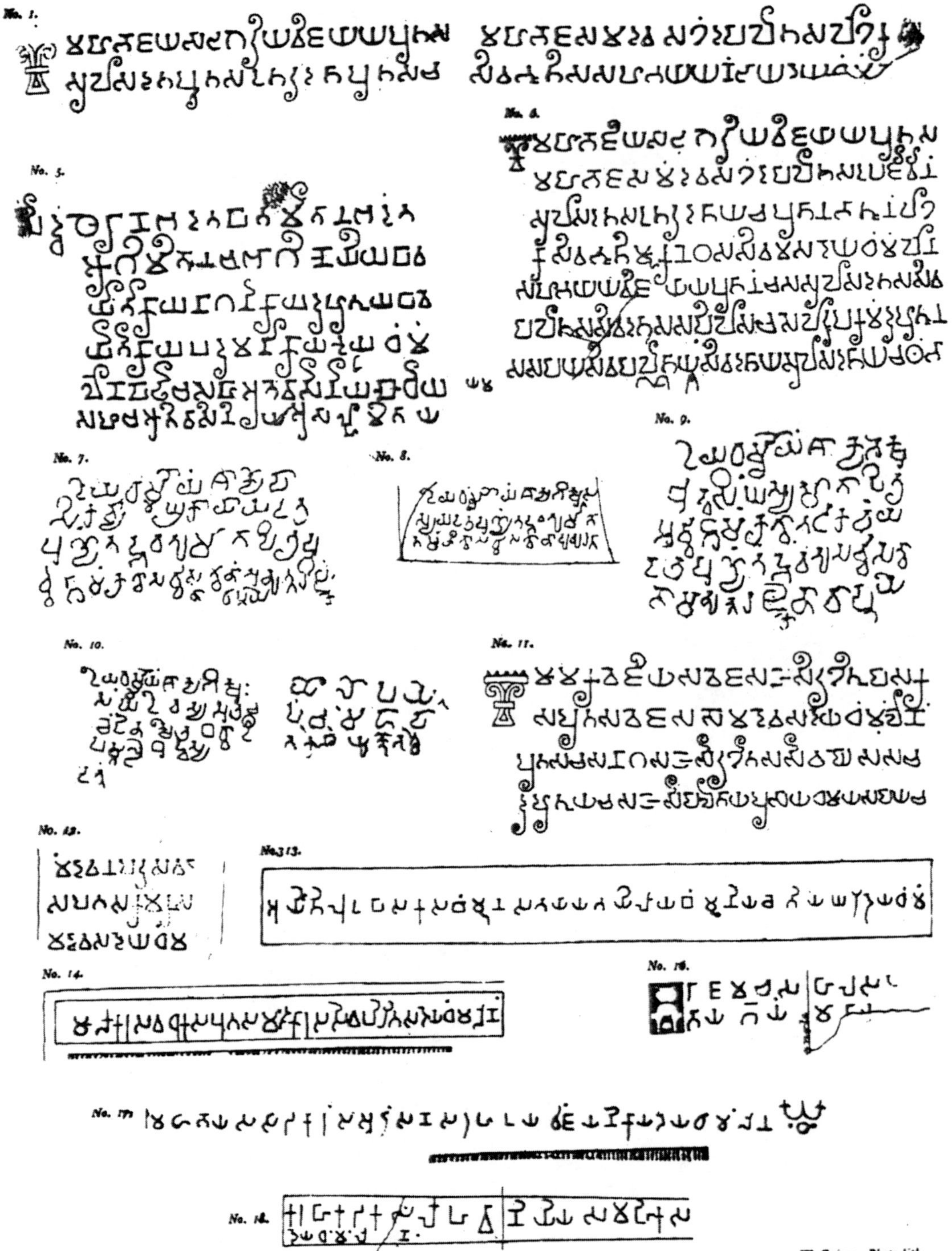

J. Burgess.

W. Griggs, Photo-lith.

INSCRIPTIONS AT KUDA, MAHAD & KOL.

PLATE XLVI.

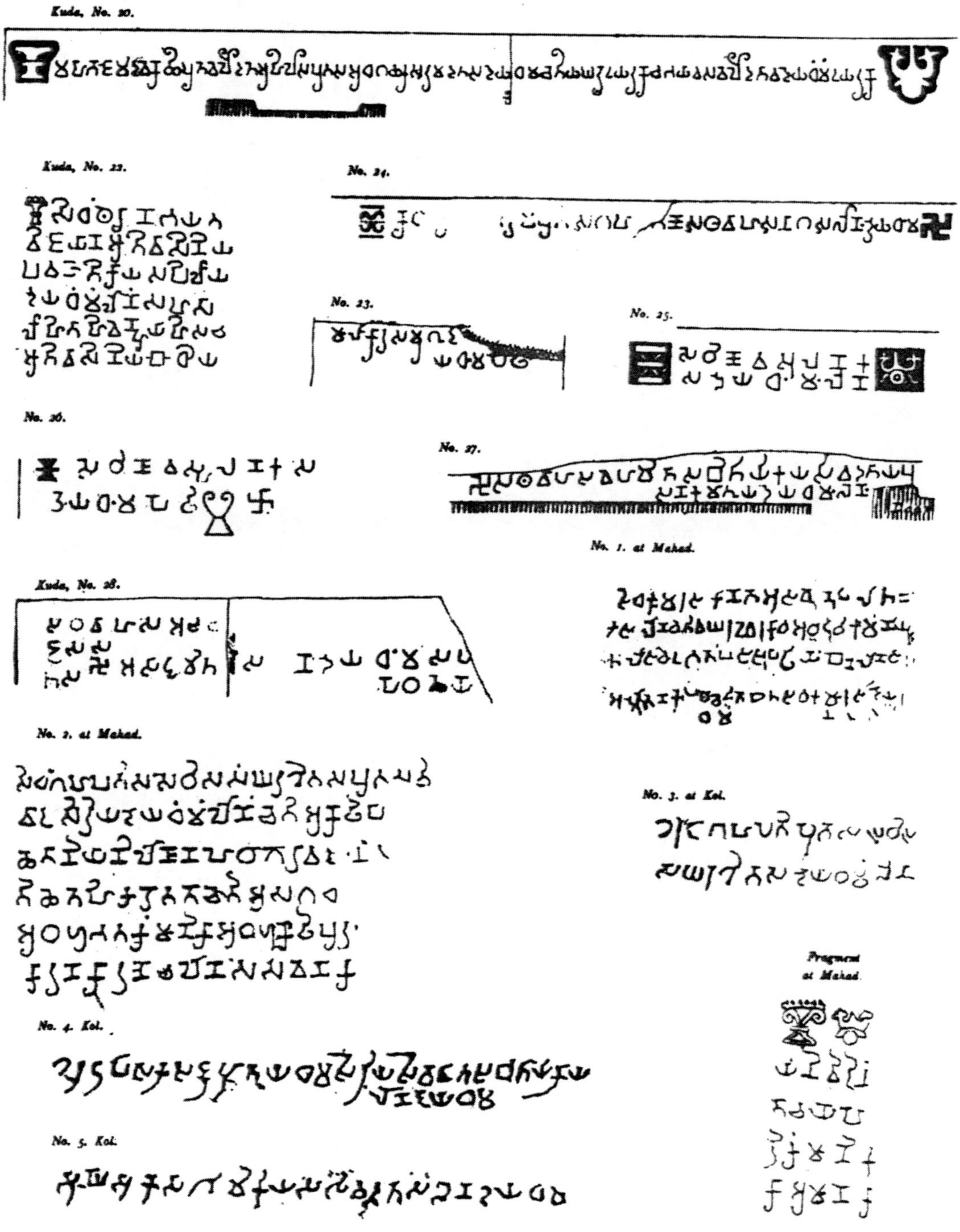

J. Burgess. W. Griggs. Photo-lith.

BEDSA & KARLE INSCRIPTIONS.

Bedsa No. 1.

No. 3.

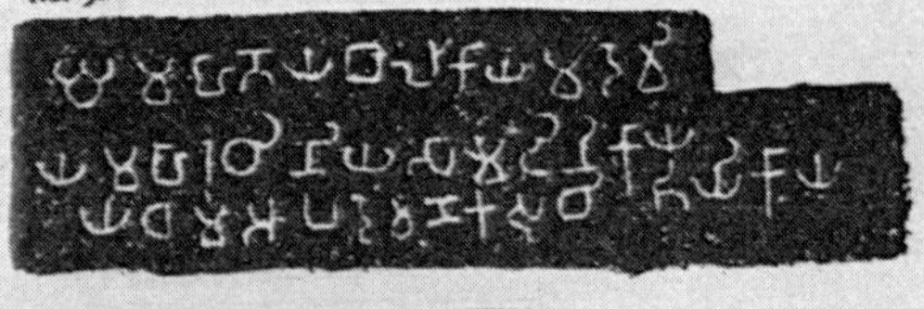

No. 2.

EARLIEST KARLE INSCRIPTIONS.

Karle No. 1.

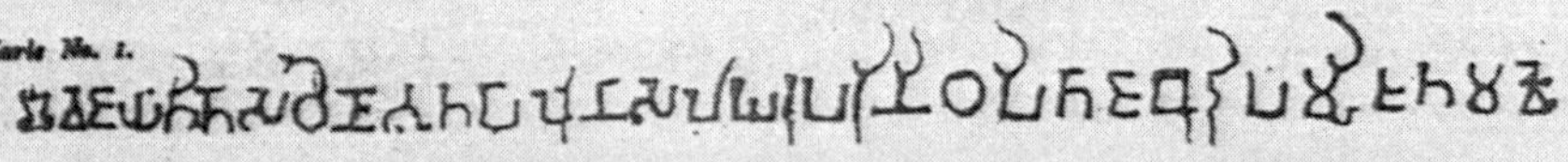

No. 2.

No. 3.

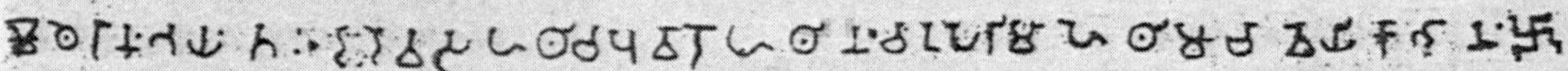

No. 4.

No. 5.

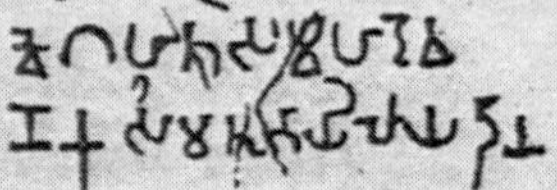

No. 6.

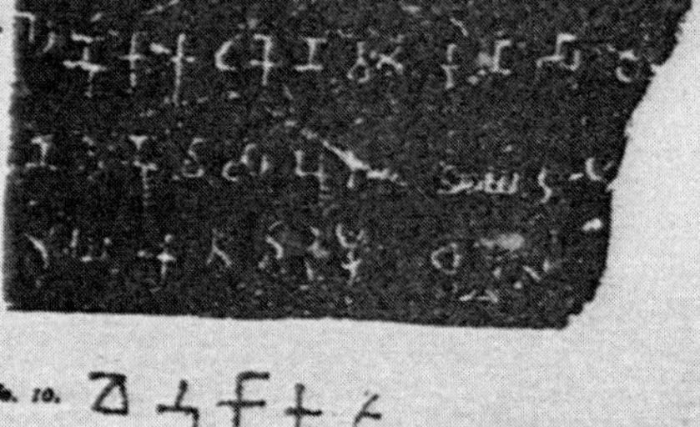

Nos. 8. & 9.

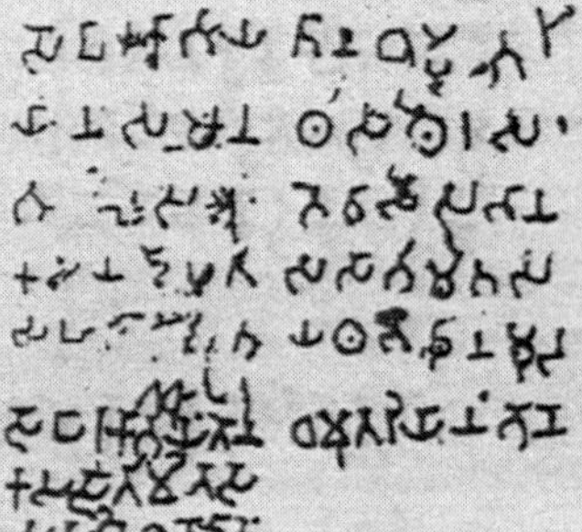

No. 10.

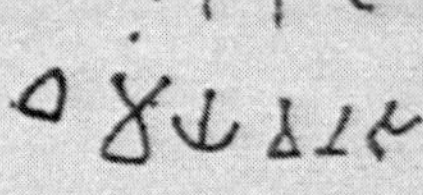

No. 7.

J. Burgess. & Pandit Bhagwanlal Indraji fecit. W. Griggs, Photo-lith.

Karle No. 11.

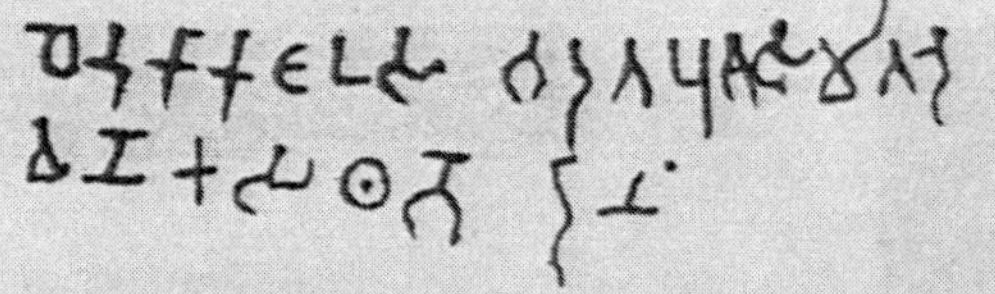

No. 12.

No. 13.

No. 14.

No. 15.

Karle No. 17.

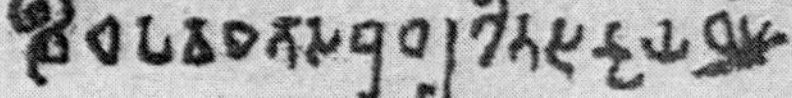

No. 16.

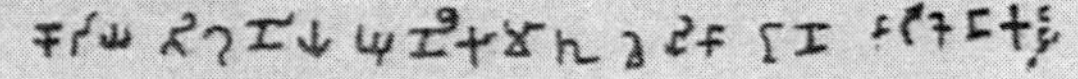

No. 18.

No. 19 Sailarwadi.

JUNNAR INSCRIPTIONS.

No. 1.

No. 2.

No. 3.

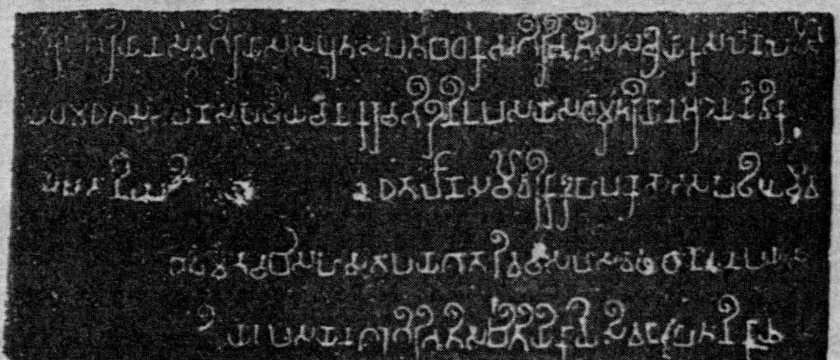

J. Burgess. & Pandit Bhagwanlal Indraji fecit. *W. Griggs, Photo-lith.*

No. 4.

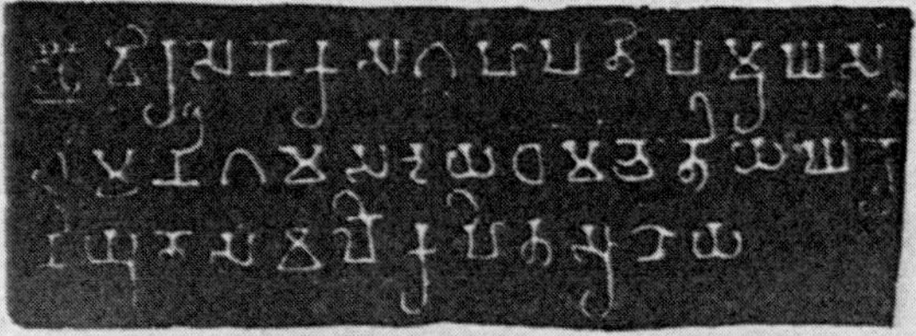

No. 7.

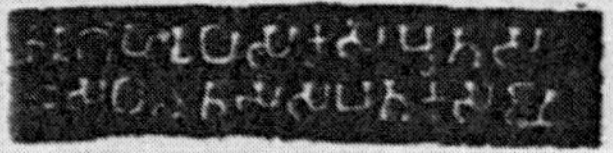

No. 8.

No. 5.

No. 6.

No. 9.

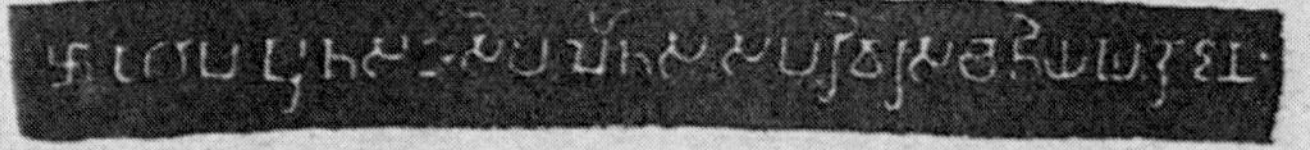

No. 10.

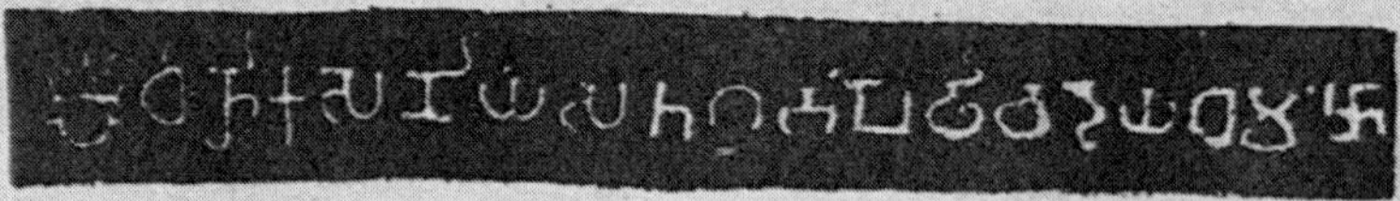

No. 11.

No. 12.

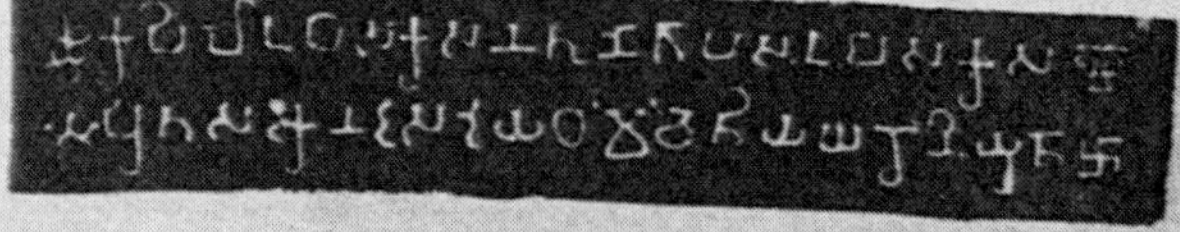

No. 14.

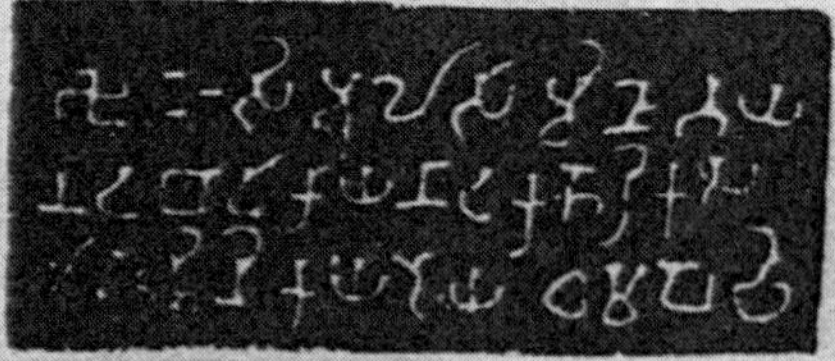

No. 13.

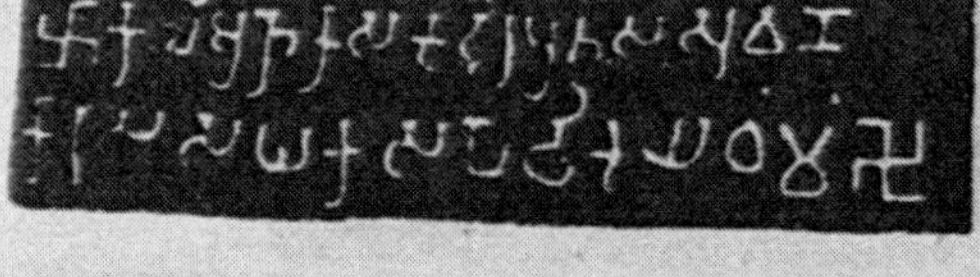

No. 15.

Pandit Bhagwanlal Indraji fecit.

W. Griggs, Photo-lith.

Pandit Bhagwanlal Indraji fecit.

W. Griggs, Photo-lith.

Junnar No. 31.

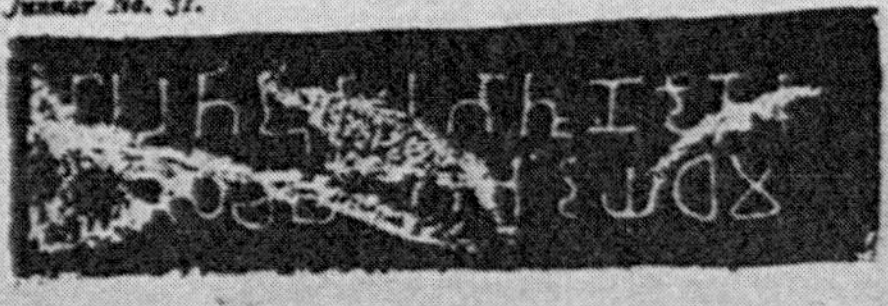

No. 34.

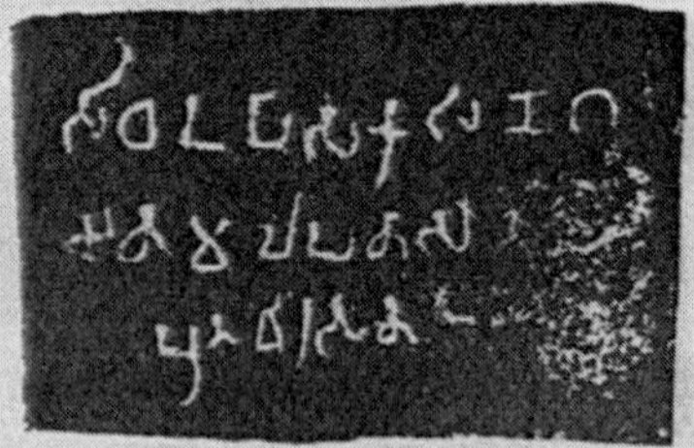

No. 33.

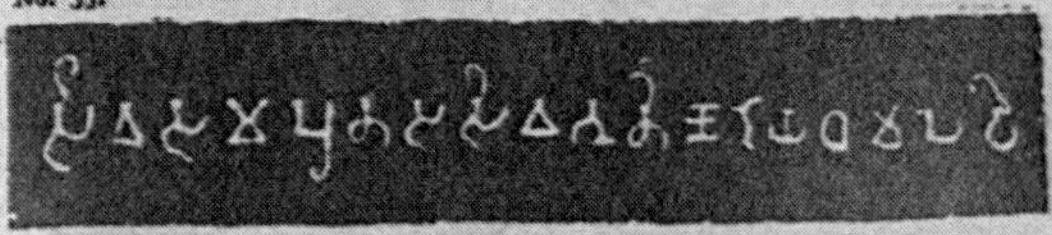

KSHATRAPA & ANDHRA INSCRIPTIONS FROM NASIK, KARLE &c.

Nasik No. 1.

Nasik No. 2.

Nasik No. 3.

Nasik No. 4.

Karle No. 19.

J. Burgess. *Pandit Bhagwanlal Indraji fecit.*

NASIK INSCRIPTIONS.

PLATE LII.

No. 5 Nasik.

No. 10a.

No. 9.
Nasik No. 7

No. 10b (Nasik No. 8.)

Nos. 18 & 19 (Nasik Nos. 14-15.)

W. Griggs, Photolith.

7. Nasik No. 6a.

8. Nasik No. 6b.

No. 12.

Nos. 13. 14. Nasik

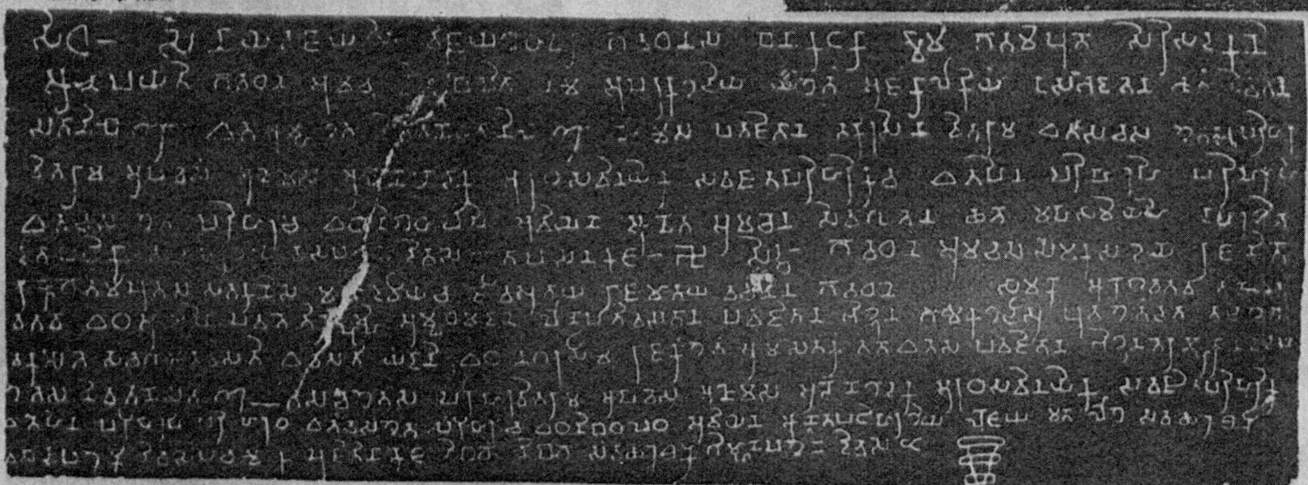

Pandit Bhagwanlal Indraji fecit.

KSHATRAPA & ANDHRA INSCRIPTIONS. PLATE LIV.

No. 11. (Junnar No. 32.)

No. 15. (Nasik No. 12.)

No. 16. (Nasik No. 13.)

No. 17. (Karle No. 20.)

No. 20. (Karle No. 21.)

No. 21. (Karle No. 22.)

J. Burgess. Pandit Bhagwanlal Indraji fecit.

NASIK INSCRIPTIONS.

No. 22. (Nasik No. 16.)

NASIK PRIVATE INSCRIPTIONS.

No. 1. (Nasik No. 17.)

No. 4. (Nasik No. 20.)

No. 3. (Nasik No. 19.)

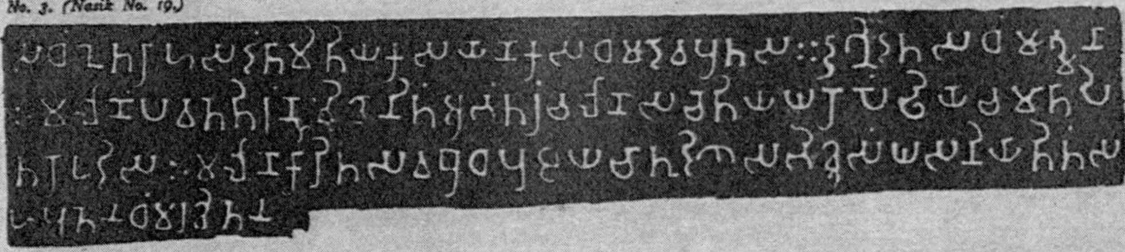

No. 2. (Nasik No. 18.)

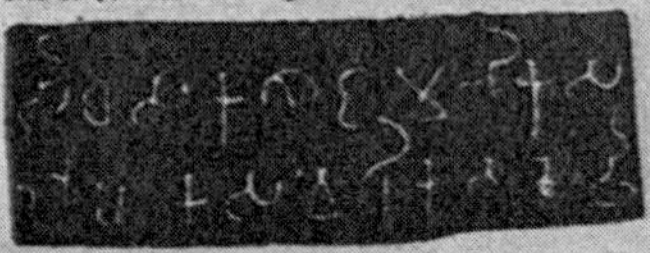

No. 5. (Nasik No. 21.)

No. 6. (Nasik No. 22.)

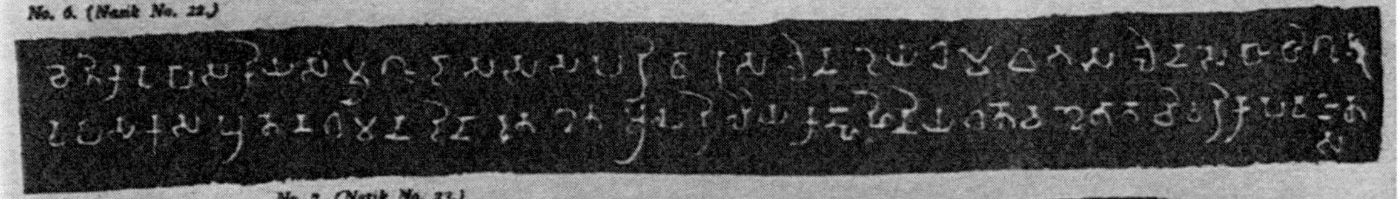

No. 7. (Nasik No. 23.)

No. 8. (Nasik No. 24.)

No. 9. (Nasik No. 25.)

J. Burgess.

Pandit Bhagwanlal Indraji fecit.

No. 1

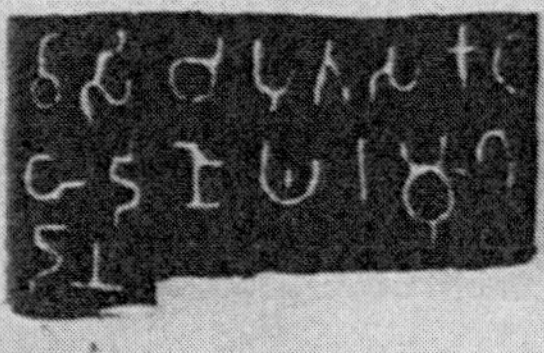

No. 2

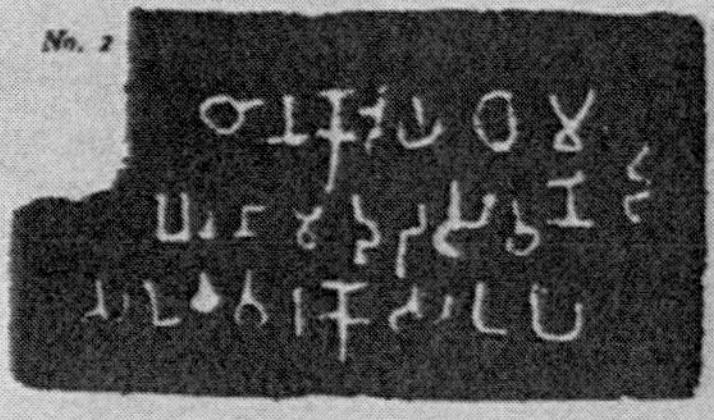

No. 4.

Pandit Bhagwanlal Indraji fecit.

W. Griggs, Photo-lith.

J. Burgess. Pandit Bhagwanlal Indraji fecit.